OFFICIAL HISTORY
OF THE
SUDAN CAMPAIGN

COMPILED IN THE INTELLIGENCE
DIVISION OF THE WAR OFFICE

COLONEL H. E. COLVILLE
GRENADIER GUARDS

• VOLUME II •

The Naval & Military Press Ltd

published in association with

FIREPOWER
The Royal Artillery Museum
Woolwich

Published by
The Naval & Military Press Ltd
Unit 10 Ridgewood Industrial Park,
Uckfield, East Sussex,
TN22 5QE England
Tel: +44 (0) 1825 749494
Fax: +44 (0) 1825 765701
www.naval-military-press.com

in association with

FIREPOWER
The Royal Artillery Museum, Woolwich
www.firepower.org.uk

In reprinting in facsimile from the original, any imperfections are inevitably reproduced and the quality may fall short of modern type and cartographic standards.

OFFICIAL COPY.

[All rights reserved.

HISTORY

OF THE

SUDAN CAMPAIGN.

IN TWO PARTS, WITH A CASE OF MAPS.

PART II.

BY

COLONEL H. E. COLVILE, C.B.,
Grenadier Guards.

COMPILED IN THE INTELLIGENCE DIVISION OF THE
WAR OFFICE.

LONDON:
PRINTED FOR HER MAJESTY'S STATIONERY OFFICE,
BY HARRISON AND SONS, ST. MARTIN'S LANE,
PRINTERS IN ORDINARY TO HER MAJESTY.

And to be purchased, either directly or through any Bookseller, from
EYRE & SPOTTISWOODE, East Harding Street, Fleet Street, E. C.; or
ADAM AND CHARLES BLACK, 6, North Bridge, Edinburgh; or
HODGES, FIGGIS, & Co., 104, Grafton Street, Dublin.

Price Fifteen Shillings for Two Parts and Case of Maps.

To face page 108.

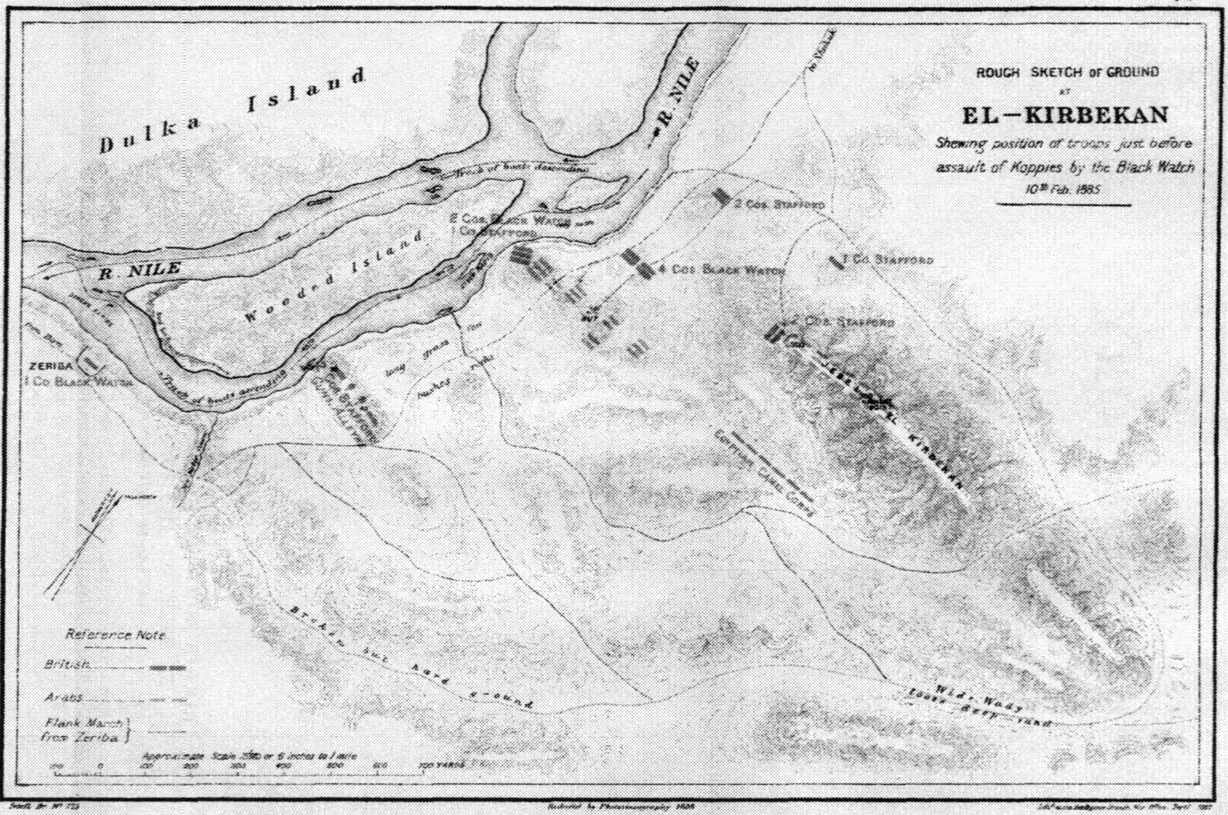

(Wt. 15076 1000 12 | 89—H & S 251)

PART II.

FROM THE DEPARTURE OF THE DESERT COLUMN
TO THE CONCLUSION OF THE CAMPAIGN.

WITH APPENDICES AND A SKETCH MAP.

TABLE OF CONTENTS.

PART II.

CHAPTER VI.—THE DESERT COLUMN.

	PAGE
December 16th, 1884. Arrival of Lord Wolseley at Korti	1
Decision to form post at Jakdul	1
Orders for march of convoy	2
December 30th. Departure of the convoy	3
January 2nd, 1885. Arrival at Jakdul	4
Desert march a surprise	4
Jakdul Wells	4
Water supply	5
Return of convoy. Garrison of Jakdul	5
January 5th. Convoy reaches Korti	5
January 7th. Colonel Clarke's convoy for Jakdul	6
January 8th. Orders to Sir H. Stewart	6
Orders to Sir C. Wilson	8
Orders to Lord C. Beresford	9
March of main body for Jakdul	10
January 12th. Arrival at Jakdul	10
Colonel Burnaby's convoy	10
Letter from Sir H. Stewart of January 14th	10
Review of the situation in the theatre of operations	12
January 14th. Force leaves for Metemmeh. Composition	13
Garrison of Jakdul	14
January 16th. Touch of the enemy	15
Bivouac before Abu Klea	15
January 17th. The advance towards Abu Klea	16
Line of advance	17
The battle of Abu Klea	17
Arrival at the Wells of Abu Klea	20
Casualties during the day	20
January 18th. Sir H. Stewart's plans	21
Departure for Metemmeh	21
Confusion among transport during the night march	22
Peculiar difficulties of this march	22
Arrival at the Shebakat bush	23
January 19th. Halt at dawn	23
The Nile in sight	24
Force halted and laager formed	25
Sir H. Stewart wounded	25
Advance determined upon	25
Composition of square	25
Skirmishers dispensed with	26

TABLE OF CONTENTS.

	PAGE
Charge of the enemy against the square	26
Nile reached	27
January 20th. Occupation of Gubat	27
Remainder of force brought to Gubat	28
Position of the village	28
January 21st. Attack on Metemmeh	28
General Gordon's steamers in sight	29
News from Khartum	30
Sir C. Wilson on the situation	30
Dispositions in view of an expected hostile movement from the south	31
Two forts built	31
January 22nd. Reconnaissance to Shendi	31
January 23rd. 3 p.m. Steamers reported ready to proceed to Khartum	32
Messages from the Queen and Khedive	32

CHAPTER VII.—THE VOYAGE TO KHARTUM.

	PAGE
January 24th. Departure of Sir C. Wilson from Gubat	33
Description of steamers	33
January 25th. "Bordein" run aground in the 6th cataract	34
January 26th. Delay of a day caused by the accident	34
January 27th. Fire opened by the enemy	34
Report of General Gordon's death	35
January 28th. Preparations for running the blockade	35
First view of Khartum	35
Tuti Island in enemy's hands	36
Khartum found to have fallen. Steamers retire	37
"Telahawiyeh" aground for a short time	37
Heavy fire on the steamers	37
Crews show signs of disaffection	37
Difficulties of situation	38
January 29th. Wreck of "Telahawiyeh"	38
Letter from the Mahdi	39
Answer to Mahdi's letter	41
Disaffection among native troops	41
January 30th. Passage of Shabluka	41
January 31st. Descent of last rapid	42
Wreck of "Bordein"	42
Mernat Island	42
Lieutenant Stuart-Wortley starts for Gubat	43
Sir C. Wilson's dispositions	44
Desertions	44
February 3rd. "Safieh" sighted	45
Sir C. Wilson quits Mernat Island and marches down to the "Safieh"	45
The voyage of the "Safieh"	46
Fort at Wad Habeshi	46
The boiler struck	47
Dangerous position of the "Safieh"	47
Repair of the boiler	47
February 4th. Relief of Sir C. Wilson's party	48

CHAPTER VIII.—THE RETURN OF THE DESERT COLUMN.

	PAGE
Events at Gubat during Sir C. Wilson's absence. Convoy for Jakdul	49
Condition of Animals	50
Proclamation by Lord C. Beresford	50
Reconnaissances by the steamers	50
January 31st. Return of Colonel Talbot's convoy from Jakdul	51
February 1st. Arrival of Lieutenant Stuart-Wortley	51
Departure of 2nd convoy for Jakdul. Some of the wounded sent off	51
Return of Sir C. Wilson on the 4th	52
February 2nd. Sir R. Buller assumes command in the desert	52
Reinforcements sent across to Jakdul from Korti	52
February 7th. Reinforcements leave Jakdul for the front	53
Orders to Sir R. Buller on the 4th and 5th	53
Memorandum to Sir R. Buller of February 5th	53
February 11th. Sir R. Buller, with Colonel Talbot's convoy, and the Royal Irish reaches Gubat	55
February 12th. Sir R. Buller's despatch announcing his intention to retire from Gubat	56
Lord Wolseley's correspondence with the Home Government as to the course to be pursued	57
Lord Wolseley's Despatch on the fall of Khartum	60
February 10th. Orders sent to Sir R. Buller to take Metemmeh, and move on Berber	62
February 12th. Further orders to Sir R. Buller to the same effect	63
February 13th. Sick and wounded sent back to Abu Klea	66
Skirmish on the way	66
February 17th. Death of Sir H. Stewart near Jakdul	67
Sir E. Wood sent to consult with Sir R. Buller	67
February 14th. Retreat from Gubat	67
February 15th. Arrival at Abu Klea	68
Lord Wolseley's report of the withdrawal from Gubat	68
February 16th. Appearance of the enemy round Abu Klea	70
February 18th. Major Wardrop sent to Jakdul to prepare for a march on Berber	70
His dispositions on finding orders at Jakdul for Sir R. Buller to retire	70
All hope of taking Berber before Autumn abandoned	71
Reasons for this change of plan	72
February 23rd. Evacuation of Abu Klea	74
Sir R. Buller's report	74
Lord Wolseley's covering despatch	75
Withdrawal from the desert	75
March 16th. Last troops reach Korti from the desert	76
Lord Wolseley's report of the situation on 16th March	76
Review of the events that led to the abandonment of operations till the Autumn	77

CHAPTER IX.—THE RIVER COLUMN FROM ITS ORGANIZATION TO THE ACTION OF KIRBEKAN.

December 27th, 1884.—General Earle's orders	81
December 28th. Departure of leading battalion from Korti	83
Change in character of country beyond Belal	83
January 4th, 1885. Arrival of General Earle at Hamdab	84

viii   TABLE OF CONTENTS.

	PAGE
Arrangements at Hamdab..	84
January 15th. Fresh orders; River Force to be a flying column	85
Arrangements for economising rations	85
Lord Wolseley anxious that two battalions should advance at once	85
General Earle's objections to this arrangement..	86
Organization of the column hospital	86
Pay department	87
Arrangements for the boats	87
Protection of the flanks	87
Mudir's troops	87
January 23rd. Concentration complete..	87
Review of the situation at this time, as it was known at Hamdab	88
January 24th. Advance of force..	89
Difficulties of the advance..	89
January 25th. Passage of Edermi	90
Traces of the enemy	90
Difficulties of this cataract..	90
January 27th. First touch of the enemy	91
Reconnaissance along right bank to opposite Berti	91
January 28th. Ascent of the Kab el-Abd Cataract	91
Skirmish with the enemy near Berti	92
January 30th. Report of spy that there is a strong hostile force at Berti	92
January 31st. Concentration at Ghamra	92
General Brackenbury's reconnaissance to Berti	93
February 1st. Retreat of the enemy. Occupation of Berti	93
Difficulties of the Rahmi Cataract	93
Grain found in Berti	94
February 4th. Advance beyond Berti	95
February 5th. News of fall of Khartum	96
Halt ordered in consequence	96
Reported advance of the enemy	96
State of supplies at this time	97
February 7th. Advance ordered by Lord Wolseley	97
Letter from Lord Wolseley written on this day..	97
Review of the situation at this time	97
February 8th. Fresh advance from Berti	100
Mudir's troops moved across to left bank	100
Touch of the enemy near Dulka Island ..	100
Colonel Butler's report of enemy's position	101
February 9th. General Earle's reconnaissance towards Kirbekan	101
Decision to move round the left of the hostile position and attack in rear	102
February 10th. Column formed for attack	103
Advance of column	104
Action of Kirbekan	105
Death of General Earle	106
Command assumed by General Brackenbury	107
Return to camp	108
Casualties, and ammunition expended	108

CHAPTER X.—THE RIVER COLUMN, *CONTINUED*, FROM THE ACTION OF KIRBEKAN, TO ITS RETURN TO MEROWI.

February 11th. The Shukuk Pass	110
Difficulties owing to weakness in cavalry	110
Arrival of the remainder of the force	111

TABLE OF CONTENTS.

	PAGE
Letter found on the battlefield, announcing the capture of Khartum by the Mahdi	111
February 12th. Advance of the column into the Shukuk defiles	112
Orders to General Brackenbury from Korti, for his operations against Berber	112
February 14th. Advanced troops reach the Uss rapid	113
February 15th. Reconnaissance to Salamat	114
February 16th. Arrival of detailed instructions from Lord Wolseley as to the advance on Berber	115
February 17th. Concentration at Salamat	117
Destruction of Wad Gamr's property	117
February 19th. Reconnaissance to opposite Hebbeh	117
February 20th. Arrangements for crossing the Nile	118
Time taken in crossing	119
Visit to the wreck of the "Abbas," and scene of murders	120
Destruction of Hebbeh	120
February 22nd. March continued along the right bank	120
Fresh orders issued by General Brackenbury	121
February 23rd. Limit of Monasir country reached	122
Signals to Major Rundle	122
February 24th. Telegram ordering return of column	122
General Brackenbury's reply to order	123
Order issued to the troops	124
Instructions to officers in charge of boats	125
Commencement of retreat	125
Reconnaissance towards Mograt	125
February 25th. Orders issued to guide the descent in boats	126
Instructions for passing Sehirri rapid	127
Conditions of navigation reversed from what they were in ascent	128
Advanced and rear guards	128
Enemy in pursuit	128
February 27th. Uss rapid. Three wrecks	128
February 28th. Passage of the Shukuk rapids	129
March 1st. Rahmi Cataract	130
March 2nd. Um Habwa Cataract. Difficulty of the descent	130
March 3rd. Kab el-Abd rapid. Loss of six boats	131
March 4th. Another boat swamped, and three men drowned	132
Leading troops reach Hamdab	132
Time of descent of cataracts	132
Arrival at Merowi on February 5th	132
Pursuit by the enemy	132

CHAPTER XI.—PROGRESS OF AFFAIRS DURING THE ABSENCE OF THE DESERT AND RIVER COLUMNS, AND PREPARATIONS FOR AN AUTUMN CAMPAIGN.

The Line of Communications	133
District Commandants	133
Station Commandants	134
State of supplies in December	134
Deficiences in supplies ordered to be kept up, at stations on the Line of Communications	134
State of supplies at the departure of the Desert Column	135
Difficulty gradually overcome	135
Camel question	136
Grain supply running short in the province of Dongola	137

TABLE OF CONTENTS.

	PAGE
Hired convoys. Difficulties attending their organization	137
Care of sick camels..	137
Donkey convoys	139
Arrival of "Lotus"	139
Fuel for steamers	139
Coal for the Sudan railway	140
Transport of sick	140
Censorship of telegrams at Dongola	140
Watering posts established in the desert..	141
Head Quarters staff at Korti	142
Suakin Expedition, first proposed on receipt of Gordon's message of 14th December	143
Proposal for a fleet to be sent to Suakin..	143
Government proposal to send reinforcements to Suakin	143
Lord Wolesley's reply	144
January 18th. A battalion and some cavalry and artillery sent to Suakin..	145
Fall of Khartum. Lord Wolseley requests the despatch of a force to crush Osman Digna	145
February 7th. Lord Wolseley's estimate of force necessary for Autumn campaign	145
February 10th. Government propose Suakin-Berber railway	146
February 11th. Lord Wolseley's reply. His plans ..	146
February 18th. Lord Wolseley doubtful as to advancing on Berber	147
The Suakin Expedition. Sir G. Graham in command..	148
February 21st. Capture of Berber definitely postponed	148
Effect of this change of plan on the Suakin Expedition	148
Dispositions necessitated on the Nile	150
Nile, main route for supplies	150
March 3rd. Lord Wolseley insists on extension of Halfa railway	150
The Suakin-Berber railway. Communications between the Government and Lord Wolesley	150
March 6th. Despatch of Lord Wolseley giving his views on the situation	152
Transport and supply arrangements for the Autumn	158
Available transport. Assiut to Wady Halfa	158
Steamers, etc., for the Autumn	159

CHAPTER XII.—THE SUMMER QUARTERS AND EVACUATION OF THE SUDAN.

February 22nd. Selection of camps	161
Disposition of troops for the summer	161
Fatmeh, the advanced post of Line of Communications	164
Troops in quarters. Arrangements in case of a hostile advance	164
Huts built by the troops	165
March 30th. Departure of Lord Wolseley for Cairo	166
April 3rd. Departure of Mudir	166
April 13th. Lord Wolseley informed that expedition to Khartum would probably be abandoned	167
April 21st. Orders for retirement	167
Steps taken to secure quiet in district of Dongola	167
General Dormer assumes command	167
Instructions for withdrawal of sick	167

	PAGE
The retreat from above Abu Kussi	167
Destruction of forts	169
Appointment of civil governors for the abandoned districts	170
Withdrawal of civil employés	170
June 17th. Rear guard entrusted to General Brackenbury. His orders	170
Arrangements made by him	172
June 26th. Proposed re-occupation	173
Lord Wolseley's views on the abandonment of the Sudan	173
Difficulties of proposed re-occupation	174
Position of force at this time	174
Supplies available in June	176
Decision to continue retreat	177
July 1st. Lord Wolseley informed of this decision by the Secretary of State	177
Decision to hold railroad	178
July 5th. Evacuation of Dongola	179

CHAPTER XIII.—THE SUAKIN EXPEDITION.

February 17th, 1885. Contract for railway	180
February 20th. Sir G. Graham appointed to command. His instructions	180
Force available previous to the assembly of the Suakin Field Force	182
Organization of the British Troops	182
Indian Brigade. Its composition	183
New South Wales Contingent	183
Animals, etc., supplied by the Indian Government	184
Arrival of Sir G. Graham	184
March 13th. Commencement of railway	185
Organization of Water Supply.	
Condensing ships	185
Supply Depôts	186
Distribution of water	186
Railway supply	186
Field supply for the zeribas as these were formed	187
Supply for animals	187
Commissariat and Transport.	
Difficulties at the outset	188
Daily consumption of food	189
Nature of provisions supplied to the troops	189
Forage for horses and camels	189
Fuel and water	189
Transport sent from England. Animals whence supplied	190
Organization into seven sections	190
Labour required by the Commissariat Department	191
Ordnance Store Department.	
Medical Department. British Troops.	
Personnel	191
Bearer Companies	192
Hospitals	192
Hospital ships	192

TABLE OF CONTENTS.

PAGE

Medical Department. Indian Contingent.
Personnel 192
Hospitals 192
Hospital Ships 193
Ambulance Transport 193
Veterinary Department.
Personnel 193
Sick Horse Depôts 193
Camel Lazaretto 194
Shoes and Shoeing 194
Balloon Detachment.
Changes in the *order de bataille* of the expeditionary force 194
Night Alarms 194
Letter from Osman Digna 195
Two phases of the contemplated Campaign 195
Features of the country 195
Tactics of the enemy 196
Direction of the railway 196
Position of enemy round Suakin 196
Reason for advance on Hashin 196
March 19th. Reconnaissance to Hashin 197
March 20th. The action at Hashin 197
Return of force to Suakin 199
March 22nd. Force sent out to establish post on road to Tamai under Sir J. McNeill. Composition of force 200
Formation and advance of force. Sir J. McNeill's orders 200
Force halted at Tofrik 202
Disposition and construction of zeribas 202
Arrival of a second squadron from Suakin. Its return 203
The attack on the Tofrik Zeriba 204
Major Graves' two Squadrons 206
Casualties 207
Subsequent movements. Convoys sent out 23rd to 30th of March .. 208
April 2nd. Force marched for Tamai 210
Halt at Tesela 211
April 3rd. Advance on Tamai 211
Occupation of Tamai 211
Return of force 212
Second phase of operations 212
Attempted alliance with neutral tribes 212
Formation of No. 1 Station 213
April 8th. Occupation of Handub 214
April 10th and 19th. Occupation of Otao and Tambuk 214
Progress of the railway 214
Camel Corps formed 214
Reconnaissances westwards 215
May 2nd. Arrival of Lord Wolseley 215
Hostile gathering at T'Hakul 215
May 6th. Advance on T'Hakul. Suakin Column 216
Otao Column 216
Return to Suakin 217
Offers of Submission 217
Orders for withdrawal 217

CHAPTER XIV.—CONCLUSION.

	PAGE
June 27th. Departure of Lord Wolseley for England	219
Evacuation of the province of Dongola	219
July 10th. Reported death of Mahdi	219
July 17th. Evacuation of Fatmeh	220
July 21st. Command of frontier handed to General Grenfell	221
Lord Wolseley's recommendations for the protection of Egypt	221
Movements of the Mahdieh	223
Fall of Sennar and Kassala	224
Advance on Dongola	224
20th June, 1885. Death of Mahdi. Advance delayed	224
August 17th. Dongola occupied by Dervishes	225
December 30th. Battle of Ginnis	225
Lord Wolseley's final despatch	225

APPENDICES.—PART II.

Appendix 39.—Distribution of the Nile Expeditionary Force, and State of troops at Korti previous to the departure of the Desert Column .. 243
Appendix 40.—Sir H. Stewart's despatch reporting the occupation of Jakdul .. 246
Appendix 41.—Sir H. Stewart's report on his second march to Jakdul 247
Appendix 42.—Work done at the Jakdul wells .. 251
Appendix 43.—Approximate State of troops at Abu Klea on 17th January, 1885 .. 254
Appendix 44.—Despatches on the battle of Abu Klea.. 255
Appendix 45.—Despatches on operations near Metemmeh .. 259
Appendix 46.—Sir C. Wilson's explanation of delay at Gubat .. 267
Appendix 47.—Notes on the fall of Khartum by Major Kitchener .. 270
Appendix 48.—General Brackenbury's report on action at Kirbekan 277
Appendix 49.—Estimated amount of supplies to be with River Column on reaching Berber .. 281
Appendix 50.—Marching out State from Abu Klea, 23rd February, 1885 .. 282
Appendix 51.—Medical arrangements of the River Column .. 283
Appendix 52.—Orders for troops in boats issued by General Earle at Hamdab .. 291
Appendix 53.—Report on the Mudir's troops .. 293
Appendix 54.—Despatches on the operations of the River Column .. 295
Appendix 55.—Lord Wolseley's telegram of the 11th February with regard to steamers required .. 298
Appendix 56.—Report by the Director of Transport on the organization of Camel Transport for the Autumn Campaign .. 299
Appendix 57.—The hutting of troops .. 303

TABLE OF CONTENTS.

	PAGE
Appendix 58.—Instructions issued to the Principal Medical Officer for the withdrawal of the sick during the evacuation	305
Appendix 59.—Movement of the Nile force from the Sudan in June and July, 1885	306
Appendix 60.—Indian transport for the British Force at Suakin ..	312
Appendix 61.—Staff of the Suakin Field Force	315
Appendix 62.—Embarkation Table of troops for Suakin expedition ..	317
Appendix 63.—Sir G. Graham's final despatch	320

Sketch Map to illustrate the History of the Sudan Campaign.

PART II.

HISTORY OF THE SUDAN CAMPAIGN.

CHAPTER VI.

THE DESERT COLUMN.

Maps 1 and 2.

ON the 15th of December Sir H. Stewart arrived at Korti, with the Guards and Mounted Infantry, Camel Regiments and detachments of the South Staffordshire Regiment and Royal Engineers. On the following day Lord Wolseley, with his personal staff, and Sir C. Wilson, arrived, and was joined on the 24th of December by Sir R. Buller, and the remainder of the Headquarters Staff. December 16th, 1884. Arrival of Lord Wolseley at Korti.

The two tables given in Appendix 39 show the troops, &c., at Korti, and along the whole line, on the 25th December.

Supplies for the troops were at the front in sufficient quantities; but the supply of forage for camels was, as had been anticipated, very deficient, as owing to its bulk, which precluded the possibility of bringing it from Egypt, it had to be obtained almost exclusively from local sources, which were far from being abundant. This scarcity of forage necessitated the reduction of the camel transport to the lowest possible limits. But the amount actually available fell below what had been counted upon.

On his arrival at Korti, Lord Wolseley had expected to find the Chief Saleh, of the Kababish tribe, with a number of camels which that chief had, according to the Mudir, undertaken to supply. No camels were, however, forthcoming, and as, owing to insufficiency of camel transport, it was not possible to move the whole of the force intended for the capture of Metemmeh across the desert in a body, with their supplies, and at the same time to form a depôt at Jakdul, it was decided to send a convoy, the composition of which is Decision to form post at Jakdul.

Orders for march of convoy.

given below,* to the wells of Jakdul, there to form a post; the camels which had carried the garrison there, returning to bring on more men and supplies.

On the 29th, orders were issued by Sir H. Stewart for the force to march on the following day. It was directed to form up on the desert plateau, south-east of the village. Officers Commanding were instructed to see that the rations to be carried regimentally were present, in addition to the commissariat stores to be convoyed, and that water skins and water bottles were well filled and did not leak. Dates were issued to be carried in the haversacks, and strict orders were given that no water was on any account to be taken out of a water skin without a brigade order. All animals were to be watered about two hours before starting, great care being taken that they had every chance of drinking their fill. Officers were reminded that the pace of the column would depend upon each individual camel proceeding without checking, and to ensure this result, great attention to the loading of the camels was enjoined. Watches were set to the same time.

The Heavy Camel Regiment and Light Camel Regiment acted as transport, each camel carrying about 230 lbs., and one man leading 3 camels. These regiments, with the Royal Artillery Battery and the Commissariat and Transport Corps, were placed under the command of Colonel Stanley Clarke, Light Camel Regiment, who was appointed Baggage-Master of the force. Assistant Commissary-General R. A. Nugent, C.B., was in charge of the Commissariat and Transport Corps, and

	Officers.	N.C.O.'s and men.	Natives.	Camels, R. and B.	Horses.
Brigade Staff	5	3	2	11	5
19th Hussars	2	32	—	24	40
Heavy Camel Regiment	6	100	—	215	—
Light Camel Regiment	9	81	—	250	—
Guards' Camel Regiment	19	365	—	406	—
Mounted Infantry	24	359	1	413	—
Royal Artillery	3	20	31	164	—
Royal Engineers	2	26	—	40	—
Commissariat and Transport Corps	2	27	153	601	—
Medical Staff	6	16	35	82	—
Total	78	1029	221	2206	45

Surgeon-Major Fergusson of the Field Hospital and Bearer Corps; Major Kitchener accompanied the force as representative of the Intelligence Department. Major T. H. Phipps, Mounted Infantry Camel Regiment, and Lieutenant Count Gleichen, Guards' Camel Regiment, were directed to make a reconnaissance sketch of the road. The Officer Commanding the rear guard, composed of 19th Hussars, was authorised to use the spare camels preceding his detachment, or the cacolets of the Bearer Company, and was held responsible for no one being left behind.

At 3 p.m. on the 30th, the column marched off in the order given below,* and with the exception of a halt from 5 p.m. to 7.15 p.m., marched till 7.30 on the following morning, when a halt was made for the day, 34 miles having been covered. Frequent short halts had, however, to be made to allow straggling camels to come up and to re-adjust the loads. The track was found to be good, and for the most part easily discernable, and lay across an undulating gravel plain. *December 30th. Departure of the convoy.*

At 3 p.m. on the 31st, the column again marched off, halting at 5.15 p.m. to 8 p.m., and arrived at 8.30 p.m. at the wells of Hambok, where a short halt was made, and a small quantity of white muddy water was found.

At 1.15 a.m. on January the 1st, the well of El Howeiya was reached, and a halt was then made till 8.30 a.m. The supply of water was found to be very scanty and of bad quality. A detachment of mounted infantry was left here to improve the well.

The column again halted from 1 p.m. to 3.30 p.m., and then

---

* Advance guard, 20 men 19th Hussars.
  Scouts of Guards' Camel Regiment (two scouts per company) not extended.
  Guards' Camel Regiment.
  Royal Engineer detachment.
  Moveable Field Hospital.
  Half detachment Bearer Company, with all reserve water camels.
  Baggage camels, 19th Hussars.
  Heavy Camel Regiment.
  Light Camel Regiment.
  Royal Artillery.
  Commissariat and Transport Corps.
  Mounted Infantry Camel Regiment.
  Half detachment Bearer Company.
  Six spare camels from Commissariat and Transport Corps.
  Scouts of Mounted Infantry (two per company), not extended
  Rear Guard, 12 men, 19th Hussars.
  Distance between corps 30 yards.

continued its march till dusk (7 p.m.). It halted till the moon rose, at 8.30 p.m., and then continued marching throughout the night, and reached the gorge leading into Jakdul at 6.45 on the morning of the 2nd January.

January 2nd, 1885. Arrival at Jakdul.

At 2 a.m., before reaching Jakdul, the Abu Halfa wells were seized by a detachment of the mounted infantry. The latter part of the journey had lain through a district thickly studded with mimosa, and showing signs of a considerable rainfall at some periods of the year. The road for the last 12 miles had been flanked on the left by the escarpment of the Jebel Gilif range.

The total distance of 98 miles from Korti to Jakdul had been traversed in 63 hours and 45 minutes, $32\tfrac{3}{4}$ of which had been employed in actual marching.

Desert march a surprise.

Traces of Arabs were seen along the desert tracts, but not in any numbers, and the march was manifestly a complete surprise to the inhabitants. As a rule these retired before the advancing force, but several were interrogated and sent away with directions to bring in cattle and supplies to the troops. One, a hill robber of some importance, named Ali Loda, was retained, and rendered good service as a guide.

On nearing Jakdul a party of men wearing the Mahdi's uniform was captured. They were *en route* from Metemmeh, and were supposed to be emissaries of the Mahdi to Wad Kinkain, a Sowarab Sheikh, who had for some time past been conducting raids on the villages between Korti and Merowi, and who had several times been instrumental in cutting the telegraph wire.

Jakdul wells.

Map 3.

The wells, or rather reservoirs, of Jakdul were found to be situated about two and a quarter miles to the north of the Korti-Metemmeh road. The three main ones were situated one above the other, in the bed of a watercourse, running into an amphitheatre of rocks. The lower pool was of an irregular shape, and had precipitous sides. Its mean length was 85 feet, breadth 55 feet, and depth 12 feet. The water was found to have been much polluted by animals. The second pool, about 50 feet in length by 16 feet in breadth, with a mean depth of 6 feet, was of an irregular "diamond" shape, and was almost inaccessible, being connected with the lower pool by a narrow gorge about 30 feet long by 8 feet broad. The level of the water in this pool was about 15 feet higher than that in the lower one. The upper pool was situated at the head of a narrow and tortuous gorge about 50 feet long, and with precipitous sides about 80 feet high. Its general direction was at a right angle to that of the middle pool. It was about 80 feet long by 15 feet broad, and had a mean depth of 12 feet 6 inches. Excellent drinking water was found in the two upper pools. From the water marks on the sides of all of them it was evident that after the rains their contents were much greater.

On the date of Sir H. Stewart's arrival these pools contained:— *Water supply.*

Upper pool, 84,080 ⎫
Middle pool, 34,970 ⎬ = ⎰ 119,050 gallons of good drinking water for men.

Lower pool, 420,000 gallons of water for animals and washing purposes.

Besides these main reservoirs there were pools named by the troops "Gazelle," "Jackal," and "Pot hole," having a joint capacity of about 10,432 gallons.

The position of the pools and the general configuration of the ground is well shown in the sketch survey (Map 3), by Count Gleichen.

At 8 p.m. on the 2nd January, the day of his arrival, Sir H. Stewart marched out on his return journey to Korti, with the whole of the troops except the Royal Engineers and the Guards' Camel Regiment, 422 of all ranks, with nine horses and 10 camels, which were left as garrison of Jakdul under the command of Lieutenant-Colonel the Hon. E. E. T. Boscawen. Major Kitchener remained at Jakdul. *Return of convoy. Garrison of Jakdul.*

After the departure of Sir H. Stewart and his force, pumps were rigged to convey water from the middle pool for the men, and from the lower one for the animals, the latter conveying the water into a row of canvas troughs having a total length of 80 feet. A trench was also dug from the lower pool to convey the water to the mouth of the narrow gorge. Watering the camels had taken the whole day on the 2nd.

At noon on the 5th of January, Sir H. Stewart's convoy returned to Korti, having left a small detachment at Hambok to improve the water supply. Captain Lord Cochrane, Heavy Camel Regiment, had been sent on with despatches to Lord Wolseley the previous day and had arrived at 7 p.m.* *January 5th. Convoy reaches Korti.*

This first march of 196 miles, at the beginning of which the animals were comparatively fresh, caused a loss of 31 camels out of the 2,195 which started. It had told, however,

---

* Sir H. Stewart's report on the march is given in Appendix 40.

(S.C.2)

very severely on the camels generally. Most of them had been marching for a long time and were in low condition. Many returned to Korti with large sores and were incapacitated for service for the remainder of the campaign.

No cases of sickness had occurred among the troops.

January 7th. Colonel Clarke's convoy for Jakdul.

On the 7th of January a convoy of 1,000 camels, escorted by three sections of the Light Camel Regiment under Colonel S. Clarke, left Korti for Jakdul; 100 of the camels were laden with small-arm ammunition, 80 with medical stores, 30 with artillery stores, and the remainder with supplies.

Having deposited his load at Jakdul, Colonel Clarke had orders to return with the unloaded camels to Korti.

January 8th. Orders to Sir H. Stewart.

On the 8th of January, Sir H. Stewart and the main body of the Desert Column again left Korti for Jakdul. The following orders were issued to him:—

"On the 8th you will arrange to start yourself with the following force:—*

Half Battery Royal Artillery.
1 Squadron 19th Hussars.
Heavy Camel Regiment.
Mounted Infantry Camel Regiment.
Headquarters and 400 all ranks, Sussex Regiment.
1 Company, 50 men, Essex Regiment.
All the Naval Brigade now here.
2 Sections Bearer Company.
1 Section Moveable Field Hospital.
As many transport camels carrying supply as can be provided.

"Of this force, you will leave the 50 Essex at El Howeiya, and take on the mounted infantry now there.

"150 Sussex Regiment at Jakdul under command of Colonel Vandeleur.

"After such rest as your animals require, you will proceed to Metemmeh with following force:—

1 Squadron 19th Hussars.
3 Guns Royal Artillery.
Guards' Camel Regiment.

* Total strength :

Officers	98
Non-commissioned officers and men	1,509
Natives and interpreters	296
Egyptians	8
Camels	2,228
Horses	155
Mules	2

Heavy Camel Regiment.
Mounted Infantry Camel Regiment.
250 Men Sussex Regiment.
Naval Brigade.
Detachment Royal Engineers.
and a convoy taking eight days' supply for the force, 25,000 rations for the post at Metemmeh, and 3,000 rations for a post to be established at Abu Klea, as hereafter ordered ; 400 boxes small-arm ammunition ; 1 section if possible, 2 sections, Moveable Field Hospital ; 2 sections Bearer Company.

"On reaching Abu Klea,* you will establish a post there garrisoned by from 50 to 100 men, Sussex Regiment, as the nature of the ground may require, 300 rounds per man, and 3,000 rations.

"You will then advance on Metemmeh, which you will attack and occupy. For this it may be advisable to laager your convoy at the wells of Shebakat.

"Having occupied Metemmeh, you will leave there the Guards' Camel Regiment, the detachment Sussex Regiment, the Naval Brigade, detachment Royal Engineers, and three guns Royal Artillery, 25,000 rations, and 300 rounds small-arm ammunition per rifle ; and return with the convoy to Jakdul.

"You will give strict orders to all officers commanding posts that a cordon is to be established round their several posts, within which no Arabs are to be allowed to come.

"You will post at all stations a detachment of Mounted Infantry as express riders.

"For the present it is not advisable that less than four men should be sent with a message.

"Arrangements should be made to keep a supply of water in each post.

"You will be particular to use every endeavour to keep me as well and as quickly informed of your movements as possible.

"On your return to Jakdul you will continue to forward stores by convoy to Metemmeh.

"It may be necessary for you to leave Jakdul with more camels than you leave Korti with, in that case you will take camels from Colonel Clarke's convoy.

---

* If you think it desirable you may leave the establishment of this post until you return.

"Colonel Sir C. Wilson, D.A.G., and Captain Verner, D.A.A.G., will accompany you for intelligence duties.

"Sir C. Wilson has been directed to show you his instructions, He will be in command of Metemmeh when you leave."*

The following orders were also issued to Sir C. Wilson:—

Orders to Sir C. Wilson.

"You will accompany the column under the command of Brigadier-General Sir Herbert Stewart, K.C.B., which will leave Korti to-morrow for Metemmeh. Your intimate knowledge of Sudan affairs will enable you to be of great use to him during his operations away from these Headquarters.

"You will endeavour to enter into friendly relations with the Hassaniyeh tribe, and to induce them, if possible, to carry supplies for us across the desert, and to sell us sheep and cattle, &c.

"As soon as Metemmeh is in our occupation Sir H. Stewart will dispatch a messenger to Korti with an account of his march, &c., and you will be good enough to send me by same opportunity all political information you may have obtained, all news of General Gordon, the so-called Mahdi, &c., &c.

"I am sending Captain Lord Charles Beresford, R.N., with a small party of seamen, to accompany Sir H. Stewart to Metemmeh, where, if there are any steamers, Lord C. Beresford will take possession of one or two of them, as he may think best. Any Egyptian (Fellaheen) soldiers on them can be converted into camel drivers, and come back here with the empty camels.

"As soon as Lord C. Beresford reports that he is ready to proceed with one or more steamers to Khartum, you will go to that place with him and deliver the enclosed letter to General Gordon. I leave it open so that you may read it.

"Orders have been given to Sir H. Stewart to send a small detachment of infantry with you to Khartum. If you like you can, upon arriving there, march these soldiers through the city, to show the people that British troops are near at hand. If there is any epidemic in the town you will not do this. I do not wish them to sleep in the city. They must return with you to Metemmeh. You will only stay in Khartum long enough to confer fully with General Gordon.

* This was afterwards changed, as Colonel Burnaby, Royal Horse Guards, who had been detailed for duty with the River column, was posted, on the 10th of January, to the Desert column, to act as commandant of Metemmeh when Sir C. Wilson proceeded to Khartum.

Having done so, you will return with Lord C. Beresford in steamers to Metemmeh.

"My letter to General Gordon will explain to you the object of your mission. You will confer with him both upon the military and upon the political position. You are aware of the great difficulty of feeding this army at such a great distance from the sea. You know how we are off in the matter of supplies, the condition and distribution of the troops under my command, the dates when General Earle will be able to move on Abu Hamed, &c.

"I am sending with you the three officers named in the margin* who will accompany you to Khartum, and remain there to assist General Gordon until I am able to relieve that place.

"Upon your return to Metemmeh from Khartum you will rejoin my Headquarters at your earliest possible convenience.

"It is always possible that when Mohammed Ahmed fully realises that an English army is approaching Khartum he will retreat, and thus raise the siege. Khartum would, under such circumstances, continue to be the political centre of our operations, but Berber would become our military objective. No British troops would be sent to Khartum beyond a few red coats in steamers for the purpose of impressing on the inhabitants the fact that it was to the presence of our army they owed their safety.

"The siege of Khartum being thus raised, all our military arrangements would be made with a view to the immediate occupation of Berber, and to a march across the desert to Ariab on the Suakin road.

"Upon arrival at Metemmeh it is very possible you may find papers or letters from General Gordon awaiting us. You will be good enough to send them to me by the first messenger coming here."

The orders issued to Lord C. Beresford, were as follows :—

"The Section Naval Brigade now here, will march with Sir H. Stewart's convoy on the 8th for Metemmeh.

Orders to Lord C.

"You will report yourself to Sir H. Stewart, to receive instructions regarding the march.

Beresford.

"On arrival at Metemmeh, you will at once take over and man any steamer, or, if you can, steamers that are there or

---

* Major Dickson, Royal Dragoons, Lieut. Stuart Wortley, King's Royal Rifles; the third to be named on arrival at Metemmeh.

in the vicinity; and you will use every means in your power to put one or more of the steamers that will, it is believed, be available, into an efficient state.

"You will do this under the direction of the senior military officer at the post, and will take his instructions regarding the steamers when ready."

March of main body for Jakdul.

The force marched till sunset, and then halted till the moon rose at 3.30 a.m. on January 9th. It then marched till 9.30 a.m., when a four hours' halt was made at Wady Abu Gir. It again marched till sunset and then halted till the moon rose, when a march was made straight to El Howeiya, which was reached at about 10 on the morning of the 10th. Here, unfortunately, the wells were found to have been drained by Colonel Clarke's convoy, and some discomfort consequently ensued.

January 12th. Arrival at Jakdul.

In the afternoon of the same day the force marched for the wells of Abu Halfa, which were reached on the following afternoon, a halt of nine hours having been made after sunset, and another short halt in the morning. On the morning of the 12th January it arrived at Jakdul, and the day was spent in watering and grazing the camels, which had already began to suffer from hard work and privations.*
During the nine days that Colonel Boscawen and his men had been left alone, they had effected great improvements in the post. The work done is best described in the report by Major Dorward, R.E., which is contained in Appendix 42.

Colonel Burnaby's convoy.

On January the 13th, a convoy of 125 camels from Korti arrived under Colonel Burnaby, and the whole force was then ready to advance.

The following private letter from Sir Herbert Stewart, one of the last he wrote, is of interest as showing his view of the situation.

"*Jakdul, January 14th,* 1885.

Letter from Sir H. Stewart of January 14th.

"My dear General,

"I have endeavoured to give you everything up to this officially, but I write one line privately to tell you that everything is going on swimmingly except as to time. In the absence of dhura, I am sure you would not have wished the camels to be tried beyond what they ought to be called

---

* Sir H. Stewart's report on, and itinerary of, the march, is given in Appendix 41.

upon to bear, and this, coupled with the operation of watering the number of camels and horses now here, has consumed time which I could wish had been employed marching.

"To see 3,000 camels and more watered from a pool, and all waterskins, tanks, and waterbottles filled up, is a sight to be seen to be appreciated. I am sorry to tell you that a considerable amount of Nile stores are useless. It seems incredible, but whilst flour has been soldered down, the tea has only been fastened up with canvas, and so has easily got wet. That which has got wet is spoiled. Fortunately the loads thus spoiled have not used up much transport, but most unfortunately they are our most valuable stores.

"I am very much obliged for the 29 red coats* which arrived quite safely.

"The more I see of this road and its work, the more convinced I am that you will have largely to supplement the supply of camels. The camels with my force are very well, but the transport animals will want a deal of replenishing, and we also are bound with time to make calls upon you.

"The water on the road could be vastly improved. Bad as Hambok turned out, I still think it capable of improvement. If a little shafting such as is used for mines was sent here in the shape of a few planks, I am sure a supply might be obtained for small convoys. El Howeiya will afford a really good supply, and at Abu Halfa where I halted, there could soon be an unlimited quantity. There are also other places on the road where we found water. I wont bother you with any more, but hope to write to you from Metemmeh and send off Sunday afternoon.

"Yours very truly,
"HERBERT STEWART."

Lord Wolseley attached very great importance to the appearance of British soldiers in their red coats on board the steamers at Khartum. It was not alone supplies that the defenders of the place stood in need of, although the stores that the steamers would bring were sorely needed. The garrison required encouragement. The very sight of the British soldiers would be sufficient to bring it home to the defenders that the relief, of which rumours so often reached

* For the use of the detachment intended to proceed to Khartum with Sir Charles Wilson.

them from the north, and in which their chief expressed such confidence, was really at hand.

As long as General Gordon held out at Khartum, the Expedition had a definite object to achieve, and success was certain. From the first Lord Wolseley's object in despatching the Desert Column to Metemmeh was to get one or more steamers up to Khartum at the earliest possible date, with a few red coats on board. And to accomplish this end he deliberately accepted the difficulties and dangers involved in the march across the Bayuda Desert. As the event proved, it was only when the garrison lost all hope of succour that Khartum fell into the hands of the Madhi.

And here, before proceeding with the narrative of Sir H. Stewart's advance, it may be well briefly to review the situation as then known to the military authorities.

Review of the situation in the theatre of operations.

The latest news of General Gordon was that received in the little letter and the verbal message delivered to Lord Wolseley on the 30th of December, which told that Khartum was holding out, but was hard pressed, and that five of General Gordon's steamers were awaiting our orders at Metemmeh.*

On the date of this messenger leaving Khartum, Omdurman was still in the hands of General Gordon, and the bulk of the Mahdi's army was concentrated round that place and Khartum.

Small raiding parties were scouring the desert between Debbeh and Khartum, but with the exception of a post of 80 men under Ez Zein at Sarni on the Dukeiyat-Berber road, and some unimportant raids, the Bayuda Desert was believed to be quiet. That this was so, as far as the country to the west of Jakdul is concerned, is proved by the fact that on the 8th of January, Mr. Piggott, Reuter's correspondent, arrived at Korti, having ridden from Jakdul accompanied only by a native camel driver, and having been invariably received with signs of friendship by the few Arabs whom he met on the road.

As regards the garrison of Metemmeh, a native who had left that place on the 15th of December, had reported to Lieut.-Colonel Colvile, at Merowi, on the 25th of December, that there were about 3,000 Arabs there, armed with Remingtons and fowling pieces, and two brass mountain guns; and that

---

* The steamers were, as a matter of fact, at Nasri island, about 25 miles above Metemmeh.

STAFF OF DESERT COLUMN. 13

Mohammed Ahmed was sending them another mountain gun and a Gatling; that there were also 1,000 men on the opposite bank near Shendi, and that Metemmeh had been fortified.

The only direct information as to opposition on the Korti-Metemmeh road, had been a telegram from the Mudir of Dongola to Lord Wolseley on the 30th of December, stating that the enemy were going to send 20,000 men to Bayuda or Jakdul to stop the road. The advance of the first convoy to Jakdul was, however, well known (although its advance was in itself a surprise), and it was evident that once knowing the route which we intended to follow, the enemy would make every effort to oppose the British force on it, before it reached the river. It was not, however, known that Omdurman had fallen during the second week in January, and that a large force of Mahdieh had thus been liberated.

The formation of a depôt at Jakdul before the final advance on Metemmeh had been necessitated by want of camels, of camel drivers, and of camel equipment. Not only had it been found impossible to obtain large numbers in the neighbourhood of Korti, but there was also a want of food for them in the district. The whole neighbourhood was in a short time almost completely drained of the necessary dhura.

At 2 p.m., on January 14th, the following force left Jakdul for Metemmeh:— January 14th. Force leaves for Metemmeh. Composition.

2 Troops 19th Hussars, Lieutenant-Colonel P. Barrow, C.B., C.M.G., commanding.

1 Division Naval Brigade, 1 Gardner gun, Lord C. Beresford commanding.

1/1 S.D. R.A. (Camel Battery, 3 guns) Captain G. Norton, R.A., commanding.

Royal Engineers, Major Dorward, R.E., commanding.

Heavy Camel Regiment, Lieutenant-Colonel Hon. R. Talbot commanding.

Guards' Camel Regiment, Lieutenant-Colonel Boscawen commanding.

Mounted Infantry Camel Regiment, Major Hon. G. H. Gough, 14th Hussars, commanding.

250 Royal Sussex Regiment, on camels, Major M. Sunderland commanding.

Moveable Field Hospital, Surgeon W. H. Brigg.

Bearer Company, Surgeon A. Harding.

In all about 1,800 combatants of all ranks,* accompanied by 1,118 transport camels.

The Staff were as follows :—

Brigadier-General Sir H. Stewart, K.C.B.
Aide-de-Camp Captain F. Rhodes, 1st Royal Dragoons.
Deputy Assistant Adjutant and Quartermaster-General Major Wardrop, 3rd Dragoon Guards.
Brigade-Major Captain the Earl of Airlie, 10th Hussars.
Deputy Adjutant-General, Intelligence Department, Colonel Sir Charles Wilson, K.C.M.G., R.E.
Deputy-Assistant Adjutant-General, Intelligence Department, Captain Verner, Rifle Brigade.
Attached to Intelligence Department, Major J. B. B. Dickson, 1st Royal Dragoons. Captain R. F. Gascoigne, Yorkshire Hussars (late Royal Horse Guards), and Lieutenant Stuart Wortley, King's Royal Rifles.
Colonel F. Burnaby, Royal Horse Guards (Special Service).
Assistant Commissary-General Nugent, C.B.
Assistant Commissary-General Rainsford.
Principal Medical Officer, Surgeon-Major Fergusson.
Lord Cochrane was appointed baggage master to the force.

On the same day (January 14th) Colonel Clarke left Jakdul for Korti with 482 "empty" camels to bring up more supplies. He was accompanied by Major Kitchener, whose services were placed at the disposal of the General of Communications.

Garrison of Jakdul.

A garrison of 150 of the Royal Sussex Regiment was left at Jakdul under the command of Colonel Vandeleur.

Sir H. Stewart marched for four hours, doing ten miles, and then halted for the night. The force started again at five on the following morning and marched till 9.30, when a halt was then made opposite Jeble El-Nus (the halfway hill) till noon, when the march was continued till 5 p.m., at which hour the force halted for the night near Jebel Es-Sergain. During the day fresh tracks of horses, passing to and from Metemmeh, were frequently observed.

This march fatigued the camels greatly, as the day was very hot and the route lay for a considerable distance through heavy sand. They had been marching for sixteen days, almost without a rest, on a short allowance of food and with little water.

* A detailed state of the force is given in Appendix 43.

ADVANCE ON ABU KLEA.

At 5.15 on the morning of the 16th January the march was continued. The Hussars were pushed out a considerable distance to the front, and gained touch of the enemy during the morning. The force advanced till 11.30 a.m. A halt was then called, a short distance to the northward of the range of hills over which lay the track to the wells of Abu Klea. About the same time news came from the cavalry that the enemy was in sight.

January 16th.

At about noon Colonel Barrow came in and reported the enemy in position between the British force and the wells.

Touch of the enemy.

At 1 p.m. the column moved off again in the following formation. On the right the Guards' Camel Regiment, in the centre the Heavy Camel Regiment, on the left the Mounted Infantry Camel Regiment, the baggage behind them, and the rear brought up by the Royal Sussex. The whole was massed together in close formation. The cavalry were in front watching the enemy.

Sir H. Stewart and Sir C. Wilson pushed on to the front, the former to select a bivouac ground and the latter to reconnoitre. On his return Sir C. Wilson reported that he had seen a large force, part of which at least belonged to the Mahdi's army, and that something more serious than mere desert Arabs would be encountered.

Bivouac before Abu Klea.

The force moved forward slowly, over two ridges, crossed some rough ground, and descended into the narrow valley leading to the Abu Klea wells; it halted about 3½ miles from the wells. The enemy showed in considerable force. Considering it too late to attack that day Sir H. Stewart ordered a zeriba to be constructed.

The spot chosen for the bivouac was near the foot of some rising ground that lay to the right of the line of advance on Abu Klea, and near the head of the wady leading to the wells. On either side of this wady there lay a long line of hills, those to the west, or right, throwing out a succession of low spurs and underfeatures. A piquet was placed some little distance to the front, and from the spot which it occupied, the enemy's chief position could be seen, marked by a long line of flags across the valley. About 2,000 yards to the right was one high rocky peak and a group of smaller hills; about 1,000 to 1,200 yards to the left and left rear was a chain of lower hills. These latter were occupied by the mounted infantry, who built a small fort on the summit of one of them; but the hills to the right being considered out of range were not occupied, and before night-fall they had been lined by groups of the enemy's sharpshooters, who kept up throughout the night a brisk but comparatively harmless fire.

The enemy were on the move all night, beating their tom-toms and evidently preparing for battle. At dawn the force stood to arms, and a company of Mounted Infantry was sent out to keep down the hostile fire.

January 17th. At 8.30 a.m. the Arabs occupied the high ground to the left of the valley in force, but soon retired again. They appeared to have got the range, as casualties became more numerous, and Sir H. Stewart, judging that the Mahdieh intended to harass him from a distance, determined to take the offensive.

The advance towards Abu Klea. Breakfast was served out under a warm fire, which caused several casualties, and at 9 a.m. orders were given to form square preparatory to an advance. The square was formed thus :—

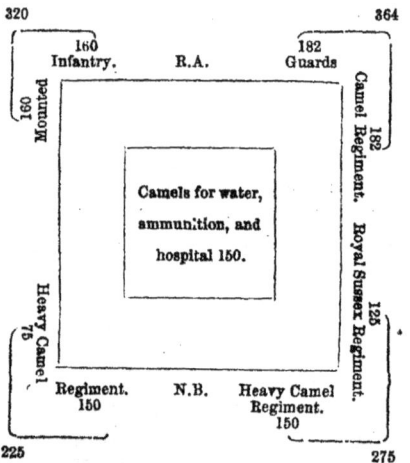

While the square was forming, Colonel Barrow and the cavalry moved off to the left to keep the enemy on the hills in check, while part of the Mounted Infantry, under Captain Campbell, and a detachment of Scots Guards under Lieutenant Romilly, were sent to the left and right flanks respectively to skirmish. The sick and baggage were left in the zeriba under the protection of a guard of the Royal Sussex. As the square was forming, Major Gough was wounded, and the command of the Mounted Infantry devolved on Major C. T. Barrow. Major Dickson and Lieutenant Lyall, R.A., were wounded about the same time.

As the men rose from the slight hollow in which they had bivouacked, a heavy fire was opened by the enemy, chiefly on the right flank, causing several casualties.

The square then moved very slowly forward, feeling its way, the skirmishers keeping in check as much as possible the brisk fire which the enemy kept up from the front, right and right rear, and the left being protected by the cavalry. After moving a short distance, the guns were taken off the camels, and were brought into action against hostile bodies on the high ground to the right and right rear. The cavalry kept in check bodies of hostile horsemen and spearmen who endeavoured to work round towards the zeriba. The guns were not replaced on the camels, but were dragged by the men. It was during this period that Captain Viscount St. Vincent, Adjutant of the Heavy Cavalry Regiment, received the wound which afterwards proved fatal; Surgeon J. Magill, Coldstream Guards, was also wounded at this time.

The line of advance selected by Sir Herbert Stewart was at first down the centre of the valley, along which ran a broad sandy khor studded with clumps of long grass and bushes. The column soon, however, took ground to its right, and then moved parallel to the khor, by a route which gave some little command, and at the same time kept clear of ground in which the enemy might lie concealed. It had, however, the disadvantage of crossing ground that was undulating and difficult for camels and guns. As a consequence, it became necessary for the square to move very slowly, and halt constantly to avoid having its rear face forced out. *Line of advance.*

When within about 1,500 yards of the line of flags already mentioned, a halt was made and a few shells were sent among them, which had the effect of making some hundreds of the enemy spring up and retreat. This, combined with the fact that our fire had almost completely silenced that of the enemy on that flank, led to a belief that no serious opposition would be encountered. The march was then continued, without incident, until the skirmishers got to within 200 yards of the flags, which were placed diagonally across the khor, as shewn in the sketch facing page 20. The square was still about 500 yards distant from the flags.

The square had been marching by the right, and the right front corner happened to be on a slight rise of ground. A *The battle of Abu Klea.*

Map 4.

halt was made at this point to allow of the rear face of the square, which had been bulged out by the lagging camels, closing up, and also to enable the files to close to their right. This movement was greatly impeded by the slowness of the camels and their drivers, and before it was completed a mass of about 5,000 of the enemy rose up from behind the line of flags, advanced at a quick run, in a deep serrated line headed by horsemen, and charged towards the left front corner of the square.*

The skirmishers at once retired, but as they did so directly in the line of advance of the enemy, they screened him from the fire of the square during the first stage of his charge, and it was not until the spearmen were within 200 yards of the square that the fire could be developed. Two of the 7 prs. were run out in advance of the front face, and the other was brought into action in front of the left face, close to the left front corner.

The fire from the front and left faces was such that the Arabs were forced to take ground to their right, and they thus brought the whole weight of their charge to bear on the left rear corner, defended by the Heavy Camel Regiment and the Naval Brigade. The Mahdieh appeared indeed to have recognised instinctively that the left rear, which was not at the moment properly formed, was the weak point. The left rear angle was still partly screened by its own skirmishers, the last man of whom was, in fact, speared by the enemy just as he was reaching the square. This part of the attack was also more hidden by folds of the ground than that on the left front; for while the Mounted Infantry were able to bring a constant fire on the advancing Arabs, these were often concealed from the Heavy Camel Regiment. Captain Verner's sketch (Map 4) shows the folds of the ground very clearly.

The Arabs came down on the left rear of the square with lightning rapidity. The last 100 yards were crossed in a few seconds, although during this brief space numbers fell before the fire of the Heavies and of the Gardner Gun, which the Naval Brigade had run out 20 yards outside the left rear face. But the number of rifles, however well used, was insufficient to annihilate the mass of Arabs which charged; and hardly had the enemy's flank movement been perceived, when the left rear corner was pressed back by sheer weight of numbers. Unfortunately, too, the Gardner gun, which had

* Some of our wounded were outside the square throughout the charge.

BATTLE OF ABU KLEA.   19

been doing good service at the beginning of the charge, jammed, and caused the loss of nearly half the Naval Brigade, who gallantly stood by it until they were swept into the square by the rush of Arabs. Many of the rifles also jammed, thus reducing the fire, which at its best was inadequate against such overwhelming odds.

The onslaught on the left rear corner of the square was so sudden that some difference of opinion exists as to what occurred while the Arabs made their charge. The left face had been weaker than the right, and there were gaps in it when the attack occurred.*

Part of the Heavy Camel Regiment from the rear face appears to have moved somewhat to its right, to strengthen the left face, and thus to have created a gap in the rear face. This gap the Royal Sussex endeavoured to fill up, and when, in the mêlée that ensued, the Heavies in the rear face were borne back by the masses of fanatic spearmen, they carried the Royal Sussex with them.

The camels, which up to this time had been a source of weakness to the square, now became a source of strength. The spearmen by weight of numbers forced back the rear face of the square on to the camels; these formed a living traverse that broke the rush and gave time for the right face and front face to take advantage of finding themselves on higher ground, and to fire over the heads of those engaged in a hand-to-hand struggle, on to the mass of the enemy behind. A desperate conflict ensued in the centre of the square, but the slaughter caused by the musketry from the rising ground caused the rearward Arabs to waver and then to fall back. Within the square the din of battle was such that no words of command could be heard, and each man was obliged to act on the impulses of the moment.

Officers and men alike fought well in this short hand-to-hand encounter, and many acts of heroism were performed. Colonel Burnaby was killed in the mêlée at the left rear corner. The Heavies suffered terribly in the struggle at this point. Two privates of the Heavy Camel Regiment remained outside the square throughout the charge, guarding their officer, Lord St. Vincent, who was lying helpless and wounded under his camel, and almost by a miracle both their lives were spared. But before five minutes had elapsed the little band of less than 1,500 British soldiers had by sheer pluck and

* See the diagram page 16.

muscle killed the last of the fanatics who had penetrated into their midst. At the same time the fire of the Heavies and Royal Sussex had checked a formidable charge of the enemy's cavalry.

The inside of the square cleared, its outside assailants sullenly withdrew, halting anon, apparently to throw back one more curse at the "infidels" who had again defeated them; and then, a ringing cheer broke forth from the little band of British soldiers. The enemy fled across the khor, and up the hills on its other side, till well out of range. There small bands remained hovering on the high ground watching Sir H. Stewart's force till dark, while the remainder disappeared over the hills.

While the wounded were being collected and dressed, and the enemy's arms, ammunition, &c., burnt, the cavalry were sent off to find the wells. Some delay occurred in discovering them, and the Arabs made a momentary stand; but a few volleys from the Hussars sufficed to drive them off. The square in the meantime moved slowly forward, the men suffering greatly from thirst, and the transport of the wounded causing delay. About 5 p.m. information reached it from the Hussars that the wells were close by, and unoccupied.

Arrival at the wells of Abu Klea. They were found to consist of a number of holes in the sandy bed of the valley, in which the water gathered slowly. The water was muddy but good.

The force here bivouacked in square and awaited the arrival of the baggage and stores which had been left in the zeriba of the previous night.

Our losses were found to be as follows:—

Casualties during the day. *Killed*—Colonel Burnaby; Majors L. M. Carmichael, W. H. Atherton, and W. A. Gough, Captain J. W. W. Darley, Lieutenants C. W. A. Law and R. Wolfe, Heavy Camel Regiment; Lieutenants A. Pigott, and R. E. De Lisle, Naval Brigade (nine officers); and 65 non-commissioned officers and men.

Wounded.—Lord Airlie, slightly; Lord St. Vincent,* severely; Lieutenant R. J. Beech, slightly, Lieutenant H. Costello, slightly, both of the Heavy Camel Regiment; Major Gough, severely; Major Dickson, severely; Lieutenant Lyall, dangerously; Lieutenant J. D. Guthrie,* Royal Artillery, severely; Surgeon J. Magill (nine officers); and 85 non-commissioned officers and men.

* Died of wounds.

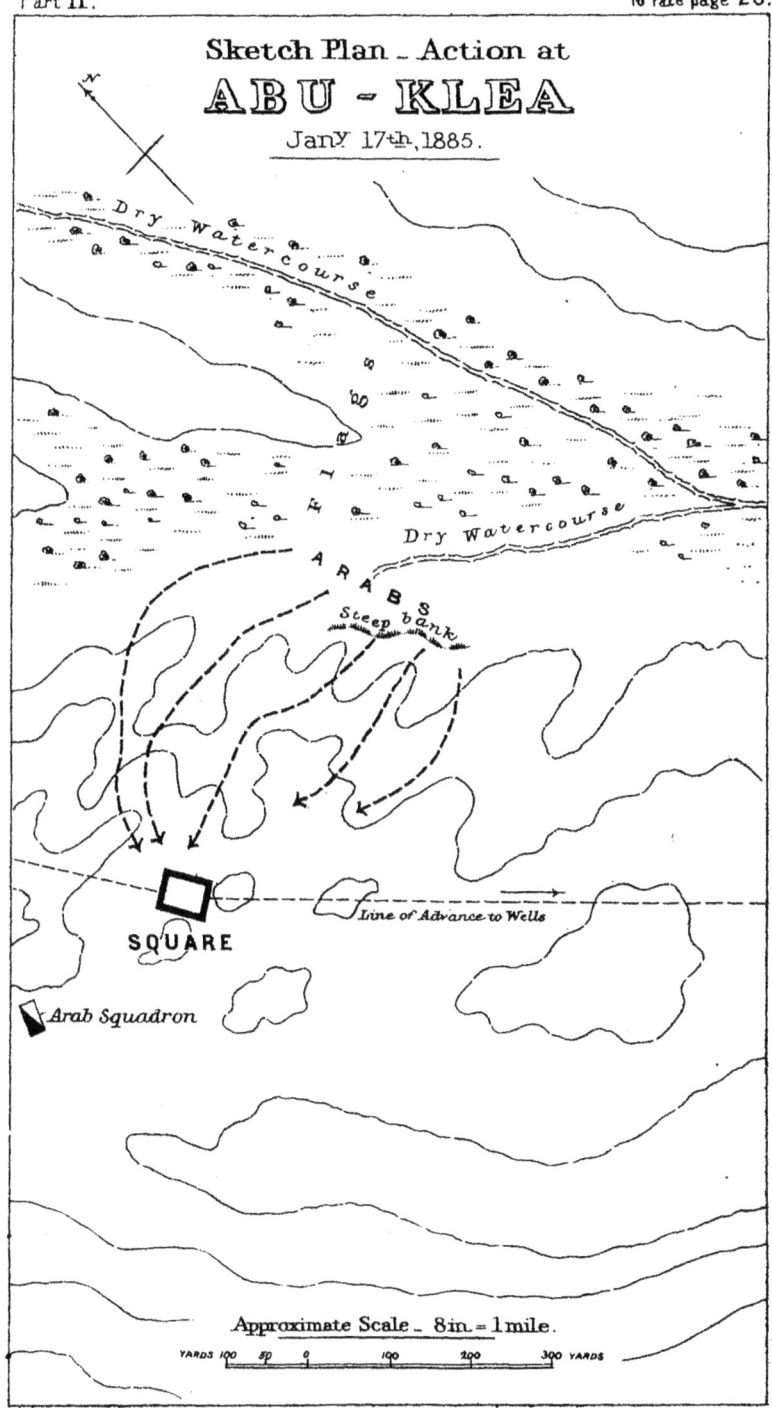

The enemy's loss was very heavy, 1,100 bodies were counted in the immediate proximity of the square, and all prisoners stated that their loss in wounded had been exceptional.

Sir H.. Stewart's despatch on this action is given in Appendix 44. As will be seen from Sir C. Wilson's report, enclosed in the despatch, it was ascertained from prisoners that Omdurman had fallen. A large force liberated from Omdurman had taken part in the day's fighting.

At sunset a party of 300 volunteers under Major Phipps, Mounted Infantry, was sent back to the zeriba to bring up the camels and impedimenta. It was a dark night and, as the loads of the camels had been utilised for improving the defences, it was 7.30 on the following morning (18th January) before the party returned. The troops in consequence spent a very miserable night, without food, coats or blankets—a serious matter in the desert during the winter.

The early part of the day was spent in building a small fort for the protection of the wounded, who had to be left behind under a guard of 100 men of the Royal Sussex. This detachment had instructions to entrench itself and to hold the wells. January 18th.

Sir H. Stewart had determined to push on to the Nile, and to make a night march in the hope of reaching the river without fighting. He decided to follow the route to Metemmeh till the column had passed the Shebakat wells and then to move to the right, so as to strike the Nile two or three miles above the town. Ali Loda, the robber, who alone professed to know the country, was consulted and said that the proposed route was possible, although he expressed doubts as to passing the Shebakat bush on a dark night. It was afterwards found that this bush could have been avoided by taking a direct route from Abu Klea to Abu Kru, but this would have entailed leaving the track and striking across an unknown country, and such a course never suggested itself. Sir H. Stewart's plans.

At a little after 4 o'clock in the afternoon the column moved off for Metemmeh. The distance to be traversed was about 23 miles. The order of march was as follows:— Departure for Metemmeh.

Combatants in front and transport in rear. The camels of the latter numbered 1,000, and marched in column of sections (of 30 camels front) at close interval.

Each of the drivers, mostly Aden natives, had charge of three or four camels, and rode the leading one, the others, tied head to tail, following in a string.

In rear of the baggage were some 50 spare camels, which

(s.c.2)

had either left their loads at Abu Klea, or had belonged to the killed or wounded left there.

The whole column covered about 600 yards, exclusive of the advanced and rear guards.

Ali Loda acted as guide and was accompanied by Captain Verner.

The pace was at first somewhat fast for the baggage camels, exhausted as they were, and the spare animals soon began to be heavily drawn upon, so that before long it became necessary to give orders that when a camel broke down its load was to be abandoned, unless it happened to be ammunition or a man. At nightfall, two companies of the Guards' Camel Regiment, and two companies Mounted Infantry, were dismounted, to act as an advanced guard.

Confusion among transport during the night march.

During the evening and early part of the night the order of march was well maintained; but as the night wore on and the native drivers fell asleep in their saddles, the camels, left to themselves, either forged ahead, crushing through the ranks, or lagged behind, throwing the rear sections into confusion, or, ravenous with hunger as they were, turned off the track to graze.

Even at the commencement of the march all ranks were fatigued, and it is probable that the usual amount of care was not expended in adjusting and securing the loads. As, time after time, these got knocked off as the camels crushed through the ranks, they were put on by the worn out drivers each time with less care, and therefore with more certainty that they would again fall off.

Peculiar difficulties of this march.

Previous night marches had always had the advantage of moonlight. This night there was no moon. Moreover, previously, on the march, both by day and by night, the column had always been halted by the bugle of the officer commanding the transport when he considered it necessary. On this night, however, owing to the proximity of the enemy and to the fact that the march was intended as a surprise, no bugle sounds were permitted, and it was therefore necessary to pass the word "Halt in front" by word of mouth. At first this worked well enough, but as the men, many of whom had been without sleep for two nights, got sleepy, they omitted to pass it, and finally it was found impossible to communicate with the front, unless a responsible officer himself carried the communication. Apart from the exhaustion of the men, the difficulty of communication was greatly increased by the fact of the Aden drivers not understanding English. They were also physically incapable of the exertion they were called upon to perform, and being civilians, could not be made to understand the importance of keeping proper interval. The regimental baggage trains kept together for a time in a fairly compact formation, as these were driven by our own men, but gradually the inroads of strings of leaderless baggage camels threw even these into confusion.

As the column approached the Shebakat bush the country traversed became more and more difficult, and the confusion in rear increased. Frequent halts were made in front, but the rear found great difficulty in following the troops at the head of the column, and appears to have left the track. About midnight the head of the column reached a thicket of acacia which Ali Loda had described as being close to the Shebakat Wells. The bush was now very troublesome, and even the advanced troops found difficulty in passing through it; but about 1 a.m. the head of the column arrived on the open ground beyond the bush. A long halt took place to enable the rear to close up, but although the mounted troops got clear of the thicket without great difficulty, the baggage camels were in the utmost confusion. Sir H. Stewart fully realised the state of affairs; but being anxious to reach the Nile before daybreak, and being well aware that the only chance of getting work out of a worn-out animal is to keep him on the move, he did not deem it safe to order a prolonged halt, and thus allow camels and men to become stiff. *Arrival at the Shebakat bush.*

The column therefore again advanced, leaving the road and striking off towards a point some three or four miles above Metemmeh, still under the guidance of Ali Loda. The direction was checked by Captain Verner and also by Colonel Barrow from compass bearings and by the stars. The country was open, with scattered trees, but the column had been greatly disorganized and progress was extremely slow. At dawn (about 6 a.m.) Sir H. Stewart ordered a halt, and, as is always the case, the reappearance of daylight acted as a stimulus to men and animals. In a very short space of time the column was again organized and ready to march. *January 19th. Halt at dawn.*

The spot where this halt was made was subsequently discovered to be 18 miles in a straight line from the Abu Klea Wells, or about five miles from the river. To traverse this distance had taken about 14 hours. During the 14 hours the head of the column had been halted for $4\frac{1}{4}$ hours, but the rear, delayed by stragglers and by the confusion of the march, was scarcely halted more than 1 hour. The distance traversed had

24   HISTORY OF THE SUDAN CAMPAIGN.—PART II.

been nearly 19 miles. It is very probable that, if a direct line had been taken to Abu Kru across the country to the right of the Abu Klea-Metemmeh road, which was afterwards found to be free of impediments, the column would have reached the Nile by daybreak, since fewer delays would have been necessary to enable the rear to close up.* Ali Loda, however, although he had pointed out that the Shebakat bush might prove a source of danger, never suggested such a route being followed.

As soon as the transport had been reorganised the column again moved on, making a quarter turn to the eastward, as Sir H. Stewart believed that he was too far south.

The Nile in sight.

At 7.30 a.m., on the 19th January, a gravel ridge was topped, and the Nile, Shendi, and Metemmeh appeared in sight. Out of the latter crowds of Arabs were seen to be

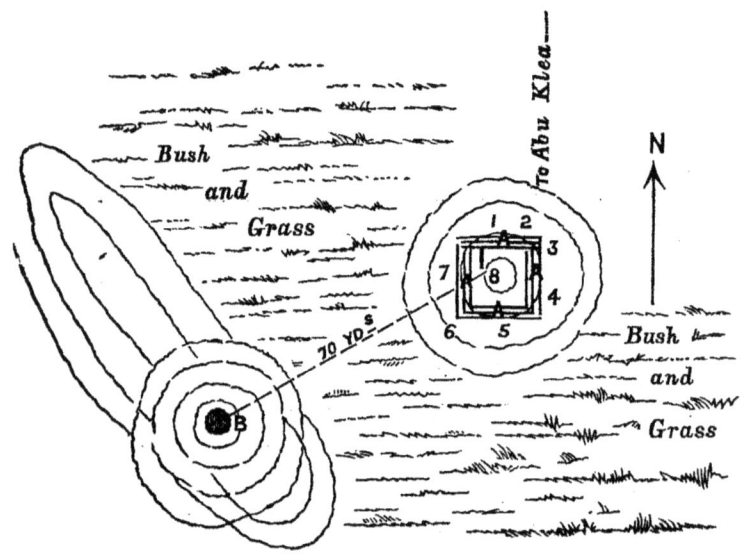

1. Hussars ; 2. Royal Engineers' Detachment ; 3. Navy and Gardner gun ; 4. Mounted Infantry and Royal Artillery ; 5. Guards ; 6. Heavies ; 7. Sussex ; 8. Hospital ; AA, camels ; B, redoubt.

* The only other night marches between the River and Abu Klea were those of the convoys of the 23rd of January and the 1st of February. These took 10¼ hours of actual marching.

streaming, while a force had already taken up a position between the column and the river, with the intention of contesting the advance.

Seeing that there was now no hope of reaching the river without a fight, Sir H. Stewart determined to laager his transport, and march straight to the river with the fighting force. The laager was formed on open ground, upon a small hill of gravel, giving command over the surrounding sea of grass and bush, and about 4 miles from the river. *(Force halted and laager formed. Map 5.)*

Sir H. Stewart, however, shortly afterwards modified his first plan and settled to let the men have their breakfasts before advancing.

He accordingly formed them up in the order shown in the accompanying diagram, round the camels. These had been parked in a square, with an opening at the right rear corner, closed by a traverse of biscuit boxes. In the centre of this square was the hospital. At the same time a rough parapet of camel saddles, biscuit boxes, and whatever the men could lay their hands on, was thrown up in front of the men, and a detachment was sent to occupy the knoll B, to prevent its occupation by the enemy.

While these preparations were being made, the enemy were gradually creeping closer, and kept up a hot fire from the long grass in which they were concealed, and which prevented the fire being returned with much effect.

At about 10 a.m. Sir H. Stewart received the wound which afterwards proved fatal, and the command thus devolved on Sir C. Wilson, the next senior military officer, who, after consultation with Sir H. Stewart, determined to repeat the tactics of Abu Klea, and, leaving his baggage, &c., in the zeriba, to fight his way to the water. Before doing so, however, it was necessary to put the zeriba and the fort, which had been formed on the knoll B, in a state to resist a sudden rush. This operation, partly owing to the mass of camels crowded round the baggage, and partly to the heavy fire encountered in crossing the open space to the fort, occupied a considerable time, and it was 2.30 before the square was formed up in rear of the zeriba, ready to march. The executive command was entrusted by Sir C. Wilson to Colonel Boscawen, the next senior Military Officer. *(Sir H. Stewart wounded. Advance determined upon.)*

The square was composed in the same manner as that at Abu Klea, with the Guards and Mounted Infantry in front and the Sussex and part of the Heavy Camel Regiment in rear. Half the Heavies, the 19th Hussars, the Royal Artillery, and *(Composition of square.)*

Naval Brigade, with their guns and the Gardner were left behind for the protection of the zeriba, under command of Colonel Barrow, the senior military officer, Lord C. Beresford, commanding the Naval Brigade, being the actual senior. A hot fire was kept up by the enemy while the square was forming. About this time were killed Mr. St. Leger Herbert, correspondent of the *Morning Post*, and acting as private secretary to Sir H. Stewart, who was shot through the head; Mr. Cameron, of the *Standard*, Quartermaster A. G. Lima, of the 19th Hussars, and others. Lieutenant C. Crutchley, Adjutant of the Guards' Camel Regiment, was severely wounded.

At 3 p.m. the square marched off, guided by Captain Verner. Small reserves were held in readiness at the corners of the square, these being the points that experience had shown to be the usual objective of Arab attacks. It soon became evident that the enemy were in considerable force to the front, and that the expected reinforcements from Omdurman had arrived. The gravel ridge, which ran between the zeriba and the village of Abu Kru on the river, was alive with foot and horse, and in every direction their banners could be seen rising out of the long grass, streaming in the breeze.

Skirmishers dispensed with.

As the cavalry had been left in the zeriba, and as the experience gained at Abu Klea had shown that, with such an enemy and in such a country, skirmishers were a source rather of danger than a protection, the square had to feel its way as best it could. Every precaution was taken against surprise, and a somewhat erratic course was followed, in order to keep as much as possible in ground clear of grass. Every now and then, when the enemy's fire became perilously hot, a halt was made, and volleys were fired at the puffs of smoke that issued from the grass, until it had somewhat abated, when the march was recontinued. The guns in the zeriba gave the square great assistance by an effective shrapnel fire whenever the enemy showed in force, and the Gardner also did good service.

The continual fire from an invisible enemy was exceptionally trying to the men, and it was with cheers of relief, as they neared the gravel ridge, that they greeted the Arabs, who were seen suddenly preparing for a charge.

Charge of the enemy against the square.

Running down hill as they were, the Arabs probably charged with even greater impetus than at Abu Klea, but the fire of the square was not masked by its own skirmishers. While the spearmen advanced a very heavy rifle fire was brought to bear on them from the very commencement of their rush, and with such effect that only one Arab succeeded in getting within 100 yards of the square. The hostile cavalry, as at Abu Klea, threatened the rear of the square after the onslaught of the spearmen, but kept at a distance, and in less than five minutes from the beginning of the charge, the whole scene had changed. The seething mass of fanatics, who had headed the charge, were now a heap of lifeless bodies, their comrades in rear had melted away into the distance, and the British troops (sadly reduced in numbers since their first fight at Abu Klea), made the echoes ring with a loud cheer. It was afterwards ascertained, that the column had on this day been opposed by another contingent that had come from Omdurman under Nur Angar.

No further opposition being encountered, the square then marched for the Nile. The direction was changed slightly to avoid a village in front, and the square entered a narrow valley leading down to the river, which was reached half-an-hour after dark, Sir C. Wilson having gone on ahead to select a bivouac ground.* *Nile reached.*

The position that was taken up on the river, although not a naturally strong one, was rendered secure by piquets, and the dispositions against attack that were hastily made, rendered it, with little labour, safe for the night.

A thorough rest was enjoyed by all but the surgeons, who, in spite of this being their fourth night of work, were unremitting in their attentions to the wounded. Rest was greatly needed by all, for this was the night of the 19th January, and the greater part of the force had either been under fire, or marching, or working since the evening of the 16th. This in a trying climate, and accompanied with unusual privations as regards food and water. The losses on the 19th amounted to 1 officer and 22 non-commissioned officers and men killed; and 8 officers and 90 non-commissioned officers and men wounded.

On the following morning (January 20th) the greater part of the force moved back to the zeriba, making a detour towards Metemmeh, and occupying the village of Gubat on the gravel ridge, where the wounded were left under a guard of the Heavies, and of a detachment of the Royal Sussex, under *January 20th. Occupation of Gubat.*

---

* Sir C. Wilson's despatches, on this action and immediately subsequent events, with Lord Wolseley's covering despatch, are given in Appendix 45.

command of Major Lord A. Somerset, Heavy Camel Regiment. The village was hastily placed in a state of defence.

During the return to the zeriba a demonstration in some force was made by the enemy out of Metemmeh, but was checked by a few well directed volleys, and the zeriba was reached without opposition.

Remainder of force brought to Gubat.

Steps were at once taken to move the stores and wounded to Gubat, and by 4 p.m. the whole force had taken up its position near the water, with the exception of a detachment under command of Major T. Davison, Heavy Camel Regiment, left to guard a few stores which could not be moved from want of camels. This detachment occupied the redoubt on the knoll, the zeriba being dismantled.

Position of the village.

Map 6.

As already stated, the village of Gubat is situated on the gravel ridge which runs between the desert and the river, and is distant from the latter 780 yards, and about 3,500 from Metemmeh, from which it is screened by a curve in the ridge. The village itself was occupied by the Royal Sussex, the wounded, and the Commissariat; the Hussars and camels were bivouacked on the side facing the Nile, the Guards on the opposite side, the Heavies to the south, and the Mounted Infantry on the side nearest to Metemmeh.

With the occupation of the village, the first part of Sir H. Stewart's mission was accomplished, in spirit if not in letter. Metemmeh, it is true, had not been taken, but British troops had established themselves within two miles of it, in a defensible position, which, judging by their performances in the open, they were capable of defending against any odds. The main object of the desert march, the opening of communications with Khartum, would apparently be capable of accomplishment the moment General Gordon's expected steamers should arrive. It now became a question whether the political effect of the capture of Metemmeh would be worth the loss of life which it would entail.

Its possession was of considerable military importance, and Sir C. Wilson decided that unless the operation proved to be more difficult than he had then reason to anticipate, the capture of the town should be attempted.

January 21st. Attack on Metemmeh.

On the following morning (January 21st) the force, with the exception of the Royal Sussex, the Naval Brigade, part of the Heavy Camel Regiment and one gun R.A., which were left to garrison Gubat, paraded at daybreak and advanced in double column, with guns, ammunition, cacolets, and water between the two columns. The 19th Hussars were sent on in advance to reconnoitre to the north, whence it was intended to deliver the attack. They took with them a captured slave, who was to be sent into the town with a letter calling on the inhabitants to surrender, and promising that they should not be molested if they did.

A little before eight Colonel Barrow, 19th Hussars, sent in to say that a small body of the enemy's cavalry had advanced out of the town, but had retired before his fire to the north-east.

The Hussars were then at G (*see* Map 5), and the rest of the force at H, where it was halted for some time, while Sir C. Wilson went to G to reconnoitre. While he was away, Colonel Boscawen moved the force to the village D, and opened fire on a body of Arabs who were moving along the river bank with the intention, as it was believed, of attacking Gubat. He informed Sir C. Wilson of what he had done and seen. {Map 5.}

The force having moved so far to the south, Sir C. Wilson considered it best to continue the attack from that quarter. He accordingly continued the advance to the point K, nearly due south of the centre of Metemmeh, leaving a detachment of Mounted Infantry and Engineers at the house near I. The advance from I was continued in square.

As the square advanced the enemy opened fire from Metemmeh, which was replied to with rifles and guns. Fire was also opened from the village with two guns, but this did little damage. At length, finding that his force suffered considerable loss and that the shells produced but little effect on the mud walls of the town, and being moreover afraid of the Artillery ammunition running short, Sir C. Wilson determined to move back towards D. As he was doing so a message was brought in from Colonel Barrow, saying that the expected steamers from General Gordon were in sight, and before the village D had been regained, a contingent of blacks and Shaikiyeh, under Khashm-el-Mûs Bey and Abd el Hamid Bey, had landed and joined the force. They were brought up by Captain Verner, who had gone on board one of the steamers at Gubat, and were moved to I with their guns to open fire on the west end of Metemmeh, which it was then Sir C. Wilson's intention to attack. But hearing from Khashm-el-Mûs that a large force under Feki Mustapha was on its way down from Khartum, and might be expected at Gubat within the next twenty-four hours, Sir C. Wilson did not consider that he was justified, with his already enfeebled force, in risking a further loss, and accordingly gave {General Gordon's steamers in sight.}

orders to retire. During his retreat he destroyed the three villages between Metemmeh and Gubat. Major C. Poe, commanding the Marine Company of the Guards' Camel Regiment was severely wounded.

News from Khartum.

The steamers which had arrived were the "Bordein," "Safieh," "Tewfikia," and "Telahawiyeh." They brought with them the journal kept by General Gordon since the departure of Colonel Stewart, a letter to the Officer Commanding Her Majesty's Troops, and several private letters, amongst which was one to Major Watson (Colonel, Egyptian Army), dated December 14th, in which General Gordon stated that he expected a catastrophe in the town, after ten days' time, also a scrap of paper on which was written:—"Khartum is all right. Could hold out for years. C. G. Gordon, 29-12-84."

The flotilla was commanded by Nusri Pasha, an Egyptian; but in consequence of an urgent request from General Gordon, that no Egyptians should be allowed to return to Khartum, he was superseded, and the Shaikiyeh chieftain Khashm-el-Mûs, put in command.

The situation at this time is thus described by Sir C. Wilson.*

Sir C. Wilson on the situation.

"I had every reason to believe that forces of the enemy were advancing against us from the north and south, and I could not leave the small force in its position on the Nile without ascertaining whether it was likely to be attacked. I knew that Omdurman had fallen, and that Gordon had expected Khartum to fall on Christmas Day; but I hoped that the pressure upon the town would be relieved by the large number of men sent down by the Mahdi to meet us, and that news of our victories would have got into Khartum and given Gordon and his garrison fresh heart. At any rate there was nothing to show—and I questioned the commander of the steamers carefully—that the crisis at Khartum which had been deferred from the 25th December to the 19th of January would be hurried on, or that a delay of a couple of days would make much difference.

"I also considered that my first duty was to see that the small force which had been so roughly handled on its march to the Nile was safe from immediate attack. The result of the fight at Abu Klea was known to Khashm-el-Mûs on the evening of the 17th, and it was probably known in the Mahdi's camp and in Khartum on the 19th or 20th; I hoped

---

* "From Korti to Khartum," page 112.

this would still further delay the expected crisis. A large body of the enemy were said to be collected at Sayal below Metemmeh.

" It was these considerations taken together that made me undertake a reconnaissance down the river before starting for Khartum. My arrangements were that Barrow's Hussars were to reconnoitre as far as they could up the river early in the morning, and that if they sent back word to say that they could see nothing of Feki Mustapha's force, I would start down the river with two steamers and two companies of the Mounted Infantry."*

The total losses on the 19th, 20th, and 21st, amounted to 1 officer (Quartermaster Lima) and 22 non-commissioned officers and men killed, and 9 officers (Sir H. Stewart, Lord Airlie, Lord A. Somerset, Lieutenant Crutchley, Major Poe, Lieutenants T. D. O. Snow and C. P. Livingston, Mounted Infantry, Captain A. G. Leonard, East Lancashire Regiment, Lieutenant E. L. Munro, R.N.), and 93 non-commissioned officers and men wounded.

In consequence of the report that Feki Mustapha was advancing in force on Gubat, it was considered necessary to make some change in the dispositions there. *Disposition in view of an expected hostile movement from the south.*

As already stated, the village was situated on a gravel ridge and was at some distance from the river. As it was considered possible that an enemy might cut it off from the water, it was thought that a post should be held on the river bank. Owing, however, to the command which the gravel ridge, on which Gubat lay, gave over the banks, it was not possible to evacuate that position. It was finally determined to build two forts, one on the high ground close to Gubat, to be occupied by the Guards, the other on the river bank for the hospital and remainder of the force. Captain Verner was sent with some men to the Island of Gubat, and a small *tête de pont* was constructed nearly opposite the fort on the river; this was afterwards occupied by Egyptian troops from the steamers. Major Davison's detachment was brought in. *Two forts built. Map 6.*

In the afternoon of January 22nd, the 19th Hussars having reported no enemy to the southward, Sir C. Wilson and Lord C. Beresford, with Major Phipps and two companies of Mounted Infantry and Khashm-el-Mûs, started in the "Telahawiyeh" to reconnoitre to the north. They were accompanied by Captain Verner and Abd el Hamid Bey, *January 22nd. Reconnaissance to Shendi. Map 2.*

---

* Sir C. Wilson's official letter on this subject is given in Appendix 46.

with a detachment of native soldiers in the "Bordein," and by the "Safieh" with her own captain and crew.

As Shendi was neared, a native who was taken up from the bank reported that the town did not contain more than 300 or 400 Dervishes, and that a large party in the town were loyal. He also stated that the force from Berber had turned back on meeting the fugitives from Abu Klea. Some native soldiers were landed and made a reconnaissance, but soon re-embarked, as the enemy showed in force. After firing 60 shells into the town the flotilla withdrew, and as they did so saw a large party of the enemy entering the town.

A good view was obtained of Sayal, which was unoccupied. The party returned to Gubat shortly after sunset.

January 23rd, 3 p.m. Steamers reported ready to proceed to Khartum.

During this trip it was discovered that certain repairs to the machinery were necessary, and could not be carried out until it had cooled down. On the following morning (January 23rd) they were taken in hand, and at 3 p.m. on that day Lord C. Beresford reported to Sir C. Wilson that the steamers were ready.

On the receipt in England of the news of the occupation of Gubat by the Desert Column, the following telegram was despatched by the Secretary of State for War to Lord Wolseley, who at once forwarded it to Sir H. Stewart:—

"*28th January*, 1885, 4.10 *p.m.*

Messages from the Queen and Khedive.

"Yours No. 29. Have received the Queen's gracious commands to express her satisfaction and warm thanks to her brave troops, and her deep concern for their losses and sufferings, but especially for General Stewart's severe wound.

"Her Majesty has, in consideration of that officer's gallant service, been pleased to promote him to the rank of Major-General.

"I desire to add my own congratulations on the successful issue of this operation, so admirably designed and so brilliantly executed."

The following telegram was also sent by His Highness the Khedive:—

"*From Khedive to General Lord Wolseley.*

"Thanks for telegram which relieved late extreme anxiety caused by absence of news. I congratulate you upon glorious success gained, but deplore temporary loss of General Stewart. Please inform me when possible of his progress. I appreciate his daring and courage. When occasion permits please cause my congratulations and thanks for their valour to be given all officers and men engaged in late actions."

CHAPTER VII.

THE VOYAGE TO KHARTUM.

Map 1.

AT 8 a.m. on the morning of January 24th, 1885, Sir C. Wilson started for Khartum in the "Bordein," accompanied by Khashm-el-Mûs Bey, Captain R. F. T. Gascoigne, 10 non-commissioned officers and men Royal Sussex Regiment, 1 petty officer, one artificer R.N., and 110 Sudanese troops. *January 24th. Departure of Sir C. Wilson from Gubat.*

The "Bordein" was accompanied by the "Telahawiyeh," having on board Captain L. J. Trafford and 10 of the Royal Sussex Regiment, including a signaller, Lieutenant Stuart Wortley, one artificer R.N., Abd el Hamid Bey, and 80 Sudanese troops. She had in tow a nugger laden with dhura for Khartum, and about 50 additional Sudanese soldiers.

The steamers were small wooden boats of about the size of Thames "penny" steamers; but they had been rendered bullet proof by a casing and breastwork of boiler plating, and were also fitted with bullet proof turrets in the bows and amidships.* Neither the turrets nor sides were however proof against artillery fire. A bullet proof "crow's nest" had also been rigged at the masthead. They were armed with 9-pr. brass howitzers, two on each vessel. In consequence of General Gordon's request, all Egyptians had been removed, and the crews and native troops were entirely composed of blacks and Shaikiyeh. *Description of steamers.*

When opposite Sheikieh a portion of Feki Mustapha's force was observed on the left bank, but, with the exception of a few stray shots, it offered no opposition to the passage of the steamers. This force had left Omdurman two days after that under Nur Angar, which was encountered on the 19th, but, on hearing of the result of that action, it had halted and finally took up a position at Wad Habeshi.

The voyage was then continued without incident till dark, when the steamers were made fast to the right bank near Gos el Basabir.

* This rough armour plating had been chiefly carried out under the superintendence of the late Lieutenant-Colonel H. D. Stewart.

January 25th.

A start was made at daylight on the following morning but a halt of some duration had to be made before noon to take in fuel, of which the steamers, whose machinery was of antiquated pattern, consumed a vast quantity. These halts were of frequent occurrence, and as the fuel had to be obtained by pulling down houses in the native villages, each stoppage for this purpose occupied a considerable time.

At about 4.30 p.m. on the 25th the enemy's fort at Wad Habeshi was passed. All was made ready to run past it under a heavy fire, but it was found to be unoccupied.

"Bordein" run aground in the 6th Cataract.

The steamers then ran on without difficulty till about 6 p.m., when the "Bordein" ran hard upon a rock, and although the whole crew was kept at work till nearly midnight, they were unable to move her.

The Sixth Cataract consists of a maze of channels running between the many islands which here dot the river. Of these channels two are usually used for navigation, that on the right bank during high Nile, and that in the centre at low Nile. As the steamers had come down the right or eastern channel, the Reis imagined that he could proceed up it, and did so without difficulty until the "Bordein" struck. The "Telahawiyeh" completed the passage without accident.

January 26th. Delay of a day caused by accident.

On the following morning stores, ammunition, &c., having been taken off the "Bordein," with considerable difficulty she was hauled off, and, when reloaded, proceeded up the channel. But after proceeding a short distance she again ran aground on a sand bank. By great exertions she was again hauled off, and then the Reises said that, owing to the difficulties of the navigation, it was necessary that they should combine to take up each steamer separately. The Reis of the "Bordein" accordingly went over to the "Telahawiyeh," and having taken her to the mouth of the pass, said that it would be impossible to take his ship by the same channel. The "Bordein" was accordingly dropped down some distance and proceeded up the middle channel, the head of which she reached shortly before sunset.

The result of these accidents was that twenty-four hours were practically lost, the steamers on the night of the 26th January being only three miles nearer Khartum than they were on the evening of the 25th. A start was made at daylight on the following morning, and the gorge of Shabluka was passed without difficulty. This pass, which is from three to four miles in length, is bordered on each side by high and steep rocks, barely 300 yards apart at their bases, and the position

January 27th.

is one which could be guarded with ease by a handful of good shots. Great surprise was therefore felt by all on board at no opposition being offered here.

At Gos Nefisa, at the head of the passage, a halt was made for wood, and while this was being collected firing was kept up by the inhabitants of the village from the surrounding hills. But with this exception little opposition was encountered till about 2 p.m., when the enemy's fire from the left bank became hotter, and was continued persistently up to sunset. During the afternoon a man on the bank called out that Khartum had fallen and that General Gordon was killed. This information, however, was not believed by those on board.

Fire opened by the enemy.

Report of General Gordon's death.

At dark the steamers were made fast to the bank near the village of Tamaniat, where as much wood was taken on board as the steamers would carry.

At 6 a.m. on the morning of the 28th, the steamers got under way, as it was then believed for the last time, before entering Khartum. The orders, given with a view to running the blockade, were that the "Bordein" was to lead, and the "Telahawiyeh" to follow close astern and conform to her movements, both ships going full speed ahead. The detachment of the Royal Sussex had orders to fire exclusively at the embrasures of the enemy's batteries, which were also to be engaged by the guns.

January 28th. Preparations for running the blockade.

The Sudanese troops were to keep up an independent fire on the enemy. Lieutenant Stuart Wortley and a signaller he had with him, were to try to attract General Gordon's attention by means of the heliograph.

Seg et Taib, a steep hill close to the river, where the enemy had formerly had a battery and some guns, was passed without opposition at 7.30 a.m. Here another native hailed the "Telahawiyeh" and stated that Khartum had fallen.

At about 11 a.m. the first view of Khartum, still some miles off and partly screened by Tuti Island, was obtained. At this point another native called out from the bank that Khartum had fallen and that General Gordon had been killed.

First view of Khartum.

As Fighiaiha was approached a sharp fire was opened by the enemy. Half a mile further up the steamers got abreast of Halfiyeh, and encountered a heavy fire from four guns and a great number of rifles.

Map 7.

View of Halfiyeh.*

This fire was vigorously replied to by guns and rifles, but probably with little effect as the enemy were firing from behind good cover. Sir C. Wilson directed the operations from the midship turret, which from its height made an excellent conning tower, while its position made communication easy with the Reis and Engineer.

When opposite Halfiyeh it was noticed that it had been completely wrecked, and that some large boats were lying off the bank. As it was known that the Mahdi had no boats, it was assumed that General Gordon's troops must be there, a supposition which was, however, speedily proved to be fallacious by the heavy fire which was opened on the steamers.

On coming abreast of the lower end of Tuti Island, the fire almost entirely ceased, and as the smoke cleared off, the Government House of Khartum was clearly visible above the trees. As it was known that General Gordon always kept the Egyptian flag flying on this building, an eager search was made for it through glasses, but no sign of it could be observed.

On reaching the upper end of the island, a very hot fire was encountered from both banks, and at the same time four guns opened fire from the fort at Omdurman. The fire from the right bank was at a range of from 60 to 200 yards; that from the left about 1,000 to 1,200 yards. Owing to the slope of the bank, especially on the Omdurman side, the enemy was afforded but little cover, and the fire of the steamers must have done great execution among the crowds who lined the bank.

Tuti Island in enemy's hands.

It was now evident that Tuti Island was in the hands of the enemy, but as it was still possible that Khartum might be holding out, Sir C. Wilson pushed on till on rounding the

* This and the other woodcuts in this chapter are from sketches made on the spot by Captain Trafford.

south western point of the island, at the point "A" (see Map 7), the town came full in view. It was then observed that no Egyptian flag was flying in Khartum although the town was searched carefully with glasses, and the steamers were near enough to allow of an ensign, had there been one, being seen with the naked eye. A number of nuggers and troop boats were collected under the left bank at Omdurman, and it was known that General Gordon had always kept these moored under his guns at Khartum.

Neither of the steamers that General Gordon had retained came out to co-operate. Khartum itself was firing on Sir C. Wilson's steamers.

A number of the enemy, with banners and spears, were collected on the shore on the Khartum side of the White Nile, at "B," ready to oppose any attempt to land. No firing was heard in Khartum itself. Government House and the buildings near it were completely wrecked.

These facts, together with the heavy fire from Tuti Island, convinced Sir C. Wilson that Khartum had fallen, and considering that it would be a useless waste of life to attempt a landing, he ordered the "Bordein" to be put about, and at once ran down stream. *Khartum found to have fallen. Steamers retire.*

The "Telahawiyeh" had in the meanwhile run aground at the point "C," and was for some time in a very precarious position. However, a few moments after the "Bordein" passed, she shoved off, swung round, and followed her consort. *"Telahawiyeh" aground for a short time.*

As the steamers turned, the enemy's fire was redoubled, and it was under a hail of bullets and shell that they sped down stream. Both ships were struck by shell, but not dangerously. *Heavy fire on the steamers.*

Just after the steamers turned, a native on a camel was seen on the Omdurman shore waving a flag of truce. As, however, the enemy's fire did not abate, it was considered inexpedient to stop for the purpose of communicating with him.

At 4 p.m. on the 28th January, after having been continuously engaged for four hours, the steamers got clear of the enemy's batteries. Their escape had been little short of marvellous. The chief danger now lay in the disaffection of the Sudanese crew, who, thoroughly disheartened at the loss of their families in Khartum, were at best unwilling to make any further exertions, while many of them considering that the Mahdi's was now the winning side, showed every inclination to join the enemy. *Crews show signs of disaffection.*

(s.c.2)

38 HISTORY OF THE SUDAN CAMPAIGN.—PART II.

The steamers continued their course without opposition till dark, when they made fast to an island about twelve miles south of J. Rojan.

From this place messengers were sent out to ascertain the fate of General Gordon, and on their return stated that the town had fallen on the morning of January 26th, through the treachery of Farag Pasha, and that General Gordon had been killed. The town had been given over to a three days' pillage.*

Difficulties of situation. There was much to be done that evening, and on the following morning; the wounded had to be attended to, bullet holes had to be plugged up and a paddle wheel to be repaired; above all, a plan of operations for descending the cataract had to be decided on. This was no easy matter; the "Telahawiyeh" and "Bordein" were larger than the steamers which it is usual to send down the Nile at this season, and they were in addition heavily weighted with iron plates and guns, and were laden with a large quantity of dhura which had been taken up for the use of the garrison. The Nile too was falling rapidly. It had, indeed, been observed to diminish in height three feet in a single night at Gubat, and it is possible that the Reises had not noticed this. They were at first inclined to say that the task before them was an impossible one, but a promise of 100*l.* to each of the captains, and half of that sum to each of the Reises if they succeeded in getting the boats down safely, caused them to modify their opinion. All the dhura was thrown overboard, the boats were generally lightened and got into as good trim as possible, and at 7 a.m. on the 29th January the flotilla again started for the north.

January 29th. After about an hour and a half of steaming the "Bordein" struck on a sand bank, but was got off again without any great difficulty. At 12.30 the head of the cataract was reached, and here it was determined to concentrate the whole available navigating skill on one vessel at a time. The "Bordein" was therefore brought up while her captain and Reises took the "Telahawiyeh" down the first reach of the cataract. This operation was performed in safety, and the "Bordein" was in her turn taken down to join her consort.

Wreck of "Telahawiyeh." At the foot of the upper rapid a reach of open water was gained, and all was apparently going well when, at 4.30 p.m.

* The official account of the fall of Khartum, compiled by Major Kitchener, is given in Appendix 47.

the "Telahawiyeh" struck heavily on a sunken rock opposite Jebel Rojan, and immediately began to sink.

Wreck of "Telahawiyeh."

The "Bordein" was at once brought up against a little island close at hand, and assistance was sent to the wrecked vessel. This, however, was scarcely needed, for by the time Captain Gascoigne arrived at the scene of the wreck in the "Bordein's" boat, all the men, the two guns, and most of the stores had been removed by Captain Trafford and Lieutenant Stuart Wortley to the nugger which was in tow. All the gun ammunition and most of the small arm ammunition were, however, lost.

A few shots had been fired at the steamers during the day, but they did no damage, and were not thought worth replying to.

In the evening a messenger from the Mahdi appeared on the bank, and was received on board the "Bordein." He handed Sir C. Wilson a letter, of which the following is a translation:— *Letter from the Mahdi.*

"In the name of God, the Merciful, the Compassionate, Praise be to the Bountiful Lord, and blessings be upon our Lord Mohammed and on his family. From the servant were stands in need of God, and on whom he places dependence, Mohammed, the Mahdi, son of Abdullah, to the British and Shaikiyeh officers and their followers: God direct them to the truth. Surrender and you will be spared. Do not disobey, or you will rue it as I briefly warn you. Perchance God Almighty may put you upon the path of the righteous. Know then that the city of Khartum and its surroundings are like the garrison of a stronghold; God has destroyed it and other places by our hands; nothing can withstand his power and might; and by the bounty of God all has come into our hands. As you have become a small remnant, like a leaflet within our grasp, two alternatives are offered to you. If you surrender and prevent the shedding of your blood and the blood of God's creatures who are under your leadership, well and good, grace and security from God and his Prophet, and security from us will be upon you. But if you do not believe what we have said, and desire to ascertain the truth of the killing of Khartum (Gordon?)* send a special envoy on your part to see the truth of what we say; and to your envoy is given the security of God and his Prophet, till he comes to us and sees and returns under a guard from us, to see and be warned of God, even as God says, 'If any one of the heathen seek help of thee, help him that he may learn the word of God Almighty.' You are offered the choice of fighting or surrendering to the command of God, and returning to Him. Were it not for pity for you we would not write to you in this manner; and if you pay heed, on receipt of this my letter to you, fear nothing, for nothing will happen to you after the (granting) of the security of God and His Prophet to you; but if you refuse you shall taste evil, in that you turn away from the path of God to the torment of the other world. For it is known that the victory is unto the believers, even as God has promised them in his revealed Book. Do not be deceived and put confidence in your steamers and other things, and delay deciding until you rue it; but rather hasten to your benefit and profit before your wings are cut. Much reasoning will not convert, for it is God who converts, and he who lets go astray, and you will find no ruler over Him. What has been said is enough for him who has been reached by God."

(Sealed)

There is no God but God.
Mohammed is the Prophet of God.
Mohammed, the Mahdi, son of Abdullah (slave of God).
1293.

* The word translated killing is only applied to a man or animal.

The bearer of this letter was a certain Feki Abd er-Rahman, a Dongalawi, the same man who had appeared on the bank at Omdurman with a flag of truce.

Sir C. Wilson was averse to sending any answer to the letter, but Khashm-el-Mûs pointed out that the steamer would be completely at the mercy of the enemy while passing the narrow gorge of the cataract, and begged permission to gain time by writing a letter to the effect that he dared not give himself up unless a special safe conduct were given him, but that if this were sent he would deliver the English and the steamer over to Feki Mustapha, who was then at Wad Habeshi with a force. Sir C. Wilson, taking into consideration the gravity of the situation, gave Khashm-el-Mûs leave to write this letter, taking care that no promise was made on the part of himself or the English officers. *Answer to Mahdi's letter.*

Feki Abd er-Rahman's conversations with the Shaikiyeh officers and men had a very bad effect, which was immediately marked by the first desertion among the natives. *Disaffection among native troops.*

At daybreak on the morning of the 30th January the "Bordein," followed by the nugger, again made a start, and passed the various rapids in safety, and, to the surprise of everyone on board, met with no opposition in the narrow gorge of Shabluka. *January 30th. Passage of Shabluka.*

The intricate and difficult passage between the islands which had caused so much delay on the 25th, had still to be passed, and it was considered necessary to lower the steamer down, stern first, by hawsers made fast to anchors, a tedious operation which would have been almost impossible had any numbers of the enemy been in the neighbourhood. In spite of all precautions the "Bordein" was driven on to a shoal by a strong blast of wind, and was only got off after considerable labour. This caused such loss of time, that she had to be brought up for the night in the cataract.

Symptoms of disaffection among the Shaikiyeh were growing more and more apparent. Abd el Hamid Bey's manner was especially suspicious, and during the night it was reported to Sir C. Wilson that he was engaged in a conspiracy to wreck the ship, which had only been stopped by the interference of Khashm-el-Mûs. Fortunately at this crisis a false but opportune report reached the natives that Metemmeh had been taken by the English, whose reinforcements were swarming across the desert. The effect of this was at once apparent, and it undoubtedly did much towards deciding the wavering Shaikiyeh to remain loyal.

January 31st. Descent of last rapid.

At daylight on the following morning (January 31st) the descent of the last rapid was commenced, and by 10 a.m. was successfully accomplished, leaving a clear stretch of unbroken water all the way to Metemmeh. The one difficulty ahead was the running the gauntlet at Wad Habeshi, where it was known that Feki Mustapha had a large force and a battery. Every precaution was taken to protect the boilers as much as possible from shell, and it was hoped that by running past the fort at full speed, the enemy's not very accurate shell fire would be evaded. Sir C. Wilson also believed that the large reward which he had promised the Reises in the event of success would induce them to do their utmost. A full stock of wood was laid in to enable the steamer to keep up full speed for a good hour after passing the fort.

Wreck of "Bordein."

As in the case of the "Abbas," all was apparently going well, and the worst of the dangers were thought to be over, when at 3.30 p.m., while steaming along in smooth water, the "Bordein," as she was descending the channel to the west of Mernat Island, struck heavily on a sunken rock and immediately began to fill. Sir C. Wilson at once gave orders to lay her alongside a small sand spit running out from an island, situated about 50 yards from the larger one of Mernat. This was successfully done, and all possible steps were taken to repair the damage, but without avail. All hands were set to the pumps and buckets, and carpenters were directed to investigate the hole, which was found to be of great size, below the water line in a difficult place to get at, and the water was soon several feet above it.

The sketch plan facing page 48 illustrates the operations of Sir C. Wilson after the wreck of the "Bordein," and shows the position of Mernat Island with regard to Wad Habeshi.

Guns, ammmunition, and stores were landed as soon as possible, and Captain Gascoigne was sent to select a suitable place for a zeriba on Mernat Island, which commanded the smaller island against which the steamer was beached.

The sketch on page 43, taken looking west from the shore of Mernat Island, shows the position of the islands and wreck.

Mernat Island.

Map 1.

Mernat Island was about three-quarters of a mile wide, by two miles long, and was covered with trees and long grass. The channel to the east of the island was found to be only about 300 yards wide. The point opposite the wreck of the "Bordein" was about three-quarters of a mile from the north end of the island. Sir C. Wilson considered the position so

Wreck of "Bordein."

impossible for defence that he at first determined to make a forced march in the night down the right bank to opposite Gubat, and to send Lieutenant Stuart Wortley on to that place in the small boat, to inform the garrison of the disaster and to beg that a steamer might be sent up to protect their flank. Finding, however, that it was impossible to do anything with the native troops, and believing that they would be worse than useless in the event of an attack, the alternative was forced on him of making himself as secure as circumstances would permit, and awaiting the arrival of help on the scene of the wreck.

At 6.45 p.m., on January 31st, Lieutenant Stuart Wortley started in the ship's boat to row to Gubat, having with him four English soldiers, including the signaller, and eight natives. His start was timed to enable him to pass the enemy's fort at Wad Habeshi in the interval of darkness between sunset and moonrise. He rowed on to within about half a mile of the fort, and then, shipping his oars, ordered the crew to lie down in the bottom of the boat, which, floating down stream, gradually approached the enemy's positions. So near did it drift to the shore that the men's faces could easily be distinguished as they sat over their camp fires, and they were heard discussing whether the black object which they saw upon the stream was a boat or not. Suddenly their doubts were dispelled by the rising of the moon on the eastern horizon in a straight line behind the boat, which was at once rendered plainly visible. The shout which followed this discovery soon warned the crew that further concealment was useless, and springing to their

Lieut. Stuart Wortley starts for Gubat.

places, they gave way with a will amidst a rain of bullets which ploughed up the water on every side, but fortunately did no damage. A few hundred yards brought them to another island, by following the right side of which they were enabled to continue their journey under cover for a considerable distance; and on again emerging into the main channel they found that they were only followed by a few camel men who were apparently unarmed with rifles. At 3 a.m. on the 1st February they reached Gubat. On the receipt of Lieutenant Stuart Wortley's report, Lieut.-Colonel M. Willson, Scots Guards, commanding at Gubat in place of Lieut.-Colonel Boscawen, who was in hospital, at once ordered relief to be sent to Sir C. Wilson. At 2 p.m. on the same day (February 1st) Lord Charles Beresford started for Mernat in the "Safieh."

Sir C. Wilson's dispositions.

Sir C. Wilson had in the meanwhile, on the departure of Lieutenant Stuart Wortley, established a small post on Mernat Island, leaving his stores and ammunition and the main body of his men on the smaller island for the night. On the following morning the stores and main body were transferred to a strong zeriba which was formed on the west side of Mernat, opposite the "Bordein," while the smaller island was occupied by an outpost of native troops to prevent the chance of annoyance from any of the enemy's riflemen who might land there, were it left unoccupied.

The zeriba was formed in a semi-circle on the edge of the bank, which was here some 25 to 30 feet high, and very steep. Along this bank ran a belt of trees, which, while securing the occupants of the zeriba from view, would not have impeded their fire on an advancing enemy. The four guns were put in position in the zeriba. The north end of Mernat Island was about three miles above Wad Habeshi.

With the exception of a visit from some Shaikiyeh who confirmed the news of the fall of Khartum, and who stated that Lieutenant Stuart Wortley had safely passed the enemy's batteries, the day and the following night were passed without incident.

Desertions.

On the following morning an episode that occurred showed the remarkable conditions under which Sir C. Wilson's small force existed. This was the visit to Mernat, of Feki Mustapha, the enemy's commander at Wad Habeshi, and an interview between him and Khashm-el-Mûs, in which he endeavoured to induce the latter to desert. This, Khashm-el-Mûs refused to do, but Abd El Hamid Bey and his company of Shaikiyeh, went over to the enemy.

The night passed without incident, but soon after daylight on the morning of the 3rd of February, the report of a gun down stream, told that the expected help was arriving from Gubat; and shortly afterwards the look-out man on a neighbouring tree top announced that the English steamer was in sight. The effect of this information on the depressed native troops was almost magical, and the men who, a few moments before, had been too indifferent to move even when urged with blows, were now all energy and anxiety to please. Sir C. Wilson at once ran up a signal to show his position to the steamer, the only immediate effect of which was to bring down a sharp fire from the enemy on the opposite bank.

February 3rd, "Safieh" sighted.

Noticing that the steamer's fire was being kept up for a suspiciously long time, Sir C. Wilson sent Captain Trafford to try to ascertain the state of affairs. On that officer's return he reported that he had seen her enveloped in smoke and that she had apparently met with a serious accident. Sir C. Wilson then went himself to obtain a view of her, and saw her swinging at anchor opposite the enemy's battery, with which she appeared to be heavily engaged.

Under these circumstances Sir C. Wilson determined to attempt to effect a junction with the crew of the steamer. He therefore at once gave orders for the zeriba to be broken up and for the guns, stores, and wounded to be put on board the nugger, in command of which he placed Captain Gascoigne, with orders to float down and await the arrival of the remainder of Sir C. Wilson's force alongside the right bank, opposite the north end of the island. At the same time the small boat was sent down to take Sir C. Wilson and the land force over to the right bank from the north end of the island.

Sir C. Wilson quits Mernat Island and marches down to the "Safieh."

In spite of a sharp fire from the enemy, the zeriba was broken up and the stores were embarked without any serious casualties, and a landing was effected on the right bank without opposition. The force then marched down and established itself opposite to the disabled steamer, which was about 500 yards from the right bank, and the nugger dropped down stream to the same point.

After some difficulty, owing to the party not having a proper signaller, communication was established by signal with the steamer, and it was ascertained that she was hit in the boiler, but had hopes of being able to mend it. As however there was some doubt as to the accuracy of the message, Captain Gascoigne volunteered to go over to her in the small boat, and succeeded in doing so and returning without any casualties. He brought a message from Lord C. Beresford requesting Sir C. Wilson to keep up a fire on the fort and thus to divert the enemy's attention from the steamer while the boiler was being repaired, and in the morning to move down two or three miles to some spot on the bank where embarkation would be easy, and there await the arrival of the steamer, floating the sick and wounded, 25 in number, down in the nugger during the night.

Thereupon, part of Sir C. Wilson's force, under Captain Trafford, was sent down to select and prepare a camping place. Sir C. Wilson himself, having got one gun out of the nugger (there was little ammunition, most having been ost in the wrecks), remained with this and the native artillerymen, opposite Wad Habeshi. This gun engaged the enemy's fort till dark, after which, owing to the exhaustion of the men, it was spiked and thrown into the river. An attempt was also made to move the nugger down the right bank under shelter of a sandbank which partly screened it from the enemy, but it ran aground, and all except the very badly wounded had to be landed; it was after sunset before it was again afloat. Sir C. Wilson then, considering that he could be of no further use, left his position opposite the fort and joined Captain Trafford at the zeriba, which had been formed about two miles lower down.

The voyage of the "Safieh." It will now be necessary to go back for a few hours and narrate the adventures of the "Safieh." Lord C. Beresford had with him a portion of the Naval Brigade under Lieutenant E. B. Van Koughnet, 20 non-commissioned officers and men of the Mounted Infantry, and two Gardner guns and two 4-prs. He was accompanied by Lieutenant Stuart Wortley.

Fort at Wad Habeshi. After leaving Gubat no incident of any importance occurred on the 1st or 2nd of February, but at 7 a.m. on the morning of the 3rd, the enemy's earthworks at Wad Habeshi were sighted, and beyond them was observed the "Bordein," aground near Mernat Island.

When within 1,200 yards of the fort, Lord C. Beresford opened fire with his bow gun, and was shortly afterwards answered by the enemy. He then ordered all fire to be directed at the embrasures of the work, and proceeded to run past it, being obliged, owing to the shallowness of the water, to pass within 80 yards of it. So heavy was the fire brought to bear from the steamer with the machine guns and riflemen, that the enemy were unable to fire the two guns in the central embrasures which bore directly into the steamer when she was abreast of the work. When, however, she had passed the fort about 200 yards, the angle at which it lay prevented so heavy a fire being brought to bear on it: The enemy thus being enabled to work the guns in their upstream embrasures, succeeded in sending a shot through the "Safieh's" boiler. Observing that the paddle-wheels were still moving, Lord C. Beresford headed her towards the right bank and anchored, but within 500 yards range of the enemy, who kept up a continuous fire. *The boiler struck.*

The "Safieh" was now lying stern on to the fort, a position which although causing her to afford a smaller target for the enemy, reduced her own fire action considerably for some time. By cutting off the trail of one of the 4-prs., and cutting a hole in the afterside of the stern battery, one gun and one machine gun were however after a time brought to bear on the fort. *Dangerous position of the "Safieh."*

From 7.30 on the morning of February 3rd till past sunset so heavy and continuous a fire was kept up from the ship that the enemy was never able to get his gun to bear on her; and although a smart fusilade was kept on her during these 12 hours by the enemy's riflemen, their firing was mostly wild and did but little damage. As, however, under cover of the night the enemy would have ample opportunity of moving his guns into a position which would render their fire certainly fatal to the steamer, Lord C. Beresford saw that it was imperative to have the boilers repaired by the morning, and also, if possible, to delude the enemy into a belief that he had deserted his ship, and thus make them think it not worth their while to shift the position of their guns. With this latter object in view, he hauled his four boats alongside, as if for the purpose of escaping in them, and at dark ceased firing and remained perfectly still throughout the night.

The work of repairing the boiler had been commenced by Mr. Benbow, Chief Engineer, as soon as it had become sufficiently cool, *i.e.*, at 11 a.m. on the morning of the wreck. The artificers and nearly every one in the stokehole having been severely scalded by the escape of steam when the boiler was struck, Mr. Benbow had to do nearly all the work *Repair of the boiler.*

with his own hand, under fire. Lieutenant Van Koughnet was wounded and a petty officer was killed.

By 9 p.m. on the same night the work was completed, and at 5 a.m. on the following morning Lord C. Beresford gave orders for the fires to be lighted, but for every precaution to be taken to prevent the escape of sparks which would betray his presence to the enemy.

February 4th. Relief of Sir C. Wilson's party.

The day was just breaking when the occupants of the fort perceived that the steamer was not abandoned, and that their chance of capturing her was lost. This discovery was notified by a yell of defiance from the Arabs and by a hail of bullets. Lord C. Beresford was, however, prepared for this emergency, and before the enemy's guns had been brought to bear properly on the steamer, he had weighed anchor and was going full speed ahead. After proceeding up stream for about 200 yards, to a part of the river where there was more room, he turned round and again ran the gauntlet of the fort, bringing all his available fire to bear on the embrasures as he did so. This operation was conducted without accident, and the party on board were just congratulating themselves on the fact that their difficulties were at length over, when, in the dim light, the nugger was seen to be hard and fast on a rock about 400 yards below the enemy's battery. On board her were Captain Gascoigne and some sick and wounded. They had on the previous evening towed the nugger some little distance up stream from where it had been aground, and had then dropped down with the current; but, after floating safely past the fort they had run on this rock, and all their efforts to move the nugger off it had been unavailing.

Lord C. Beresford again anchored the steamer as near to the wreck as he could, and at once despatched Sub-Lieutenant C. R. Keppel, R.N., and a party of men, in the small boat to Captain Gascoigne's assistance. After removing the greater part of the stores, the nugger was finally hauled off, under a smart fire from the enemy, and she and the steamer proceeded to the zeriba down stream. Sir C. Wilson and his party were embarked about a mile below, this at a convenient spot. At 5.45 p.m. on the same day the party safely arrived at Gubat. Sir C. Wilson had lost altogether 2 Sudanese killed and 25 wounded.

During Lord C. Beresford's action, 5,400 rounds were fired from the Gardner, 2,150 rounds from Martini-Henrys, and 126 rounds from the howitzers.

Part II.   To face page 48.

SKETCH PLAN
to illustrate
THE WRECK OF THE "BORDEIN"
and the relief of
SIR C. WILSON'S FORCE
BY LORD C. BERESFORD.

REFERENCES

A Sir C. Wilson's force landed after breaking up Zeriba.
B Nugger waited here for Sir C. Wilson with land force.
C C' Hillocks occupied by Sir C. Wilson and Capt. Gascoigne on landing.
D Sir C. Wilson's force halted and communicated with "Safieh."
E Nugger grounded afternoon of 3rd.
F Nugger ran on rock on night of 3rd.
G Island under which Lieut. Stuart Wortley's boat gained shelter on night of 31st of January.
H Point where Sir C. Wilson embarked on the "Safieh" on the 4th Feby.

CHAPTER VIII.

THE RETURN OF THE DESERT COLUMN.

Maps 1 and 2.

ON the departure of Sir C. Wilson for Khartum on the 24th January, the military command had devolved on Colonel Boscawen, Lord C. Beresford being the actual senior officer of the force. On the previous day a convoy of 1,000 baggage camels, escorted by 300 men of Heavy, Guards' and Mounted Infantry Camel Regiments, under Colonel Talbot, left Gubat for Jakdul to bring up supplies from that station. The convoy marched after dark to avoid attracting the attention of the enemy, and halted at midnight on the confines of the Shebakat bush. Lord Cochrane acted as guide and furnished a report. The route followed, took a line direct from Gubat to Abu Klea, avoiding the Shebakat bush. The convoy arrived at Jakdul on the morning of the 26th inst. *Events at Gubat during Sir C. Wilson's absence. Convoy for Jakdul.*

Sir C. Wilson took advantage of this convoy to forward despatches to Lord Wolseley. They were carried by Captain Pigott, 21st Hussars, who, leaving the convoy at Abu Klea, lost his way, and did not reach Jakdul till the night of the 26th; whence he rode to Korti, a distance of 96 miles, in 29 hours, including halts, arriving at his destination at 3.30 A.M. on the 28th of January.

On the same day that Sir C. Wilson started from Gubat for Khartum, the River Column, which had been concentrating at Hamdab, preparatory to moving forward, commenced its advance on Abu Hamed and Berber. The force carried 100 days' supplies and was to be a flying column, without a regular line of communications with Korti. It was to replenish its supplies by means of a convoy from Korosko which would meet it at Abu Hamed.

The departure of Colonel Talbot's convoy reduced the Gubat garrison to—

    73 Officers.
   912 Non-commissioned officers and men.
   417 Camels.
   119 Horses.

The camels were in a most deplorable condition, and the horses were hardly any better; they had had but little food during their march across the desert, and during the last *Condition of animals.*

56 hours of it, no water whatever. Even at Gubat it was impossible to supply them with grain. They were able to do outpost duty, but were incapable of long journeys. Fortunately the enemy had suffered far more severely than had the British force; they were indisposed to offensive operations, and made no attempt to threaten its communications. It was believed, however, that hostile reinforcements were on their way from Khartum, and that an attack might be expected. Colonel Boscawen, therefore, lost no time in making his post as strong as the limited means at his disposal would allow; and all available hands were turned on to the construction of earth works, &c.

Proclamation by Lord C. Beresford.

The following proclamation was issued by Lord C. Beresford, to the natives :—

"To the people of the river districts.

"This is to make it known to you that we are the advanced portion of the two great English armies which are now marching on Khartum to punish the rebels.

"We do not wish to do you any harm if you will come to see us. You shall receive no hurt, and we will pay you for your cattle and crops.

"If, however, you do not tender your submission, we will punish you severely. Your cattle will be taken, your villages and sakiehs burnt, and you yourselves will be killed, even as those unfortunates who ventured to oppose us at Abu Klea and Metemmeh.

"Any person desirous of speaking with the English general should carry a white flag, and come by the river bank alone. He will not be detained, and he will be guarded from all danger.

"(Signed)   THE SIRDAR,
"Advanced Guard,
"English Army."

Reconnaissances by the steamers.

On the 26th and 27th Lord C. Beresford went down to Metemmeh in a steamer and shelled it on the latter date, covering at the same time a raiding party of 40 men from the camel regiments.

On the 27th it was also necessary to send a small party of Mounted Infantry and Guards' Camel Regiments to turn out of a neighbouring village some of the enemy who were firing at our vedettes.

On the night of the 28th firing of guns and rifles was kept up for some hours, accompanied by beating of tom-toms inside Metemmeh. This was thought at the time to indicate either

DEPARTURE OF THE SECOND CONVOY FOR JAKDUL.

the arrival of reinforcements or a native festival, but it evidently resulted from the receipt of the news of the fall of Khartum.

At noon on the 31st, Colonel Talbot returned from Jakdul with a convoy of 1,341 camels laden with supplies, details of Naval Brigade, Bearer Company, and two mountain guns, Royal Artillery, having been three days out from Jakdul. He also brought with him eight boxes of Martini-Henry ammunition, which he had picked up on the battlefield of Abu Klea. On arrival within sight of the zeriba formed on the 19th he found it occupied by the enemy, who, however, retired on his dismounting his advanced guard and flankers. Some of the enemy's cavalry also appeared and threatened his left flank, but they were dispersed by a couple of shots from the mountain guns.

January 31st. Return of Col. Talbot's convoy from Jakdul.

Colonel Boscawen being ill with fever, the command had devolved on Colonel M. Willson, Guards' Camel Regiment.

At 3 a.m. on the morning of the 1st February, Lieutenant Stuart Wortley arrived, as already described, with the report of the fall of Khartum, and the wreck of Sir C. Wilson's steamer, and Lord C. Beresford started to relieve the party.

February 1st. Arrival of Lieut. Stuart Wortley.

A good deal of firing took place during the course of the day between foraging parties and small bodies of the enemy in the neighbouring villages and dhura fields.

At 9 p.m. on the same day Colonel Talbot again left Gubat for Jakdul with a convoy of all available camels, and an escort of 400 men, taken equally from the Guards', Heavy, and Mounted Infantry, Camel Regiments. Each regiment took with it 100 spare riding camels and saddles. All wounded and sick who were fit to be moved accompanied the convoy, viz., 5 officers, 55 non-commissioned officers and men, and 6 natives. This left 7 officers, 35 non-commissioned officers and men, and 2 natives still sick at Gubat. Colonel Talbot was also instructed to pick up, at Abu Klea, all sick and wounded fit to be moved and to convey them to Jakdul. He was also ordered to increase the garrison of Abu Klea by 100 men of his escort, taking their camels on with him to Jakdul.

Departure of 2nd convoy for Jakdul.

Some of the wounded sent off.

Lord Cochrane acted as guide to the convoy and also carried despatches to Lord Wolseley, informing him of the fall of Khartum; he pushed on from Abu Klea and reached Korti on the 4th.

The convoy arrived at Jakdul on February 4th, and deposited the sick and wounded. Colonel Talbot was, however, ordered to remain at Jakdul, and did not leave it on his return journey till the 8th.

Return of Sir C. Wilson on the 4th.

On the 4th Lord C. Beresford returned to Gubat in the "Safieh," bringing with him Sir C. Wilson and his shipwrecked crew.

Sir C. Wilson left Gubat for Korti on the morning of the 6th February, with an escort of 12 men of the Guards' Camel Regiment. He reached Korti on the 9th. Lord Wolseley immediately telegraphed a report of the circumstances attending his return to Gubat, and on the 11th the following reply was received from the Secretary of State for War :—" Express warm recognition of Government of brilliant services of Sir C. Wilson, and satisfaction at gallant rescue of his party."

On receipt of Sir C. Wilson's despatch giving an account of the battle of the 19th, and the news of Sir H. Stewart's wound, Lord Wolseley at once decided to send Sir R. Buller to take command in the desert and at Gubat, and to despatch the Royal Irish and Royal West Kent Regiments to reinforce the garrison at Gubat. Sir E. Wood was appointed Chief of the Staff in place of Sir R. Buller.

February 2nd. Sir R. Buller assumes command in the desert.

Reinforcements sent across to Jakdul from Korti.

On the 2nd February, Sir R. Buller arrived at Jakdul, having left Korti on the 29th January. The Royal Irish Regiment also arrived at Jakdul on the 4th from Korti, whence they had marched by half battalions, one under command of Lieutenant-Colonel H. Shaw, V.C., and the other under command of Lieutenant-Colonel Wray, on the evenings of the 28th and 30th January. They were in charge of a considerable quantity of commissariat stores for the troops at Gubat. The men carried 70 rounds of ammunition, water bottles filled, and rolled great coats. They had carried for them by camels, one blanket and one waterproof sheet for each man, and a kit bag for every four men, also eight days' rations and a reserve of Martini-Henry ammunition of 230 rounds per man.

One gallon of water was carried as a daily ration for each man, and was distributed as follows :—1 quart for breakfast, 1 quart for dinner, 1 quart for the evening meal, and 1 quart in the water bottle.

The marches were all made at night, and were of varying length, the shortest being the first out of Korti, 10 miles, and the longest that on the fourth night into El Howeiya, 17 miles.

The first convoy of hired camels (88) had left Korti for

Jakdul on 18th of January, and before the end of that month six similar small convoys had started across the desert. But it was not till the 9th of February that these hired convoys could be got to work with the troops.

On the morning of the 7th of February the Royal Irish left Jakdul for Abu Klea, and here they were joined by Colonel Talbot's convoy, which had followed them on the 8th from Jakdul. Sir R. Buller also left Jakdul on the 8th for Abu Klea. On arriving there he assumed command, and leaving two companies of the Royal Irish under Colonel Wray as garrison, he marched with the remainder for Gubat on the 10th. February 7th. Reinforcements leave Jakdul for the front.

On receipt of the news of the fall of Khartum, on the 4th, Lord Wolseley despatched an express messenger after Sir R. Buller, conveying to him the following orders:— Orders to Sir R. Buller on the 4th and 5th.
1. To remain at Jakdul.
2. To remove to Korti all wounded.
3. Not to move any more infantry from Jakdul.
4. Not to engage in any offensive operations.

On the evening of the same day these orders were changed and Sir R. Buller was directed to go to Gubat. It was on receipt of these second orders at Jakdul on the 8th, that Sir R. Buller started for Abu Klea. On the following morning the more extended orders, given below, were sent to him. They reached him at Abu Klea on the 10th, he having left Jakdul just before the messenger arrived there, and he replied that night in a private letter, sent back by the same messenger, which spoke hopefully of the situation.

"*Korti, 5th February*, 1885.

"Major-General Sir R. Buller,

"With reference to orders sent you by express messenger last night, I have now to inform you that the first matter of serious importance which demands your immediate attention is the safety of Sir C. Wilson and his party, who have been wrecked, it is said, about four miles above a position occupied by the enemy, and between 30 and 40 miles from Gubat. A steamer had left Gubat on the 1st instant to bring him back to that place, and it is hoped that it will succeed in doing so, as Lieutenant Wortley experienced no serious difficulty in returning from the island. Memorandum to Sir R. Buller of February 5th.

"The second point to be provided for is the safe evacuation of the seriously wounded who still remain at Gubat.

(S.C.2)   E 2

"Their number is reported to be 7 officers, 35 British soldiers, and 2 natives. It is feared that most of these will require to be carried by hand on stretchers.

"You will take the earliest possible measures for the evacuation of these wounded.

"To strengthen you in camel troops I am sending you as many of the Light Camel Regiment as I can mount efficiently. They will leave Korti this evening, and should be with you on the 8th instant.

"Every arrangement must be made at Gubat for suddenly leaving that place with all troops now in it and returning to Jakdul, picking up *en route* the men stationed at Abu Klea. If possible I should like all the ammunition now at Gubat brought back to Jakdul, but any for which conveyance cannot be provided, must be thrown down wells or into the river.

"You will have the goodness to occupy the wells at Abu Halfa with a strong force for the present. Colonel Shaw, Royal Irish, or some other senior officer, to be selected by you, to command there.

"I expect to receive a telegram from home before midnight conveying to me the wishes of Her Majesty's Government and a general outline of the policy to be adopted in the Sudan. On receipt of the telegram I will send another express to you. I have no doubt the first thought of the Government will be the absolute safety of this army, and that, owing to the lateness of the season, I shall be ordered to undertake no further movements upon Khartum. Unless I am ordered to the contrary, which is unlikely, I shall, under these circumstances, concentrate the army on the line Merowi-Abu Kussi, sending all sick and wounded to Abu Fatmeh for conveyance to Wady Halfa.

"I shall send a small British garrison to Abu Fatmeh, and strengthen the garrison at Dongola.

"No more provisions will be sent from Korti and Jakdul. Please instruct officer commanding at Gubat to use every endeavour, through native means, to ascertain with certainty the fate of General Gordon.

"All soldiers and sailors of all ranks now at Gubat belonging to the steamers under Khashm-el-Mûs, who wish to come with us, to be allowed to do so. It may, in the first instance, be advisable to bring all of them with us as far as Abu Klea, to avoid the possibility of their giving information to the enemy of our evacuation of Gubat. They might be useful in carrying the wounded; every man so employed being disarmed and carefully watched.

"The West Kent Regiment will not be sent forward to Jakdul, unless you require their assistance for the safe evacuation of Gubat.

"The detachment of black troops of Egyptian army now *en route* for this place will be halted at Abu Kussi.

"As I told you in the minutes of last night* General Earle has been ordered to halt wherever he may be when the order reaches him.

"Remembering it is almost certain the English Government will not listen to any further forward movement, and that the evacuation of the army, as I have already indicated, is almost certain to be ordered from home, you will, if you find yourself temporarily cut off from communication with me, take steps for the evacuation of Gubat, and for the concentration of all the troops who have gone from here across the desert at Jakdul, and the wells of Abu Halfa and Howeiya. If, finding yourself without further instructions, you think the movements of the enemy are such as to render the evacuation of Gubat difficult, you should withdraw to Jakdul the garrison from that place, and if you think it advisable even from Abu Klea also. Looking to the degree to which we are dependent upon friendly tribes for the conveyance of stores across the desert, nothing could be more unfortunate for us at present than that our troops at Gubat should be besieged by large bodies of the enemy, which the fall of Khartum now renders available for that purpose.

(Signed) "WOLSELEY, General."

At noon, on February 11th, Sir R. Buller, Colonel Talbot's convoy and the Royal Irish arrived at Gubat where they were warmly welcomed by the troops. The news that Sir H. Stewart had been promoted to be a Major-General for distinguished service in the field caused the liveliest satisfaction.

Nothing of importance had occurred at Gubat since the departure of Colonel Talbot's convoy. The information from the south, however, tended to show that Mahdist forces were advancing from Khartum.

On the 12th, having reviewed the situation at Gubat, Sir R. Buller expressed his opinions and announced his decision in the following memorandum:—

---

* This refers to the orders sent on the evening of the 4th.

February 12th.
Sir R. Buller's despatch announcing his intention to retire from Gubat.

"Chief of the Staff.

"1. Referring to your orders of the 5th instant, and your subsequent communication enclosing copies of telegrams addressed to Lord Wolseley by the Secretary of State for War.

"2. A convoy will, I hope, leave this to-morrow, taking all the sick and wounded hence to Jakdul. The officer commanding has orders to pick up and take on all the sick and wounded now at Abu Klea.

"3. I have seriously considered the position here; it is this—

"4. Metemmeh is occupied by about 2,000 men (800 to 1,000 of whom are possibly wounded) who will fight, but who would not, if attacked, make any desperate resistance. They have two guns (brass howitzers), and say 1,000 to 1,500 rifles, but very little ammunition of any sort. They are much in fear of being attacked by us.

"5. A reinforcement of from 3,000 to 4,000 men with five or seven guns, only one of which in either case is a Krupp, is on the way. This reinforcement has a good deal of ammunition, both artillery and small arms with it.

"6. Metemmeh is a large closely built town, of well built thickly walled houses. I do not think it ought to be difficult to take after we have made a lodgement in one part of it. Of course, if it is to be taken, it should be attacked before the expected reinforcements arrive.

"7. This, I think, is a step from which I am precluded by your orders of the 5th instant.

"8. Metemmeh could equally be surely taken, I think, after the arrival of the reinforcements, but of course at greater risk; and the knowledge that they were asked under these circumstances to do what might have been done before, would have a bad effect on our men, and possibly would increase the risk.

"9. There are two steamers here, one a small one, the other an old one. Lord Charles Beresford reports that neither of them are of the slightest use for offensive purposes, that the old one can only ascend 22 miles, and descend 25 miles, from here, till after the Nile rises.

"10. Our camels are emaciated, and their carrying power is small. Indeed I do not think we have enough camels to get this force out at one go.

"11. I understand from your letter of the 5th that you have ordered General Earle to halt wherever he may be.

"12. I have about 12 days' supply here, 12 more at Abu Klea, and to keep up supply should have to send all my

LORD WOLSELEY REQUESTS INSTRUCTIONS.

camels at once to Jakdul, to which place, by last advices, you have ceased sending supply.

"13. Camels hence to Jakdul and back cannot do the journey in less than 10 days in their present weak state.

"14. Consequently, I have concluded that it is my duty to take action at once, and shall withdraw to Abu Klea and Jakdul.

"15. I regret to have to express now an opinion different to that which I expressed to Lord Wolseley in a letter dated the night of the 10th instant; but when I then wrote, I was not aware of the condition of the steamers and of the fact that the big one could not pass a sandbank 25 miles below this. Lord C. Beresford considers it doubtful if the other one can either.

"16. I am still of opinion that it would be advantageous to occupy Berber; but having weighed all the circumstances of the case, I think that one-half of the force now here, marched viâ Jakdul and Merowi to Abu Hamed and Berber, will be more valuable and entail less risk than if we march past Metemmeh and draw the force of the Mahdi after us.

"17. Since writing this I am confirmed in my opinion by the news that Mohammed Ahmed left Khartum en route here on the 9th instant.

"18. I will send further news of any movement.
"REDVERS BULLER,
"Major-General.
"Gubat, 12th February, 1885."

In forwarding the news of the fall of Khartum by telegram to the Secretary of State for War on the 4th of February, Lord Wolseley had added "It is now for the Government to decide what policy they wish me to pursue, as the fall of Khartum leaves me without instructions, the object of my mission to this country being no longer possible. .... If you wish, I could still advance on Khartum and could defeat Mahdi; but operation under present conditions is much more difficult than before, and owing to the lateness of the season, would be somewhat hazardous, for our serious enemy would be the hot weather, not the Mahdi. Force under my command is in no danger whatever. I can concentrate it whenever it is desirable to do so. I could not possibly reach Khartum with sufficient force to attack Mahdi for six weeks from this date. If you do not wish us to enter upon a campaign against him under

Lord Wolseley's correspondence with the Home Government as to course to be pursued.

present circumstances, at this late season, I could concentrate all my force in neighbourhood of Debbeh and await events."

To this telegram the following reply was sent on the 6th of February by the Secretary of State for War:—

" Objects to be aimed at now are—

" 1. Safety of Gordon, if alive, which must be assumed till we are certain of his death.

" 2. To check advance of Mahdi in districts now undisturbed.

" Whether it will be ultimately necessary to advance on Khartum or not, cannot now be decided; but a hazardous operation at this season does not appear essential to the above objects.

" From political point of view there would be disadvantages in a retrograde movement unconnected with military concentration, but all such considerations must yield to military necessities.

" We have absolute confidence in your judgment, and give you the fullest discretion to use the forces at your disposal for accomplishment of above main object. We are prepared to give you any further assistance in our power, either by despatch of troops to Suakin, or in any other manner you indicate."

To this Lord Wolseley replied on the same day as follows:—

" I will make every possible effort to secure safety of Gordon if he be alive. Have to-day sent messengers into the Mahdi's camp to ascertain his fate, and will send others to-morrow, and others again in a few days. No military operations I can now undertake will ensure his safety. The Mahdi may send him beyond reach of all possible help, but I shall certainly ascertain his fate. Your telegram gives me no information as to the policy with reference to the Sudan you mean to pursue. My pushing forward now will not help Gordon, if he be alive, but the capture of Berber will secure us a great advantage if you mean to send me away to Khartum next cold weather.

" If you do not mean to overthrow the Mahdi's power at Khartum, I regard the movement on Berber as unwise from a military point of view.

" In fact, if you do not mean sooner or later to overthrow the Mahdi's power at Khartum, and you cannot under present conditions make certain of taking that place this cold season, your best course would be to take Abu Hamed and hold the road from thence to Dongola, which would secure your object No. 2. There would be no risk in this policy except from climate, but all force now here would have to remain for hot season in Sudan.

"I would, if this course be approved, withdraw at once from Gubat, and by degrees from posts in desert.

"If the troops now in Sudan were to remain here this hot weather, I would recommend the immediate despatch of a force to Suakin sufficient to destroy Osman Digna's power.

"If you decide upon army remaining this hot weather in Sudan, railway from end of present line near Sarras must be extended to Absarat.

"If you decide to embark on a campaign next cold season against the Mahdi at Khartum, more troops will be required here.

"Pending a further expression of your views as to the military policy to be pursued, and the objects you wish this army to secure, I have, owing to the general tenour of your telegram, ordered Earle to push on to Abu Hamed.

"Report received from Gubat, given, I assume, on authority of Khashm-el-Mûs, says that capture of Khartum has placed at the Mahdi's disposal 15,000 rifles, and 15 camel guns, with plenty of ammunition.

"This renders the Mahdi now a much more formidable opponent than when he was badly provided and seriously engaged with all his troops in besieging Khartum. These reports may be exaggerated."

On the evening of the 7th Lord Wolseley received a telegram from the Secretary of State for War, in answer to his request for information as to the policy which was to be pursued in the Sudan. This telegram ran as follows :—

"Your military policy is to be based on the necessity, which we recognize on the state of facts now before us, that the power of the Mahdi at Khartum must be overthrown. We leave you to decide the military measures best calculated to attain this object, and whether advance should be made this season or next. On this statement of our policy tell us at once what additional force you desire, and when and where to be sent; also whether, on the plan you adopt under your instructions, you wish immediate despatch of force to attack Osman Digna."

Lord Wolseley replied by telegraph on the 8th, thanking the Secretary of State for his explicit statement of policy. He requested that Osman Digna might be dealt with at once. While expressing a slight hope that General Gordon might possibly be still holding out within Khartum, he stated that unless this was the case, he would probably have to content himself with the capture of Berber. He pointed out that reinforcements could not now reach him in time for the present season's campaign on the Nile.

On the following day Lord Wolseley wrote this despatch on the situation:—

From General Lord Wolseley to the Secretary of State for War.

CAMP KORTI,
9th February, 1885.

Lord Wolseley's despatch on the fall of Khartum.

MY LORD,

I have the honour to report that on the 4th instant I received a despatch from the Officer Commanding at Gubat, of which I forward a copy herewith, informing me that Khartum had without doubt been taken by the Mahdi's troops on the 26th ultimo. Lieutenant Stuart-Wortley's report, which is amongst the enclosures of this despatch, describes the attempt made by Colonel Sir Charles Wilson to reach Khartum for the purpose of communicating with General Gordon.

Up to the moment of my writing this, no native here believes that Khartum has fallen, as no rumour on the subject has been received in any neighbouring village. The Mudir of Dongola, who is in my camp, says it is impossible that Khartum should have been taken on the 26th ultimo, without the fact being long since known far and wide.

There can be no doubt that the enemy have captured Omdurman and Tuti Island, as an artillery fire was opened from both those places on the two steamers carrying Colonel C. Wilson and party. It is not, however, clear that any shots were fired from Khartum itself on those steamers, thus leaving us a gleam of hope that, although the positions, above referred to are certainly in the Mahdi's possession, the city itself may still be uncaptured.

One rumour is—as will be seen from enclosed papers—that General Gordon and a party of determined men had taken refuge in the Roman Catholic Church, which is strongly built of stone. The accompanying rough sketch of the city shows its position.

I have not yet heard the result of Captain Lord Charles Beresford's expedition up the river from Gubat to bring back Sir C. Wilson and party from the island, where their steamer was wrecked. The navigation there for steamers had become very difficult, owing to the river having fallen three feet in three days.

The wounded from Gubat and Abu Klea, except seven officers, 35 British soldiers, and two natives, still at Gubat, had reached Jakdul safely, having stood the journey very well. They are now on their way to Korti, where every arrangement has been made for their comfort.

Major-General Sir Herbert Stewart is still on board a steamer at Gubat, and the latest reports of his condition are most hopeful.

I shall not attempt to disguise from your Lordship how deeply the reported fall of Khartum is felt by all ranks in the Army under my command. If it be literally true—and it is difficult to disbelieve it—the mission of this force, which was the relief of Khartum, falls to the ground.

The strength and composition of this little army was calculated for the relief, not the siege and capture of Khartum, the two operations being entirely different in character and magnitude.

The former meant one or more engagements in the open with an enemy who, owing to the geographical position of Khartum could not concentrate his forces without raising the siege, and who, in order to concentrate, would have had to pass his troops, guns, ammunition, &c., over two unfordable rivers of considerable breadth, in the face of General Gordon's armed steamers.

If he opposed my advance along the right bank of the Nile upon Khartum, he must have fought in a position where defeat would have been his destruction.

I think I may say, that as long as Khartum held out, he could not have prevented my entering it, although he might afterwards have awaited my attack, in a selected position on left bank of White Nile to the south or south-west of the city.

With Khartum in the enemy's possession, the whole conditions are reversed, and the Mahdi—strengthened by the large number of rifles, guns, ammunition, &c., taken in that place, and by the captured troops, who would certainly fight on his side—could concentrate an overwhelming force to oppose my advance; and, if defeated, could still fall back upon the city, the siege and capture of which, situated as it is in the fork of two unfordable rivers would be an impossible operation for the little army under my command, more especially as it would then be encumbered by a large number of wounded men.

As I have already said, the force under my command was not intended for any operation of that magnitude, nor was such an operation even contemplated in the instructions I received from Her Majesty's Government.

Khartum in the hands of the enemy cannot be retaken until the force under my command has been largely augmented in numbers and in artillery.

I have, &c.,
(Signed) WOLSELEY, General.
The Right Hon. Marquis of Hartington, M.P.

<small>February 10th. Orders sent to Sir R. Buller to take Metemmeh and move on Berber.</small>

On receipt of the telegram announcing that Her Majesty's Government had decided that the Mahdi was to be crushed, a special messenger was despatched to Sir R. Buller, on the morning of the 10th, bearing instructions :—

1. To take Metemmeh as soon as he felt himself strong enough to do so, and to use his discretion as to the necessity for also occupying Shendi.

2. To arrange approximately for the following party on the desert line :—

El Howeiya	70 of all ranks.
Abu Halfa	50 „
Jakdul	200 „
Gubat or Metemmeh	400 „

3. Having taken Metemmeh to combine with General Earle in an attack on Berber.

4. To endeavour to open up negotiations with the Hassaniyeh tribe with a view to inducing them to establish convoys of hired camels to ply between Jakdul and Gubat or Metemmeh.

He was also informed that Her Majesty's Government were sending a force to Suakin to crush Osman Digna.

Sir R. Buller received these orders late on the night of the 13th, when he had already partly evacuated Gubat and had made all arrangements for leaving it at daylight the following morning. He wrote, explaining that he thought it advisable to adhere to the opinion expressed in his letter of the 12th, and to evacuate Gubat at once and occupy Abu Klea Wells, without first attacking Metemmeh.

He gave as his principal reason for this that he felt convinced a force of some sort was *en route* from Khartum, and that if that force, on arrival, took up a position in the bush between Gubat and Abu Klea, he would experience great difficulty in keeping up his communication. At Abu Klea, on the contrary, he could be perfectly safe, as no enemy could exist in the desert between that place and Jakdul; and from Abu Klea he could either retire comfortably, or march through Metemmeh on Berber, as he might be ordered.

On the 12th February, Lord Wolseley received at Korti the news of the success of the River Column at Kirbekan. On that same date the following orders were sent to the Desert Column:—

"*From Chief of Staff to Major-General Sir R. Buller, V.C.*
"*Korti, 12th February, 1885.*

"SIR,

"(1). Enclosed is a copy of Brigadier-General Brackenbury's despatch,* reporting result of his very successful action of 10th inst., and the sad news that General Earle was killed upon that occasion.

"(2). In a private letter of the 10th instant, 9 p.m., General Brackenbury reports that, of the amounts telegraphed on the 2nd inst. to the Chief of Staff as in possession with his column, 30 per cent. of the biscuit is unfit for food.

"(3). The enclosure marked C† shows the amount of provisions according to amended scale, as they will be when General Brackenbury receives Lieutenant Rundle's first convoy from Korosko; that is to leave for Abu Hamed next Sunday, the 15th instant, and should reach its destination on 20th or 21st instant.

"(4). General Brackenbury, leaving behind a garrison of 150 or 200 with rations for 60 days, would be able to leave Abu Hamed on 22nd instant, but, as I cannot expect to receive an answer from you to this before the 22nd or 23rd instant, and as it will take three days for a messenger to reach Abu Hamed from Merowi, I shall halt Brackenbury at Abu Hamed until he hears from me again. I cannot, therefore, calculate on his leaving Abu Hamed before 26th February, or on his reaching the neighbourhood of Berber before the 13th or 14th of March. With what force could you reach that place on that day, having left behind, at or near Metemmeh, the garrison as detailed in my previous instructions of the 10th inst. What date would you propose starting, and for what number of days could you carry rations for the

February 12th. Further orders to Sir R. Buller to the same effect.

* See Appendix 48.   † See Appendix 49.

force you take with you, beyond the 21 days which it is calculated you will be absent from Metemmeh? With reference to my instructions of the 10th instant, you will perceive from enclosure (C) that you cannot depend upon General Brackenbury's column for any provisions from their boats.

"(7). In case you cannot accomplish this operation without obtaining from Jakdul another convoy, please send me a special messenger to report when you think you would be able to reach Berber as intended, with, at all events, three weeks' supply for the force you intend taking with you.

"(8). I enclose herewith a return, giving you the number and composition of the daily convoys that have lately left Korti for Jakdul, and the amount of supplies sent forward by them to that place.

"(9). The remaining detachment of the Royal Sussex Regiment left here on the 9th inst., and three companies of the Royal West Kent on the 10th inst. It is not intended to send forward any more troops from Korti to Jakdul. All infantry lately sent over the desert have taken three hundred rounds per man.

"(10). Enclosure gives a return of the gun ammunition that will I trust leave this on the 14th inst, and should reach Jakdul on the 18th inst.

"(11). When Berber is taken, a garrison of 2 guns Egyptian battery, Guards' Camel Regiment, Royal Irish, Detachment R.E., one thousand men maximum strength of all ranks, corps, departments, and others, will be left there under the best officer available; and with it will be left all the ammunition which can be spared by General Brackenbury's column, and all the rations that his and your column can afford to leave them.

"(12). Unless you receive other orders you will then return with your column, minus the Royal Irish, which will form part of the Berber garrison, all sick and wounded being handed over to General Brackenbury, to take in his boats down the river to Korti *viâ* Abu Hamed. He should leave Berber the same date that you do, which should be the 20th of March, assuming that you and he had reached Berber on the 10th March.

"(13). It is hoped that the two steamers now at Gubat may be of great use to you in these operations, although it is feared the river between Berber and Metemmeh will soon be too shallow in places for the navigation of these steamers.

"(14). The Naval Brigade under Lord Charles Beresford will eventually form part of the garrison of Berber, but will not be counted in the one thousand men already referred to. It is to be hoped they may be able to repair one or both of the steamers now in the enemy's possession there.

"(15). When you return to Metemmeh, which place I presume you will reach on the 27th of March, you will make every arrangement for evacuating that place, bringing back with you all the infantry and mounted infantry, and the battery Royal Artillery, to Jakdul *viâ* Abu Klea, picking up *en route* the force at that place.

"(16). The two regiments of Cavalry Camel Corps will then return to Berber, taking with them as much provisions, ammunition, and money as you can send with them, together with all the boats they can collect and the two steamers. They will remain at Berber until further orders, which they will possibly receive *viâ* Suakin, but will always be ready to march across the desert to Suakin. If they have not enough camels for the march, they must endeavour to purchase more locally.

"(17). A force of about 9,000 men is now being moved to Suakin to crush Osman Digna, and it is hoped that operation may be effected in the first week in April. As soon as this is accomplished, it is hoped the road between Berber and Suakin can be safely traversed by the two cavalry regiments of Camel Corps.

"(18). These orders are based on the assumption that Khartum has been taken and General Gordon murdered. No news in corroboration of these statements has yet reached this neighbourhood, and the story is entirely discredited by the Mudir of Dongola.

"(19). Please forward all Berber and Khartum news you possess, and do all you can to send people into both places to obtain news of the Mahdi's plans and intentions. It is possible that Khashm-el-Mûs may be of great aid to you in this respect. You are authorised to take him on the pay of your Intelligence Department.

"I have, &c.,
(Signed)   " EVELYN WOOD, Major-General.
                                          " C. of S."

This despatch crossed those written by Sir R. Buller on the 12th and 13th, and that officer had evacuated Gubat before it reached him. As will presently be seen, from Lord Wolseley's telegram to the Secretary of State for War on the 18th, he thoroughly approved of the course taken by Sir R. Buller.

February 13th. Remainder of sick and wounded sent back to Abu Klea.

Sir R. Buller's first despatch was forwarded to Korti, with a convoy which started on the morning of the 13th February under command of Colonel Talbot, and which took with it Sir H. Stewart and all the sick and wounded; those who were unable to walk being carried on stretchers by Egyptian soldiers.

The sick and wounded, 75 in number, were in charge of the Bearer Company under Surgeon-Major Conolly. They were accompanied by 300 Egyptian soldiers and camp followers, and a portion of the Commissariat and Transport Corps. The escort was composed of a wing of the Heavy Camel Regiment, the Marine company and another of the Guards' Camel Regiment, and a company of the Mounted Infantry Camel Regiment.

After proceeding eight or nine miles, a halt was made for breakfast in the bushy district of Shebakat, after which, just as the column was about to proceed on its march, the scouts reported a large convoy of camels with Arab drivers, in sight.

Skirmish on the way.

On receipt of this information, Colonel Talbot sent out the Marine company of the Guards' Camel Regiment in skirmishing order to reconnoitre, and, if possible, to take the convoy. Captain A. C. Pearson, commanding the Marines, however, found the enemy too strong for him, and Colonel Talbot accordingly reinforced him with the Guards' Company. Colonel Talbot then extended the men of the Heavy Camel Regiment to the right front and formed up the Mounted Infantry Company in rear of the column. The Egyptian soldiers were formed in line on both flanks of the column, and sick and wounded were placed in the middle of the camels.

In the meanwhile the enemy had extended round three sides of the convoy, and kept up a fairly well directed fire for about an hour and a half. At the end of this time a body was seen advancing towards the convoy's left flank and was received with a volley; fortunately not a well directed one, as the body turned out to be the Light Camel Regiment, under command of Colonel Clarke, which had arrived on the scene from Jakdul.

At 1.15 P.M. the enemy fired a parting volley and withdrew, and the convoy proceeded on its way to Abu Klea accompanied by the Light Camel Regiment.

The casualties in the skirmish were 2 killed and 6 wounded.

The convoy arrived at Abu Klea on the morning of the

14th, and halted there for the day to rest the sick and wounded, marching again at 8.30 a.m. on the 16th.

On the following day, while in bivouac seven miles north of Jebel El Nus, occurred that great national misfortune, the death of Sir H. Stewart, who had lingered for nearly a month, and who now succumbed to his wounds within a few miles of the spot where he had so lately won his laurels in his first independent command. *February 17th. Death of Sir H. Stewart near Jakdul.*

He was buried on the following day near the wells at Jakdul.

On arrival at Jakdul the convoy found Sir E. Wood in command. His place as Acting Chief of the Staff, in the absence of Sir R. Buller, was filled by Colonel G. B. Wolseley, A.D.C., A.A.G. The garrison of Jakdul consisted of 4 companies of the Royal Sussex, and 3 companies of the Royal West Kent. *Sir E. Wood sent to consult with Sir R. Buller.*

Lord Wolseley's instructions to Sir E. Wood before leaving Korti on the 15th, were to proceed to Gubat to consult with Sir R. Buller. Lord Wolseley proposed that, after the departure of Sir R. Buller's force to co-operate with the River Column in an attack on Berber, the garrisons in the desert, including that which the orders to Sir R. Buller of the 10th and 12th directed him to leave at Metemmeh, should be withdrawn under Sir E. Wood's personal direction. These troops were to strengthen the Line of Communications between Hannek and Merowi. Lord Wolseley, however, left it open to Sir E. Wood, to modify this plan should circumstances at Gubat be such as to necessitate its variation, or even to abandon it altogether.

But in the meanwhile the evacuation of Gubat had taken place. The day that the convoy left (the 13th February) was devoted to the destruction of such stores as it was impossible to find transport for. The six brass howitzers brought down from Khartum were spiked, and the eccentric straps were taken off the two steamers, thus rendering them useless.

Before daylight on the following morning (14th February) the troops were ready to move, and as the day broke the force (1,700 strong) marched out of Gubat. Officers and men were all on foot, with the exception of the 19th Hussars. One camel was allowed to every four men to carry suleetahs (saddle bags) and blankets. The rear guard, which was under command of Colonel Shaw, was composed of the *February 14th. Retreat from Gubat.*

Royal Irish Regiment, with 2 guns, a small detachment of Hussars, and General Gordon's black troops.

It is a noteworthy fact that during the whole of the desert march and the occupation of Gubat, there never once occurred the slightest suspicion of a night alarm or scare of any kind, a fact which considering the very trying circumstances in which they were placed, speaks volumes for the *morale* of the troops of all arms.

The force was followed by a small body of the enemy's cavalry, who, however, kept at a respectful distance, much to the disappointment of the troops. The men, after their weary march across the desert and the trying inactivity at Gubat, were anxious for a final brush with the enemy.

After a 13 miles march a halt was made in a good natural position, and the night was passed without any disturbance.

<small>February 15th. Arrival at Abu Klea.</small>

At 5.30 on the following morning, February 15th, the march was resumed and the wells of Abu Klea, 10 miles distant, were reached at 11 a.m. Here Sir R. Buller found in addition to the garrison, the Light Camel Regiment, which Lord Wolseley had sent to relieve the Heavy Camel Regiment. Sir R. Buller now halted for further instructions.

On receipt of Sir R. Buller's despatch announcing the evacuation of Gubat, Lord Wolseley sent the following telegram to the Secretary of State for War:—

"*Korti*, 18*th February*, 1885, 11.40 *p.m.*

<small>Lord Wolseley's report of the withdrawal from Gubat.</small>

"Despatch just received from General Buller, from Abu Klea, reports that he evacuated Gubat on the morning of the 14th inst., and reached Abu Klea on the 15th without any attempt by the enemy to interfere with his movements. He now awaits instructions at Abu Klea.

" I think he acted with wisdom and discretion; for since the fall of Khartum, the whole of the Mahdi's army is disposable, and could have invested him at Gubat with a large force, not only of men but of guns; this they cannot do either at Abu Klea or at Jakdul.

"My instructions to General Buller were on no account to allow himself to be shut in near Metemmeh; and, with the information he had of the Mahdi's movements, in proceeding to Abu Klea he has rightly interpreted the spirit of these instructions.

" The army under my command was intended for the relief of General Gordon and of his beleagured garrison.

Its strength and constitution were not fixed with the view of its attacking the Mahdi entrenched in Khartum, especially after he had been strengthened by the large quantity of arms captured there, and his numbers augmented by the many thousands of well drilled soldiers, whom Gordon had trained, but who have now transferred their allegiance to the False Prophet.

"The fall of Khartum set free for the Mahdi a considerable army, and furnished him with an arsenal containing a great number of guns and rifles, and about 100,000 rounds of rifle ammunition. Operations, which before could be carried out under the ordinary hazards of war, cannot now be undertaken without incurring inordinate risks. When Khartum fell, moreover, the main object for which General Stewart's force was sent to Metemmeh ceased to exist. That object was to be prepared to march at once, even at considerable hazard, to the assistance of Gordon, should it be found that he required immediate aid.

"The capture of Khartum left his force without an objective, while at the same time it greatly increased the insecurity of its position. Its isolated situation, separated from me by 180 miles of desert, and liable at any moment to have its communications cut by a movement of the Mahdi down the Nile, has latterly caused me considerable anxiety. It is now freed from this exposure, since our possession of the wells precludes any operations of the enemy in the desert, and it is at my disposal to divert to points where it can act with equal effect and with less risk. General Buller reports that the health and spirits of his men are excellent; the sick and wounded are doing well; but I regret to add that Sir Herbert Stewart's case was less hopeful, as his fever had increased."

Lord Wolseley on the same day sent fresh instructions to Sir E. Wood and to Sir R. Buller. Sir R. Buller, with the Camel Regiments, 19th Hussars, the Camel Battery, and details, was to march to Merowi, while Sir E. Wood was to withdraw the remainder of the troops and all stores from the posts in the desert to Korti.

On inspecting the wells of Abu Klea on the 15th, Sir R. Buller had found that they could not be relied on to water his whole force, and he had also found that he was, though well supplied with rations and ammunition, deficient of food for his horses and camels.

On the morning of the 16th, therefore, he sent:—

The 19th Hussars, except 1 officer, 6 men, and 8 horses,
Guards' Camel Regiment.
Remainder of Heavy Camel Regiment,
Transport Corps with all spare camels,
and all the Sudanese in camp, to Jakdul.

Later in the day, finding that the camels were suffering from want of food, he sent 100 of the Light Camel Regiment with 150 camels to Jakdul, under Lieutenant-Colonel J. P. Brabazon.

February 16th. Appearance of the enemy round Abu Klea.

On the evening of the 16th the enemy were discovered to have occupied a hill commanding the camp and about 1,200 yards to the north-east of it, from which they kept up a harassing fire throughout the night; they were, however, driven away with loss on the following morning. Their retreat was in a great measure due to the action of Major F. M. Wardrop, D.A.A.G., who, with only three other mounted men and Lieutenant R. J. Tudway, Mounted Infantry, by appearing rapidly and firing from several points in succession, made the enemy believe that their position (which was a very strong one) was threatened in rear, and caused them to evacuate it.

On the afternoon of the 17th, Lieutenant-Colonel H. McCalmont, Light Camel Regiment, arrived with the Chief of the Staff's despatch of the 12th, containing the news of the successful action at Kirbekan. This despatch, however, written on the assumption that it would find Sir R. Buller at Gubat, or Metemmeh, contained no instructions as to what course should be pursued now that his force had withdrawn to Abu Klea. All was quiet in the evening.

The casualties on the 16th and 17th amounted to 3 men killed and 4 officers (Captains H. A. Walsh, Mounted Infantry, and H. Paget, Light Camel Regiment, Quartermaster W. Jamieson, Royal Irish, and Surgeon S. L. O'Neill) and 23 men, wounded.

February 18th. Major Wardrop sent to Jakdul to prepare for a march on Berber.

On the 18th Major Wardrop was sent to Jakdul. He carried detailed instructions respecting Sir R. Buller's requirements in the event of his being ordered to march from Abu Klea to Berber, or from Abu Klea to Jakdul.

His dispositions on finding orders at Jakdul for Sir R. Buller to move to Merowi.

On arrival at Jakdul, he found Sir E. Wood in command and also learnt that orders had been received for Sir R. Buller to move on Merowi. He at once made all the necessary arrangements for this retrograde movement, despatching a convoy with grain and water to Abu Klea, and taking steps for the formation of two depôts on the road. One depôt of 1,200 gallons of water and 10,000 lbs. of dhura he placed 20 miles from Jakdul, the other of 2,500 gallons of water and 15,000 lbs. of dhura about half way between there and Abu Klea.

Major Wardrop then left for Abu Klea, and arriving there on the 21st before his convoy, brought Sir R. Buller the despatches containing instructions to move on Merowi. The convoy, which was under Colonel Brabazon, arrived on the 22nd with 782 camels.

Throughout these operations, one of the main difficulties with which Lord Wolseley had had to contend was that of communicating with the Desert Column. While Lord Wolseley was issuing his instructions to Sir R. Buller for his march from Metemmeh on Berber on the 12th, that officer was already preparing for his retreat on Abu Klea. During this march Sir R. Buller had satisfied himself that his camels were completely broken down, and it was only on receipt of the reports from Abu Klea on the 18th, that Lord Wolseley became fully aware of the collapse of the transport in the Desert.

All hope of taking Berber before the autumn abandoned.

The terrible strain not only on the camels, but also on the cavalry horses, had rendered it impossible for the Desert Column to undertake active operations unless supplied with a large number of fresh camels and horses, and these were not available.

Sir E. Wood's opinion on this point is shown in the following extracts from a minute written by him on February 20th:—

"It is desirable that it should be distinctly understood that in my opinion it is impossible for General Buller to march to Merowi, unless he gets the fresh camels mentioned in my letter of yesterday,* and the 19th Hussars will require at least half their number of fresh horses.

"Moreover the troops cannot get to Korti without transport to move all of them, as also for the stores. I assume every effective will walk.

"I do not think the debilitated state of our transport is realised at Korti. The Heavy Camel Regiment has now 22 riding and 10 baggage camels only. The Guards have 228, but they are in a wretched state."

---

* "The Heavy Camel Regiment and Guards will require nearly all new Camels, the Light Camel Regiment will require at least 100, the Mounted Infantry 200; all the Transport here should be remounted."

Reasons for this change of plan. About the same time that this minute was received from Sir E. Wood, private letters from Sir R. Buller also arrived. In these he not only drew attention to the fact that the transport of the Desert Column was completely exhausted, but further stated that the boots of the men were thoroughly worn out, and that many of them were almost shoeless.

The receipt of these letters, coupled with the intelligence received from General Brackenbury that, taking into consideration his present position and the state of his supplies, he could not guarantee leaving any rations for the proposed Berber garrison, forced upon Lord Wolseley a complete change of arrangements. Up to this time the various orders issued to Sir R. Buller and General Brackenbury and the reports and communications from headquarters to the Home Government, had all been based on the intention to capture Berber and Abu Hamed, and to hold those places with garrisons during the summer, preparatory to an advance in force on Khartum during the ensuing cool season. It will further be apparent, when the account given later on in this work of the origin of the Suakin expedition is read, that all the initial arrangements of that expedition were made with the view of co-operating towards this end. But during the second and third weeks of February, Lord Wolseley became aware that the transport, without which it was impossible for the Desert Column to undertake the march on Berber, had completely given out under the hard and continuous work to which it had been subject, and that the marching power of the men themselves was seriously crippled, and was every day becoming more crippled by the fact that their boots were rapidly going to pieces. Further, the unusually low Nile had caused the advance of the River Column, which, from the latest reports would not be concentrated at Abu Hamed before the 29th, to take longer than had been anticipated. The period during which this force could be kept separated from its base had been reduced by a month owing to one third of its biscuit supply having been found useless. Calculations had been originally based upon the arrival of the column at Berber at such a date, that, with the replenishment its supplies would receive at Abu Hamed by the Korosko convoy, it would have rations in hand for a considerable space of time. But the loss of one third of the biscuit supply carried with the column, had already materially affected the time during which it could operate. And now it transpired that the physical difficulties in the way of its rapid progress had

REASONS FOR POSTPONEMENT OF ADVANCE ON BERBER. 73

been such that unless a second convoy could be got across from Korosko, the column would only have sufficient supplies for its own consumption for the time taken in advancing to Berber and returning to Korti. The withdrawal from Gubat —a withdrawal that was dictated by military exigencies—was in itself, as apart from the advance of the River Column, a retrograde movement. And it was a retrograde movement of that section of the Expeditionary Force that had been most severely engaged with the Mahdieh. This would tend to enhance the prestige of Mohammed Ahmed, already grown enormously, consequent on the success of his combinations at Khartum. Lord Wolseley foresaw that the moral effect of the Mahdist achievements, actual and apparent, might render the Ababdeh tribe disaffected, might forbid a second food convoy to Korosko, and might thus deprive the garrisons of Berber and Abu Hamed of their necessary supplies.

In view of all these considerations the Commander-in-Chief felt that he was no longer justified in persevering with the combined movement of the Desert and River Columns on Berber, and he was forced, reluctantly, to abandon all hope of taking that place before the autumn. The intention to take Berber being given up, the capture of Abu Hamed became unnecessary; it would only have led to a useless waste of life, and have unnecessarily prolonged the line of river to be defended during the summer months. The retention of the Desert Column in its exposed position in the desert was equally without object. A concentration on the Nile became the only course open to Lord Wolseley. Orders were accordingly sent on the 20th, directing the River Column to return, and fresh instructions as to the withdrawal of the force from the desert were sent to Sir E. Wood. Sir R. Buller was, at the same time, directed to return to Korti.

This period, therefore, namely the end of the third week in February, marks a change in the objects aimed at in the Headquarters' plan. The safe housing of the troops in summer quarters on the Nile, from Merowi northwards, now became the chief matter of consideration; and in conformity to the altered conditions, the plan for the Suakin force underwent a modification, as will be seen in the sequel.

On the 19th and 20th, patrols, sent out from Abu Klea, had come in contact with small parties of the enemy, and ·deserters stated that the enemy's camp contained about 1,000 men from Metemmeh, and that the Mahdi, who had started northwards, had returned to Omdurman.

On the 23rd, after sending off in the afternoon a convoy of all the sick, Sir R. Buller quietly withdrew the garrisons of the forts after dark, and marched off with the whole force at 8 P.M., leaving the ordinary camp fires burning and sounding the first and last post. In the morning a large force of the enemy had been reported by our piquets as entering the enemy's camp.

The account of the evacuation is given in the following report by Sir R. Buller:—

"Chief of the Staff,

"1. I left Abu Klea on the 23rd instant, and arrived here with the whole force about noon to-day.

"2. About 11 a.m. on the 23rd the enemy received a strong reinforcement which was estimated to be not less than 8,000 men. This compelled me so far to alter my plans that, instead of destroying the forts and leaving the wells untouched, I left the forts standing but filled in all the large wells.

"3. At 2 p.m. I sent out all my baggage with a convoy of 300 men under Colonel Stanley Clarke, with instructions to camp on the Oh Mit Handel plain, out of gunshot range of the Abu Klea Hills.

"4. At 6.40 p.m. I withdrew the garrisons of my outposts, and at 7.30 p.m. marched out of Abu Klea; we were not interfered with.

"5. The enemy's scouts turned up about mid-day on the 24th, and fired a few shots, they then retired and we have seen nothing of them since.

"6. Having barely camels to move my stores and supplies, all the men and officers had to march; this, in this weather, on three quarts of water per man per day, was most exhausting, but nothing could have been better than the spirit shown by all ranks.

"7. I attach a state.* We brought in here 32 all ranks, sick and wounded; all the wounded have done well on this march.

"8. I wish expressly to remark on the very excellent work that has been done by the small detachment of the 19th Hussars, both during our occupation of Abu Klea and during our retirement. Each man has done the work of 10, and it is not too much to say that the force owes much to Major French and his 13 troopers.

"REDVERS BULLER, Major-General.

"Jakdul, 26th February, 1885."

---

* Appendix 50.

This report, together with one of the 18th from Abu Klea, was forwarded to the Secretary of State for War with the following covering letter from Lord Wolseley:—

"*Camp, Korti, 1st March,* 1885.

"My Lord,

"I have the honour to forward herewith copies of two despatches received from Major-General Sir Redvers Buller, K.C.M.G. They contain an account of the attack of the enemy on his camp at Abu Klea Wells on the 16th and 17th ultimo, and also of his march to Jakdul, where he arrived on the 26th.

Lord Wolseley's covering despatch.

"The manner in which the movement from Gubat to Jakdul has been carried out reflects the greatest credit upon General Buller as a leader, and upon all ranks under him. Every retrograde step is regarded by uncivilised races as a sign of weakness and of fear, and to withdraw troops in the face of a savage enemy is neither an easy nor a grateful task. Sir Redvers Buller has, however, done this with little loss, and in a way which has won him the confidence of all who served under him. "I have, &c.,

(Signed) "WOLSELEY, General.
"The Right Hon. Marquis of Hartington."

Colonel Talbot's convoy left Jakdul on the 23rd February, and arrived at Megaga on the following day, where a halt was made, as Colonel Talbot had orders to form a post there. He spent the 25th and 26th in improving roads, building three "pepper-box" forts, making ovens, and improving access to the wells. On the 27th the remainder of the Heavy Camel Regiment arrived, and a halt of some days was made.

Withdrawal from the desert.

On the 27th February, Sir R. Buller left Jakdul for Korti to resume his duties as Chief of the Staff. On the same day all the sick and wounded were removed from Jakdul.

The Guards' Camel Regiment had left Jakdul on the 21st for Abu Halfa, where they remained till the 4th of March, strengthening the post and improving the water supply, and arriving at Korti on the 9th March. The Heavy Camel Regiment, Naval Brigade, and part of the Camel Battery, had reached Korti the previous day.

On the 3rd March, the remainder of the troops, under Sir E. Wood, marched out of Jakdul at 4.30 p.m. for Megaga wells, which were reached in three marches of about 10 miles each at 7 p.m. on the 4th March. The heat of the weather, and the fact that the heavy march across the desert had almost completely worn out the men's boots, combined with the reaction following all the recent excitement, made this march a very trying one for the men. Sir E. Wood therefore made a two days' halt at Megaga.

At midnight on the 6th March, the left half battalion of the Royal Irish left Megaga for Korti, which they reached on the morning of the 11th, the right half battalion reached Korti with Sir E. Wood on the 14th March. The regiment had marched on foot the whole way from Korti to Gubat and back.

March 16th. Last troops reach Korti from the desert. On the 16th of March, part of the Royal Sussex and Mounted Infantry Camel Regiments, with some detachments, the last troops of the desert column, marched into Korti, and the following telegram was sent by Lord Wolseley to the Secretary of State for War :—

"*Korti*, 16*th March*, 1885, 6 *p.m.*

Lord Wolseley's report of the situation on 16th March. "The last troops of the desert column arrived at Korti this morning, and the concentration on the line Abu Kussi-Merowi is now complete. I think it is very desirable that the military reasons which have rendered a concentration on the Nile necessary, should be clearly known and understood by all.

"As I said in my No. 91,* the strength and composition of this army were not fixed with a view to its undertaking the siege of Khartum. Its mission was to relieve Khartum, in doing which, had that town held out, it would have had the assistance of Gordon's army, with all its guns, ammunition, and war material. The fall of Khartum has given the Mahdi the power of turning against us, all the troops who before were bound to that town by the necessity of keeping up the siege, and it has also given him, in addition, all Gordon's trained army, his war material, and his arsenal.

"Under these circumstances, not only would a forward movement on either Khartum or Berber have been exceedingly rash, but a concentration on a line, whence I could ensure uninterrupted communication with my base, was practically a military necessity. I could not, with any due regard to safety, leave a portion only of my force to face the

---

* Telegram of February 18th, 1885 (see page 68).

greatly increased power of the Mahdi, in a position where its communications might be severed at any moment, and where such an occurrence would have necessitated a difficult and perilous retreat.

"The object for which Stewart's column was sent across the desert disappeared with the fall of Khartum. That object was to be in a position to send immediate assistance to Gordon, should his situation be found to be one requiring help without delay. For such a purpose I was prepared to incur great risk, and in pushing Stewart forward as I did I went to the extreme limits of the risks to which a commander should expose his troops. To have kept the column at Gubat, when the risks had greatly increased and the object no longer existed, would have been at once unjustifiable and useless.

"Very similar reasons operated with regard to Brackenbury's column. To have taken Abu Hamed under the existing condition of things would only have wasted life to no good purpose. My whole force is now about to take up its summer quarters, and I trust that, as I have said, the reasons for the present concentration may be made generally known."

The disaster at Khartum had completely revolutionized the situation in the theatre of war. For some months the Expedition had had for its object the relief of General Gordon. That an advance of British troops actually to Khartum might be necessary, had been foreseen by its Commander long before the Expedition was despatched. Now all was changed. *Review of the events that led to the abandonment of operations till the autumn.*

Lord Wolseley had thrust Sir H. Stewart's force across the desert into the heart of the enemy's country, to establish in the first place, a post at Metemmeh, and thence to open up communications by steamer with Khartum. The steamers were to replenish the food supply of the town. The presence, on board, of a few British soldiers was to nerve the garrison to fresh efforts. The object of the Desert Column had in fact, in the first place, been to ensure that Khartum should hold out till the British forces were ready to strike their final blow.

The River Column had been ordered to press on up the Nile. It was to proceed by Abu Hamed, where a food convoy was to meet it from Korosko, to Berber.

The possession of Berber was of great importance. It was here that the great desert route from Suakin met the Nile. The town itself was one of the chief places in the Sudan, and its recovery from the followers of Mohammed Ahmed could not fail to exercise a great moral effect over wavering tribes. General Gordon had, in his message of the 14th December, uttered a warning against the place being left in hostile hands, in rear of the force moving to relieve him at Khartum. General Earle had therefore been instructed that his first object was to be the occupation of Berber. And then, from there, supplies were to be forwarded to the force that had proceeded across the desert. But till the exact position of affairs at Khartum could be ascertained, Lord Wolseley was unable to definitely decide as to the arrangements for a final advance.

When the news arrived that Khartum had fallen, it became necessary to make entirely fresh dispositions for the future. The expedition had had a definite mission to fulfil. It had undertaken the relief of a fortress isolated in a hostile country, and beleaguered by a formidable army. But the fortress was held by friendly troops under a brilliant leader. It possessed an arsenal, and contained great stores of war material. It was, moreover, so situated in the fork between two great meeting rivers, that its siege was an operation of exceptional difficulty; for the steamers in possession of the defenders commanded the passages of these obstacles which split up the investment line into distinct camps. Now that this fortress, with its guns, its rifles, its ammunition, and its steamers, had fallen into the hands of the enemy, and that the hostile forces had been almost certainly swelled by a considerable part of its garrison, not only had the general situation in the theatre of war as it affected the Expedition altered very materially for the worse, but the object for which the Expedition had been undertaken had really ceased to exist. The question, therefore, that first presented itself when the intelligence reached Korti—a question that Lord Wolseley was not able himself to decide—was whether the victorious Mahdi was or was not to be overthrown. Pending the decision of the Home Government on this point both columns were ordered to stand fast.

The decision of the Government was that the Mahdi was to be crushed at Khartum. A plan of campaign with this end in view had, therefore, to be determined upon.

Lord Wolseley, recognising that Khartum could not be taken with the forces at his disposal, and that no reinforcements could reach him for several months, saw that an autumn campaign would be necessary. But the possession of Berber would be a great step towards the eventual capture of Khartum, and he determined that the former place should, if possible, be taken by a combined movement of the Desert and River Columns. Nor did this operation appear to be a very difficult one as far as could at the time be judged at Korti. The troops at Gubat were less than 100 miles from Berber, and would have the assistance of two steamers on a reach of the Nile that was not believed to present at the time any serious difficulties to navigation. The River Column was already nearly half way through the Monasir Cataracts, and its progress after passing these would certainly be rapid. A force was being sent to Suakin to destroy the power of Osman Digna, and this would eventually assist in opening the Suakin-Berber route. When, therefore, a few days later, news arrived of the success of the River Column at Kirbekan, and information was about the same time received of the condition of its supplies, Lord Wolseley issued detailed instructions as to the conduct of the proposed operations. These were framed with a view to the direct march of Sir R. Buller's force northwards from about Metemmeh to meet the River Column at Berber.

But it was not known at Korti that Sir R. Buller had found it necessary, in the meantime, to withdraw from Gubat to Abu Klea, that his transport was crippled, that the boots of his men were worn out, and that his steamers would probably not have been able to descend the Nile to Berber. Nor was it known that the River Column was encountering unexpected difficulties owing to the unusually low condition of the Nile. When Sir R. Buller's despatch announcing his retreat from Gubat arrived, Lord Wolseley, still unaware of the condition of the transport and the state of the men's boots, decided that part of the Desert Column should march to Merowi as a support to the advancing River Column. As a result of this retrograde movement of the Desert Column—which was to be accompanied by the withdrawal to Korti of all the detachments and stores from their exposed positions at Abu Klea, Jakdul, and elsewhere on the Metemmeh route—the whole expeditionary force would be once again assembled on the River Nile, which must be, both in the case of the impending operations against Berber, and of the subsequent autumn campaign, the main line at once of advance and of supply. But soon after issuing the necessary orders to this effect, Lord Wolseley received information that the troops in the desert had, for the reasons stated above, become practically incapable of undertaking any enterprise involving mobility. The reports from the River Column, moreover, showed that the rapids to be ascended were very difficult, that the progress of the boats was necessarily much retarded, and that, in consequence of the space of time that would elapse while the troops advanced to Berber and then fell back to Korti, all supplies that could be calculated upon would be consumed by the column itself, and none could be left for the proposed summer garrisons of Berber and Abu Hamed. The operations that had been contemplated had, therefore, to be abandoned until the autumn, and orders were sent to the River Column to fall back, whilst preparations were commenced for the withdrawal of the whole expeditionary force into summer quarters on the Nile from Hafir to Merowi

CHAPTER IX.

THE RIVER COLUMN FROM ITS ORGANIZATION TO THE ACTION OF KIRBEKAN.

Maps 1 and 8.

On the 27th of December, 1884, the following instructions were issued to Major-General Earle by the Chief of the Staff:—

December 27th, 1884. General Earle's orders.

"Lord Wolseley has decided on continuing his advance by two lines.

"1. By water.
"2. On camels.

"You will command the force proceeding by water, and the following Officers from Headquarter Staff have been detailed to act on your Staff:—

"Colonel H. Brackenbury, C.B., as principal Staff Officer and second in command.*
"Lieutenant-Colonel Alleyne, R.A., A.A.G.
"Lieutenant-Colonel Colvile, D.A.A.G.
"Major Slade, D.A.A.G.
"Colonel Burnaby, Royal Horse Guards.†
"Captain Beaumont, Signalling Officer.
"The force under your command will consist of—
  1½ Squadrons 19th Hussars.‡
  The South Staffordshire Regiment.
  The Duke of Cornwall's Light Infantry.
  The Black Watch (Royal Highlanders).
  The Gordon Highlanders.
  Battery Egyptian Artillery.
  The Egyptian Camel Corps.
  Headquarters and 400 camels of 11th Transport Company.

"In addition to the above, the Essex Regiment, or some other one regiment, will be placed at your disposal to form posts on your line of communications between Merowi and Abu Hamed.§

---

* Appointed Brigadier-General on the 7th January, 1885.
† Colonel Burnaby was afterwards detailed to the Desert Column, and Colonel Butler, C.B., to the River Column.
‡ Only one squadron was actually given to the River Column.
§ This extra regiment was afterwards withheld.

"You will inform the General Officer commanding Communications, of the posts which you form.*

"It is desirable that you should concentrate your force at Hamdab and start thence as soon as you have 100 days' supplies per man in hand to take with you.†

"Major Rundle, R.A., has undertaken to have some supplies at Abu Hamed, from Korosko, four days after your arrival at the first-named place.‡

"200,000 rations of groceries, 100,000 rations of biscuit, and 50,000 rations of preserved meat are at Korosko awaiting transport.

"You must use every endeavour to keep Major Rundle informed of your movements.

"A portion of the army of the Mudir of Dongola has been told off to accompany your force. You will employ them as you think fit. It is suggested that it might be well to employ them to collect and store supplies in the Monasir country, on the understanding that they will be paid for the supplies so collected.

"Having filled up at Abu Hamed with supplies, you will advance upon Berber, and having secured that place, you will use every endeavour to forward as many supplies as possible to the force which will have proceeded by land to Khartum.

"During the advance you will be guided by the following instructions in your dealings with natives:

"You will treat all tribes, except the Monasir, as friends, if they will meet your advances; if they will not accept them, you will enforce your demands.

"You will treat the Monasir as friends if they deliver up the murderers of Colonel Stewart and his party for punishment, not otherwise.

"You will occupy Abu Hamed and Berber, and such other places as may be necessary for the safety of your line.

"You will consider that it is, above all things, of the first importance that you should place 75,000 rations at Shendi at the disposal of the force which has operated by land, by as early a date as possible."

---

* As will be seen later, p. 85, the idea of forming these posts was abandoned, and General Earle was informed that he must consider his force a flying column.

† At the time this order was issued, the South Staffordshire, the first regiment to leave Korti in boats, had only 30 days' rations, the remainder having been taken to supply the Desert Column.

‡ These supplies were to have been conveyed across the desert by the Ababdeh tribes of whom Major Rundle had charge.

On the date of issue of this memorandum, orders were telegraphed to Colonel Colvile, who was then at Abu Dom, the advanced post of the Mudir's troops, requesting him to at once commence the purchase of such supplies as could be obtained locally.

On December 28th, the South Staffordshire Regiment, 545 of all ranks, left Korti in their whalers, accompanied by two boats containing a detachment of the 26th Company R.E.

December 28th. Departure of leading battalion from Korti.

On the following morning, half a troop of the 19th Hussars, 26 of all ranks and 30 horses, left Korti for Abu Dom, and on the afternoon of the same day, Colonel Brackenbury, who was in command of this column till it was joined a few days later by General Earle, left Korti with the following Staff Officers: Major Slade, Captain Beaumont, and Deputy-Assistant Commissary-General Boyd. On the 30th December, the messenger bearing General Gordon's famous dispatch, "Khartum all right.—C. G. Gordon, 14. 12. 84," and the verbal message, quoted on p. 182, Part I, came into Abu Dom.

On the two following days, the South Staffordshire Regiment were engaged in bringing over supplies from Merowi, and a site for a bivouac was selected at the foot of the Ulad Garbar Rapids.

On the morning of the 2nd, the South Staffordshire Regiment left Abu Dom, and halting for the night at Belal, reached Hamdab, 19 miles from Merowi, at the head of the rapid, on the afternoon of the 3rd. This rapid offered no difficulties, the men being able to row up it all the way.

A great change takes place in the character of the country after Belal. From Abu Fatmeh to that place, the river is broad and smooth, bounded on its right bank by a vast expanse of yellow sand, and on its left bank by a broad strip of alluvial soil, beyond which lies the rolling hard shingle of the Bayuda Desert. On either side the endless creaking of the sakiehs may be heard, and an almost continuous chain of villages and palm trees points to the fertility and populousness of the district. At Belal the river begins to be choked by islands known as the Ulad Garbar. The pent-up stream becomes more rapid, and sand and alluvium give place to tumbled masses of black rock, which encroach in places almost to the water's edge, leaving only at wide intervals scant room for a meagre patch of cultivation. The creaking of the sakieh is replaced by the roar of the Nile, and the most

Change in character of country beyond Belal.

(s.c.2) G

cursory glance shows the district to be one in which inhospitable nature has not yet been conquered by the energy of man. From a military point of view, the conditions are as adverse as from an agricultural. Instead of the rolling plains, so favourable to long range fire, and so fatal to an enemy whose strength lies in the impetuous charge of his spearmen, are here found cramped and tortuous passes, down which a company could scarcely march in line. The rocky ground is almost impassable for cavalry. On every side extend rugged ridges, behind any one of which thousands of Arabs might be concealed, ready to spring out on a column, with a minimum of exposure to themselves in the open.

The country beyond Hamdab was practically a *terra incognita*. Colonel Colvile had reconnoitered as far as that place in November, but beyond it the only information available was that to be obtained from the journals and maps of the officers who accompanied Mehemet Ali's expedition in 1820. These maps were found to be so inaccurate as to be practically useless. Colonel Brackenbury, with some other Staff officers, reconnoitred to the front on the 4th, as far as Jebel Kulgeli, a prominent hill about 5 miles beyond Hamdab. This hill was ascended and a good view of the river obtained as far as Auali Island, where a sharp bend shut off further view. Enough, however, was seen to make it certain that there was no serious impediment to the progress of the boats between Hamdab and Auali.

January 4th, 1885. Arrival of General Earle at Hamdab.

On the afternoon of the 4th January, General Earle arrived at Hamdab, accompanied by his aide-de-camp, Lieutenant J. T. St. Aubyn, Grenadier Guards, and his Brigade Major, Major M. C. Boyle, King's Royal Rifle Corps. On the following day, Major C. H. Flood, 19th Hussars, arrived with a troop and a half of his Regiment, completing the squadron to 91 sabres.

Arrangements at Hamdab.

General Earle had received orders from Lord Wolseley to advance beyond Hamdab when his force was concentrated, and when he had accumulated 100 days' supplies per man. As he could not hope to complete the concentration under a fortnight at least, everything was done to make the bivouac as comfortable as circumstances would permit. A market was established; the natives were invited to bring in supplies, such as milk, dates, dhura, and bread; a bakery was constructed capable of turning out 600 loaves a day; and there being no telegraph, a daily camel post was organized from Abu Dom. Lieutenant Stuart, R.E., was also instructed to restore the old Egyptian telegraph line from Berber, which struck the river at Dukeiyat, 3 miles from Hamdab, and then followed its left bank. This had been destroyed by the enemy, but a considerable quantity of the wire was still lying on the ground.

On the 15th January, General Earle received fresh orders to the effect that it would be impossible to give him the fifth battalion promised for the formation of his line of posts, that the General of Communications was unable to establish any line of communication beyond Abu Dom, and that consequently the river force was to be a flying column, and could hope for no fresh supplies after it had once left its point of concentration. January 15th. Fresh orders; River Force to be a flying column.

These new orders made it of vital importance that the troops should start with their full complement of 100 days' rations. Every endeavour was, therefore, made to prevent the necessity of eating boat rations at Hamdab before the start. With this end in view, troops starting from Korti, brought with them "way rations" in addition to their 100 days' boat rations, which took them to Abu Dom, where they were again supplied with "way rations" of meat and bread, procured locally, to carry them to Hamdab. Flour and forage for horses and camels were also purchased at Merowi, and forwarded daily to Hamdab by donkey convoys. Moreover, meat was obtainable in sufficient quantity at Hamdab. So with the exception of groceries,* no drain was made on the boat stores during the concentration at Hamdab. The supply was, however, only just equal to the demand, and General Earle, knowing that the concentration would not be complete for another fortnight at least, determined to keep the remainder of his troops back, within touch of Korti, till the last moment. On the arrival of the Duke of Cornwall's Light Infantry at Abu Dom, a boat convoy of the South Staffordshire Regiment was sent down to that place, to take over their boat rations, and complete the advanced battalion to 100 days. The Duke of Cornwall's in turn filled up from the Royal West Kent Regiment, which was sent up from Korti for that purpose, and then returned. Arrangements for economising rations.

It was now Lord Wolseley's desire that General Earle should advance through the Monasir country as soon as he had Lord Wolseley anxious that two battalions should advance at once.

* A small quantity of coffee and some rough rock salt were obtained locally and served out in rations.

concentrated two battalions, letting the others join him at Abu Hamed for the attack on Berber. Lord Wolseley's object was to open up the Korosko-Abu Hamed road as soon as possible, and to get a store of rations at the latter place.

General Earle's objection to this arrangement. General Earle, however, represented that it would be unwise for him to advance in boats through an unknown and hostile country without his small force of cavalry, and that his cavalry could not move without camels to carry their forage, and that he had then not a single baggage camel. He also pointed out that the South Staffordshire Regiment and Duke of Cornwall's Light Infantry could not complete their 100 days' supplies before the 22nd of January, and that, owing to the impossibility of replenishing supplies after he had once started, it was of the utmost importance that he should start with his full complement. He pointed out that he had received orders to leave at Abu Hamed a garrison of 300 men, and at Berber a garrison of 700, each with 60 days' supplies, besides 40,000 complete rations to be left at Berber for the use of the column which was to return from that place to Suakin. He proposed, therefore, that, if 40 baggage camels were sent him, he should start on the 23rd. But he pointed out that this limited transport would deprive him of the means of making any turning movements in the desert, which might require a day's absence of the infantry from their boats, and that, should difficult rapids render portaging necessary, the whole labour would have to be performed by the men.

This date of departure was accepted, and it was found possible, by that date, to give General Earle the 11th Transport Company of 330 camels.

Organization of the Column Hospital. Owing to difficulties of transport the hospital had to be reduced to the lowest possible limits. Material for a field hospital of 200 beds had been forwarded to Abu Dom, but as it was on far too extensive a scale for a flying boat column, it was arranged that the hospital should be divided into eight sections, each to have one boat, with a ninth boat for the Senior Medical Officer, in which he could take extra comforts for the sick and wounded. The crews were to be formed partly of men of the Medical Staff Corps, and partly of men of the regiments. Each corps was to carry its own sick and wounded in its boats, and the sick and wounded of each mounted corps were to be carried by the boats of the battalion to which it was attached for rations. Each battalion was to be accompanied into action by eight stretchers, carried by its bandsmen. Medical Officers of corps were authorised to draw from the field hospital at all times whatever was wanted to keep the regimental medical equipment complete. A full report on the hospital arrangements of the River Column is given in Appendix 51.

A paymaster accompanied the column with about 10,000*l.* in money; but after leaving Hamdab his office became almost a sinecure, the country being destitute alike of supplies and inhabitants. Pay Department.

A number of Canadian voyageurs, under Lieutenant-Colonel Denison, were attached to the column and distributed among the boats, and two boat repairing parties were organized. A naval detachment of 1 officer and 11 men, with 1 whaler was added to the column. Arrangements for the boats.

The arrangements for the advance of the boats were under the direction of Colonel Alleyne, assisted by Staff Captains C. R. Orde, Rifle Brigade, W. F. Peel, 2nd Life Guards, H. G. Morris, D.C.L.I., J. McCrae, Black Watch, and up to the time of his death by Lord Avonmore, Hampshire Regiment. Colonel Butler was told off to command the advanced guard both by land and water.

The right flank of the column was protected by a squadron of the 19th Hussars, under Major Flood, and the Egyptian Camel Corps, under Major R. A. Marriott, E.A. (Lieutenant R.M.A.). Protection of the flanks.

The left flank was covered by 300 of the Mudir of Dongola's black troops under command of Ahmed Effendi Suliman. They were accompanied by Jaudet Effendi, the Vakil or Deputy-Governor of Dongola, whose mission it was to take over the Civil Government of the Monasir country, and by Colonel Colvile. It had originally been intended that a portion of these troops should make a flank march through the desert to Berti; but it was afterwards considered inadvisable to divide so small a force, and they were all concentrated on the right bank. Mudir's troops.

On the 23rd January, the 11th Transport Company arrived, and orders were given for the advance of the troops on the following morning. January 23rd. Concentration complete.

The column was then concentrated at Hamdab, with the exception of part of the Gordon Highlanders, and of the Duke of Cornwall's Light Infantry, which, with the Mudir's troops, were still at Abu Dom.

The situation in the Sudan, as known at that time was as follows:—

Review of situation at this time, as it was known at Hamdab.

Sir H. Stewart after a successful but hard won fight at Abu Klea was continuing his advance on Metemmeh. The latest news from Khartum was that contained in the letter which arrived on the 31st December "Khartum all right, 14th December," and the verbal message, delivered at the same time, that the relieving force must make haste.

Reports received from Berber showed that on the 23rd of December it was strongly entrenched, but contained no formidable garrison, and that there was a fortified camp with six guns at Gobush on the opposite bank. Mohammed-el-Kheir, the Mahdi's Emir, had applied to Headquarters for reinforcements, and they had been refused.

From Abu Hamed news had been received as late as the 3rd of January; a small force was reported to be there under Hassan Wad-el-Haj Said and Ali Basha, but cultivation was being carried on and there were no signs of unusual military preparations. Abu Hejel,* the powerful chief of the Robatat tribe was living quietly at a village half-way between Abu Hamed and Berber.

News from Berti was received almost daily, and spies were stationed there who could be trusted to bring news of any fresh movement on the part of the enemy.

The force there was under command of Abd-el-Majid el-Kalik, a relation of Mohammed-el-Kheir, the Emir of Berber; it consisted of 1,500 Dervishes, about 1,200 fighting men of the Monasir tribe, and about 300 of the Robatat, under their Sheikh's son, Musa. Suliman Wad Gamr, the Sheikh of the Monasir, was at Salamat where he had gone to bring up reinforcements. There was every reason to suppose that these men meant fighting. Their position was said to be a strong one, and behind them was the Shukuk Pass, a gorge which native evidence represented as capable of defence by a handful of determined men against an army. The native accounts in no way exaggerated the ruggedness or narrowness of this pass, but did not take into account that the nature of the surrounding country would have allowed a turning movement to be executed almost anywhere.

Colonel Butler had reconnoitered as far as Auali Island, and had selected a site for a camp. He reported the river free from obstacles to that point.

---

* This man had formerly been Vakil of Dongola, but was removed from his post by General Gordon in consequence of his extortions.

REVIEW OF SITUATION.

At 7 a.m. on the morning of the 24th, the force moved off in the following order:— *January 24th. Advance of force.*

By land	{ 19 Hussars	} at 7.
	{ Half Camel Corps	
	⎧ 2 Companies S. Staffordshire Regiment	
	⎪ Royal Engineers (2 boats)	„ 7.15.
	⎪ Remainder S. Staffordshire Regiment	„ 7.30.
	⎪ 1st half battalion Black Watch	„ 7.45.
By water	⎨ Repairing party	⎫
	⎪ Senior Medical Officer	⎬ „ 8.
	⎪ Half Field Hospital	⎪
	⎪ Headquarters boats	⎭
	⎩ 2nd half battalion Black Watch	„ 8.15.
By land	⎧ Baggage and remainder of mounted troops	„ 10.
	⎩ Headquarters	„ 11.

The masts of all whalers were unshipped and stowed away, as, owing to the bend of the river, no fair wind could now be expected till after Abu Hamed was passed.

By 7 p.m. the whole force was concentrated opposite Auali Island, about eight miles from Hamdab. The Black Watch bivouacked on the right bank, the remainder of the force on a "high Nile Island," *i.e.*, a peninsula, the isthmus of which was covered at high Nile.

In the meanwhile, the Mudir's troops had reached Um-Merikh on the right bank opposite Auali Island, having marched from Kasingar, opposite Belal, that morning. These troops had provided themselves with donkeys to carry their kits, ammunition, and scanty rations, and were, therefore, enabled with ease to make marches of considerable length. Some information with regard to them is given in Appendix 54.

A reconnaissance was sent forward along the left bank as far as Kabur, and reported the country to be deserted. The river was also reconnoitered to the front by two boat officers.

These reconnaissances showed that the river was impracticable for boats along the left bank, and it therefore became necessary to send the flotilla round the far side of Auali Island. But it was also necessary to occupy the point where the boats would again debouch into the main stream, *Difficulties of the advance.*

and, to do this, a portion of the force had to be sent along the left bank by land. As the enemy was then known to be in force only 18 miles distant, General Earle did not consider it safe to allow his very small force of cavalry to advance, and bivouac alone in the difficult country ahead of them. He, therefore, determined to disembark half a battalion of the Black Watch and march them with the mounted troops to the head of the channel, there to form a post, till they were joined by the advanced boats of the South Staffordshire Regiment, when they would return to Auali by land, and bring their boats up the rapid. The difficulties of the country and river necessitated frequent resort to these manœuvres.

January 25th. Passage of Edermi. On the morning of the 25th, Colonel Butler advanced with the mounted troops to select their post, which he established just above the head of Sofieh Island. The South Staffordshire Regiment at the same time moved in their boats into the right bank channel and commenced the ascent of the Edermi cataract, with their left flank protected by the Mudir's troops who had taken up a position at Mushra el-Obeid at the head of the rapid.

Traces of the enemy. Opposite the worst part of the cataract a strong breastwork of stones was discovered, with traces of recent fires; this had been constructed and occupied by a rebel Shaikiyeh chieftain named Wad et-Turki and his followers, with the intention of contesting the passage of the rapid.

Difficulties of this cataract. During the day, only three companies of the South Staffordshire Regiment succeeded in ascending the rapid, which was so bad that all arms, ammunition, and accoutrements had to be taken out to lighten the boats, and carried three-quarters of a mile. Three boats' crews were required to haul each boat up the rapid. On reaching the head of the rapid these companies at once received orders to push on to the advanced post, to relieve the half battalion Black Watch.

Colonel Butler had, in the meanwhile, reconnoitered five miles further on to the Kab el-Abd Cataract, and reported the country and water fairly clear up to that point. On the following day, the remainder of the South Staffordshire Regiment, and two Companies of the Black Watch passed the Edermi Cataract. As a spy, who returned from Berti on the evening of the 26th, reported that the enemy intended to attack while our boats were scattered in the cataract, it was thought advisable to concentrate as soon as possible. Orders were, therefore, given for the Staffordshire and leading Companies

THE EDERMI CATARACT.

of the Black Watch to push on to Kab el-Abd, and there form a post and await the rear battalion. The Mudir's troops were ordered to take up a position opposite Kab el-Abd. On the 27th, the South Staffordshire Regiment and Royal Highlanders commenced the concentration at the new advanced post about a mile short of Kab el-Abd, and the Duke of Cornwall's Light Infantry entered the Edermi Cataract. The Mudir's troops took up a position at Shebebat on the opposite bank. *January 27th.*

On this day, Colonel Butler on the left bank, and Colonel Colvile on the right, almost simultaneously obtained the first touch of the enemy. Colonel Butler, while reconnoitering with the mounted troops about two and a half miles beyond the advanced post, sighted about 120 of the enemy, with seven or eight horsemen. Shots were exchanged at about 1,000 yards, and the enemy retired. The Egyptian Camel Corps succeeded in capturing 4 camels, 6 oxen, and 60 sheep, a welcome addition to the Commissariat. *First touch of the enemy.*

Colonel Colvile, advancing from Shebebat, with ten of the Mudir's troops mounted on camels, succeeded in reaching Howsh el Jerun, opposite Berti, about fourteen miles distant. He obtained a good view of the enemy's camp, of which he was able to make a sketch. He believed that the enemy were not more than 1,000 strong, but, owing to the broken ground in which they were bivouacked, he found it impossible to estimate their numbers with accuracy. He was followed on his return journey by a small body of the enemy's horse and foot armed with spears, but no shots were exchanged. *Reconnaissance along right bank to opposite Berti.*

Both Colonel Butler and Colonel Colvile reported the country ahead to be rough and difficult, and the former officer also gave a very unfavourable account of the river for boat work.

On the morning of the 28th January, the boats commenced the ascent of the Kab el-Abd Cataract, and the South Staffordshire Regiment and Black Watch succeeded in reaching Kandi Island, about two miles above their bivouac of the previous night, and bivouacked on the Island, and on a ridge of rock on the left bank opposite to it. On the following morning, six companies of the Black Watch were sent by land to Warrak at the head of the Um Habwa Cataract, and there formed a post for the protection of the boats ascending that very difficult piece of water, returning to their boats as soon as they could be relieved by troops advancing in boats. *January 28th. Ascent of the Kab el-Abd Cataract.*

On the same morning the mounted troops, under Colonel

Butler, had been moved on with orders to push on to Berti, and bring back information of the enemy's strength. On his return, Colonel Butler reported that he had advanced to within a mile of Berti, and had come in sight of a body of the enemy about 700 to 800 yards distant. Having taken up a position on clear ground, he despatched Major Slade to reconnoitre from a neighbouring hill from which he obtained a good view of the enemy's camp, and estimated their number to be about 2,000. At the same time, Major Marriott, commanding the Egyptian Camel Corps on the right, had fallen in with a scouting party of the enemy and exchanged a few shots, losing one camel. He also obtained a view of the enemy's camp.

Skirmish with the enemy near Berti.

On the morning of the 30th, a deserter from the enemy's camp came into the bivouac at Mushani, where Headquarters still were, and reported that the force at Berti consisted of 5,000 Monasir, 4,000 Robatat, and 6,000 Bisharin and Berberines, but that they had only 300 rifles and 30 rounds of ammunition per rifle. As one of Colonel Colvile's spies had reported on the previous day that large reinforcements were then advancing from Salamat, this man's evidence, confirming as it did the previous report,* was taken to be substantially correct, and General Earle considered that the time had arrived when he must concentrate within striking distance of Berti.

January 30th. Report of spy that there is a strong hostile force at Berti.

On the 31st, the South Staffordshire Regiment marched to Ghamra, a place about seven miles from Berti, where there was a good, open camping-ground, and anchorage for boats. They had orders to form a zeriba and protect the head of the rapid until the arrival of the Black Watch in their boats, when the South Staffordshire Regiment would march back, and, in their turn, ascend in boats. The mounted troops and the Duke of Cornwall's Light Infantry were also to be concentrated at Ghamra.

January 31st. Concentration at Ghamra.

This concentration again brought the English force into touch with the Mudir's troops, who had taken up a position on Um Kombatat Island opposite Ghamra, having been separated from the main body, since leaving Mushra El Obeid on the 27th.

On the 31st, while this concentration was going on, General

---

* There is reason to believe that both these reports were spread with the object of forcing General Earle to halt and concentrate, and thus give the enemy time for the evacuation of Berti, which had been decided on, on receipt of the news of Sir H. Stewart's victories.

ADVANCE TO NEAR BERTI. 93

Brackenbury made a reconnaissance into the desert to the south-east. Ascending a high detached hill about four and a half miles from the enemy's camp, he obtained a good view of the rear of his position, round which ran a broad sandy khor leading from the desert. Several branches of the khor were visible, evidently leading into the centre of the enemy's camp. As it was known that the ground by the river bank was extremely rough and had been fortified by the enemy, it was evident that the best way of attacking him would be from the desert, and down the khor already mentioned. General Brackenbury did not push his reconnaissance down the khor for fear of showing his hand to the enemy, although tempted to do so by the total absence of outposts on the enemy's side. This circumstance was, in the course of the evening, fully accounted for by a statement of the deserter, that the enemy had evacuated Berti on the previous evening—a statement wholly at variance with that which he had made in the morning, but which was afterwards found to be correct. *General Brackenbury's reconnaissance to Berti*

On the following morning, 1st February, Colonel Butler, with the mounted troops, and supported by half a battalion of the Black Watch, pushed into Berti and found it deserted. As soon as his report was received, all troops were ordered to advance, the other wing of the Black Watch into the Rahmi Cataract, and the South Staffordshire Regiment and Duke of Cornwall's Light Infantry to Ghamra. The Artillery and convoy were also ordered up to Ghamra from their bivouac in rear of Mushani. *February 1st. Retreat of the enemy. Occupation of Berti.*

The disposition of the force was then as follows:—

½ Battalion Black Watch.—In Rahmi Cataract.
Headquarters ⎫
Mounted Troops ⎪
Artillery ⎬ Ghamra.
South Staffordshire Regiment ⎪
½ Battalion Black Watch ⎪
Convoy ⎭
Mudir's troops.—Um Kombatat Island (opposite Ghamra).
½ Duke of Cornwall's Light Infantry.—Warrak.
½ Duke of Cornwall's Light Infantry.—In Um Habwa Cataract.
Gordon Highlanders.—Kab en-Nat.

On receiving Colonel Butler's report that Berti was deserted, General Earle himself rode on there, and there fell in with Hussein, the stoker of Colonel Stewart's ill-fated steamer, the "Abbas," who gave him a detailed account of the murder of Colonel Stewart and his party.

On the 2nd February, Colonel Butler, with the mounted troops, was sent forward to form a zeriba at Berti and hold it. Having done so, he reconnoitered for five miles in advance, and came across some abandoned baggage and provisions of the enemy. He reported the river smoother, but the country to be exceedingly rough, with rocks coming down to the water's edge.

Difficulties of the Rahmi Cataract.
Map 8.

In the meanwhile, the advanced infantry were struggling up the Rahmi Cataract, which was found to be so bad, that they only succeeded in ascending half of it by sunset.

During the course of the day, a deserter from the enemy's camp reported that the Mahdieh were in full retreat on the other side of the Shukuk Pass. Colonel Colvile's spies, however, reported that the enemy had halted in the defile, prepared to contest the passage.

The 3rd February was, like the previous day, occupied by the infantry in struggling through the Rahmi rapids. Five companies of the South Staffordshire Regiment arrived at Berti at sunset, having only succeeded in traversing the seven miles of water between Ghamra and Berti after 24 hours of unremitting toil. The Black Watch, who had started in advance, were still in the rapid. They had, as the pioneers of the force, to find their own way, and had, unfortunately, got into an extremely difficult rapid, which delayed their arrival till the 4th.

Grain found in Berti.

In the meanwhile, the town had been carefully searched by the Intelligence Officers, who made a catalogue of the property of Suliman Wad Gamr and his relatives, with a view to its destruction. This was carried out on the following day. A mass of native correspondence was found, and a few relics of Colonel Stewart's party, but nothing of great importance. A large quantity of grain was also found concealed among the rocks, a great gain to the Commissariat, who now reported that the horses were rationed with grain up to the 6th March, and the natives with flour up to the 23rd March, without counting six tons of unground wheat, to be used for either natives or horses as most required. They were also enabled to issue a small grain ration to the camels, which had hitherto been subsisting on growing crops only. Compared to the country which the force had just been passing through, Berti was a perfect garden, with plentiful crops and palm groves. The houses were also much more substantially built, than those even in the Dongola district. The town is partly built on the mainland and partly on the island of Atrab, which is only separated from the left bank by a narrow channel, dry at low Nile. The mainland portion of the town is enclosed by a semi-circle of rocky hills, the extremities resting on the river. It was towards the western, or down stream, end of this semi-circle that the enemy's camp had stood. After inspection of their camping ground, it was estimated that the enemy's number had been from 1,500 to 2,000.

On the 4th February, the rear companies of the South Staffordshire Regiment arrived at Berti, and the six leading companies were pushed forward to a spot, christened by Colonel Butler Castle Camp, about a mile and a half down stream of Dulka Island. They reached this bivouac at noon, having had the novel experience of encountering no bad water. *February 4th. Advance beyond Berti.*

During the day, the Black Watch concentrated at Berti, having been four days in the Rahmi cataract working from dawn to dusk, and having lost one man drowned and two boats. The Duke of Cornwall's Light Infantry were still in the cataract, and the Gordon Highlanders were at the head of Kab el-Abd. A boat officer was sent back to pilot them through the Rahmi rapids.

On the morning of the 5th February, the Black Watch and the remainder of the South Staffordshire Regiment were sent on to Castle Camp, and Colonel Butler received orders to send them on on the following day, as soon as the river in front had been reconnoitered. Colonel Alleyne was to push a boat reconnaissance up on both sides of Dulka Island, to find the best channel. He was also to examine the ground with a view to sites for camping. Colonel Butler was also ordered to push on a reconnaissance by land. On his return, he reported that he had ascended a range of hills about two miles south of the Shukuk Pass and that his guide (a deserter from the enemy) had pointed out some rising ground about a mile ahead, behind which, he said, lay the enemy's camp. As after events proved, this reconnaissance was of the utmost value, for the ridge which Colonel Butler ascended was that on which five days afterwards, the action of Kirbekan was fought, and as the news of the fall of Khartum caused the enemy to return and occupy this ridge on the following day, the reconnaissance would have been impracticable on any later date. On this afternoon the news of the fall of Khartum was received by General Earle, in the following cipher telegram* from the Chief of the Staff, "4th February, 8.50 p.m. I am ordered by Lord Wolseley to inform you that to his deep regret Khartum was found by Wilson to be in possession of the enemy. Wilson, in returning, was wrecked, but steamer has gone for him, and there is no apparent danger for him. You are to halt where you are until further orders."

<small>February 5th. News of fall of Khartum.</small>

On receipt of this sad news General Earle at once sent word to Colonel Butler that none of his troops were to move without further orders, to Colonel Colvile to keep the Mudir's troops on the opposite bank, and to the Gordon Highlanders, who were still in rear, to concentrate at Ghamra.

<small>Halt ordered in consequence.</small>

As General Earle considered that this news might entail a prolonged halt at Berti, he gave orders for improving the sanitary and watering arrangements of the camp, and generally making provision for a standing camp.

The contents of the telegram from the Chief of the Staff were kept secret.

On the following day (6th February) the troops had a much needed day of rest, the first for a fortnight, which gave them a chance of washing their clothes, and attempting to mend the rags, which, both for officers and men, General Earle had described, in a telegram to the Chief of the Staff, as "not sufficient for decency."

A party of the Egyptian Camel Corps was also sent back to Abu Dom to act as carriers of messages. Major F. Ventris Essex Regiment, who was the Commandant there, was requested to forward all messages from Lord Wolseley in duplicate, one copy to be entrusted to two of the Egyptian Camel Corps, and another to a native messenger.†

<small>Reported advance of the enemy.</small>

In the evening Colonel Colvile signalled that one of his spies had just returned from the enemy's camp and had reported that the enemy had advanced out of the Shukuk Pass and taken up a position at Kirbekan. The spy stated that they were not more than 1,000 strong and had about 150 rifles, and that they had no outposts at night but sent out a patrol before daylight. This information was at once sent to Colonel Butler.

* Forwarded by messenger from Merowi.
† On the departure of the Gordon Highlanders from Hamdab the telegraph office at that station had been closed, troops to garrison the place not being available.

The 7th February was employed in improving the sanitary condition of the camp and collecting supplies.

General Earle had taken advantage of the halt to obtain an exact return of the state of his supplies, and on the 8th he sent a telegram to the Chief of the Staff, informing him of the number of days' rations he had of each article for the 2,966 officers and men drawing rations,* and requesting him to arrange that the supplies forwarded from Korosko to Abu Hamed by Major Rundle, should be so apportioned as to equalise the various articles. He added that although he had 30 days' grain for his 140 horses, he had none for his 580 camels, which had hitherto subsisted on the growing crops, and that, if a prolonged halt was made, it would be difficult to feed them. Soap was also urgently called for, there being only 30 days' supply left.

State of supplies at this time.

On the 8th General Earle received orders dated the 7th from the Chief of the Staff desiring him to push on to Abu Hamed, and await further orders there.

February 7th. Advance ordered by Lord Wolseley.

On the 7th, Lord Wolseley also wrote a private letter to General Earle, congratulating him on his progress, and explaining more fully his views on the situation, and the part which General Earle's force was to take in the forthcoming operations.

Letter from Lord Wolseley written on this day.

In giving the substance of this communication, it will be well to briefly show how the fall of Khartum immediately affected the River Column. How completely this event altered the aspect of the Sudan Campaign has been already explained in the last chapter.

Review of the situation at this time.

General Earle had been originally ordered to advance to Abu Hamed with 100 days' supplies for his force, leaving posts on his line of communications through the Monasir country. At Abu Hamed he was to meet a food convoy from Korosko and replenish supplies; he was then to advance to Berber. That important strategical point secured, he was to push on as fast as possible supplies to Shendi for the Desert Column, holding Abu Hamed, Berber, and such other places as he might deem necessary. But before the force left Hamdab, these instructions had been somewhat modified, and as a result of fresh orders, the River Column had become a flying column. General Earle had been moreover informed that Abu Hamed and Berber must be held by 1,000 men with 60 days' rations, and that an additional 40,000 rations, must be left at the latter place.

* The Mudir's troops provided their own supplies.

Although when the River Column commenced its forward movement from Hamdab, it was not known for certain that Sir H. Stewart's column had reached the Nile near Shendi, there could be little doubt that this first part of Lord Wolseley's plan had been successfully carried out. The first object for the river force was therefore to advance as rapidly as possible.

Officers and men had greatly profited by their prolonged struggle with the Nile cataracts below Dongola. The whalers were no longer manned by untutored crews, such as had embarked at Serras and Gemai. Experience had taught the troops how to manage their boats in broken water, and how to get the fullest advantage out of the means of propulsion at their disposal. But even so, and although the men were in admirable condition for performing severe and continuous labour, the constant succession of rapids and the intricate channels of rushing water through a wilderness of rocks, taxed their capabilities and their endurance to the utmost. In spite of the strenuous exertions of the troops, progress was slow, and as the river was falling, advance became more and more difficult from day to day. But up to the present time the struggle had been merely against nature. Although it was known that a hostile force was in the broken rocky country to the front, and although traces of the enemy shewed that resistance had been contemplated at more than one point between Hamdab and Berti, the Mahdieh had shirked a conflict.

At the time that the news arrived of the disaster at Khartum and that Lord Wolseley halted the River Column, its leading troops were about half-way through the Monasir Cataracts. Native reports all tended to show that the rapids ahead, and also the country to be traversed by the portion of the force marching by land, were more difficult than anything that had been yet encountered. There could moreover be little doubt that the hostile gathering that had been falling back sullenly step by step before the British advance, would elect to give battle before the River Column had got clear of these rugged defiles on to the level open country below Abu Hamed.

Now that Khartum had fallen, and that the original object of the Nile Expedition had ceased to exist, Lord Wolseley had been obliged to request fresh instructions from Her Majesty's Government. The telegraphic correspondence that ensued has been given already in Chapter VIII. In Lord Wolseley's letter to General Earle of the 7th, written before the receipt of the despatch acquainting him with the decision of the Government that the power of the Mahdi must be overthrown, he gave the substance of the first instructions received, and his reply.

He said that he had been informed by the Government that he was now to keep two objects in view, the safety of Gordon, should he still be living, and the security of districts as yet undisturbed by the Mahdi. The Government had not decided whether the force should, under the altered circumstances, advance to Khartum, but they had left the question of taking Berber to his own discretion.

Lord Wolseley went on to inform General Earle that he had replied, that his future operations must depend on the decision of the Government as to whether the power of the Mahdi at Khartum was to be overthrown or not; if it was, an advance on Berber would be necessary, but otherwise such a movement would be unwise. He considered that the second object of the Government could be best carried out by holding the Nile from Abu Hamed to Abu Fatmeh. He had asked for a force to be despatched at once to Suakin to crush Osman Digna, but did not consider that this would fulfil its mission before the 1st of April at the earliest. In the event of its being necessary to take Berber, Lord Wolseley informed General Earle that he proposed to do so by a combined movement of Sir R. Buller's force from Metemmeh and General Earle's from Abu Hamed ; he would then send a portion of his mounted troops across from Berber to Suakin to open the road. Lord Wolseley said that the Mudir of Dongola refused to believe in the fall of Khartum, urging that he would have certainly heard of it by that date, had it occurred as stated on the 26th January. "It is pleasant," Lord Wolseley said in conclusion, "to let one's mind rest, even for a moment, on such a chance as that Gordon still holds out in Khartum, but I cannot flatter myself by believing the report."*

On the evening of the 7th, Lord Wolseley received the telegram from the Secretary of State for War, given on page 59, which informed him that the power of the Mahdi was to be overthrown at Khartum. Lord Wolseley at once decided that Berber should be taken. His plans, which are explained by the instructions sent to Sir R. Buller on the 10th and 12th of February, and which are given on pages

* This letter was not received by General Earle till the eve of the action at Kirbekan, and was never answered by him.

62 and 63, were framed with the view of securing that important strategical point, by a combined attack of the two columns. Fresh telegraphic orders were sent to General Earle on the 8th, informing him of the Government's decision, ordering him to advance to Berber, stating that a force was about to be sent to Suakin, and adding that Sir R. Buller would co-operate with the River Column in taking Berber.

The fall of Khartum did not therefore at the time affect the earlier part of Lord Wolseley's original programme for the River Column. This force was to push on up the Nile as had been intended from the first. Nor was it probable that the Mahdi's triumph would have the immediate effect of greatly increasing the hostile forces known to be gathered between Berti and Abu Hamed. The force liberated from the investment of Khartum would almost necessarily gravitate towards Metemmeh, and would be involved in operations against the Desert Column. At the same time the news of Mohammed Ahmed's great success could not fail to inspirit his followers confronting General Earle, and this greatly increased the probability of an early conflict.

February 8th. Fresh advance from Berti.

On receipt of the Chief of the Staff's telegram of the 7th, orders were at once issued for the Gordon Highlanders to advance by the northern channel to Berti, and for the South Staffordshire Regiment, covered by the mounted troops, to advance from Castle Camp to a point to be selected by Colonel Butler. As General Earle did not wish to commit more than one battalion to the rapids, until their nature was more thoroughly known, he left the Black Watch at Castle Camp. Wishing to keep the Gordon Highlanders near to the Duke of Cornwall's Light Infantry, he also ordered half of the latter to halt for a day at Berti. The Black Watch and a wing of the Duke of Cornwall's Light Infantry were ordered to advance on the 9th.

Mudir's troops moved across to left bank.

The Mudir's troops were ordered to cross over to the left bank and occupy the Monasir country during the advance of the British. Lieutenant-Colonel Colvile was instructed to join General Earle's Headquarters as soon as he had placed these troops in a suitable position, and had seen the last of the British off the ground. He was to inform the Vakil that General Earle relied on him to obtain and forward supplies of grain and cattle, to send information of the intentions and movements of the enemy, and to forward messages to and from Abu Dom.

Touch of the enemy near Dulka Island.

Colonel Butler, taking command of the whole, advanced

ADVANCE FROM BERTI.

guard, left the South Staffordshire Regiment at the head of the first rapid, and directed Lieutenant-Colonel P. H. Eyre, commanding the battalion, to make his camp on Dulka Island. He then advanced with Major Flood and twenty Hussars along the left bank. At 2.30 p.m., his scouts fell in with some of the enemy posted on some rocky ground commanding the track by which the cavalry was advancing, and all of which had been patrolled by the mounted troops on the 5th. The Hussars took up a position opposite them and fired a few volleys, which made them leave the front faces of the rocky knolls, but they still held their sides and summits. At about 4 p.m., four exploring boats arrived just below the cavalry, and Colonel Butler landed two boats' crews and fired some volleys. He estimated the enemy's number at 200. On the approach of sunset, he returned to Castle Camp, the enemy following him as far as his outposts.

Colonel Butler reported the enemy's position as being about two miles from Colonel Eyre's camp at Dulka Island. He considered that the South Staffordshire Regiment could be moved from Dulka Island to the spot where he had engaged the enemy, in less than two hours, and the Black Watch could be moved to the point from Castle Camp, in six hours. He proposed to move these regiments up on the following day, covering their landing with the mounted troops. He asked for two guns: these he proposed to place on Dulka Island, from the upper end of which, he said, the enemy's position could be taken in reverse. *Colonel Butler's report of enemy's position.*

General Earle approved, in the main, of this proposition, but did not sanction the guns being taken over to Dulka Island. He cautioned Colonel Butler that great care must be taken in effecting the crossing of the South Staffordshire Regiment, so that it should be impossible for them to be attacked while landing, in case the enemy should advance and compel our cavalry to retire. He notified his intention of himself reconnoitering the position on the following day.

Owing to the officer sent to guide him losing his way among the rocks, General Earle's arrival at the advanced post on the 9th was somewhat delayed, and it was noon before he reached the ground where the South Staffordshire Regiment was to encamp. *February 9th.*

Meanwhile, the mounted troops had re-occupied the ground evacuated by them on the previous evening, and this done, Colonel Butler had sent for the South Staffordshire Regiment.

102 HISTORY OF THE SUDAN CAMPAIGN.—PART II.

General Earle's reconnaissance towards Kirbekan.

General Earle, accompanied by his Staff, then personally examined the enemy's position, from a point about 300 yards distant from it. (See the sketch facing page 108.) Immediately in front of him was a chain of four hillocks from 50 to 80 feet high, formed of tumbled masses of trap rock. The central ones of these were occupied by the enemy, who had constructed some rough stone breastworks on the side facing our troops, and also on their inner sides. The base of the western-most hillock touched the river. The track from Berti to Salamat ran between this hillock and the centre ones. About 600 yards beyond these hillocks, and running parallel to them, was a remarkable ridge of trap rock about 300 feet high and 600 yards long, forming a serrated wall, springing out of steep moraine-like slopes of trap *debris*. This ridge, broken at intervals, continued across the river. It formed a remarkable feature on Binni Island, and extended into the desert on both sides, as far as the eye could reach. When viewed obliquely it had the appearance of a gigantic wall built across the desert. Its western slope commenced some 200 yards from the river, and through the defile thus formed ran the Salamat road. All along its broken summit, men with spears and banners could be seen, moving among the rocks. This was the ridge which Colonel Butler had ascended on the 5th instant. It was known as Jebel Kirbekan.

As the enemy's occupation of this position completely blocked the road to Abu Hamed, both by road and river, it was obvious that they must be turned out, before any further advance could be made. There were four ways of effecting this:—

1st. A direct attack upon the hillocks, aided perhaps by flanking fire from Dulka Island. The objections to this were, that it would entail heavy loss, and would not cut off the enemy's retreat through the Shukuk Pass.

2nd. To march round the hillocks and attack them from the north, *i.e.*, from between them and the ridge. This, however, would have exposed the force to a double fire, if the enemy stood. General Earle was, moreover, of opinion that, on seeing that an attempt was being made to outflank him, the enemy would retire from the hillocks.

3rd. To advance against the ridge and storm it, afterwards bringing fire to bear from it upon the hillocks, to assist an attack upon these. This would, also, have exposed the assailants to a double fire, and would not have cut off the enemy's retreat.

4th. To attack the ridge and hillocks simultaneously from the rear, having marched round the ridge under cover of broken ground. This plan had the advantage of cutting off the enemy's retreat, taking his breastworks to a certain extent in reverse, and allowing the assault to be delivered up the most gentle of the steep slopes leading up to the ridge. The practicability of the operation, however, depended on the nature of the ground to the eastward, which, at this time, was unknown. Colonel Butler was, therefore, despatched with orders to make a wide detour of the ridge, and to see if there was a fair road for infantry and camels, by which the position could be turned.

On his return, he reported that the enemy's position could be turned by an easy march through a wide, sandy khor, and that he had noticed a road, by which the khor could be approached without any great exposure. The fourth plan was, therefore, decided on by General Earle, who, believing that the enemy was not in great force, and remembering the manner in which they had given him the slip at Berti, resolved to attack on the following morning with the force he then had at hand, viz., the mounted troops, two guns, E.A., the South Staffordshire Regiment, and the Black Watch. Decision to move round the left of the hostile position and attack in rear.

General Earle then sent back to Castle Camp for the two guns, and for Surgeon-Major Harvey, the Senior Medical Officer, whom he informed of what was in comtemplation and told to bring up what assistance he might require.

Having done this, the General made the final arrangements for the morrow.

During the afternoon some of the enemy opened fire from a small island above Dulka and struck one of our vedettes. They were, however, soon turned out by a company of the South Staffordshire Regiment, who were sent over to occupy the island and bivouacked there. The orders of the previous day as to the River Column pushing on to Berber, and also Lord Wolseley's private letters to General Earle of the 7th, arrived during the afternoon.

Before dawn on the morning of the 10th February, the cavalry vedettes were again in their position of the previous day, and, as the growing daylight enabled them to see, they reported the enemy still in position. February 10th.

The company on Dulka Island was recalled, baggage was packed, and camels were loaded to accompany the column.

At 7 a.m. the troops, having breakfasted, formed up as ordered, South Staffordshire Regiment in red, Highlanders in kilts. Column formed for attack.

The British strength was as follows:—

	Officers	Men	Horses
Staff	10	2	
19th Hussars	5	78	86
S. Staff. Regt...	23	533	
Black Watch	20	417	
Medical Staff Corps	7	12	
Chaplain's Department	1		
Egyptian Artillery	2	22	
Egyptian Camel Corps	5	42	

Total combatant strength:
	Officers	Men
British	56	1042
Egyptian	7	64

Total 1,169 all ranks.

Lieutenant-Colonel C.J. Eden's company of the Royal Highlanders, was told off to form a small zeriba to cover the boats and baggage. Two companies of the South Staffordshire Regiment were sent, with the two guns, to occupy some low hillocks between the zeriba and the enemy's positions. This detachment was under Colonel Alleyne, who had orders not to open fire until the column had reached the outer flank of Kirbekan.

Advance of column. At 7.15 the column moved off, led by Colonel Butler, the South Staffordshire Regiment (six companies) under command of Colonel Eyre leading in line of half battalion columns at an interval of two companies, the Black Watch* (six companies) under command of Colonel W. Green, C.B. following in the same formation. Company stretcher bearers followed their own companies. The Field Hospital camels and reserve small arm ammunition camels (nine and one spare), were massed between the South Staffordshire Regiment and the Black Watch, and moved with the left column.

General Earle's object in ordering this formation was to enable each column to take advantage of convenient ground for marching as long as the force was moving among rocks, but at the same time to be able, in case of sudden attack, to get rapidly into formation for forming square, with the stretcher bearers and camels inside. The front was covered by the cavalry, and the left flank by the Egyptian Camel Corps.

The line of march led, at first, in an easterly direction over hard but broken ground; after half an hour a wide khor, with a bottom of deep loose sand was reached, along which progress was slow. This khor was followed, till, at 8.30, the force came in line with the east end of the ridge of J. Kirbekan, and, as it did so, the two guns under command of Colonel Alleyne were heard to open fire. Although the

---

* One company of this battalion had not yet reached the camp.

column must have been visible from the ridge, no shot was fired by the enemy.

While a short halt was being made at this point, a message was received from Colonel Butler, who was forward with the cavalry, to the effect that about 200 or 300 of the enemy were visible on some low rocky hills to the immediate north of, and at right angles to, J. Kirbekan. Shortly afterwards a second message was received, saying that this body was retiring.

On resuming the march, the column turned to the left, round the eastern end of J. Kirbekan, and entered a rocky valley leading towards the river, barred by a low spur on which Colonel Butler had just seen some of the enemy.

As the column rounded the eastern end of the ridge the enemy opened fire, and two or three men were hit. After a short further advance, General Earle halted the column under cover, and sent one company of the South Staffordshire Regiment to occupy the spur, and another to line the rocks on the left of the advance, and keep down the fire from J. Kirbekan. The column was then advanced about 300 yards over the spur into a narrow valley bounded by rocky ridges, leaving the company of the South Staffordshire Regiment in occupation of the spur to keep down the fire from the summit of J. Kirbekan. Finding, however, that this fire increased in vigour, General Earle ordered Colonel Eyre to take two companies of his regiment, and endeavour to storm the ridge by its western shoulder. These companies were, however, exposed to such a heavy fire from the summit, as well as from the hillocks to the south, that, after climbing one-third of the way up the shoulder, they were forced to take shelter under a cluster of rocks. It was while in this position that Colonel Eyre received his death wound.

At the same time, two companies of the Black Watch were moved to some high ground to the right front, and obtained a good view of the river about 400 yards distant. As they reported that parties of the enemy were making their way to it and swimming over, General Earle ordered them to establish themselves on the bank so as to cut off the enemy's retreat in this direction. At the same time the three remaining companies of the South Staffordshire Regiment, and the four remaining companies of the Black Watch under Colonel Green, were ordered to advance and swing round to their left so as to face the four koppies which appeared to be held by a strong body of riflemen. General Earle then ordered the

Action of Kirbekan.

two advanced companies of the Black Watch, which now formed the extreme right, to leave their position and advance in line along the river bank towards the hillocks, clearing the bank of the enemy. At the same time the main body of the South Staffordshire Regiment and Black Watch brought a heavy fire to bear on the hillocks, gradually advancing from one vantage point to another, till they attained a position on the rocks about 400 yards distant from them, the intervening space being perfectly open and swept by the enemy's fire. To the right, however, a further advance under cover was possible, by the now dry foreshore of the Nile. Along this General Earle ordered the two right companies of the Black Watch supported by one company of the South Staffordshire Regiment, to advance, and to storm the hillock nearest to the river, from its river side. This operation having been successfully accomplished, a flanking fire was brought to bear from the summit of this hillock on the two main central ones. The defenders of these, however, sheltered by the natural cover of the huge boulders of which the koppies were composed, and by the breastworks which they had thrown up, showed no signs of giving way.

General Earle, seeing that the time had arrived for assaulting the koppies, was just about to give the order, when suddenly a body of the enemy's spearmen charged down towards the nearest company of the Black Watch which, under Colonel Green, was somewhat advanced to the left front. The Highlanders stood firm and poured a withering fire on the gallant Arabs, who beat a precipitate retreat. It was during this period that Lieutenant-Colonel R. C. Coveney of the Black Watch was killed.

The order was then given to charge, the officer commanding the troops on the western hillock, having been previously ordered to advance simultaneously with the frontal assault.

With pipes playing, the Highlanders charged at a steady double over the open ground, gained the bases of the two rocky pyramids, and took them, never halting, except to scramble from one boulder to another, till the last Arab in their way had fled. A desperate stand was made by some few of the enemy on the summits of the koppies.

Death of General Earle.

Just at this moment of victory, occurred the lamentable death of the General Commanding. His death is thus described by General Brackenbury, who was near him when he fell :—

"The assault was over, and the two main koppies were in

our hands; the troops were searching the sconces and holes among the rocks; and there was, as there must always be after such an effort, some need to collect them and form them up for fresh work. Between the crest of the two main koppies there was a depression forming a small flat plateau, on which was built a stone hut some 10 feet square, with a thatched roof. General Earle was engaged in forming up the men in the ranks on this plateau, not more than 10 yards from the hut, when a sergeant of the Black Watch said, 'There are a lot of men in that hut, and they have just shot one of our men.' General Earle ordered the roof to be set on fire; but on its being said that there was a quantity of ammunition in the hut, he ordered the roof to be pulled down, and himself approached the hut. I was close to him and said, 'Take care, sir; the hut is full of men.' Our men had set the roof on fire, and my attention was attracted for a moment by seeing a native, who rushed out from the side door of the hut, bayoneted by one of our men. As I turned my head back towards the General, I saw him fall, shot through the head from a small square window in the hut, close to which he had approached. He lived only a few minutes, tended to the last by his Aide-de-Camp, Lieutenant St. Aubyn, and by the Senior Medical Officer, Surgeon-Major Harvey." *

The command then devolved on General Brackenbury, who ordered two companies of the Black Watch to remain as a picket on the hillocks, and was sending to the South Staffordshire Regiment to assemble them, when it was brought to his knowledge that the two companies of the regiment, sent to take J. Kirbekan, had failed to get more than one-third of the way up. He learnt that Colonel Eyre had been killed, shot through the heart; that Captain Horsburgh and Lieutenant Colborne had been severely wounded; that the loss in men had been considerable; that the ammunition was exhausted, except four rounds per man which had been reserved; and that the enemy was still holding the ridge. He therefore assembled four companies of the Black Watch as a reserve at the foot of the koppies, and instructed Lieutenant-Colonel H. Beal, on whom had devolved the command of the regiment on Colonel Eyre's death, to take the remainder of his regiment, including the company left to watch the hill early in the day, to reinforce the two companies on the hill with troops and ammunition, and then

Command assumed by General Brackenbury.

* From "The River Column," by Major-General Henry Brackenbury, C.B.

to assault and take the position. This order was carried out with promptitude, and the South Staffordshire Regiment had an opportunity, which they made the most of, of rivalling the Highlanders' charge up the hillocks. Climbing the steep slope of broken trap by alternate rushes, they reached the rocky summit, and bayoneted the enemy who remained there fighting to the very end. This charge, which drove the enemy from their last position, took place at 12.30 p.m.

In the meanwhile, Colonel Butler, with the Hussars, had, early in the day, struck the river above J. Kirbekan, and following its bank, had perceived scattered groups of Arabs, who had beaten a retreat early in the action. He had gained the entrance to the Shukuk Pass, and in the centre of the rocky gorge there, had come upon the enemy's deserted camp, where he captured a number of standards, some camels, and some donkeys.

The Egyptian Camel Corps had, throughout the action, maintained a position to the south of J. Kirbekan. They had materially assisted, by their fire, in keeping down that from the heights, and had cut off the retreat of such of the enemy as attempted to escape into the eastern desert. Their position, stationary for four hours under a smart fire, was a most trying one, and the two companies of the South Staffordshire Regiment, who remained so long upon the shoulder and were witnesses of their conduct, were eloquent in their praise.

Return to camp. Two companies of the Black Watch were left as a piquet on the hillocks, and two more were sent to occupy a high Nile island at the head of the rapid, and the remainder of the troops were ordered back to camp.

At sunset, the bodies of General Earle, Colonel Eyre, and Colonel Coveny, were buried side by side at the foot of a solitary palm tree on the river bank.

Casualties, and ammunition expended. The losses were 3 officers and 7 men killed ; 4 officers and 43 men wounded.

The ammunition expended was as follows :—
19th Hussars, Martini-Henry carbine, 395 rounds.
South Staffordshire, Martini-Henry rifle, 15,450 rounds.
Black Watch, Martini-Henry rifle, 5,745 rounds.
Egyptian Camel Corps, Martini-Henry rifle, 2,450 rounds.
Egyptian Battery, common shell, 17 ; shrapnel, 6.

General Brackenbury's report on the action, is given in Appendix 48.

Surgeon-Major Harvey's report on the medical arrangements during the action is given in Appendix 51, Annexure A.

It was reported by prisoners that the total hostile force that had held the Kirbekan position amounted to between 1,500 and 2,000, belonging principally to the Monasir and Robatat tribes. There were not, however, more than 800 present when the British force commenced its march to the attack, and a large number of them retired before the attack begun.

CHAPTER X.

Maps 1 *and* 8.

THE RIVER COLUMN, *CONTINUED*, FROM THE ACTION OF KIRBEKAN TO ITS RETURN TO MEROWI.

February 11th.
The Shukuk Pass.

THE telegraphic despatch describing the action of Kirbekan ended as follows: "If it" (the victory) "enables us to pass the Shukuk Pass, which is still before us and to get through the rapids ahead without more fighting, it will, indeed, be a valuable day for us." This Shukuk Pass had been a bugbear, from the moment that the Intelligence Department first turned its attention to the Monasir country. Native reports all agreed in describing it as one of those typical positions, that a few men could hold against a thousand, and Colonel Butler's reconnaissance to its mouth had not tended to throw discredit on these accounts. The rapids in rear of the force had been ascended, and it was felt that the men and boats that had surmounted them were equal for any combination which rocks and water could produce. Still, the experience of the column up to the present time, in the Monasir country, did not hold out much hope of rapid progress in the future, unless the physical conditions changed materially for the better. And the reports of the boat officers showed that little hope of such a change could be entertained for the present.

Difficulties owing to weakness in cavalry.

It was fully realised that the first rule of Arab warfare is to follow up a victory before the enemy has time to rally, and that it was therefore desirable at once to seize the heads of the pass and rapids. Had the cavalry been strong enough, they could have passed through the defile in half a day and have occupied its further end. But after deducting the necessary guards, the mounted troops, British and Egyptian, barely numbered 100; and, to have pushed on this small force to encamp on the far side of a long and difficult pass, without any infantry in support, would have been to court disaster. The infantry were tied to their boats, and every man who marched a yard beyond his boat, had to be marched back again to it sooner or later.

There was, therefore, no alternative but to keep the infantry and cavalry together, and feel the way through the difficult country ahead.

On the morning of the 11th a wing of the Duke of Cornwall's Light Infantry, two companies of the Black Watch, and two of the South Staffordshire Regiment, all troops that had not been engaged on the previous day, advanced by boat to the high Nile island at Kirbekan, and relieved the two companies of the Black Watch which had bivouacked there. The mounted troops covered the advance, and Colonel Butler reconnoitered some distance into the Shukuk Pass. *Arrival of the remainder of the force.*

On the same day the other wing of the Duke of Cornwall's Light Infantry, the remainder of the Artillery, and the convoy, arrived at the camp opposite Dulka Island, while the Gordon Highlanders reached Castle Camp.

While the Duke of Cornwall's Light Infantry were tracking their boats up the rapid, they noticed a donkey grazing on the bank, with a pair of saddle bags on its back. One of the men, examining the saddle bags to see what they contained, found an Arabic document, which in accordance with a column order on the subject, he handed to his officer for the information of the Intelligence Department. The following is a translation of the document :—

"Copy of a letter received from the Governor-General, addressed to the Commandant-General of the station (*sic*) *Letter found on the battle field, announcing the capture of Khartum by the Mahdi.*

"In the name of God the merciful, the compassionate, &c., from the servant of God, Mohammed-el-Kheir Abdulla-Khojali, the Governor-General of Berber and its neighbourhood, to his esteemed, &c., the Governor Abd-el-Majid el-Kalik, &c.

"My beloved after, peace, mercy, and blessings from God, I inform you that this day, after midday prayer, I received a letter from the Khalifa of the Holy Man, the Khalifa Abdulla, son of Mohammed, to the effect that Khartum had been conquered on Monday, the 9th Rabia, the second 1302, from the Hanai side, and the manner of the conquest was that the Imam the Mahdi, on whom be peace, and his Khalifas, moved out and stormed the trench, and took Khartum in a quarter of an hour, and killed Gordon, the accursed one, and took possession of the steamers and boats, and God gave victory to Islam. Therefore rejoice and be glad and praise

God, and worship God for this grace which cannot be overvalued. Rejoice and give the glad tidings to those who follow you.

"(Dated)   13th Rabia the 2nd, 1302."*

It was evidently the receipt of this document that induced el-Kalik, who, disheartened at the news of Sir H. Stewart's success, was retiring, to send back part of his force so as to make a stand at the mouth of the Shukuk Pass.

February 12th. Advance of the column into the Shukuk defiles.

On the 12th, the Duke of Cornwall's Light Infantry advanced about a mile up the rapid, reaching the mouth of the Wady el-Arku, and the Gordon Highlanders reached Dulka Island, the remainder of the force being between these two stations.

Colonel Alleyne reconnoitered a mile and a half up stream and reported a very bad rapid ahead, and Colonel Butler, making a detour through the desert, returned by the Shukuk Pass, without finding any signs of the enemy. From the reports of both these officers it was evident that the force was about to be entangled in a long and difficult defile, both by land and water.

Orders to General Brackenbury from Korti for his operations against Berber.

In the morning, General Brackenbury had received a telegram from the Chief of the Staff, informing him of the decision of the Government that the troops were to be retained in the Sudan until the Mahdi's force at Khartum was overthrown; and that if this could not be done before the hot weather, they must wait till the autumn. It was added that Sir R. Buller had left Jakdul on the 6th for Gubat, and was to take Metemmeh as soon as the Royal Irish Regiment reached Gubat. It was assumed that the River Column would be at or near Berber on the 28th February, but, if General Brackenbury did not think he would be near it by that time, he was to name a date, in order that Sir R. Buller, who would be in the neighbourhood with six guns and about 1,500 men, might co-operate in the attack. In any case, General Brackenbury was to push on with all possible speed compatible with safety. He was to leave a garrison of 200 men at Abu Hamed, instead of 300, as previously ordered, with 250 rounds of ammunition per man and 60 days' rations.

---

* This letter was written on the 29th or 30th of January, and gives the date of the fall of Khartum as the 25th or 26th. The Hanai side is that between the two Niles. The Khalifa Abdulla, here spoken of, succeeded the Mahdi on his death. The document was docketted as having been received on the 6th February.

PASSAGE OF SHUKUK PASS. 113

To this telegram General Brackenbury replied, that he did not think it possible to reach Berber by the 28th February, and that any date given, must be pure conjecture, the time being dependent upon unknown rapids and unknown movements of the enemy, but he did not think he would reach Berber before the 12th of March.

On the morning of the 13th of February, Lord Avonmore died of enteric fever, at the Dulka Island camp. He was buried by the side of his comrades in arms, who had fallen in action at Kirbekan.

On the same day, the Duke of Cornwall's Light Infantry and four companies of the South Staffordshire Regiment advanced about five miles, to a camp under J. Shukuk. The remainder of the South Staffordshire Regiment, the Gordon Highlanders, and two companies of the Black Watch closed up to Wady el-Arku, to which place Headquarters were also moved.

Colonel Alleyne reconnoitered four miles of clear and not very swift water. Colonel Butler moved with the mounted troops to the upper end of the Shukuk Pass, where it debouched on the river opposite Uss Island. Here he reported another rapid, but not so formidable a one as that just passed. He also reported that the country opened out a little after the pass, but that there were no traces of cultivation.

On the 14th the Duke of Cornwall's Light Infantry entered the Uss rapid; the South Staffordshire Regiment and Gordon Highlanders reached its foot before nightfall; Headquarters were also moved to the foot of the rapid. The Black Watch, the Artillery, and the convoy reached Wady el-Arku. By making a slight detour into the desert, the artillery and convoy were enabled to avoid the central portion of the defile, but the narrow gorges by which it gained the river at both ends, could not be turned. Writing of this defile General Brackenbury says, "About noon I had the pleasure of seeing the head of the convoy and battery emerge from the pass. That pass had long been a subject of anxiety to us, and rightly so. In the course of the day I rode back some two or three miles through it, and an uglier place it was difficult to conceive. In some places there was barely room for a loaded camel to pass between the perpendicular rocks; in others, where the path was wider, the rocks had been prepared for defence by loopholed stone sconces, in the same way as the koppies and ridge at Kirbekan. There was no order or regularity in the plan of the rocks. They seemed to have

February 14th. Advanced troops reach the Uss rapid. Map 8.

been upheaved, in a mass, in some great volcanic convulsion, and to have fallen one upon another in every direction, covering a space, some six miles long by three or four broad. With our infantry tied to the boats, as it were, and with so small a force of mounted troops, it would have been a most difficult task to dislodge an active and determined enemy from such a position, of which he knew every outlet, and of which we knew nothing. It was an oppressive place to remain in. It had not even the redeeming element of grandeur, such as great massive features give to the most rugged mountain ranges. It represented low sullen savagery. It was typical of the tribes to whom it belonged."

By the evening of the 14th all the troops, with the exception of the Black Watch, were concentrated at Uss. This enabled the General to bring to the front the Duke of Cornwall's Light Infantry and the Gordon Highlanders, whom, not having taken any part in the action at Kirbekan, he was anxious to place in a good position in the event of another brush with the enemy. The infantry advance was therefore continued in the following order:—

> Duke of Cornwall's Light Infantry.
> Gordon Highlanders.
> South Staffordshire Regiment.
> Black Watch.

February 15th.

The Uss rapid proved to be a very bad one, and by 2 p.m. on the 15th, *i.e.*, after seven hours' work, only the Duke of Cornwall's Light Infantry and two companies of the Gordon Highlanders had got through it.

Reconnaissance to Salamat.

In the meanwhile Colonel Butler with the mounted troops reconnoitered as far as Salamat, which they entered at 1.30 p.m. on the 15th and found to be deserted. One of the spies stated that the inhabitants had all fled into the desert or into the Robatab country, on the 12th instant. Colonel Butler reported that there was another bad rapid opposite Sherari Island, but above that clear water, apparently for some miles.

In the evening the leading boats reached the island of Showar, about four miles above Uss.

On receipt of Colonel Butler's report General Brackenbury sent the following report to Lord Wolseley:—

"Cavalry entered Salamat to-day, and found it deserted. Leading infantry are within four miles of Salamat, but a bad rapid intervenes opposite Sherari Island, which will probably require 500 yards portage. The rapid opposite Uss Island is not marked on my map, nor had we any information of its existence; but it takes three days to get the troops through it. Under conditions of exceptionally low Nile and unexpected rapids, any estimate of time must be mere guess work. I hope I may reach Abu Hamed in ten days but I do not think I can concentrate there in less than fourteen, as I have all my camels and horses to cross over."

The 16th was occupied in the ascent of the Sherari rapid, which was only difficult on account of the extreme narrowness of its passage; this took some time to discover, and necessitated the boats passing up it in single file. By nightfall only six companies of the leading battalion had succeeded in reaching its head.

On this day, detailed instructions arrived as to the operations that were to be undertaken by the River Column in combination with the troops in the desert, for the capture of Berber.

<small>February 16th. Arrival of detailed instructions from Lord Wolseley as to the advance on Berber.</small>

The River Column had started with sufficient supplies for its own consumption up to the beginning of May. But, unfortunately, it had been found that, owing mainly to bad soldering of the cases, 30 per cent. of the biscuits were unfit for food. Thus the date up to which, apart from other sources of supply, the column was independent of its base, became the beginning of April instead of the beginning of May.

The Korosko convoy, the detail of which had been somewhat modified, was now to bring 100,000 breadstuff rations and only 10,000 rations of preserved meat. 100,000 rations for the River Column of 3,000 men was equivalent to a little more than a month's supply. Therefore, as will be seen from the detailed estimate given in Appendix 49, General Brackenbury's force could only calculate on supplies of preserved meat and biscuit up to the early days of May.

Previous to the fall of Khartum, Lord Wolseley had intended that the River Column, during any subsequent operations, was to leave garrisons, respectively of 300 and 700 men at Abu Hamed and Berber, with supplies for 60 days; also that 40,000 rations were, in addition, to be left at Berber for the column he proposed sending to Suakin. The deficiency in the biscuit supply, the serious character of which was only ascertained on the 10th, and the slow rate of

(S.C.2) I

progress that the boats were making through the difficult Monasir country, rendered it, however, very doubtful whether any rations would be available from the supplies with the River Column, and from those being brought to it from Korosko for the proposed garrisons. Nor did the reduction of the proposed Abu Hamed garrison, from 300 to 200, materially affect the question.

When, after the fall of Khartum, Lord Wolseley formulated his plans for the capture of Berber, it was with the intention that garrisons should be left there and at Abu Hamed during the summer. The River Column was in the meantime to withdraw down the Nile, and the Desert Column to retire by Metemmeh and Jakdul, the two Cavalry Camel Corps eventually proceeding by Berber to Suakin. Actually, therefore, the necessity of supplies being left by the River Column for garrisons at Abu Hamed and Berber remained much the same as before.

When the detailed instructions, given on page 63, were sent to Sir R. Buller for his move on Berber, corresponding orders were sent by telegram to General Brackenbury. He was informed that Major Rundle's convoy should reach Abu Hamed on the 20th or 21st of February. The strength of the garrison to remain at that place during his advance to Berber was left to his discretion. Lord Wolseley hoped that he might commence his advance from there to meet Sir R. Buller on the 26th, and that Berber would be reached on the 13th or 14th of March. The garrison to be left at Berber would consist of 1,000 men drawn chiefly from the Desert Column, and while Sir R. Buller moved back to Jakdul the River Column would return to Korti bringing all the wounded, and leaving 250 men at Abu Hamed. The instructions recognized that the River Column, even after replenishing supplies from Major Rundle's convoy, probably would not be in a position to leave 60 days' rations for the Berber garrison as had been hoped, but General Brackenbury was ordered to leave such supplies as he could spare. This telegram, dated the 13th, arrived on the 16th, and on the same day Captain R. G. Kekewich, D.A.A.G., arrived with despatches to the same effect, having travelled through in three days.

On the following day, General Brackenbury replied that he would only be able to leave groceries for the garrison of Berber, unless a second convoy reached Abu Hamed from Korosko. He stated that he could fix no dates, the rate of progress being dependent upon unknown conditions. He further pointed out that the descent of the cataracts by his troops after the capture of Berber would take considerable time. This telegram reached Korti on the 19th, soon after the arrival of the reports from Abu Klea which showed how seriously the Desert Column would be crippled in any future movements, owing to the collapse of the transport and the condition of the men's boots.

Lord Wolseley had in the meantime altered his plans for Sir R. Buller's force, owing to the evacuation of Gubat, and had arranged for the withdrawal of all troops from the desert. This withdrawal, and the spread of the Mahdist propaganda consequent on the military successes of the False Prophet, rendered it doubtful whether the Ababdeh tribe could be depended upon for a second convoy to Korosko. The unsatisfactory news thus almost simultaneously received from his two detached forces, obliged Lord Wolseley, as has been already explained on page 73, to abandon all hope of taking Berber for the present.

On the 17th, the cavalry, the Duke of Cornwall's Light Infantry, three companies of the Gordon Highlanders, the Naval boat, the Royal Engineers, and Headquarters, bivouacked at Salamat. February 17th. Concentration at Salamat.

Colonel Butler reconnoitered as far as J. Ausma, which he ascended, and from which he obtained a good view. He reported good water for nine miles ahead, and no sign of the enemy.

Salamat, which was the headquarters of Suliman Wad Gamr, was a long scattered village, containing some very good houses, and surrounded by a fair amount of cultivation. The whole of Suliman Wad Gamr's property and that of his family, with the exception of his uncle Abu Bekr, was destroyed. Very strict orders had been issued forbidding the promiscuous destruction of property, and admirable discipline was preserved in this respect. Some interesting relics of Colonel Stewart, Mr. Power, and M. Herbin were discovered. Destruction of Wad Gamr's property.

On the 18th the Gordon Highlanders and the South Staffordshire Regiment closed up to Salamat, and the Black Watch entered the Sherari rapid.

On the 19th the Black Watch entered Salamat; the head of the column continued its advance, and reached Sulimaniyeh about nine miles ahead, by the evening. February 19th.

Colonel Butler reconnoitered as far as opposite Hebbeh, the scene of the wreck of Colonel Stewart's steamer, of which he obtained a view, at the same time seeing two of the enemy's scouts on the opposite bank. He also captured a prisoner Reconnaissance to opposite Hebbeh.

(S.C.2)   I 2

who stated that there were 2,000 Ababdeh, 1,000 Bisharin, some Robatat, and a number of men from Berber, holding a strong position near the foot of Mograt Island with the intention of contesting our advance on Abu Hamed.

As it was necessary to cross the river at some point before reaching Abu Hamed, General Brackenbury was naturally anxious to do so, where it could be effected without opposition. Judging from a sketch forwarded with Colonel Butler's report, that a favourable crossing place would be found near Hebbeh, he directed that the leading troops were not to advance beyond that place on the following morning.

<small>February 20th.
Arrangements for crossing the Nile.</small>

At 8.30 on the morning of the 20th General Brackenbury rode on to opposite Hebbeh and ordered the crossing to be undertaken there. He sent orders to Sulimaniyeh for the guns and baggage to be brought on by their escort, and for the whole of the troops and the convoy, on their arrival there, to be pushed on to opposite Hebbeh. At the same time he sent the Duke of Cornwall's Light Infantry over in their boats to establish themselves on high Nile Island to cover the crossing, and placed half the Gordon Highlanders on the high ground on the left bank, where they were ordered to form a zeriba. The sketch of the environs of Hebbeh, page 100, Part I, illustrates the passage of the Nile by the column.

As some of the enemy's scouts were visible on the sand-hills on the opposite bank, Colonel Butler crossed over with a party of Hussars and drove them away, placing vedettes in commanding positions about a mile out into the desert. A chain of vedettes was also thrown out on the left bank, on a radius of about a mile and a-half from the point of crossing.

At eleven o'clock two guns arrived from Sulimaniyeh and were at once placed in position.

The troops and baggage were crossed over in the following order :—

Scouting party 19th Hussars.
Support, consisting of half Egyptian Camel Corps.
Two guns of the Egyptian battery with three camels.
Cavalry baggage.
Camel Corps baggage.
Remainder of 19th Hussars (relieved off vedette duty by half Camel Corps).
Camels of remainder of Egyptian battery.
Headquarters baggage and horses, and infantry regimental horses.

PASSAGE OF THE NILE.

Transport company, camels, and loads.
Cattle and donkeys.
Remainder of Egyptian battery.
Remainder of Camel Corps.

Each animal was towed over in a boat, its saddle, load, and driver or rider, being as a rule ferried across in that boat. A rope was securely fastened round its head by one of the Blue Jackets, and it was led into the water; the loose end of the rope was handed to a man in the stern of the boat which was then rowed off, the animal followed till it was out of its depth, when it began to swim, or, in the case of camels, often lay on its side and allowed itself to be towed across. As the horses swam freely, it was found to be important to let them have ample length of rope, to free their heads from any strain. With the camels on the other hand it was found necessary to have a very short rope, and to hold the animals' head well above water close to the stern, as their long necks had a tendency to get under water while their hind quarters rose. The Egyptian artillerymen counteracted this by sitting on the rumps and thus forcing the hind quarters down. The camels which were least exhausted, were those that lay on their sides and made no attempt to swim. Only three camels were lost, one being drowned through the breaking of a head rope, and two being suffocated, their halter having slipped over their nostrils. Six others, which crossed late in the evening, suffered afterwards from a complaint similar to staggers.

Veterinary Surgeon Queripel with his assistants were stationed on the bank, and administered restoratives to any animals suffering from exhaustion.

General Brackenbury says "I have noticed, for future guidance, that the points chiefly to be attended to in addition to the length of rope, are the tying of the head rope, great care being necessary to prevent its slipping or getting round the animals' nostrils; the hours of crossing, which should not be very early or very late, but when the sun is well up, so that there is less risk of chill; the pace of the boats, which in the case of horses and camels should be regulated by their pace of swimming; immediate administration of restoratives to exhausted animals; and gentle exercise after crossing, for all."

The actual crossing occupied $13\frac{1}{2}$ hours, during which time 780 animals, with their equipment and loads, and drivers or

Time taken in crossing.

riders, and six guns, were taken across. The crossing was effected under the superintendence of Colonel Alleyne, assisted by all the available staff officers.

Visit to the wreck of the "Abbas" and scene of murders.

While the crossing was in progress, the wreck and scene of the murder were visited. The steamer was impaled on a large rock about two hundred yards from the proper right bank of the river, with her keel then sixteen feet above the level of the water. She was seventy feet in length from stem to stern, and twenty-two feet in breadth over her paddles; the depth of her hold was four feet six inches, her sides were protected by ¼-inch iron plates, which, on her starboard side, were literally covered with splashes of bullets, and in some cases penetrated by case shot or splinters of shell—signs of the heavy fire she had been subjected to in passing Berber. She had been stripped of everything portable, and no relics of any extent were found on her.

The house of Fakri Wad Otman, where the murder had been committed, was a single-roomed mud hut, with a low, narrow doorway. No traces of the terrible scene which had taken place there six months previously were visible in the hut itself, the floor of which had been strewn with fine sand; but in the neighbouring house a blood-stained shirt sleeve, a few of Colonel Stewart's visiting cards, and some minor relics were discovered.

Destruction of Hebbeh.

On the 21st inst., while the crossing of the troops was being completed, the property of Fakri Wad Otman and the village of Hebbeh were destroyed under the superintendence of the officers of the Intelligence Department, who searched everywhere for papers and relics. Little or nothing of interest was discovered.

Up to the present time the only troops marching along the right bank had been those of the Mudir. It appears that the enemy had originally intended to offer resistance to the advance on both sides of the river, and the Mudir's contingent was probably the cause of the hostile change of plan.

February 22nd. March continued along the right bank.

At 6.45 a.m. on the 22nd, the column continued its march, the Gordon Highlanders leading. The character of the country to be traversed, and of the opposition likely to be encountered, had now entirely changed. Instead of intricate labyrinths of rocky gorges, and rapids running between abutting cliffs, the column had now entered a district of gently undulating sand hills, and a reach of the river in which the stream, if swift, was broad and smooth.

FRESH ORDERS FOR ADVANCE.

Physically the conditions were all in favour of disciplined, well armed troops. On the other hand it was probable that if the enemy made a stand, it would be with fresh troops undaunted by defeat, and there was reason to believe that a large percentage of these would be nomad Bisharin, who might be expected to rely, less on elaborate tactics than on furious charges of fanatic spearmen. To meet these altered conditions the following orders were issued:—

"In the further advance of the column by river, every effort must be made to keep the boats well closed up, not by constant delays on the part of the leading boats to wait for the remainder, but by strenuous exertions on the part of the boats in rear to keep up with those leading the advance.

Fresh orders issued by General Brackenbury.

"Commanding officers will impress upon all officers, non-commissioned officers, and men, that the success of the expedition, and its safety while moving by river, depends mainly upon the amount of energy which they put into their work.

"The advance will be covered on the right bank by the mounted troops, who will give warning to the leading boats of any aggressive movement of the enemy. Should the officer commanding the mounted troops report the enemy advancing to attack, the leading boats will fall back on the rear boats of the leading half battalion, and the rear half battalion will close up. As soon as the leading half battalion is concentrated, the troops will be landed, and at once formed up to meet attack in the strongest available position. All following battalions, unless specially ordered to the contrary, will close up on the leading battalion, land, and await orders.

"The orders for an unexpected landing, issued by the late Major-General Earle on 19th January* will be strictly adhered to. Water bottles should always be kept full.

"In case of a landing of this nature, stretchers in charge of two stretcher-bearers per company, and three boxes S.A.A. per company, must be landed with the troops.

"As a rule two sections of the field hospital will advance in the centre of each battalion, and the Headquarter boats and P.M.O. will advance between the second and third battalions.

"The Royal Engineers will advance in the centre of the leading battalion, in advance of the Field Hospital boats, and on the troops landing, will immediately strengthen the position taken up.

* See Appendix 52.

"The repairing boats will, as a rule, advance in rear of the leading company of the 1st and 3rd battalions.

"The advance by land of the guns and convoy and their escort, must be guided by circumstances, which may change from day to day, therefore no precise rules can be laid down, but all transport must be kept well together and move on as wide a front as the nature of the ground permits, and must invariably be protected by flankers well thrown out into the desert."

On the evening of the 22nd, the infantry bivouacked at El Kab, a remarkable stone fort overlooking the river. The mounted troops bivouacked about a mile higher up stream near a rock standing out in mid-stream, known as Hajar el-Baida, or the "white rock," having previously reconnoitered six miles to the front without coming across any trace of the enemy.

February 23rd. Limit of Monasir country reached.

On the 23rd, the whole force reached a small cluster of huts named Huella, said to be the last habitation in the Monasir country. The boats had done $10\frac{1}{2}$ miles in the day, against a swift stream.

The mounted troops made the usual reconnaissance to the front, and reported good water. They encountered none of the enemy but saw traces of his camel scouts.

Signals to Major Rundle.

In the evening two rockets were fired, at intervals of five minutes, a preconcerted signal to inform Major Rundle's scouts that the force was within thirty miles of Abu Hamed. The troops having done an exceptionally good day's work on the previous day, orders were given that *réveillé* should not sound till 5.30 on the 24th.

February 24th.

At seven A.M. on the 24th the leading boats of the Gordon Highlanders had moved off, when a native messenger appeared and handed a letter from the Chief of the Staff to General Brackenbury. The letter was mostly in cipher, but some words in clear catching the General's eye gave him a clue and caused him at once to sound the halt. The letter when deciphered ran as follows:—

"TELEGRAM.

"*From Chief of Staff to O.C. Abu Dom.*

Telegram ordering return of column.

20th, No. 30. Send on, following to General Brackenbury by special messenger to-day, and by another special messenger to-morrow, promising liberal backsheesh if answer is brought back quickly. Message begins.

"Korti, 20th February. Buller evacuated Gubat. His main body went to Jakdul with all sick and wounded. He remains with 1,500 men at Abu Klea. Enemy have now begun to fire into his camp there, and have killed and wounded some of his men. He awaits camels to fall back on Jakdul, which I hope he will begin to do to-morrow, 21st instant, but owing to weak state of camels all men must go on foot. I have abandoned all hope of going to Berber before autumn campaign begins. You will therefore not go to Abu Hamed, but, having burnt and destroyed everything in neighbourhood where Stewart was murdered, you will withdraw all your force to Abu Dom, near Merowi, bringing all the Mudir's troops with you.

"Please express to the troops Lord Wolseley's high appreciation of their gallant conduct in action, and of the military spirit they have displayed in overcoming the great difficulties presented by the river.

"Having punished the Monasir people for Stewart's murder, it is not intended to undertake any military operations, until after the approaching hot season.

"Further orders will be sent to you on your reaching Abu Dom. Until you have occupied the Shukuk Pass, and made sure of every one through it, you had better keep this telegram entirely to yourself and Butler. Of course if you are in presence of enemy when you receive this, you must defeat him before turning back.

"If you do not receive this before you have reached Abu Hamed, or so near to it that it is merely a question of occupying it without opposition, you must halt there and send back information at once to me, when I will start convoy from Korosko, which I do not otherwise mean to despatch.

"Of course it is impossible at this distance to give you positive orders to meet all contingencies, but Lord Wolseley has every confidence in your military discretion."

The following reply was sent to the Chief of the Staff:—

"*Desert Camp*, 16 *miles above Hebbeh*,

24*th February*.

"I received your telegram, No. 30, this morning, just as the troops were starting up river.

"I am by the map about 26 miles from Abu Hamed. I am

General Brackenbury's reply to order

not in the immediate presence of the enemy, nor have the patrols, who have seen 6 miles beyond this, had any touch of the enemy. Nor do I anticipate meeting the enemy to-day should I continue my advance.

"My latest information is that the enemy intend to fight at Abu Hamed, and I anticipate opposition if I advance upon it. There is a cataract between this and Abu Hamed, and if opposed, it might take some days before I could occupy the place.

"Therefore, although I am confident I can beat any force opposed to me, I feel it my duty, in view of the facts contained in the first part of your telegram, to fall back immediately to Abu Dom, and I shall fall back to Hebbeh to-day. I shall return by the right bank. Please telegraph to Korosko for all letters, papers, and parcels of this force to be sent to Korti immediately."

The following morning order was also issued:—

Order issued to the troops.
"I. The Brigadier-General commanding announces to the troops that since they entered the boats this morning he has received a telegram from Lord Wolseley, stating, that after the Monasir people has been punished for Colonel Stewart's murder, it is not intended to undertake any further military operations until after the approaching hot season. The furthest limits of the Monasir country having now been reached, and the punishment for Colonel Stewart's murder having been so far as possible inflicted, the troops will now return through the Monasir country to Berti. The column will therefore move upon Hebbeh to-day.

"II. In the above-mentioned telegram Lord Wolseley desires the Brigadier-General Commanding to express to the troops Lord Wolseley's high appreciation of their gallant conduct in action, and the military spirit they have displayed in overcoming the great difficulties presented by the river.

"III. The Brigadier-General Commanding has to remind the troops that the descent of this swift river will require even greater care than its ascent. All will depend upon the vigilance of the men in the bows, and the coolness and resource of the men steering."

The following instructions for officers in charge of boats were also drawn up by Colonel Alleyne:—

Instructions for Officers in Charge of Boats descending the Nile.

"1. Owing to the swiftness of the stream, the boats will move over it at a rapid rate; consequently if a boat strikes a rock she will probably receive a severe injury. {Instruction to officers in charge of boats.}

"Accidents of this nature can be avoided, *first*, by the vigilance of the polemen, who should sound frequently; *secondly*, by not allowing boats to close up or crowd upon each other, when descending a rapid.

"2. As a rule, when descending a rapid the crew must row, otherwise the boat will not steer.

"3. The last two boats of each battalion should be nearly empty, so that, in the event of a boat being severely injured in a rapid, they may be able to take in her cargo, or return to her assistance. All other boats should have equal draught of water.

"4. Coxswains must follow the lead given by boats with pilots in them.

"5. After descending a rapid the leading boats must halt until the rear boats join them.

"6. In difficult rapids special arrangements will be made for taking each boat through with Canadian pilots."

At noon the boats commenced to move down stream, led by Colonel Denison, commanding the Canadian Voyageurs. The column moved in reversed order from its progress up stream, the South Staffordshire Regiment leading, followed successively by the Black Watch, Duke of Cornwall's Light Infantry, and the Gordon Highlanders, who brought up the rear. The three leading battalions reached Hebbeh, while the Gordon Highlanders, the convoy, Camel Battery, and part of the Camel Corps, bivouacked at Um Saiyal, about three miles above Hebbeh. {Commencement of retreat.}

While the boats were commencing their downward movement, Colonel Butler with the Hussars and part of the Camel Corps, reconnoitered as usual to the front, partly with the object of an ordinary reconnaissance, and partly with a view to leading the enemy to believe that the advance was being continued. They reached a point where the river bends away to the eastward, and saw at a distance of about two miles the rocky hill, behind which the enemy was said to be encamped, but saw no traces of the enemy.* At a {Reconnaissance towards Mograt.}

---

* A deserter afterwards stated that the party had been seen from the enemy's camp.

distance of about five miles, the river was seen to divide into two branches, between which lay the large rocky island of Mograt. To the north-east an uninterrupted succession of sand hills appeared to lead on to Abu Hamed.

It was long past sunset before the party reached El Kab, and Colonel Butler therefore determined to halt there for the night, instead of joining the main body at Hebbeh. The day had been a long one for the mounted troops, and four camels and one horse died of exhaustion.

While the troops were halted at Hebbeh, another messenger arrived, with despatches of earlier date than that received in the morning, and not containing the order of recall; also messages from Abu Dom and Berti, saying that no more messengers for the column could be obtained.

February 25th.

The 25th was employed in completing the destruction of the sakiehs and houses at Hebbeh, and in equalising the supplies among the regiments in proportion to the number of boats, so as to bring all boats, as nearly as possible, to the same draught of water.

The following orders were issued to guard against the unnecessary abandonment of boats, and to ensure the destruction of boats which were necessarily abandoned :—

Orders issued to guide the descent in boats.

"The second in command of each of the three leading battalions is held responsible for bringing on all boats of his own battalion, and of details moving with his battalion, or between it and the preceding battalion. He will not move on himself, until every one of these boats that can be brought on, has preceded him.

"The Officer Commanding the rear battalion will bring up the rear of the whole column. He will tell off four companies of his battalion as a rear guard, and he will move with this rear guard in rear of all boats not abandoned. He is responsible that no boat of this column is left behind unless necessarily abandoned, and that all abandoned boats are destroyed.

"On arrival in camp he will report verbally to Headquarters that every boat has arrived.

"Should he be unable to reach the camp, he will report to the Officer Commanding the rear guard on shore.

"The two Royal Engineer boats will, for the future, carry material for the repair of boats. By this arrangement the number of repairing boats will be increased to four. The numbers of these boats are 35, 43, 490, and 779.

"One of the four, will move in rear of each of the four

battalions, and assist in repairing any boats that may be damaged and cannot be repaired regimentally."

Major Flood, 19th Hussars, was ordered to cover the rear of the column with the mounted troops, and the command of the rear guard by land and water was entrusted to Colonel Butler.

On the 26th the troops moved to Amarim, opposite Salamat, the convoy and leading boats arriving there at noon. On arriving there, the channel between the right bank and Sehirri Island, was found, from its shallowness, to be impracticable.

The Brigadier General Commanding thought it desirable to keep to the boats while they were passing the series of rapids between Salamat and Auali Island, leaving the immediate command of the mounted troops and convoy, moving down the river bank, to Colonel Butler. That Officer was ordered to keep touch with the boats, but, failing that, to make his way to Howsh el Jerun, and there await their arrival.

The following instructions were issued by Colonel Alleyne for boats passing through Sehirri Island rapid. *Instruction for passing Sehirri rapid.*

" 1. The two boats of a battalion that are passed first down the rapid will not put into shore, but will remain in the stream at the foot of the rapid, one near each bank, ready to push to any boat that may require assistance. There should be an officer in each boat, and life belts will be placed in the boats. The two boats of the leading battalion will be relieved by the two leading boats of the following battalion, and so on.

" 2. Canadians will take the first set of boats through the rapids, and there should be a Company Officer in each boat, who, on his return, would be able to steer a boat of his company down the rapid.

" After the first set of boats are through the rapid, a Canadian will be placed in every second, third, or fourth boat, as may be found necessary. At the hour named for the first boat to start, adjutants of battalions, will collect the voyageurs of battalions, and hand them over to Lieutenant-Colonel Denison.

" 3. When the boats have passed the rapid they will be anchored on the sand-bank on the right bank. When that anchorage is full they will be anchored on the sandbank on the left bank.

" 4. The life-buoys should always be so placed in the boats that are descending the river that they may be thrown without delay to a man in the water."

By sunset the Headquarters and the three leading battalions were in bivouac on Sehirri Island near a central channel between it and Sherari Island. The Duke of Cornwall's Light Infantry had been halted at Amarim for the purpose of handing over six days' rations to the mounted troops. They left at daylight on the following morning.

One boat of the South Staffordshire Regiment had struck on a rock in the Sehirri rapid, and had to be abandoned as a total wreck, but all the arms and ammunition and most of the stores were saved, and no lives were lost.

Conditions of navigation reversed from what they were in ascent.

The conditions were now wholly different from those in the ascent of the river.

In ascending, the main points were to avoid great rushes of water and to choose passages close either to the mainland or to an island, to enable the boats to be tracked whenever the stream was too swift for rowing; consequently the passages selected for the ascent were often narrow and between rocks, and generally very shallow.

In descending these conditions were reversed. To have attempted these shallow and narrow passages would have been to court destruction to the boats, and the main point now was to secure sufficient depth of water, no matter how swift or turbulent the stream. Consequently as a rule the descent was made in mid-stream of those channels which, in the ascent, the boat officers had noted as most likely to be full of water.

Advanced and rear guards.

The advanced guard, throughout the descent, was formed by the Gordon Highlanders and the naval boat, under command of Commander Hammill, C.B., and the rear guard by the Royal Highlanders under Colonel Green.

Enemy in pursuit.

Just before the Headquarters moved off, a deserter came into camp, who stated that he had been one of the Mudir's soldiers and had been taken prisoner at the battle of Korti and taken to Mograt, whence he had escaped on hearing that the English were near. He stated that the enemy were in great force, mostly spearmen, and that they had heard of the retreat of the column, and had left their camp on the previous evening in pursuit.

February 27th. Uss rapid. Three wrecks.

At 7 a.m. on the 27th the boats moved off from the Sehirri Island bivouac, and ran the rapid with the loss of one boat, no lives being lost. Later in the day the Uss rapid was run, and, owing to a sharp turn in broken water, proved a very troublesome one, and caused the total loss of one boat and severe damage to two more. The total wrecks in the day were three.. The force bivouacked in two camps about 1,000 yards apart, at the upper and lower ends of the Uss rapid. A few native spearmen were seen, but kept out of rifle range.

The mounted troops had also started at 7 a.m., and passing through a rugged rocky district, at some distance from the river, bivouacked at Selamiyeh on the river bank, about five miles due west of the infantry bivouac at Uss. Rockets were fired by both parties as a signal of their whereabouts.

The same evening Colonel Colvile reached Berti, and communicated to the Vakil the orders for the retirement of the Mudir's troops to Abu Dom.

On the following morning the rapids of the Shukuk district were to be descended, and it was felt that if any attempt was made to dispute the passage of the boats it would be while they were in that cliff-bound labyrinth of rock and torrents. After the heavy defeat which the enemy had suffered at Kirbekan, General Brackenbury did not apprehend any serious opposition, but he did not consider it improbable that a small body of riflemen might be posted to oppose his passage, and that it might be necessary to land a force to turn them out. Orders were therefore issued for two men in each boat to remain in the bows with loaded rifles in their hands, and with their accoutrements and ammunition ready. In the event of any shots being fired at boats these men were at once to return the fire. The column was not to be halted for mere stray shots; but, should any serious amount of firing take place, the nearest boats were at once to pull to shore and land their men, the landing being covered by the armed bow men. Wooden plugs were made and issued to each boat to stop bullet holes if necessary. These orders were verbally explained to the commanding officers of regiments by the General, whose object it was, to so regulate the movement as to obtain the greatest possible rapidity consistent with power of concentration in case of attack.

February 28th. Passage of the Shukuk rapids.

The leading boats were halted at the foot of Uss rapid, until two and a half battalions were concentrated there, the advance was then continued, and the Shukuk was passed without any opposition. Headquarters and the advanced guard bivouacked for the night on Dulka Island, and the remainder of the force between the old Kirbekan camp and

Wady el-Arku. No boats were lost during the day, although some very awkward rapids had been passed. The mounted troops marched off at the usual hour and reached a point opposite Binni Island in the course of the afternoon. The country they passed through, although excessively rough, was found to be far easier than that on the left bank; as, however, the route entailed complete separation from the boats, it would not have been practicable for the upward march.

March 1st.

On the 1st of March, as soon as the rear battalions had closed up to Dulka Island, the march was continued. The troublesome rapid at Castle Camp was successfully passed and also a new rapid which had sprung into existence above Berti during the absence of the column.

Rahmi Cataract.

After a short halt, during which the mounted troops were again rationed up to six days, the troops again moved off and entered the Rahmi Cataract, in which it was found necessary that each boat should be piloted by a voyageur. This caused considerable delay, as, after taking a boat down, each voyageur had to walk back to the head of the rapid to bring down another. As there were more than 200 boats, and only 67 voyageurs, each voyageur had to make three or four trips, if only one was required in a boat, and seven trips where two were required.

Headquarters, the Duke of Cornwall's Light Infantry, and the South Staffordshire Regiment, bivouacked on the left bank about the middle of the rapid; the Gordon Highlanders on a sandy island opposite, the Black Watch three-quarters of a mile above the cataract; the mounted troops at Howsh el Jerun, and the Mudir's troops at Berti.

During the day two boats were wrecked and ten badly injured, but no lives and few stores were lost.

March 2nd. Um Habwa Cataract. Difficulty of the descent.

On the 2nd, the march was resumed, and the swift water at the top of Um Habwa Cataract entered. This rapid was found to be the worst that had been encountered in the descent. There were two passages. One was straight and fairly open, but with a clear fall of three feet in one place. The other was without an actual waterfall, the whole passage being one inclined plane of rushing water, with a sharp turn at right angles in the very worst part of the shoot. This latter channel was selected; but it was thought so difficult, that all except the two voyageurs (bowman and steerer) and six men as crew for each boat, were ordered to walk, and all arms were portaged.

"The passage of this rapid seemed as bad as bad could be. The channel turned to the left, and then sharply at right angles to the right. Just at this turn two great rocks stood out in mid stream. It was necessary to pass between them. The least error in steering would be fatal. To make the turn too soon would bring the boat on the right hand rock; to wait too long would sweep her on to the left hand rock. The descent was a triumph of skill over a difficulty that seemed at first almost insuperable. Boat after boat came down at lightning speed, the men giving way with might and main to give steering power; the bowman standing cool and collected, watching the water, and only using the oar should the steersman seem to need help. Now and then an error of half a second would bring a boat on to the edge of the left hand rock. Then the boat rose and fell like a horse jumping a fence. But in the day's work only two boats out of the whole number, came to grief." *

In the evening half the infantry bivouacked below the rapid at Mushani ridge, and half above it at Warrak, the mounted troops at Shebebat, and the Mudir's troops at Kab el-Abd.

On the following morning, the passage of the rapid was continued, the leading battalions halting until the rear had closed up. By 11.30 the force was concentrated at the foot of the rapid and the advance was continued till the Kab el-Abd cataract was reached. This cataract was found to have changed in a remarkable manner with the falling Nile, showing that no chart of the river, made at any particular season, can be even approximately correct for another. The eastern channel was chosen for the descent, in preference to the western one which had been employed in ascending the river. This rapid, a mile and a half of swift water studded with rocks, proved a very formidable one, and caused the wreck of six boats, three of which had to be abandoned.

March 3rd. Kab el-Abd rapid. Loss of six boats.

The Gordon Highlanders, and eleven boats of the Duke of Cornwall's Light Infantry, bivouacked below the rapid, and the remainder of the infantry above. The mounted troops bivouacked on the right bank near Auali Island, and the Mudir's troops half a mile above the British Infantry on the left bank.

On the morning of the 4th, the remainder of the boats passed the cataract. Owing to the channel having become

* From 'The River Column." Major-General H. Brackenbury, C.B.

blocked by a boat stuck on a rock, the boats in rear were by some error directed off into mid stream, instead of being turned into the bank to wait till the channel was clear. The result of this was that the boats of two and a-half battalions had to shoot a fall three feet high, like a Thames weir. Strange to say only one of them, a South Staffordshire boat, was swamped (a fact that speaks volumes for the seaworthiness of these craft); but unfortunately the unlucky boat contained two wounded men, both of whom, with a serjeant, were drowned. One of the wounded men, Private Barber, had been specially distinguished by his gallant conduct at Kirbekan. A badly wounded private of the Royal Highlanders also died while passing through the cataract.

Another boat swamped and three men drowned.

In the evening, the main body of the infantry bivouacked at Hamdab, the mounted troops at Belal and the Mudir's troops at Dukeiyat.

Leading troops reach Hamdab.

The descent of the cataracts had been accomplished in nine days; they had taken thirty-one days to ascend.

Time of descent of cataracts.

On the 5th, the River Column reached Merowi, and the mounted troops were at once crossed to Abu Dom. The Mudir's troops were halted at Duaim, and afterwards returned to garrison Dukeiyat at the head of the Berber road.

Arrival at Merowi on February 5th.

Information was received at Abu Dom that the enemy, 6,000 strong, had pursued as far as Berti, which place they reached on the evening of the day the Mudir's troops left it. They were said to be halted there, awaiting reinforcements, under Mohammed-el-Kheir.

Pursuit by the enemy.

On the morning of the 7th, Headquarters and all the troops proceeded to Korti, except the following, who remained at Abu Dom under Colonel Butler.

1 troop 19th Hussars.
The Egyptian Camel Corps.
2 Guns Egyptian Artillery.
Detachment Royal Engineers.
Black Watch.
Detachment 11th Company Commissariat and Transport Corps, with 100 camels.

On March the 8th, General Brackenbury arrived at Korti. His report on the operations is given in Appendix 54, with Lord Wolseley's covering despatch.

133

CHAPTER XI.

PROGRESS OF AFFAIRS DURING THE ABSENCE OF THE DESERT AND RIVER COLUMNS, AND PREPARATIONS FOR AN AUTUMN CAMPAIGN. *Map* 1.

DURING the month of January, 1885, the really engrossing question to the Headquarter Staff was that of supplies. This period, therefore, in the history of the Nile Expedition, when the work on the line of communications had reached its climax of importance, appears to be a convenient one for glancing at that work.

Sir E. Wood was at this time at Korti with the Headquarters of the Army, and General Grenfell, with the Line of Communications Headquarter office, was at Dal, a central position in the Batan el Hajar, whence he was able to exercise a general superintendence over the work of passing stores up the cataracts by whalers, native boats, and camels.* The Line of Communications.

District Commandants had been appointed whose duties were to see that the Station Commandants carried out their orders, and that the regulations as to the passage, management, and working of the whalers, and as to the supply and passage of convoys, were carried out in their districts; to exercise a general supervision over the several reaches in their charge, and to hasten the passage of boats and supplies; to see that detachments in whalers did not loiter in working hours, and that the upward stream of boats was constant; to make sure that no wrecked boats, which were repairable, were abandoned, and that all stores, unavoidably dropped, were taken in proper charge, and forwarded with all possible despatch; to render all possible assistance to Station Commandants, officers employed at rapids, and those in charge of native labourers ; to co-operate with the officers working the neighbouring districts ; to keep the General of Communications informed of their movements. District Commandants.

* On the despatch of Sir R. Buller to Gubat and the assumption of the post of Chief of the Staff by Sir E. Wood, General Grenfell proceeded to Korti and took over the duties of General of Communications, and was relieved at by Colonel C. F. Clery, C.B., who was brought up from Cairo.

(S.C.2) K 2

Station Commandants.

The various Station Commandants were responsible that no unavoidable delays occurred at their stations, and had orders to see that all boats arriving at portages were unloaded, and that the loads were despatched at once and re-embarked. They were responsible for the maintenance of the roads and telegraphs in their districts, and for the supply of guides. They were, also, the arbitrators in all disputes between the troops and the natives. They were responsible for the rationing of the troops passing through their stations, and had orders to keep the General of Communications informed of the state of supplies (including firewood) and specie at their stations.

For purposes of medical supervision the Line of Communications had been divided into four sections,* Deputy Surgeon-General S. A. Lithgow being appointed Principal Medical Officer of the Line of Communications.

State of supplies in December.

It had been found in the middle of December, that the progress of supplies to the front was proceeding more slowly than had been originally anticipated. There were, then, still remaining at the Railhead (Moghrat), 405,600 whaler rations, or forty days' supply for 10,000 men. These were being forwarded with all possible despatch, 400 camels working daily between Railhead and Ambako, whence stores were forwarded by river, and 300 camels and 21 whalers working between Sarras and Semneh, whence stores were forwarded by native craft to Ambako.

At one period, in consequence of the length of the portage there, a serious block had occurred at Dal. This, however, had been relieved by the exertions of Colonel Alleyne, so that by the middle of December, the accumulation of boats had been entirely removed, and, with the help of 150 camels for portage work, stores were being forwarded as quickly as they arrived.

Deficiencies in supplies ordered to be kept up at stations on the line of communications.

It was calculated that stores were forwarded from Halfa to Korti at a daily rate of 15 tons, yet the supplies at the various stations on the line of communications had fallen considerably below the amount ordered to be reserved at them. Abu Fatmeh, for instance, was 10,000 rations short. But at this post, Colonel Maurice, the Commandant, was able to collect some supplies locally.

---

* 1 Assiut to Korosko, inclusive; Field Inspector, Brigade-Surgeon Norris.
  2 Wady Halfa to Ferkeh; Field Inspector, Surgeon-Major Will.
  3 Absarat to Abu Fatmeh; Field Inspector, Surgeon-Major Corban.
  4 Dongola, southward; Field Inspector, Deputy Surgeon-General Lithgow.

These deficiences were chiefly owing to the systematic robbery of stores which was carried on along the line of communications, and which, owing to the great length of the line and the impossibility of finding a sufficient number of officers to control it, it was difficult to prevent.

The deficiences had to be made up from stores which would otherwise have been forwarded to the front; moreover, besides bringing up food, a considerable portion of the carrying power had to be expended in forwarding ordnance stores, ammunition, medical comforts, and specie.

At the date of the departure of the Desert Column (December 31st), it was expected that three months' supply would be required for the force of 10,000 men south of Korti, and that on the return journey, rations for 10,000 men would be required for— *State of supplies at the departure of the Desert lumn.*

10 days at Korti.
15 ,, ,, Abu Fatmeh.
15 ,, ,, Wady Halfa.
20 ,, ,, Assuan.

About 8,000 refugees were expected from Khartum, in which town there was practically no food. But it was believed that when the siege was raised, the country would supply them as far as Metemmeh, whence to Wady Halfa, a thirty days' journey, they would have to be fed.

On the 3rd January, 1885, it was calculated by the Chief of the Staff that there were, south of Assuan, sufficient rations for the whole British force for five months. Of these there were, either at Korti or to the south of it, about $25\frac{1}{4}$ days of bread stuffs, and $12\frac{1}{4}$ days of preserved meat for the whole force, in addition to which there was a considerable amount of fresh meat.

The difficulty of forwarding supplies along the Line of Communications to the front was however, gradually overcome. *Difficulty gradually overcome.*

The following table shows the daily tonnage carried upwards on the different reaches, as calculated on the 20th of January :—

Reach.	Number of portage camels.	Number of		Daily Tonnage Carried.	
				Separate	Total
Semneh / Ambako	14	Boats / Whalers	15 / 44	11 / 22	33
Ambako / Tanjur	62	Boats / Whalers	2 / 27	3 / 18	21
Tanjur / Dal	51	Boats / Whalers	6 / 33	7 / 16	23
Dal / Kajbar	108	Boats / Whalers	22 / ...	11	11
Kajbar / Fatmeh	20	Boats / Whalers	15 / 20	8 / 8	16
Fatmeh / Dongola	...	Mahdiehs*...	10	2	2
Fatmeh / Korti	78	Boats / Whalers as required	21 / ...	14	?
Dongola / Korti	...	S.S. "Nasif-el-Kheir" / 2 powerful picquet boats / 3 weak ,, ,,	...	14 used to help boats.	14 sailing

* Small native craft generally used as ferry boats.

Camel question.

The camels were used on those reaches where boats experienced the greatest difficulty, so as to prevent a congestion of traffic.

The river was, however, rapidly falling, and means of communication by any craft, except whalers, were daily becoming more restricted. It was foreseen that, before long, the steamers would have to cease running altogether. Nor was there much hope of substituting camel transport for that of boats.

On the 3rd of January there had been at Korti and in the desert, 2,659 camels fit for use, but only 2,160 saddles, and even this number had only been collected with great difficulty. Indeed so meagre was the supply of saddles, that in spite of the urgent necessity for camels, orders had to be issued that none were to be bought unless furnished with a saddle.

By the end of January the lack of camels was causing great inconvenience. Nearly the whole available organized camel transport was at the front with the fighting columns. Forced desert marches and casualties in action, were reducing the transport company with the Desert Column to a mere skeleton.* The Remount Depôt had been emptied in attempting to replenish it. No more camels were to be had, and the country had been so drained of camel fodder that no small difficulty was experienced in keeping the available camels effective.

Nor was there any chance of getting more camels from the north. As early as the 29th December, 1884, when General Gordon's necessities at Khartum compelled Lord Wolseley to launch his force into the desert, before his supplies were in a state to have justified such a move under ordinary circumstances, every available ration and camel had to be concentrated at Korti. This had not only depleted stations on the line of communications of any surplus rations, but had taken away the camels at the portages by which alone rations on their way up could be conveyed round the cataracts. Thanks to the energy of General Grenfell and the officers under him, this deficiency was soon made up, but another such strain on the line of communications would probably be more than it could bear.

The Arabs were moreover found to be exceedingly loth to part with their best animals, and those which they offered for sale were generally from extreme youth or extreme age, wholly unfit for rough work. The difficulty of feeding even the few animals which remained was also so great, that it is doubtful whether, under any circumstances, a great increase in the establishment would have been possible.

The inroad of 10,000 men, with camp followers and animals, had almost exhausted the grain supply of the province of Dongola, and even to meet the requirements of the animals in hand, the Chief of the Staff had found it necessary to order the General of Communications to purchase large quantities of grain in Egypt. *(Grain supply running short in the province of Dongola.)*

The only possible means of supplementing the failing river transport and augmenting the weakened desert transport, was to hire camels from the Arabs. This was eventually done with a fair amount of success, but even at the best it was an uncertain means of transport, owing to the impossibility of *(Hired convoys. Difficulties attending their organization.)*

---

* The following is a return of the camels remaining at the conclusion of the desert march:—

Fit for work	556
Sick, but fit to be retained	799
Sick, recommended to be cast	636
Total	2,303

persuading the native drivers to accompany convoys in districts where there was the slightest possibility of opposition. Moreover, at first, the greatest difficulty was encountered in persuading the Arabs to hire out their camels at all, and to go where they were wanted when they had done so.

The following extract from the Chief of the Staff's diary, for January 12th, 1885, gives an example of these difficulties:—

"A contract entered into with Sheikh Mohammed-el-Kheir of the Sowarab tribe to supply camels for transport to Jakdul, the Sheikh undertaking to provide 50 camels to commence with in five days. The price to be 15 Medjidieh dollars per load of 320 lbs.

"The history of the negotiations preceding this contract are worth recording, as they are a fair instance of the way we are harassed, thwarted, and plundered by the Egyptian authorities.

"On the 18th December, Lord Wolseley made a contract with the same Sheikh for camels to carry to Metemmeh, the price named and accepted by the Sheikh being 10 dollars a load.

"No camels coming, a spy of the Intelligence Department was sent, who reported that the Sheikh was not going to fulfil his contract because he believed the Mudir did not approve of his doing so.

"Lord Wolseley then telegraphed to Sir Evelyn Baring, begging that he would press the Khedive to send a telegram in the strongest language to the Mudir on the subject. He also sent Zohrab Bey to speak to the Mudir.

"In due time the Mudir arrived here, having summoned the Sheikhs.

"The Mudir expressed the greatest surprise at our wanting camels. If he had only known it he would have got them. He also thought 10 dollars a fair price. The Sheikh arrived, and, in conversation with the Chief of the Staff, refused to carry to Metemmeh at all, and to Jakdul only for 20 dollars a load.

"This was refused.

"The matter was then referred to the Mudir, who suggested the contract made, and said he considered it a just one—viz., 15 dollars a load to Jakdul. Camel transport being necessary, the bargain was closed. It remains to be seen how it will be carried out."

Care of sick camels.

An arrangement was made with the Kashif of Ambukkol, by which we were relieved of the burden of the large number of sick camels on our hands. The Kashif contracted for a sum down, and for a further sum for every camel returned sound, to take charge of the sick animals and provide them with good grazing, medical treatment, and attendance. He was to produce a piece of the skin of the neck with the Government brand on it, for every camel that died, and was to pay a fine for every camel not so accounted for, or produced alive. The camels were to be kept till cured or for two months.

The hired camel convoys were also supplemented on a small scale by hired donkey convoys, which, as far as they went, answered well; but they were not organized till February, and the system had never time to be developed. Donkey convoys.

In the meanwhile, however, the s.s. "Lotus" had arrived at Korti, and was of the greatest assistance on the Fatmeh-Korti reach, being able to carry 45 tons and tow 20 tons. She had been constructed by Messrs. Yarrow, and sent out to Egypt in pieces, arriving at Alexandria on the 22nd September, and at Wady Halfa on the 19th October. Thence she was forwarded by train to a point above the Semneh Cataract, where her construction was commenced on the 4th November, by a detachment of the Royal Sussex Regiment, under the superintendence of the engineer sent out with her from England. Arrival of "Lotus."

On the 2nd December, she was launched and christened the "Lotus," and on the 2nd January started on her voyage up the river, during which the only serious difficulty she encountered was in the passage of the Ambako Cataract, up which she was successfully taken by Colonel Wynne, after the ascent had been attempted and declared impossible by the naval officer and pilots in charge.

On the 29th January, she arrived at Abu Fatmeh, whence after a short halt for repairs she proceeded to Korti, arriving there on the 3rd February. She was at once set to work, and after the wreck of the "Nasif-el-Kheir" on the 5th March, became quite invaluable. Both these steamers, however, and also the steam pinnaces, consumed enormous quantities of wood (the "Nasif-el-Kheir" notably so), and careful organization was required to keep them supplied. A responsible native agent, whose good faith was guaranteed by the Mudir, was placed in charge of each wooding station, and received a commission on each kantar (100 lbs.) of wood stacked. A Commissariat Officer visited the stations once a month, to audit accounts and pay for the wood issued to steamers. Fuel for steamers.

Coal for the Sudan Railway.

The maintenance of the coal supply for the Sudan railway and for the steamers on the lower reaches, also required careful consideration, and in consultation with the Senior Naval Officer, the General of Communications decided that coal, then in transit, should be allowed to accumulate until the following amounts were stored at the places named below:—

Assuan	3,000 tons.
Shellal	1,200 ,,
Korosko	500 ,,
Halfa	{ 450* ,,
	{ 244 ,,

Transport of sick.

Besides the stores, &c., to be brought up, there was a constant stream of sick and wounded to be sent down the river. These were for the most part sent to Abu Fatmeh or Dongola by steamer, and thence by whalers to Railhead. Two large barges were also fitted for sick by Captain Boardman, R.N., under the superintendence of the Principal Medical Officer.

The work of the Medical Staff had been very heavy during the absence of the fighting columns, and on the 17th of February, Lord Wolseley telegraphed to the Secretary of State for War, demanding the following augmentation to the department to be sent out as soon as possible. To complete establishment, 2 quartermasters, 27 non-commissioned officers, and 10 privates. To act as servants to medical officers, 112 privates. For extra duty during the summer, when a larger proportion of sick was expected, 23 medical officers, 28 non-commissioned officers, and 101 privates. This made a total demand for 23 medical officers, 2 quartermasters, 55 non-commissioned officers and 223 privates.

Censorship of telegrams at Dongola.

In order to ensure Her Majesty's Government having the earliest information of all facts, and to prevent the circulation of false reports of disasters, which it was believed the sympathisers with Mohammed Ahmed were likely to attempt to promulgate, it had been found necessary to establish a strict censorship of telegrams at Dongola,‡ to the Commandant of which station the following order was given:—

---

* For steamers.
† For railway, being ten months' supply.
‡ The office of examination was afterwards removed to Korti.

WATER SUPPLY.

"No telegram whatever will be allowed to pass Dongola from the front, without having been previously seen by you. The line is not to be cleared for any one except Lord Wolseley and Major-General Earle.

"No report of any action with the enemy, or of any success or failure, or of any rumour of disaster, is on any account to be allowed to pass, unless it be confirmation of news, previously sent through by Lord Wolseley or Major-General Earle."

A copy of these instructions was also sent to the General of Communications, and he was directed to use every endeavour to ensure their being carried out at all stations.

Mr. McCullough was also posted at Assuan, as Arabic censor, with similar instructions; and General Stephenson was requested, in the event of rumours being current in Cairo, at once to enquire of Mr. McCullough if such rumours had passed through his station. The Director of Army Telegraphs was also directed to give similar instructions at all stations.

During the advance of the Desert Column, the force had been able to subsist on the water which it carried from the Nile, and on that which it found at the various desert wells; but on the latter becoming exhausted, and the carrying power of the transport companies becoming less, it was found necessary to establish watering posts on the line of march. *Watering posts established in the desert.*

The first step in this direction was to send Lieutenant-Colonel Todd, R.E., to El Howeiya, to report on the water supply at that place, and at Megaga (14 miles to the east of it). He found that the wells at El Howeiya were rapidly decreasing, yielding on the date he visited them (February 14th), only 310 gallons daily, of which the garrison consumed 200 gallons. He considered that the wells would not hold out for more than another three weeks. He ordered three new wells to be dug, but found that they would not increase the supply much. He also visited the so-called wells of Megaga, which he found to consist of two natural reservoirs in the rock. The lower one, the water in which was fit for animals only, contained about 5,000 gallons, and the upper one about 100 yards beyond, contained 100,000 gallons of good clear water. Both pools were considerably below their highest level, and there was no water running into either of them.

The officer commanding the detachment of Essex Regiment at El Howeiya also visited the Megaga tanks and the wells of Abu Alik, about 12 miles to the east of his post; he found them to be very inaccessible, and did not consider that they contained sufficient water to justify convoys in making a detour to reach them. At Miljik, a spot 6 miles distant from El Howeiya, which was reported to contain water, several natural tanks were found, but they were all dry.

In consequence of these reports, it was determined to establish two auxiliary watering posts between El Howeiya and the Nile. The first was established at a hill 12 miles east of Korti on the 22nd February, a party of 19th Hussars being sent there to start it, taking with them a number of waterskins and bags.

On the 25th February, the second watering post was established at a hill 30 miles east of Korti, by a detachment of 19th Hussars, with seven transport camels laden with 40 tin-lined biscuit boxes roughly fitted up as reservoirs for water. These boxes held 13 gallons each.

It was arranged that this post should be supplied from No. 1 post (12-Mile Hill) which was in its turn filled from the Nile by means of convoys of weak and sickly camels, unfit for heavy loads or making long journeys. Every available animal was requisitioned for this purpose, officers' private camels even being employed, and the service was also supplemented by hired donkey transport.

By the 27th February, two days after its establishment, 630 gallons of water had already been stored at 30-Mile Hill.

Convoys proceeding to Jakdul also left water at El Howeiya, carrying on their bags and tanks to Jakdul, where the water supply was still fairly plentiful, and then refilling them for the return journey. Rations were also sent to these stations for the returning troops. 6,000 rations for men, and 3,500 rations for horses and camels, equivalent to two days' supply for the Desert Column, were sent to 30-Mile Hill on the 4th March, to furnish food for the march into Korti.

Headquarters Staff at Korti.

Various changes took place in the Headquarters Staff during the absence of the Desert and River Columns. Sir R. Buller Sir E. Wood, and Colonel Wolseley in succession acted as Chief of the Staff. Captain H. C. Sclater, R.A., succeeded Captain Kekewich as D.A.A.G. at Headquarters, on the departure of the latter to join the River Column. During the absence of Sir C. Wilson, Major Turner, R.A., D.A.A.G., acted as head of the Intelligence Department at Korti. Lieutenant-Colonel Swaine, C.B., Rifle Brigade, Lord Wolseley's Military Secre-

QUESTION OF SENDING TROOPS TO SUAKIN.

tary, was invalided early in February, and was replaced by Lieutenant-Colonel Grove.

Colonel Hon. E. Primrose, Grenadier Guards, had been appointed Commandant at Korti, but was invalided in February, and on the 22nd Major-General Hon. J. C. Dormer, who had been acting as Chief of the Staff to Sir F. Stephenson at Cairo, was appointed Commandant in his place.

Besides his duties as Commander of the Nile Expedition, Lord Wolseley, as Commander-in-Chief in Egypt, was, at this period, in constant communication with Her Majesty's Government on the question of an expedition to Suakin This idea had been mooted by the Government at an earlier date, but it may be said to have definitely taken shape on receipt of the verbal message received from General Gordon on the 30th December, 1884,* which at once drew from Sir E. Baring a suggestion, that, in order to ensure the safety of Lord Wolseley's force, and to prevent an attack on Berber, it was desirable that a demonstration should be made from Suakin against Osman Digna. *[margin: Suakin expedition, first proposed on receipt of Gordon's message of 14th December.]*

To this Lord Wolseley replied that he would strongly advise Her Majesty's Government to send all available men-of-war to Suakin, to anchor there till Khartum was relieved; and he suggested that the men, and especially Marines in red coats, should be frequently landed and exercised, and the belief spread as much as possible that an attack on the tribes was intended. He believed that such a demonstration, which would cost nothing, would be sufficient to prevent Osman Digna sparing any men for Berber. *[margin: Proposal for a Fleet to be sent to Suakin.]*

The Secretary of State for War replied to this that he and his colleagues did not consider that a mere naval demonstration would answer the purpose intended, but that a real demonstration could be made by sending to Suakin two battalions of infantry, four squadrons of cavalry, a mule battery, and four Field or Horse Artillery guns from Cairo, with a transport company. Lord Wolseley was requested to telegraph if he thought these measures would be desirable to support his operations, as apart from all other questions. He was also informed that a battalion from Malta had been put under orders for Egypt in case he wanted more troops at Assuan. *[margin: Government proposal to send reinforcements to Suakin.]*

To this Lord Wolseley replied as follows:—

---

* See page 138, Part I.

"*Korti, 8th January,* 1885.

Lord Wolseley's reply.

"Do not send battalion from Malta until I ask. I do not think it will be required.

"The measures you propose will not assist my operations against Khartum, 'as apart from all other questions.' In all my letters and telegrams to you I have from first endeavoured to impress on Government that I am strong enough to relieve Khartum, and believe in being able to send a force when returning, by way of Berber to Suakin, to open road and crush Osman Digna.

"I have, therefore, always regarded the despatch of a force from home to Suakin as unnecessary, and an expensive luxury, but that if you could afford it, the result would be of advantage from a political point of view, provided the force at once attacked and crushed Osman Digna.

"To send a force as now proposed, without means of attacking at once on landing, would be simply a waste of money.

"Our occupation of Berber will, without doubt, seriously affect feeling of tribes towards Osman Digna, which by latest information, is already shaky. There is no such thing as certainty in war; but, please God, I shall duly relieve Khartum and open Berber-Suakin road when returning, if Amarars do not do so when I take Berber.

"Troops could only reach me by Nile route in whalers, as they must bring their own food with them. Journey here by native boats impossible. A force sent from Suakin would require vast amount of camels, far more than you could obtain or manage to feed, and the force would starve on reaching Berber.

"My only difficulty is supplies, and yet every man lands at, or passes, this place with about 100 days' food. If I were defeated, no amount of troops in Egypt could help me, but to calm public mind, stronger garrisons at Assuan, Cairo, and Alexandria would be required.

"I still strongly urge collection of fleet at Suakin, as I proposed to Baring. It will give confidence to those who wish to desert Osman Digna and join Amarars.

"I hear you are pressed to construct railway to Berber. It will certainly take at least a year to make, and could have no influence in any way on my operations, although eventually it would be of great value to Sudan.

"Please send me 2,000 strong thick white umbrellas at

once, packed in strong bales bound with iron, each bale to weigh about 70 pounds. I shall want them going to Suakin."

In consequence of this telegram, the proposed concentration of troops at Suakin was for the time being abandoned, and as there were already seven ships of war there and no more could be spared, the proposed naval demonstration was not carried out. On the 18th January, however, the Secretary of State for War decided to send to Suakin from Cairo, a battalion of infantry, two guns Horse Artillery, and some cavalry. A battalion of Royal Marines was already there. The matter then dropped till the beginning of February, when the news of the fall of Khartum was received.

January 18th. A Battalion and some Cavalry and Artillery sent to Suakin.

In the telegraphic correspondence that ensued between Lord Wolseley and the Secretary of State for War, as to the course to be pursued under the totally altered conditions that had now to be met, and which has been given in Chapter VIII., Lord Wolseley recommended the despatch of a force capable of crushing Osman Digna. He recommended that this force should consist of three squadrons of cavalry, four battalions of infantry, and the remaining four guns of the Horse Artillery battery from Cairo, in addition to the troops already at Suakin.

Fall of Khartum. Lord Wolseley requests the despatch of a force to crush Osman Digna.

On the 7th of February Lord Wolseley also telegraphed to the Secretary of State for War, that to enable him to undertake offensive operations against the Mahdi in the autumn, he would require four extra battalions for field service and one for garrisons of Korosko, Assuan, &c.; a battery of Horse Artillery; 100 men to complete 19th Hussars, and 200 Commissariat and Transport Corps, with proportion of Army Hospital Corps. He added that for reasons of supply, it would be necessary to send back most of the mounted troops to Wady Halfa, but that the remainder of the force could be fed in the Mudirieh of Dongola, or might be extended to Berber.

February 7th. Lord Wolseley's estimate of force necessary for an autumn campaign.

When Lord Wolseley was informed that his military policy was to be based on the necessity of crushing the Mahdi, he was at the same time asked to state what additional force he required, and when and where it was to be sent, also whether he wished for the immediate despatch of a force to attack Osman Digna.

In reply, Lord Wolseley said that he was sure the policy of the Government was the correct one, as the power of the Mahdi was incompatible with peace and good government in Egypt. He stated that he considered that the sooner Osman

Digna was now dealt with the better, and recommended the despatch to Suakin of a brigade of Indian infantry and one regiment of Punjab cavalry to hold it during the summer, and to co-operate with the Nile force in keeping the road open, while the English troops summered in the mountains. He concluded by saying "No troops you could send now could possibly reach me in time for the cold season's fighting, as I could not feed them unless they came up river in English boats, bringing their own food for 100 days with them. And that is now out of the question."

Lord Wolseley was thereupon informed that the Indian brigade and cavalry demanded by him had been ordered, but was asked whether the force proposed by the Government of six battalions of infantry, 4 squadrons of cavalry, two batteries of artillery, and two companies of engineers, might not be reduced. He replied that last time we had fought Osman Digna, the force employed was six battalions of infantry, two regiments of cavalry, Naval brigade, and artillery, and that therefore he did not think the present proposed force too large.

February 10th. Government propose Suakin-Berber railway.

In reply, the Secretary of State for War said it was necessary that he should clearly understand the proposed ultimate object of the Suakin force, and he suggested the reconsideration of the railway scheme, on the ground that Lord Wolseley might not be able to supply his force during the summer, from the country or by the Nile route, and that it would be of use for forwarding the heavy artillery and steamers which Lord Wolseley would require for his final advance. The Secretary of State for War expressed his opinion that the railway would probably be completed during the summer.

February 11th. Lord Wolseley's reply. His plan.

In reply to this, Lord Wolseley sent the following telegram:

"Present objective of Suakin force, destruction of Osman Digna's power and to join hands with me at Berber along road between.

"If good position on hills could be found, Suakin force should go there for summer, Indian troops taking their place at Suakin and at posts along the road to Berber. If no suitable places in hills can be found, it will be a question to what extent they should return to Cairo for summer, but it is most advisable if possible to retain them in country. I will find garrison for Berber.

"For convenience of feeding camels, as I have drained this country of grain, I shall most probably send three camel

OBJECT OF SUAKIN EXPEDITION.   147

corps to vicinity of Suakin for summer, keeping only mounted infantry here. During summer, troops now here to hold Berber, Abu Hamed, and river down to Hannek Cataract. Egyptian army to hold river from thence to Wady Halfa, Cameron Highlanders to remain at Korosko, where I have ordered them to construct huts. When supplies asked for from England have arrived, can feed them in those positions during the summer, and collect reserves for operations in autumn, railway being pushed on to Dal, and possibly to Absarat.

"For autumn campaign, to enable us to advance on Khartum and destroy Mahdi's power there, the following is, I consider, minimum strength of fighting column to advance from Shendi neighbourhood on Khartum:—Two batteries Horse Artillery to come *viâ* Suakin, the four squadrons British and one native cavalry regiment now going to Suakin, the 19th Hussars strengthened by at least 100 men, 6,000 British infantry, and one brigade Indian Infantry, and proportion Departmental Corps. Engineers now here and going to Suakin, ample. Artillery now here to be distributed with fighting force, or on communications, as may be required.

"For lines of communication from Suakin to Berber, and Hannek Cataract to Shendi:—Marines to hold Suakin, with five British and one Indian battalions for other posts. Korosko to be held by Cameron Highlanders, and Assuan as at present. You can calculate accordingly the troops and numbers required. My battalions when they reach Gubat or Berber, will not number on an average more than 550 men each, remainder have become non-effective.

"By all means make railway by contract to Berber, or as far as you can, during summer. It will be invaluable as a means of supply, and I recommend it being begun immediately. Contract to be, if possible, for so much per ton military stores and supplies, and men carried, per mile. I will telegraph later about steamers."*

On the 18th February Lord Wolseley telegraphed to the Secretary of State for War that the first object of the Suakin expedition must be the overthrow of Osman Digna and the military occupation of the Hadendowa territory near the Berber road. In this despatch, and also in one of the previous day, Lord Wolseley expressed doubts as to the possibility of taking Berber before the autumn, and pointed out that, in

February 19th. Lord Wolseley doubtful as to advancing on Berber.

(s.c.2)   * See Appendix 55.   L

such case, the railway from Suakin could only be constructed for a certain distance.

In a later telegram on the 18th, Sir R. Buller's evacuation of Gubat was reported. This telegram has been given in full on page 68.

On the following day, Lord Wolseley again pointed out that, should the capture of Berber be delayed, the railway could only be carried to about Ariab; he further questioned the advisability of this railway being of broad gauge as the Government had contracted. He requested that the railway from Wady Halfa should be extended to Absarat.

The Suakin expedition. Sir G. Graham in command.

Lieutenant-General Sir G. Graham, V.C., K.C.B., &c., had been appointed to command the Suakin force, and on the 20th was given his instructions by the Secretary of State. These are given in full at the commencement of Chapter XIII, which narrates the operations at Suakin. They fully contemplated that Berber would not be occupied till the autumn.

February 21st. Capture of Berber definitely postponed. Effect of this change of plan on the Suakin expedition.

On the 21st Lord Wolseley telegraphed that he did not propose to attempt the capture of Berber for the present, and that the River Column was to be recalled.

Although the garrison of Suakin had already, before the news of the fall of Khartum reached Korti, been considerably reinforced, the additional troops had been sent thither rather as a precautionary measure than with a view to undertaking serious operations against Osman Digna. This restless chieftain had succeeded in assembling a considerable force near Suakin, and was causing its garrison some trouble. When, on the fall of Khartum, the object of the Nile Expedition disappeared, and it became necessary to overthrow the victorious Mahdi, now installed in the capital of the Sudan, the necessity for a campaign in the Hadendowa country at once arose. Not only was the destruction of Osman Digna's power in itself a matter of vital importance owing to the moral effect it would have, and also as a step towards the final settlement of the Sudan when the Mahdi had been disposed of, but the possession of the Suakin-Berber road became necessary to Lord Wolseley for the operations which altered circumstances had now forced upon him.

The overthrow of the Mahdi was, for the present, quite out of the question. The forces on the Nile were insufficient for an enterprise of such magnitude. No means existed for increasing them. They could not be brought up to the strength demanded by the nature of the task they had in hand, nor could the stores necessary for the undertaking be conveyed to the theatre of war, till the rise of the Nile in the late summer made the river available for water transport on a great scale. An autumn campaign thus became unavoidable.

Lord Wolseley determined, if possible, to establish himself at Berber, during the period still at his disposal before the hot season. With a firm grip on this important strategical point during the summer, he would be in a position when the favourable season came round to commence operations at once against Khartum. Established at Berber and Abu Hamed, and with the Expeditionary Force in summer quarters down the Nile, he could, if the Suakin-Berber route were secured, send a considerable portion of his mounted troops to Suakin where forage was abundant, to wait there till required. And so, with this in view, and also with the intention of eventually bringing part of the reinforcements that were needed for the execution of his autumn plans, across from the Red Sea Littoral to Berber, Lord Wolseley requested that an expedition might be dispatched to Suakin.

The expedition was to be capable of dealing effectually with Osman Digna. After accomplishing this it was to occupy the Hadendowa territory in the vicinity of the Suakin-Berber route. Then it was to join hands with the Nile force, which would have by that time captured Berber. And thus, when the time came to compass the downfall of the Mahdi at Khartum, the two great lines leading to that city from Egypt and from the Red Sea coast would both be in the hands of British and Indian troops.

Her Majesty's Government approved of the Suakin expedition. They also proposed that the construction of a railway to Berber, which had already been the subject of some correspondence, should be proceeded with in conjunction with the Suakin expedition. Lord Wolseley gladly acquiesced in this proposal. It was doubtful, indeed, whether a line even of narrow gauge could be completed to Berber before the autumn. But its existence for even a part of the distance would be of great advantage to the Suakin force in its operations after crushing Osman Digna, and could not fail to be most valuable when the time of concentration came for the campaign against the Mahdi at Khartum.

When, however, circumstances were found to render the proposed capture of Berber before the hot season impracticable, and arrangements had, in consequence to be made to withdraw the Nile force into summer quarters in the province of Dongola, the plan of operations for the Suakin expedition had also to be modified. Co-operation could not now take place between the two forces before the autumn; and the route from Suakin to the Nile could not be opened till Berber had been taken by the troops on the river. The instructions to Sir G. Graham, therefore, while they contemplated the crushing of Osman Digna and the military occupation of the Hadendowa territory, were not framed with a view to his advancing beyond Ariab. The railway was to be finished to that point if possible, and plant was to be there collected so that the remaining 100 miles across a waterless desert should be completed as soon as the terminus, Berber, was taken by the Nile force in the autumn.

Dispositions necessitated on the Nile.

The question of arranging for the supply of the forces on the Nile and of distributing the troops in summer quarters now exercised the Headquarters Staff. Although Lord Wolseley considered that the Suakin-Berber railway, or as much of it as could be made, would be a valuable auxiliary means of supply, he was still of opinion that he must depend mainly on the Nile route, and on the 3rd of March he sent the following telegram to the Secretary of State for War:—

Nile main route for supplies.

March 3rd. Lord Wolseley insists upon extension of Halfa railway.

"When can I calculate upon receiving first instalment of rails for extension of Halfa railway? Even five miles of rails would be now most acceptable. I earnestly beg that Nile railway may have preference over Suakin. Former is a certainty, and I believe all troops for autumn campaign against Khartum will have to come up Nile and be fed by Halfa railway."

The Suakin-Berber railway. Communications between the Government and Lord Wolseley.

The Secretary of State for War replied (No. 144), that he was much embarrassed by this telegram, and told Lord Wolseley, that it was on his recommendation that the Suakin-Berber railway had been ordered at great expense, and that now he appeared to place no reliance on it, and to mean depending entirely on the Nile route. He asked Lord Wolseley whether he had considered the possibility of getting siege artillery up by the Nile route, and the great difficulty of moving the plant, &c., for the Halfa railway, in addition to the supplies for his own force.

When Lord Wolseley, in his telegram of the 11th, approved of the project for constructing a railway from Suakin to Berber, it was under the impression that the line was to be of the metre gauge. He also, at that time, still hoped to reach Berber in the early spring. The circumstances had now, however, greatly altered, and the Government had concluded a contract for a line of normal and not metre gauge. Lord Wolseley, therefore, replied on the 5th of March to the Secretary of State for War as follows :—

"For this summer, at all events, I do not contemplate carrying line beyond Ferkeh. . . ."

"Your No. 144. Please see passages referring to Suakin-Berber line in my Nos. 90* and 93.* My view throughout has been that this line will eventually be of great value as a means of supply. It will also have a most powerful effect in the pacification of the Sudan. But I do not believe that a railway of the gauge ordered can be completed to Berber even by the end of the year; and I cannot advance in October, trusting for my supplies to an unfinished line.

"For the immediate needs of the autumn campaign I consider the extension of the Halfa railway imperatively and absolutely necessary. Remember that when I wrote my No. 66†, I contemplated a narrow-gauge line, and also that I had not then been obliged to abandon all hope of taking Berber this spring. Neither of these conditions now obtains; and both reinforcements and supplies for my autumn advance must come to me by Nile route.

" . . . .

"With reference to the last part of your No. 144, I do not contemplate taking siege artillery either to Berber or Khartum; and the requirements for the extension to Ferkeh will not exceed 10,000 tons. I am making arrangements for transport up the Nile.

"Stephenson has just forwarded to me an unnumbered telegram he has received from you asking for a number of estimates that I certainly cannot give. The length of the Ferkeh extension, exclusive of sidings, is, however, 47 miles, instead of 62, as given in your telegram.

"Without entering into all the details you ask for, I can state positively that without the extension of the Halfa line the autumn campaign cannot proceed. If you send the men and material I have demanded I will have the line ready in time."

On the following day, Lord Wolseley sent the following

---

* Lord Wolseley's telegrams of 18th and 19th of February, in which he pointed out that, if Berber remained in the hands of the Mahdists, the railway could only be completed to Ariab.

† Telegram of 11th. See page 146.

written despatch, explaining the altered condition of affairs and his plans for the future:—

March 6th. Despatch of Lord Wolseley giving his views on the situation.

"*Camp, Korti, 6th March,* 1885.

"My Lord,

"My despatch, No. 66,* of the 9th ultimo, informed your Lordship of the reported fall of Khartum on the 26th January last, only two days before the arrival there of the detachment of troops I had ordered forward in steamers from the neighbourhood of Metemmeh, to open up communication with General Gordon.

"2. I have now the honour to report that, in my opinion, there can no longer be any doubt that Mohammed Ahmed's troops took possession of Khartum, and killed General Gordon, on the date I have named.

"3. The scope and object of the military operations to be undertaken by the army under my command were thus defined in the instructions I received from Her Majesty's Government, dated 9th October, 1884:

"'The primary object of the expedition up the Nile is to bring away General Gordon and Colonel Stewart from Khartum. When that object has been secured, no further offensive operations of any kind are to be undertaken. Although you are not precluded from advancing as far as Khartum, should you consider such a step essential to secure the safe retreat of General Gordon and Colonel Stewart, you will bear in mind that Her Majesty's Government is desirous to limit the sphere of your military operations as much as possible. They rely on you not to advance further southwards than is absolutely necessary in order to attain the primary object of the expedition.'

"4. As pointed out in my despatch, No. 66, the strength and constitution of the army were fixed and determined, after a careful consideration of the nature and extent of the operations I was ordered to carry out. Although no direct reference is made in my instructions to raising the siege of Khartum, or to the defeat of the Mahdi's troops at that place, I always considered that these operations would, probably, be necessary before General Gordon and the Egyptian garrison could safely be withdrawn from Khartum. The force at my disposal was amply sufficient for both these objects. The siege of that town, however, should it unfortunately be taken by the enemy before we could reach it,

* See page 60.

was not contemplated, much less provided for, in the instructions I received. It is almost unnecessary to add that, had any such serious operation been regarded, even as one of the possible objects to be accomplished, the force placed at my disposal must have been largely augmented. Khartum in possession of Mohammed Ahmed could not be besieged with any prospect of success, at this late period of the year by a small army provided only with mountain guns.

"5. The fall of Khartum and the death of General Gordon left me without any instructions, and found this army without any defined mission to accomplish in the Sudan. This I reported to your Lordship by telegraph, and asked for further instructions, and a clearly defined exposition of the policy that Her Majesty's Government intended to adopt under the altered condition of affairs here.

"6. In reply to my telegram, your Lordship informed me that my immediate duty was to protect the province of Dongola—the only province of the Sudan which is still clear of the enemy—and that, as soon as the necessary arrangements could be completed, Her Majesty's Government had determined to destroy the Mahdi's power at Khartum, in order that peace, order, and a settled government might be established there. This I conceive to be, in general terms, a fair description of the new mission with which I have been entrusted, and which I shall endeavour to carry out next autumn.

"7. I take this opportunity of congratulating Her Majesty's Government upon having adopted the Nile route as the line of advance for this force on Khartum. Had this army been despatched from Suakin as a base, and upon arrival at, or near, Berber, learnt that Khartum had fallen, it could not possibly have transferred its base to the Mediterranean, for it could not have been fed under those circumstances in this part of the Nile valley. The province of Dongola would have been at the enemy's mercy, and the frontiers of Egypt would have been open to his attack.

"8. Recent events at Khartum have naturally added greatly to Mohammed Ahmed's influence and power, and have gone far towards persuading many to believe in the truth of his sacred pretensions. He occupies a very different position in the Sudan now, to that in which he found himself during the three months when he was making frequent, but apparently hopeless, efforts to take Khartum. He wields an almost undisputed sway over the whole Sudan, the provinc of Dongola, which we occupy, alone excepted. All classes look up to him as a great conqueror and a very holy man, and by large numbers he is believed to be the Mahdi he claims to be. We, on the other hand, have no party here in our favour. The few tribes, or rather portions of tribes, and the small number of Sheikhs who pretend to have thrown in their lot with us, are, undoubtedly, in frequent communication with our avowed enemy, the Mahdi. They look upon us with hatred as infidels and invaders, who have come here for our own selfish ends, and who intend, if we succeed, to place in power some foreign ruler, who will tax and oppress them, much as the Egyptian Pashas did. We live in the midst of spies and concealed enemies, and few seem to feel any confidence even in our power to defeat the Mahdi. These are facts that must not be overlooked when plans for the campaign next autumn are being made.

"9. As it is impossible for me to undertake any offensive operations until about the end of summer, it is important that, in the meanwhile, Osman Digna's power in the Suakin district should be crushed. The defeat will, in some measure, act as a counterpoise to the Mahdi's capture of Khartum. This operation is not difficult, as the forces are near the seaboard, and it should be immediately followed by the occupation of the Tokar and Sinkat districts. A railway should also be begun without delay at Suakin, in the direction of Berber. Your Lordship has informed me that a contract has been entered into for the construction of this railway on a gauge of 4 feet $8\frac{1}{2}$ inches.

"10. Although I do not for a moment entertain the idea, that a railway of such a gauge can be completed over the 250 miles (about) of country lying between Suakin and Berber, in time to have any very direct or immediate effect upon our operations towards Khartum next autumn, I am convinced that active progress made upon it, will bring home to Mohammed Ahmed, and to all intelligent Sheikhs, the fact that we are now in earnest, and do not mean to leave the country until we have re-established order and a settled government at Khartum.

"11. In addition to the commercial advantages which it will eventually confer, this railroad cannot fail to have the greatest political influence upon the Sudan, whilst its strategic importance cannot be over-estimated. At present this country is cut off from the civilised world by hundreds of miles of desert on all sides, and if the power ruling at

Khartum has to be assisted from without, it is both very difficult and very costly to send troops to its aid. A railway would do away with this isolation. Had Berber been joined to Suakin by a line of rail when the Mahdi first took up arms against the Egyptian Government, his power would long since have been disposed of.

"12. In the campaign before us, the construction of this railway even as far as Ariab, will, in case of necessity, secure us a second and alternative line of communication by which supplies may be obtained, and sick and wounded taken to the coast for embarkation. It will also give to our operations an appearance of irresistible strength, which the possession of only one line of supply, and that along 1,400 miles of river, would never afford. For my main line of supply, at all events until Berber is taken, I must, it is true, depend upon this river. It is the only line of which I can be certain. I cannot trust, in an advance on Khartum, to a railway which requires that my advance should have succeeded before it can be finished. But although it would not do to rely upon the Suakin-Berber line, it is, nevertheless, one which, when completed, will afford me immense assistance, at whatever period of the campaign its completion may take place.

"13. I am now engaged in distributing this army along the left bank of the Nile, on the open reach of water that extends from the Hannek Cataract to Abu Dom opposite Merowi. Then I shall be quite prepared to meet Mohammed Ahmed at any time during the summer, should he by any good fortune be tempted to advance in this direction.

"14. During the summer, I shall collect the supplies which this army will require for its advance in the autumn. To enable me to do this, I shall be obliged to extend the existing Halfa, 3 feet 6 inch gauge, railway to Ferkeh, a distance of 47 miles beyond the point to which the line is now open. The sleepers, rails, fish plates, bolts, and spikes of this line altogether weigh about 131 tons per mile. The proposed extension is over easy ground, with the exception of some small cuttings through what seems to be soft rock. The workmen are trained and disciplined Egyptian soldiers who make very fair 'navvies.' In fact, only a few lines have ever been made under more favourable conditions. Yet I only calculate on doing ·28 of a mile per diem, and I can only work up to that amount, provided the rails I have demanded commence arriving in this country early in April, and go on arriving afterwards in a continuous stream, and the 300 platelayers, also asked for, are at Suez by April 15th.

"15. I mention these details as the data on which I base my belief that a broader gauge line with far heavier rails, sleepers, &c., cannot be made through a hostile country, across a range of mountains 3,000 feet high, at a rapid rate. Allowing the same rate of progress—which is much to expect—the railway from Suakin to Berber would take about two years and five months to complete.

"16. Between Ferkeh and the Hannek Cataract, navigation is comparatively easy. With the assistance of the light draught steamers I am obtaining from England, I do not anticipate any great difficulty in collecting the supplies I require for the autumn campaign, and in bringing here all the additional troops that will be necessary.

"17. My experience of the 178 miles of easy desert between this place and Metemmeh warns me against trusting, entirely and solely, to a desert route as a means of supply. Even supposing the wide gauge railway contracted for can be completed to Ariab by the 1st October next—which I am certain it cannot be—there would still remain to be dealt with 110 miles of desert which, both as regards water supply and the nature of the country to be traversed, compares most unfavourably with the 100 miles between Korti and Jakdul. I have never had more than about 4,000 mouths to feed in the desert here, and I have been assisted by over 1,000 excellent hired camels in addition to my own camel transport; but I have, nevertheless, experienced the greatest difficulty in feeding the small number of men I have mentioned, and, in doing so, I have, in a little over two months, completely destroyed, not only all the regular camel transport, but also almost all the camels of the four camel regiments. Most of the men of these regiments have had to make the return journey on foot, the few camels still able to work being employed in carrying food, water, ammunition, &c. Yet this 100 miles is fairly well supplied with water, and there is excellent grazing for camels all along it, two great advantages not possessed by the 110 miles between Ariab and Berber.

"18. Looking to these facts, and remembering that no advance by any force from Ariab upon Berber can be made until the latter place is in our possession, and that it may very probably be selected by the enemy as the point where he will fight a decisive battle, it is absolutely necessary that the troops advancing from this province by the Nile Valley should be strong enough to defeat any force that Mohammed Ahmed can there bring into the field against it.

"19. I do not wish in this despatch, which will doubtless be made public, to enter into minute details as to the exact strength and constitution of the army which I consider necessary for next autumn's operations. I shall content myself with saying that, in addition to the troops now in the Nile Valley between Cairo and this place, and in addition to the battalion now ordered to Assuan, I shall require here, for my lines of communication and for my fighting force together, 12 extra battalions of British Infantry, four strong squadrons of British Cavalry mounted on Egyptian or Syrian horses, and two batteries of Horse Artillery (13-pr.) similarly horsed. Events later on will enable me to report, to what extent these extra troops can be supplied from the force now at, or on its way to, Suakin. It is very desirable that the Brigade of Guards, which is at present landing at that place, should be included in the 12 extra battalions sent here for the autumn campaign.

"20. It is to be expected that, when Osman Digna's power has been thoroughly broken, the Brigade of Indian Infantry and the regiment of Indian Cavalry, together with the Marines and one or two battalions of British Infantry, will be amply sufficient for the protection of the Suakin district, and for holding and protecting the railway line during its construction. As already stated, the exact distribution of the remainder of the force now collecting at Suakin, must be a matter for later consideration.

"21. The above are the main outlines of the altered dispositions rendered necessary by the fall of Khartum and the consequent alteration in the objects to be aimed at by the British army in the Sudan. I do not propose to enter into greater detail at present, and have only to add that the arrangements for supply and other preparations for an advance from this neighbourhood next autumn, are actively progressing.

"22. I have the honour to request permission to take the necessary steps for the purchase and breaking of the Egyptian and Syrian horses that will be required for mounting the four squadrons of Cavalry and two batteries of Horse Artillery I have referred to. English horses would be of no use here. At least 200 fresh horses will also be required for the 19th Hussars, and 450 for the Mounted Infantry, which regiment I consider, for tactical reasons, it is desirable to mount on horses instead of camels.

"I have, &c.,
(Signed) "WOLSELEY, General.

"The Right Hon. Marquis of Hartington."

<small>Transport and supply arrangements for the autumn.</small>

In connection with this subject the Director of Transport's memorandum on the organisation of transport for the autumn campaign is given in Appendix 56.

The following arrangements were made by Lord Wolseley for the transport and supply of the fighting force required for the intended operations in the autumn. As already shown, in the above quoted correspondence, sufficient material and rolling stock had been demanded to extend the Halfa railway to Akasheh, and afterwards to Ferkeh. It was calculated that, if the company of Madras pioneers and 200 Indian platelayers demanded were furnished, the railway would be opened to Akasheh by the middle of July, and to Ferkeh by the middle of August.

Lord Wolseley's first consideration was the transport of material for the extension. In connection with this a difficulty arose in the fact that, while the home authorities insisted that the material demanded would weigh over 20,000 tons, the most careful calculation made on the spot gave it as less than 8,000 tons.

<small>Available transport. Assiut to Wady Halfa.</small>

Lord Wolseley believed that he had sufficient transport to carry during the month of March 4,100 tons from Assiut to Assuan, and 5,000 tons from Assuan to Halfa, thus:—

Assiut to Assuan.	Tons.
Railway sleepers	2,500
Rations, English and Egyptian army	500
Ordnance stores	100
Coal	1,000
Total	4,100

Assuan to Halfa.	
The above less 100 tons of coal	4,000
Cape rolling stock, balance of	200
Camel food, rice, and native food	800
Total	5,000

CARRYING POWER ON THE NILE ROUTE. 159

Besides the railway material and coal, carriage had to be provided for a tramway, 200 tons; eight steamers and 20 barges, 1,000 tons; rations, 560 tons a month, and ordnance 100 tons a month.

The following steamers, barges, whalers, &c., were ordered from England for the autumn campaign:— *Steamers, &c., for the autumn.*

2 50-ton stern-wheelers ⎱
3 25-ton   „   „   ⎬ To be built above the 2nd cataract.
3 30-ton Thornycrofts   ⎰

1 50-ton stern-wheeler ⎱ To be built at Cairo.
2 30-ton Thornycrofts ⎰

10 25-ton steel barges, 4 15-ton ditto, 8 10-ton ditto were also ordered.

300 Whalers with gear equipment and outfit complete. Supplies, &c., to complete whalers in hand.

It was therefore further estimated that during the month of April, May, and June, the following amounts would have to be carried each month:—

Assiut to Assuan.
Railway.

	Tons.
$\dfrac{8{,}000 - 2{,}500 + 200 \text{ for tramways}}{3}$	1,900

Coal.

	Tons.
Assuan section ⎱ steamers {	550
Halfa „ ⎰ {	450
Existing railway	150
New „	300
Material for steamers, barges, &c., $\dfrac{1{,}000}{3}$ say	350
A month's supply of coal for each of these steamers in advance, at 12 tons a day, $\dfrac{12 \times 30}{3}$	120
Ordnance stores	100

Rations.

	Tons.
8,000 English	320
3,000 Egyptian	90
1,000 natives	20
1,000 camels	130
Total per month ..	4,482

Assuan to Halfa.

The same as on other section, less the
coal (*i.e.*) 4,480 — 550, say .. .. 4,000 tons.

It was believed that the carrying power on the Assuan-Halfa section was amply sufficient for the above, being about 1,450 tons per week—viz., 890 tons towing and 560 sailing. The Assuan railway was also equal to the demand that would be made on it. The only doubt was with regard to the Assiut-Assuan section; but Messrs. Cook's agent was able to satisfy the commandants of Assuan and Assiut of his ability to provide the tonnage required, and to supply Assuan garrison also. To make certain of the matter, however, Commander Hammill, R.N., was sent over the section to report on available transport. Owing to Commander Hammill's report some more steamers were ordered in April. The Government sent out 46 barges in place of the 20 ordered, but of about the same aggregate tonnage.

CHAPTER XII.

THE SUMMER QUARTERS AND EVACUATION OF THE SUDAN.

Map 1.

HAVING decided that it was inadvisable to attempt the capture of Berber before the next cold season, Lord Wolseley's first step was to select suitable camps for his troops during the approaching hot weather. For this purpose he despatched Lieutenant-Colonel Todd, R.E., and Surgeon-Major Waters, the principal sanitary officer, on the 22nd February, to report on sites suitable for camping grounds between Korti and Abu Kussi. The positions of the camps chosen by these officers were afterwards somewhat changed. *February 22nd. Selection of camps.*

The following table shows the disposition of the troops finally decided on for the summer:— *Disposition of troops for the summer.*

Station.	Detail of Troops.	Commandant.	Staff.	Remarks.
Hafir	Heavy Camel Regiment	Col. Hon. R. Talbot, Com. H.C.R.	Captain Earl of Airlie, 10th Hussars, Brigade Major.	
Dongola	100 1st Battalion Royal Sussex Regiment 1 troop 19th Hussars 2 guns 1st Battery 1st Brigade Southern division, R.A. Guards Camel Regt. 100 Transport Camels	Col. H. B. H. Blundell	Major W. F. Spaight, R.E.	Head-quarters of Lord Wolseley, General Officer Commanding Egypt.
Khandak and Shabatut	Light Camel Regiment	Lieut.-Col. H. McCalmont, Com. L.C.R.		
Bakri	Mudir's Troops			
Abu Kussi	Detachment Naval Brigade 1 Troop 19th Hussars 2 Krupp guns, Egyptian Army 1st Batt. Royal Sussex Regiment Detachment Royal Engineers Batt. Egyptian Army 100 Transport Camels	Colonel G. B. Wolseley, A.D.C.*	Major F. M. Wardrop, 3rd Dragoon Guards, D.A.A.G.	

* Colonel Wolseley left for India in May, and was succeeded by Sir O. Lanyon.

Station.	Detail of Troops.	Commandant.	Staff.	Remarks.
Kurot (3 miles below Debbeh	Detachment Naval Brigade 4 guns 1st Batt., 1st Brigade, Southern Division, R.A. 1 Troop 19th Hussars ¼ Mounted Infantry Camel Regiment Detachment, R.E. 1st Batt. Royal Irish Regiment 2nd Batt. Duke of Cornwall's Light Infantry 1st Batt. Gordon Highlanders 200 Transport Camels	Brig.-Gen. H. Brackenbury, C.B.	Lieut. J. T. St. Aubyn, Gren. Guards, A.D.C. Maj. M. Boyle, King's Royal Rifles, D.A.A.G.* Lieut.-Colonel H. E. Colvile,† Gren. Guards, D.A.A.G. (Intelligence)	Moveable Column.
Debbeh	Mudir's troops		Col. Sir. O. Lanyon, A.A.G. Major H. H. Kitchener (Intelligence) D.A.A.G.	Head-quarters of Maj.-General Sir E. Wood, V.C., Commanding Frontier Force.
Tani (7 miles) below Korti)	Detachment Naval Brigade 1 Troop 19th Hussars 4 guns Egyptian Batty. ¼ Mounted Infantry Camel Regiment Detachment R.E. 1st Batt. Royal West Kent Regiment 2nd Batt. Essex Regt. 1st Batt. South Staffordshire Regiment. 200 Transport Camels	Maj.-Gen. Hon. J. C. Dormer, C.B.	Capt. F. Rhodes, Ryl. Dragoons, A.D.C. Col. G. S. White, V.C., C.B., A.A.G. Captain B. F. Holme, East Kent Regt. D.A.A.G. Capt. W. W. C. Verner, Rifle Brigade, D.A.A.G. (Intelligence)	Moveable Column.
Ambukkol	Mudir's troops	Col. E. Leach, R. W. Kent Regt.		
Korti	Black troops from Khartum	Com. J. A. Baker, B.N.	Lieut. W. R. Doran, Royal Irish Regt. Staff Officer	
Abu Dom	Detachment Naval Brigade 1 Troop 19th Hussars 1st Batt. Royal Highlanders Detachment R.E. Egyptian Camel Corps 2 guns Egyptian Battery 100 Transport Camels	Col. W. F. Butler, C.B.	Lieut. D. V. Pirie, 1st Life Guards, Staff Officer. Major J. H. Sandwith, Royal Marines, D.A.A.G. Major F. G. Slade, R.A., D.A.A.G. (Intelligence)	
Hamdab	Mudir's troops			

* Died of enteric fever in April, and was succeeded by Major Morgan Crofton, 1st Battalion South Staffordshire Regiment.
† Transferred to Merowi in May.

STAFF. 163

The Staff and Stations of the Line of Communications were as follows :—

Station.	Names of Staff.	Appointment.
Head-quarters Line of Communications.	Brigadier-General F. Grenfell... Colonel C. F. Clery, C.B. Colonel T. Fraser, C.M.G., E.A. Major H. H. Settle, E.A. Major E. A. Grove, Royal Wst. Kent Regt. Captain D. P. Chapman, E.A.	General of Communications. Deputy Adjutant-General. Assistant Adjutant-General. Deputy Assist. Adjutant-General. ,, ,, ,, ,, ,, ,, ,, ,,
Cairo	Lieut.-Col. J. C. Ardagh, C.B., R.E. Major E. T. H. Hutton, King's Royal Rifles Capt. H. C. Sclater, R.A.	Commandant at the base. Deputy Assist. Adjutant-General. ,, ,, ,, ,,
Assiut	Lieut.-Col. E. T. Lloyd, R.A. ... Lieut. H. A. MacDonald, Gord. Highs. Lieut. W. T. Bourke, R.N.	Commandant. Garrison Adjutant. Naval Transport Officer.
Luxor	Captain F. B. Briggs, Yorks. Regt. ...	Commandant.
Assuan	Colonel Henderson, King's Ryl. Rifles Captain H. Bowles, Yorks Regt. Capt. H. S. Fleming, Essex Regt. Captain H. A, Yorke, R.E., D.A.A.G. Lieut. H. N. Dumbleton, R.E. Lieut. C. Reeve, R.N. ...	Commandant. Staff Officer. Railway Staff Officer. Traffic Manager. Royal Engineer Officer. Naval Transport Officer.
Shellal	Col. H. Parr, C.M.G., E.A. Lieut. H. W. Lovett, E.A. Lieut. C. Napier, R.N. ...	Commandant. Staff Officer. Naval Transport Officer.
Korosko	Colonel J. M. Leith, C.B., Cameron Highlanders Lieut. J. S. Ewart, Cameron Highrs. Major H. M. L. Rundle, E.A. ...	Commandant. Staff Officer. Intelligence Officer.
Halfa	Col. F. Duncan, E.A. ... Capt. H. H. Mathias, Gordon Hghrs.... Captain Maberly, R.A. Commander T. Hammil, R.N. Lieut. E. G. Barton, R.N. Major Mulloy, R.E.	Commandant. Staff Officer. Officer Commanding Depôt. Naval Transport Officer. ,, ,, ,, Engineer Officer.
Railhead	Major J. H. Wodehouse, E.A.... Capt. A. J. W. Allen, East Kent Regt. Lieut. H. St. L. Wood, E.A. ... Lieut. F. R. Gregson, 3rd Batt. Derby Regt.	Commandant. Transport train. ,, ,, ,, ,,
Akasheh	Captain H. A. Coles, E.A.	Commandant.
Dal ...	Lieut.-Col. A. S. Wynne, E.A. Captain Lloyd, E.A. Major J. A. Man, 3rd Batt. Gordon Highlanders.	Officer Commanding District Commandant. Staff Officer.

(S.C.2)   M

Station.	Detail of Staff.	Appointment.
Absarat	Officer commanding	Commandant.
Kajbar	Lieut.-Colonel Trotter, E.A. Captain T. P. B. Ternan, E.A.	Commandant. Staff Officer.
Abu Fatmeh	Lieut.-Col. J. F. Maurice, R.A. Lieut. W. F. Peel, 2nd Life Guards Captain J. F. Brocklehurst, Royal Horse Guards	Commandant. Staff Officer. Officer Commanding moveable remount depôt.

Fatmeh, the advanced post of line communications.

For convenience of administration during the summer, and to avoid, as far as possible, the white ants, which were so terribly destructive at Dongola, the advanced post of the line of communications was at Abu Fatmeh; and there ordnance and commissariat depôts were formed. The supply of the fighting or frontier force, was supervised by the Headquarters Staff, which took up its quarters for the summer at Dongola.

Troops in quarters. Arrangements in case of a hostile advance.

On the 1st April, 1885, the troops were all located in the summer quarters in which they were to await the autumn campaign.

It will have been noticed that in the table of distribution given above, parts of the force are marked as "moveable columns." These columns were organised so as to be ready to move at the shortest notice, and attack the enemy anywhere within the zone in which it was thought possible that he might make his appearance during the summer. It was assumed that any movement required to be executed by these columns would be along the Nile, and that the whalers in possession of these columns would be sufficient for that purpose. The camel transport was, however, of course kept in as efficient a state as possible, and Sir E. Wood, whose command included all the troops from Hamdab to Abu Kussi inclusive, was authorised to purchase locally sufficient camels to complete the Kurot and Debbeh columns to 200 baggage and 100 riding camels each. The camels of the movable columns were also ordered to be carefully inspected, and those not likely to be fit for work by the 1st of August, were to be hired out to graze on the opposite bank of the Nile, or if this could not be arranged, to be sent to Railhead, where they could be fed at about half the cost of their subsistence above Dongola.

Sir E. Wood was instructed that the first consideration was to be the complete and rapid annihilation of any enemy

HUTTING.

reaching the Nile or its vicinity between Abu Kussi and Merowi; as every hour that the enemy was allowed to remain unmolested after his desert march, would be an important gain to him. His immediate destruction was therefore to be carried out at all risk to health.

The second consideration was the preservation of the men's health, by saving them from exposure to the sun in every possible way, by providing them with good cool airy huts and with bedsteads, and by supplying them, as far as possible, with amusement and occupation for mind and body.

The first of these considerations never had to be acted on, as no portion of the enemy's forces approached nearer to our posts than Dukeiyat, and then only in a very small body, which was dispersed by the Mudir's troops.

The second was carried out, as far as occupation and shelter was concerned, by employing the troops in building their own huts. These, as will be seen by an extract from Captain Barker's report on hutting (Appendix 57), were of a variety of forms and patterns. The mud or mud-brick huts require no special description. The plan and sketch given below, give a good idea of the better class of straw hut with a verandah. *Huts built by the troops.*

The mats at the sides of the hut were made of long straw, with palm branches running down their entire length at intervals. The leaves of the palm protruded at the top of the mats.

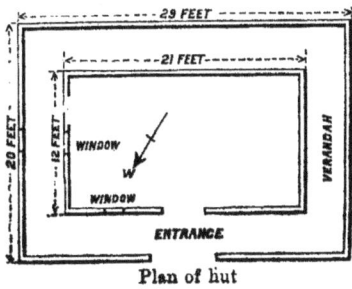

Plan of hut

Bedsteads were found in all the villages in considerable quantities, and the natives were glad to sell them. They consisted of a rough framework of mimosa poles, supported on four uprights, and covered with interlaced palm fibre ropes; they answered the purpose of keeping the men off the ground, but were mostly far too short for comfort.

Sir E. Wood was also instructed to make every endeavour during the summer, to collect as many provisions as possible at the stations under his command, and to economise wood and endeavour to collect a store of it, with a view to the advance on Khartum in the autumn.

In order to prevent commandants competing against each other in their purchases, districts were, for supply purposes, assigned to each station, and officers purchasing were ordered to confine their purchases to their own districts. Markets were also established outside the various camps, which were largely attended by the natives, and were a great convenience to the men of the force. A list of prices had been fixed by the Chief of the Staff on the 16th March, and Officers commanding districts were informed that the prices were to be the same for all districts, and were not to be exceeded without authority from headquarters.

March 30th. Departure of Lord Wolseley for Cairo.

On completion of the location of all the troops in their summer quarters, Lord Wolseley left Dongola for Cairo, as a more convenient situation for directing the two forces at Suakin and up the Nile, which were then under his command. He arrived at Cairo on the 11th of April. The Chief of the Staff remained at Dongola.

April 3rd, Departure of Mudir.

On the 3rd of April the Mudir of Dongola was despatched to Cairo, his obstructiveness having made his presence unbearable. The following extract from the diary of the Chief of the Staff of the 12th of April shows the improvement immediately caused by this step:—

"To show the difference due to the presence and absence of the Mudir of Dongola, one instance may be quoted, there are many such.

"When the Mudir was here, it was almost impossible to obtain poles for huts, and the few that were obtained were charged for at an exorbitant rate. Since the Mudir left, the Vakil has told us of a Government preserve, about seven miles from Dongola, where we have cut, in a few days, all we require. Endeavours are being made to reduce the price to which the Mudir has raised all articles."

ORDERS FOR RETIREMENT.

On the 13th of April the Secretary of State for War telegraphed to Lord Wolseley that in the then condition of Imperial affairs it was probable that the expedition to Khartum might have to be abandoned, and the troops brought back to Egypt as soon as possible. Lord Wolseley was directed to consider what measures, in that case, should be taken for the safe withdrawal of the troops.

April 13th. Lord Wolseley informed that expedition to Khartum would probably be abandoned.

On the 21st of April, it was announced in the House of Commons, that it was not intended to undertake any further offensive operation in the Sudan, or to advance on Khartum; and on the 6th of May the General of Communications was warned that the evacuation might take place. On the 11th of May, Lord Wolseley, instructed by the Secretary of State for War, ordered the withdrawal of the troops from the Sudan.

April 21st. Orders for retirement.

As it was certain that anarchy would immediately follow our withdrawal, and probable that a retreat on our part would allow the dormant hostility of the natives to find vent, it was necessary that the retreat, especially of the advanced portion of the force, should be conducted as rapidly and unexpectedly as possible. Jaudet Effendi, the Vakil of Dongola, who had taken the place of the deposed Mudir, was at once informed of the intended retreat. He begged for 15 days' start, before our policy was made generally known, in order that he might take what steps he could, to mitigate the murder and rapine for which he believed our retirement would be the signal. This was granted him, and he at once started up the river, and the movement was arranged to commence on the 21st of May.

Steps taken to secure quiet in district of Dongola.

Before the evacuation took place, Sir E. Wood left for Cairo to appear before a medical board and was succeeded in command of the frontier force by General Dormer.

General Dormer assumes command.

On the 12th May (the date on which he received orders to withdraw) the Chief of the Staff issued the instructions to the principal medical officer for the withdrawal of the sick which are given in Appendix 58.

Instructions for withdrawal of sick.

From a report of health furnished by the principal medical officer on the 13th May it appears that, of a total strength of 6,825 officers, non-commissioned officers and men, distributed between Abu Fatmeh and Merowi, there were 421 in hospital on that date.

The following table shows the manner in which the retreat of the fighting force was carried out:—

The retreat from above Abu Kussi.

May 21st.—65 whalers started from Tani to Merowi to bring down stores.*

„ 22nd.—Whalers *en route* from Tani to Merowi.

„ 23rd.—80 whalers left Kurot for Tani to bring down stores.

„ 23rd.—65 whalers from Tani arrived at Merowi.

„ 24th.—65 whalers from Tani started on return journey.

„ 25th.—Colonel Colvile with Mudir's troops left Tani.

„ 25th.—65 whalers from Merowi arrived at Tani.

„ 25th.—80 whalers from Kurot arrived at Tani.

„ 26th.—Commander Baker, R.N., and black troops left Korti and marched to Tani.

„ 26th.—Merowi evacuated.

„ 26th.—80 whalers from Kurot started on return journey from Tani.

„ 27th.—Troops from Merowi reached Tani, after which the Black Watch went on independently. Three days' rations were issued to troops marching.

„ 27th.—80 whalers arrived at Kurot from Tani.

„ 28th.—Tani evacuated. Troops bivouacked between Tani and Debbeh.

„ 28th.—Mudir's troops arrived at Debbeh.

„ 29th.—Merowi and Tani troops arrived at Debbeh.

„ 30th.—Marching column halted for the day.†

„ 30th.—Troops in whalers left Debbeh.†

„ 30th.—Black troops arrived at Abu Kussi, drew six days' rations, and were crossed to the right bank to keep them apart from the Mudir's troops, with whom they were on bad terms.

„ 31st.—General Dormer's headquarters, and troops, evacuated Debbeh.

---

* All the stores of the River Column having been left at Merowi for the autumn campaign, that station had more stores than the whalers there could carry

† All mounted and native troops marched, and all dismounted troops and Infantry went in whalers.

ARRANGEMENTS FOR EVACUATION.

May 31st.—Marching column picked up mounted party at Kurot, and proceeded to Abu Kussi, where it drew three days' rations.

June 1st.—Troops in whalers left Kurot by regiments independently.

" 1st.—Abu Kussi evacuated.

The mounted troops during this movement were under command of Colonel Butler, who picked up those at each station that he passed.

The numbers who marched from the stations south of Dongola northwards, were approximately as follows:—

From	British	Egyptian Army and Natives.
Merowi	74	155
Tani	185	199
Korti	2	257
Debbeh	—	154
Kurot	252	93
Abu Kussi	75	386
	588	1,244

General Dormer was directed to proceed to Fatmeh on the evacuation of Debbeh, and General Brackenbury to proceed to Dongola on the evacuation of Kurot. On the 23rd of May, General Dormer was directed to proceed direct to Cairo to resume his position of Chief of the Staff to Sir F. Stephenson, and Colonel R. Grant, C.R.E., was appointed commandant of the Fatmeh district.

The inhabitants during the progress of the retreat behaved very well, but reproached the British bitterly for deserting them and withdrawing all government. Many appeared anxious to leave, but were restrained by the knowledge that, should they do so, they must abandon the whole of their property. Others were prevented by inability to procure sufficient transport for their families and effects.

On evacuating the various stations, the forts and all buildings capable of defence were destroyed. Such stores, as bedsteads, &c., as it was useless to take away, were given to those natives who had assisted us most.

Destruction of forts.

Appointment of civil governors for the abandoned districts.

In order, as far as possible, to mitigate the anarchy consequent on our withdrawal, civil governors were appointed in each district. The men chosen were the descendants of the old ruling families deposed by Mehemet Ali in 1821. Of these, Mohammed Wad Kinnaish of Belal, a Shaikiyeh, was appointed Governor of the Merowi district; Said Agha, Kashif of Debbeh, Governor of the old Dongola district; and Mohammed Tumbul, Governor of the northern portion of the province of Dongola. Of these men Wad Kinnaish declared that he only accepted the post from a sense of duty, and did so at the peril of his life. The day after the evacuation of Merowi he proceeded to Khartum, made his submission to the Mahdi, and fought against us at Ginnis. Said Agha said little, but when the Dervishes came down he took to his bed, and feigned sickness. Tumbul announced his impatience for the arrival of the Mahdi, who, with his whole force, he promised to annihilate. On the arrival of the first Dervish in the province of Dongola, he and his followers beat a precipitate retreat to our outposts.

Withdrawal of civil employés.

Besides the troops to be withdrawn, provision had to be made for a large number of Government *employés* and loyal natives who could not be left behind, and who, the troops having taken up nearly the whole available means of transport, had to be carried north, with their effects and families. The organisation of this evacuation of refugees was entrusted to Major Turner, R.A., D.A.A.G. The refugees reached a total of 12,708, every one of them was naturally anxious to avoid leaving behind a single article of his or her household effects, and each clamoured long and loudly for ten times as many camels as could possibly be spared. Food for these refugees had also to be provided along the line of retreat, and diahbiehs for their conveyance from Halfa to Egypt.

The arrangements for the evacuation north of Abu Fatmeh were conducted by General Grenfell, General of Communications. The manner in which this movement was conducted is best shown in the reports which are given in Appendix 59.

June 17th. Rear-guard entrusted to General Brackenbury. His orders.

On the 17th June the Chief of the Staff left Dongola *en route* for Cairo. The command of the rear guard was then entrusted to General Brackenbury, to whom the following orders were issued :—

ARRANGEMENTS FOR EVACUATION.

"Brigadier-General Brackenbury,

"1. In accordance with instructions received from Lord Wolseley, I proceed to-morrow for Fatmeh *en route* for Halfa.

"2. Lord Wolseley wishes you to remain and come down with the last of the rear guard.

"3. Captain Boardman, R.N., remains here in charge of the steamers and pinnaces. His orders are to take the steamers to Akasheh, and such of the pinnaces as are worth it to Sarras, thence by rail to Halfa, and thence to Alexandria.

"4. I am, however, endeavouring to make an arrangement with Koki, the Sheikh of the 2nd Cataract, to take the boats down. If I succeed I will inform you.*

"5. You will on the way down give Captain Boardman any assistance he may ask for.

"6. Major Turner, D.A.A.G., Intelligence Department, has been managing all our relations with the natives, and all matters connected with refugees. I have directed him to remain here till you leave, he will then march by the west bank to Halfa, accompanied by the present acting Vakil, Talaat Bey, and a native escort which he now has; he will sweep in any stray refugees, redress any grievances, and generally arrange native affairs as he comes down.

"7. Lieutenant-Colonel Colvile, D.A.A.G., Intelligence, will in a similar manner march down the east bank, with the rear guard of the Mudir's troops, and execute similar functions on that bank. He will be accompanied by Ali Bey Rita, the commander of the Mudir's forces. As the Mudir's troops are now being ferried over, and preparing for a start, it is desirable that you should let Colonel Colvile go, when he reports himself ready.

"8. Major Turner has instructions to hand over the civil government of this province to Tumbul, Melik of Arko, who is hourly expected here for that purpose.

"9. You are aware of the general spirit of the instructions which have regulated this movement hitherto, and to which you are still to conform, namely, that there is to be no destruction of stores whatever, but that everything that is at all worth transport is to be taken down, and that the troops are to be withdrawn as speedily as the stores can be cleared out.

"10. As you are aware, Brigadier-General Grenfell is here-

* This arrangement was made, Koki being promised a bonus if he brought down the whole of the pinnaces safely, and agreeing to pay a fine, if he wrecked any, or lost any lives.

after to command the troops up Nile; it is therefore desirable that you should, so far as is convenient, consult with him, before giving a decision on any matter affecting the future of that force.

"11. The one question that I have not yet been able satisfactorily to arrange for, is the provision of camel transport for the 19th Hussars; as to this I will telegraph to you from Fatmeh or Abri.

"12. You will report all movements of troops daily by telegraph to me, and should there be any deaths you will report them by telegraph to the Commandant of the Base, Cairo.

"13. Telegrams will reach me on the 19th at Fatmeh, the 20th, 21st, 22nd at Abri, whence I will send you another address.

"By order,
"REDVERS BULLER, Major-General.

"Dongola, 17th June, 1885."

Arrangements made by him.

On the 23rd June General Brackenbury was informed by telegram, that the following further arrangements had been made for his movement.

On arrival at Fatmeh he was to send down Colonels Grant and Maurice, Major Wardrop, and all other officers not required for the rear guard.

As soon as Fatmeh was clear of stores and boats he was to proceed northwards, keeping as an absolute rear guard, the Royal West Kent Regiment and the troop of 19th Hussars intended for Halfa.

He was to see that Kajbar and all rest camps south of Abri was clear of troops, stores, and boats before passing them.

On arrival at Abri he was to hand over to General Grenfell the command of the rear guard, and proceed himself with his staff to Cairo.

On the 24th June, General Brackenbury acquainted Colonel Grant with these orders, and asked him to state as soon as he could do so with certainty, on what day he could undertake to leave Fatmeh clear of all stores and to have transport available for the mounted troops to march down.

Colonel Grant was requested to work the evacuation of his troops on the following lines :

Supposing that Fatmeh could be clear of stores and that

the camels would be available on the 30th June, he was to cross over his cavalry and guns from Hafir on the 29th, and send them on to Halfa on the 30th, General Brackenbury sending his squadron and guns from Dongola on the 28th, to relieve the others at Hafir on the 29th. These were to cross on the 30th, and march to Halfa, except one troop, which was to remain at Fatmeh as part of the actual rear guard till 1st July.

The half battalion of the South Staffordshire Regiment at Fatmeh, was to go down in its boats on the 30th, on being relieved by the rear guard, and the half battalion at Hafir on the same day as soon as the cavalry and guns had all crossed. Thus, by the afternoon of the 30th, or whatever day Colonel Grant named, Hafir would be empty, and all troops, except the rear guard, would have cleared out of Fatmeh.

General Brackenbury had orders to wait at Fatmeh till all the steamers, pinnaces, and nuggers had been passed down the Hannek Cataract, and Captain Boardman did not expect the river to be high enough for this before the 10th or 15th of July. As there were only rations for his force till the 16th July, he requested Colonel Grant to leave behind—

10 days' rations for 750 men, and
15 „ „ „ 65 horses,
15 „ „ „ 25 camels,

in order to provide against the possibility of his being further delayed.

Colonel Grant replied that he could clear out of Fatmeh on the 30th June as suggested, and the arrangements proposed were being carried out when Mr. Gladstone's ministry was replaced by that of Lord Salisbury. As Lord Wolseley had from the first protested against the precipitate retreat ordered from home, as prejudicial to the interest of England and Egypt, he was encouraged in a hope that it might still be countermanded, by a telegram from the new Secretary of State for War, enquiring how far it had been carried out. He therefore telegraphed on the 26th June detaining the troops at Dongola till further orders, and to endeavour to complete his supplies with local purchases to the end of July. On the demand by the Secretary of State for War for his view on the situation in Egypt, and the best course to be taken, Lord Wolseley replied that he believed that, if the then policy of retreat were persisted in, the Mahdi would

June 26th. Proposed re-occupation.

Lord Wolseley's views on the abandonment of the Sudan.

steadily become stronger and stronger, and we should have to increase our garrison and submit to the indignity of being threatened by him, and eventually have to fight him for our position in Egypt with a population around us ready to rise against us at the slightest reverse.* He therefore advised that the autumn campaign up the Nile should be carried out as originally intended, and that the Guards should be sent up the Nile. He pointed out that a retreat, such as that then in progress, from a province where few local supplies were to be had, and whence all military stores had to be brought away, was an operation requiring the nicest calculation, and therefore begged that he might have immediate notice of any intended change of plan.

Difficulties of proposed re-occupation. Lord Wolseley also telegraphed to Sir R. Buller informing him of the correspondence which had taken place, and asking for his report on the possibilities of re-occupation. Sir R. Buller replied that, much as he wished to remain, he thought that the difficulties of re-occupation were so great that it would be better not to go back, but to continue the retirement as far as Akasheh, and then wait till fresh supplies could be collected, as he found that the evacuation was too nearly complete for the past Nile Expedition to be in any sense revived, and that if it was intended to hold Dongola, a new expedition would have to be organised for the purpose.

Position of force at this time. It may be interesting to show the position of the force at this time.

Dongola.

1st Battalion Royal West Kent Regiment.
1 Squadron, 19th Hussars.
2 Guns 1st Battery, 1st Brigade, Southern Division, Royal Artillery.

Hafir.

2 Companies, 1st Battalion South Staffordshire Regiment.
1 Squadron, 19th Hussars.

---

* In spite of the death of Mohammed Ahmed, a Mahdist force, having Cairo for its objective, advanced to the Egyptian frontier in December, 1885, and invested the British fort at Kosheh for forty days, and had to be attacked at Ginnis on the 30th December, 1885. In consequence of this movement the British garrison up the Nile had to be increased by 6,947 men, and the whole force in Egypt had to be augmented by 2,893 men, from the Mediterranean and India.

2 Guns 1st Battery, 1st Brigade, Southern Division, Royal Artillery.

Fatmeh.

2 Companies, 1st Battalion South Staffordshire Regiment.

Kubudeh.

Commander Baker's black troops; and the 9th Battalion Egyptian Army, total strength about 600, broken up into whaler crews, forming the Fatmeh-Kajbar transport.

Shaban.

4 Companies, 1st Battalion South Staffordshire Regiment.

Kajbar.

500 Egyptian troops, mostly employed in whalers.

On march between Kajbar and Abri.

1 Squadron, 19th Hussars.
2 Guns 1st Battery, 1st Brigade, Southern Division, Royal Artillery.

Abri.

Small Egyptian garrison.

Dal.

Small Egyptian garrison.

Akasheh.

500 Egyptian troops.
300 1st Battalion Royal Sussex Regiment (on march to Halfa).

On Halfa-Akasheh Railway.

400 Egyptian troops.

Halfa.

Mounted Infantry Camel Regiment.

4 Companies, 2nd Battalion Duke of Cornwall's Light Infantry.
2 Egyptian Camel Batteries.
Egyptian Camel Corps.

Between Halfa and Assuan.

Half, Light Camel Regiment.

Assuan.

1st Battalion, Yorkshire Regiment.
4 Companies, 1st Battalion Royal Sussex Regiment.
Headquarters 26th Company Royal Engineers.

North of Assuan.

	Date of leaving Assuan.
1st Battalion Black Watch (arrived Cairo 27th June)	17th June
2nd Battalion Essex Regiment	18th „
1st Battalion Gordon Highlanders	22nd „
1st Battalion Royal Irish Regiment, half battalion	24th „
1st Battalion Royal Irish Regiment, half battalion	27th „
Guards' Camel Regiment	22nd „
Half, Light Camel Regiment	24th „
Half battalion, Duke of Cornwall's Light Infantry	27th „
Heavy Camel Regiment	27th „

Supplies available in June.

There were at Abri and south of it about three months rations for the troops then south of Abri, but forage was deficient, and most of the hospital equipment and stores had already passed to the north of Abri. Major Turner, who was then at Dongola, and who was consulted on the subject, reported that all accounts agreed that the country could not supply meat or grain to any extent before December, that the small autumn crop due in ninety days might keep off famine, but that all reports showed that this was the most that could be hoped for, that vegetable culture had gone very much to the bad, owing to the number of men employed by us and the large numbers who had left their sakiehs and gone down as refugees.

In consequence of these reports Her Majesty's Government decided that the retreat ordered by their predecessors was to be continued to a point which, in Lord Wolseley's judgment, provided for the safety of Egypt; but they stated that they were not prepared to abandon the railway, which was to be completed. Decision to continue retreat.

This decision was conveyed to Lord Wolseley in a telegram from the Secretary of State for War on the 1st July, and in the following despatch:— July 1st. Lord Wolseley informed of this decision by the Secretary of State.

"*War Office, 2nd July,* 1885.

"My Lord,

"Her Majesty's Government have had under their consideration your telegrams noted in the margin, relating to the present position of the troops on the Nile, and the possibility of arresting the retreat ordered by their predecessors.

"They were deeply impressed with the absolute unanimity which prevailed on the part of all the authorities in Egypt, both civil and military, as to the importance to the peace and security of Egypt of the retention by the Egyptian Government of the province of Dongola.

"So far as Her Majesty's Government can gather, a government existed there which appeared to be adequate for the maintenance of order over a large tract of country, and which from its natural features formed a valuable bulwark against any attack on Egypt by such forces as would be at all likely to attempt such an undertaking.

"There was also at Dongola itself, and in more or less degree at other places in the province, a settled population and a certain amount of trade and commerce.

"This state of things had been put an end to by the decision of the late Government, and Her Majesty's present Government had only to consider what it was possible to do in the existing circumstances.

"They found on taking office that the retreat on Assuan was in full operation, that the supplies of the country had been exhausted, the civil population to the number of 12,800 removed to Egypt, and that stores and supplies necessary for the maintenance of Her Majesty's troops for the limited period during which it was calculated they would be in the province, were all that remained.

"In these circumstances they were advised by you, that to occupy the province of Dongola would require a fresh expedition of considerable magnitude, and the employment in Egypt of a larger body of men than by your despatch of the 27th May, you had stated to be adequate to its protection for the present.

"They also gather that Major-General Sir R. Buller, with a full knowledge of the whole situation and the resources of the province, is of the same opinion, and, moreover, considers that it is not possible to hold Dongola with the troops now there.

"Her Majesty's Government, after a full consideration of all the circumstances, were not prepared to reverse the orders given by their predecessors by countermanding the retreat of the force of Dongola, but they considered that it was desirable for the defence of Egypt that the railway from Wady Halfa to Ferkeh, the completion of which had been decided upon, and the material provided, and which they were advised, was absolutely necessary in the event of any forward movement having to be made to meet any dangers threatening Egypt from the south, should not be abandoned.

"This decision was conveyed to you in my telegram of the 1st instant.

"Her Majesty's Government will be glad to confer with you, as to any further orders which it may be advisable to give for the adequate defence of the frontier of Egypt, and they wish you to return to this country for this purpose as soon as your duties in Egypt permit.

"Meantime the instructions which I have now given you will, probably be sufficient for the moment.

"I have, &c.,
(Signed) "W. H. SMITH.

"General Lord Wolseley, K.P., G.C.B.
Egypt."

Decision to hold railroad. In consequence of this decision Lord Wolseley made arrangements to hold the head of the railway at Akasheh with a Sudanese battalion of the Egyptian army, and, in informing the Secretary of State for War of this arrangement, he strongly urged that the extension of the railway to Ferkeh on which a considerable amount of work had already been done, should be completed, as a line as far as that point would turn all the worst cataracts and make easy any forward movements, should they be necessary. The railway was not completed to Akasheh till the 7th of August.

On the 2nd July General Brackenbury was ordered to continue the evacuation which had been interrupted on the 26th June, and on the 5th July he evacuated Dongola, bringing with him all whalers, stores, and steamers.

July 5th. Evacuation of Dongola.

CHAPTER XIII.

THE SUAKIN EXPEDITION.

<small>Maps 9 and 10.</small>

<small>February 17th, 1885. Contract for railway.</small> On the 17th February, 1885, Her Majesty's Government made a contract with Messrs. Lucas and Aird to construct a railway, of 4 feet 8½ inches gauge, from Suakin to Berber. The contractors agreed that the control, the works, and the direction of the line, should be under the General Officer Commanding, they being only responsible for labour, materials, and construction. The Government reserved to themselves the power of stopping the construction at any section.

<small>February 20th. Sir G. Graham appointed to command. His instructions.</small> On the 20th February, Sir G. Graham was appointed to the command of the Suakin Field Force, and received the instructions conveyed in the following letter from the Secretary of State for War:—

20th February, 1885.

" Sir,

" On arrival at Suakin to take command of the Force which will shortly be assembled there, you will make the best arrangements—which the shortness of the time at your disposal, before the hot weather commences, admits of — to organize a field force, and to make such transport arrangements as are possible to enable it to secure the first and most pressing object of the campaign on which you are about to enter—viz., the destruction of the power of Osman Digna.

" Owing to the short time which has been available for the collection of transport, it may probably happen that your troops may arrive before your transport is ready for them. In such case, you are authorized to detain the whole or any part of them at Suez until you are ready to receive them at Suakin, or whatever other point on the coast you may decide upon for the commencement of your operations.

" You are aware that an agreement has been made with an eminent firm of contractors (Messrs. Lucas and Aird) to construct a railway from Suakin to Berber, and on this you must greatly rely for your means of transporting supplies.

"It will therefore be of the first importance that every possible facility should be given to Messrs Lucas and Aird in the conduct of their operations.

"Your first object, as I have stated, is the destruction of Osman Digna's power, and to effect this you will, as early as possible, proceed to attack all the positions which he occupies, and to disperse the troops defending them.

"When this has been done you will then arrange for the military occupation of the Hadendowa territory, lying near the Suakin-Berber road. You will, probably, find it necessary to hold Tokar and also some position in and near Sinkat. It may be found that the Native Infantry from India will be best suited for those places, and also for the small garrison, which need then alone be kept in Suakin itself.

"The mountainous part of the Berber road, from a little beyond Tambuk Wells, to a distance of about 60 or 70 miles beyond, should be held, so far as the progress of the railway and the transport at your disposal enable you, by strong British detachments.

"It is to be hoped that good, healthy positions in the mountains may be found there for British Troops.

"The pushing on of the railway from Suakin towards Berber is the next point to which you will direct the greatest attention; but until the districts above mentioned have been entirely pacified, it will probably not be possible to push the line beyond Tambuk Wells.

"To cover the advance along the Berber line, the sooner Ariab can be occupied and held the better. Every effort should be made to clear out the wells, and increase the water supply there.

"If Berber is not taken this summer by Lord Wolseley, the railway cannot be pushed much beyond Ariab, and there, all the railway plant and material necessary for the 100 miles between it and Berber, should be collected as soon as possible, so that the advance, when the cool weather begins, and Berber is taken, may be made at once.

"During the hot weather of summer it is not advisable that a larger European force than is necessary for the occupation of the zone of country already mentioned, and the perfect protection of the railway line, should be kept exposed to the trying climate of the Soudan. Any force not required for this purpose might be sent during the extreme summer heats to the neighbourhood of Suez. On this point you will use your discretion.

"You will consider yourself under the orders of General Lord Wolseley, Commanding in Egypt, and you will place yourself in direct telegraphic communication with him.

"You will report all operations to Lord Wolseley, transmitting copies by post and telegraph direct to the Secretary of State for War.

"Within the limits of the above instructions you have perfect discretionary powers to conduct operations in any manner which you deem best.

"I have, &c.,
"(Signed) HARTINGTON."

Force available previous to the assembling of the Suakin Field Force.

Previous to the assembling of the Suakin Field Force, the following troops had been stationed there:—*

Officers.	Non-commissioned officers and men.	Horses.	Followers.	Mules and Ponies.	Camels.
109	2,526	187	63	28	339

Detachment of 19th Hussars.
G Battery, B Brigade, Royal Horse Artillery.
17th Company Royal Engineers.
2nd Battalion East Surrey Regiment.
1st Battalion Berkshire Regiment.
Royal Marines.
Detachment Mounted Infantry.
Detachment Medical Staff Corps.
Detachments Ordnance Store and Commissariat and Transport.

Major-General Sir G. R. Greaves, K.C.M.G., &c., was appointed Chief of the Staff to Sir G. Graham, and the British troops were organised as follows:—

Organization of the British troops.

Cavalry Brigade, under Colonel H. P. Ewart, C.B.
2 squadrons 5th Lancers.
2   ,,   20th Hussars.

---

* With the exception of the Royal Marines and a small proportion of Departmental Corps, these troops had arrived at Suakin between the 23rd January, 1885, and the beginning of March.

A battalion of Mounted Infantry. (4 Companies).

Artillery under Lieutenant-Colonel S. J. Nicholson, R.A.
G/B., R.H.A. (13 prs.).
5/1, Sc.D., R.A. (Mountain Battery, 7-pr. screw guns).
6/1, Sc.D., R.A.

Guard's Brigade, under Major-General A. J. Lyon-Fremantle.
3rd Battalion Grenadier Guards.
1st " Coldstream "
2nd " Scots "

Second Brigade, under Major-General Sir J. C. McNeill, V.C., K.C.B., &c.
2nd Battalion East Surrey Regiment.
1st " Shropshire Light Infantry.
1st " Berkshire Regiment.
Battalion of Royal Marines.

The Royal Engineers consisted of the 17th and 24th Field Companies, 10th Railway Company, two telegraph sections and a balloon detachment, and the Commissariat and Transport Corps of the 3rd, 5th, 7th, and 12th Companies. The 17th Company arrived later.

On the 8th February, *i.e.*, previous to the appointment of Sir G. Graham, it was decided to send an Indian Brigade to Suakin, to hold that place through the summer; and a telegram was sent to the Viceroy of India to that effect. *Indian Brigade. Its composition.*

Steps were immediately taken for the despatch of the Brigade, which was composed as follows:—

	Date of Departure from India.
15th Sikhs	22nd February.
9th Bengal Cavalry ..	23rd and 27th February.
17th Bengal Infantry ..	24th February.
28th Bombay Infantry ..	28th February and 1st March.
1 Company Madras Sappers	2nd March.

The whole under the command of Brigadier-General J. Hudson, C.B., Bengal Staff Corps.

The Brigade sailed complete with three months' supplies and all camp equipment and regimental transport. The whole force amounted to 3,000 men.

On the 15th February the Government of New South Wales telegraphed to Her Majesty's Government, offering *New South Wales contingent.*

to send to Suakin a force, consisting of two batteries of artillery, and a battalion of infantry 500 strong. This offer was accepted by the English Government, with the exception of the second battery of artillery. 9-pr. guns were sent out from home for the field battery, its 16-prs. having been left behind in Australia, as too heavy for the work. The force arrived at Suakin on the 29th March, its total strength being 26 officers and 604 non-commissioned officers and men. The entire force under Sir G. Graham amounted to about 13,000.

In addition to the actual Indian Brigade, the following corps, &c., were supplied by the Indian Government for duty with the British Force at Suakin :—

Animals, &c., supplied by the Indian Government.

6,000 Camels (for baggage only, equipped with suletahs and proper proportion of headmen and drivers), in two corps of 3,000 each. The second of these corps was not completed.

500 Riding camels (complete with saddles and proportion of attendants).

150 Ponies for mounted infantry (complete with saddles, bridles, and spare materials for repairs).

Corps of camel drivers, 1,500 (or rather 2,050, allowing for proportion of headmen and percentage for replacement of casualties), for camels purchased at Suakin.

Corps of muleteers, 300 strong.

Corps of Bhistis, 300 strong.

Corps of dhooly bearers, 500 strong, with 100 Lushai dandies.

Corps of labourers, 900 strong, of whom 400 were to be specially adapted for railway work.

The requisitions for these various corps were received by the Government of India between the 11th and 21st February, 1885, and with so good effect was exertion made for expediting the collection of animals, and recruiting men, that by the 5th April the whole of the force had been embarked and despatched from India, complete in every respect, under Lieutenant-Colonel S. Beckett. Appendix 60 shows these corps in detail.

Arrival of Sir G. Graham.

On the 12th March, Sir G. Graham arrived at Suakin, and took over the command. General Lyon-Fremantle had been in command during the winter. Sir G. Greaves and Sir J. McNeill had already reached Suakin before Sir G. Graham's arrival.

The Staff of the Suakin Field Force is given in detail in Appendix 61.

In Appendix 62 is given an embarkation table showing

WATER SUPPLY.

in detail the numbers in the different transports and dates of reaching Suakin, in the order in which the troops arrived.

On the 13th March (the day after Sir G. Graham's arrival) Messrs. Lucas and Aird began laying the railway. *March 13th. Commencement of railway.*

The work of disembarkation of men, animals, supplies, and stores, the formation of camps, the completion of the defences, the arrangements for the water supply, and the general organisation of the force, was at first very heavy on all departments.

Organisation of Water Supply.

Organisation of water supply.

As the supply of good drinking water at Suakin is practically *nil*, and the supply of indifferent water from the various wells, in the town and neighbourhood, is by no means inexhaustible, the question of water supply was one to which Sir G. Greaves, who had arrived on the 5th of March, had given his immediate attention. The troops throughout were mainly dependent upon condensed water for their drinking supply, but the animals and a large proportion of the natives at the advanced posts used well water. The arrangements, which were modified from time to time, as camps were re-arranged, were briefly as follows:—

Four Egyptian ships, fitted by the Royal Navy with extemporised condensers, lowered over the sides of the vessels, were moored at the following piers: the "Tor," at the south-east end of the harbour, for the use of the Indian Contingent, quartered at Fula redoubt. *Condensing ships.*

The "Jaffariyeh," at the Custom House Yard, Suakin Island, assisted by two large horizontal boilers on shore, for the use of troops quartered within the *enceinte*, and for the Egyptian civil establishment.

The "Mukhbar," at Ferry Pier, Quarantine Island, for troops on the island, in H Redoubt, and on the south line of the narrow gauge railway.

The "Deb el Bahr," at No. 5 Pier, north-west arm of harbour, for the Ordnance Store Depôt, camel convoys, Sandbag Redoubt, and the camp on the north line of railway.

At the date of Sir G. Graham's arrival, these ships furnished about 30,000 gallons of water daily, but by the end of March, the employment of the "Calabria" as a condensing ship had raised the daily supply to 47,000 gallons, the daily consumption being 46,000 gallons. After the end of March, four more ships, the "Edinburgh," the "International," the "Kangaroo," and the "Yurid," were employed, and from the 1st to the 18th April, the daily production averaged from 65,000 gallons to 85,000 gallons.

The steam pumping lighters "Camel," "Chester," and "Solway King," were employed in conveying water from the English condensing ships to the piers.

Supply depôts.
Two supply depôts, in connection with the north and south branches of the narrow gauge railway, were also established; one on the former, near the Sandbag Battery, for the Brigade of Guards; one on the latter, beyond H Redoubt, where a number of 400-gallon tanks were employed for storage for the 2nd Brigade and the cavalry.

Distribution of water.
Water trains, composed of 400-gallon tanks, mounted on railway trolleys, were employed, as the exigencies of the traffic permitted, in carrying water to the supply depôts from their respective piers.

The immediate distribution of water to the troops was carried out by means of regimental water carts, non-commissioned officers being appointed to attend at the different depôts, to see that no water was taken except on production of a ticket signed by the Commissariat Officer who issued the ration, specifying the number of gallons to which each corps was entitled according to the following scale:—

Officers and men .. .. 2 gallons daily.
Natives .. .. .. 1 ,,
Hospital patients .. .. 6 ,,

Working parties 1½ pints per men, each relief.

As progress was made with the railway, the advanced camps were supplied by means of tanks, mounted on ballast trucks, filled at Ferry Pier, and shunted into temporary or permanent sidings, according to the nature of the camp. At Handub a permanent platform was erected, on which was placed a row of 400-gallon tanks: water was syphoned into these from the trucks, and thence pumped into camel tins or barrels for transport.

Railway supply.
For the purpose of supplying the advanced camp on the line, two high water towers were erected at No. 5 Pier and Ferry Pier, into which water was pumped by steam lighters, to find its way thence by gravitation to a large reserve tank, holding 100,000 gallons, near the Quarry Junction. An elevated tank near H redoubt, in connection with a 8-horse power engine and a Cameron's pump, was fitted by Messrs. Lucas and Aird, with a view to forcing this water through a 4-inch main, by the side of the railway to Handub.. The work, however, was not finished before the operations were

discontinued, and in the meanwhile the camps by the side of the line were supplied by tanks mounted on trucks.

In order to furnish water at the advanced zeribas, camel convoys, carrying water barrels, indiarubber bags, tins, and skins, were organised by the Transport Department. These vessels were filled at No. 5 Pier from a series of troughs provided with cocks, and supplied by tripod pumps from the storage tanks. In this operation great assistance was derived at night from the electric search light of H.M.S. "Dolphin."

Field supply for the zeribas as these were formed.

Canvas tanks and indiarubber cisterns, 56-gallon barrels, and 400-gallon tanks, were conveyed by the Royal Engineers to the zeribas, and erected there for storage. Into these the water carried by the camels was emptied.

The tanks were always sunk in the ground to protect them from the sun.

From the moment that the expedition was decided on, a party of 40 well sinkers under Lieutenant-Colonel Wood, R.E., had been employed in sinking wells in the beds of khors or dry watercourses, numbers of which intersect the desert. Upwards of 45 of these were sunk, and water was found at depths varying from 10 to 35 feet, but in most cases it was found to be brackish. The wells were generally sunk in groups.

Supply for animals.

In addition to the above, isolated wells were dug at various points and at some of the regimental camps, to furnish washing water.

Constant attention was necessary in clearing out and deepening the various wells, as the yield of the water-bearing strata became defective.

Horse troughs for watering purposes were also erected in the various camps, the form generally adopted being a masonry trough with a concrete bottom, about 50 feet long, 3 feet wide, and 18 inches deep. Troughs of canvas or waterproof sheeting were at first tried, but were found to be soon injured by animals stepping into them. A few portable zinc troughs were also used.

Upwards of 100 labourers were employed in working the Bastier pumps (2), and, when the depth of water permitted, the tripod pumps brought from Cairo. But the water was principally drawn in native skin buckets by means of cords. These 100 labourers raised by, and at first employed under the Royal Engineers, were afterwards handed over to the Commissariat.

On the whole a fair supply of water was obtained for the

10,000 animals employed with the force; but, before the close of the campaign, the water-bearing strata began to show signs of exhaustion, and it is probable, that, had the operations been prolonged, considerable difficulty would have been encountered.

The water was nearly always free from organic matter, but was pronounced by the medical authorities to be unfit for the use of the troops, on account of the excess of chlorides which it contained. At Otao, however, the men drank the well water without any ill effects.

The supply and distribution of water was under the Commissariat Department; the arrangements and appliances for storage and the machinery for raising water from wells, under the Royal Engineers.

Commissariat and Transport.

Commissariat and transport.

The Commissariat and Transport Department was in charge of Lieutenant-Colonel J. L. Robertson, Assistant Commissary-General; Lieutenant-Colonel C. E. Walton, Assistant Commissary-General, acted as Director of Transport. Owing to the short time at their disposal, both these officers had to organise their departments under great pressure.

The transport of the Indian contingent was in charge of Major G. R. Shakespear, B. S.C.

Difficulties at the outset.
At the commencement of operations, on the 5th March, there were only three officers of the Commissariat and Transport Staff at Suakin, and hardly any transport officers. Companies of the Commissariat and Transport Corps, and camels, however, soon began to arrive, and the organisation of the transport was rapidly carried out.

By the middle of the third week in March both supply and transport arrangements were fairly efficient. Each brigade had its supply and transport establishment told off to it, and transport was detailed for hospital service, and for the carriage of water in the field.

The force to be supplied consisted of about:—

    10,600 Europeans.
    7,800 natives.
    1,850 horses.
    1,700 mules and ponies.
    7,000 camels.

COMMISSARIAT AND TRANSPORT. 189

Their consumption of food daily was in round numbers as follows:— Daily consumption of food.

European rations	20 tons.
Native „	10 „
Forage	110 „
Fuel	12 „
Medical comforts	3 „
Railway demands	5 „
Total	160

or about 10,000 tons for the two months' supply which was ordered to be maintained. All these supplies had to be piled in the open; but owing to the fine weather, but little deterioration took place.

Throughout the operation the troops were generally supplied with fresh meat, chiefly the produce of cattle supplied from Odessa. Nature of provisions supplied to the troops.

The tinned meat, at first sent out, was mostly all corned, and in 6 lb. tins; but this was found to occasion excessive thirst, and the size of the tins to cause waste. Later on sufficient supplies of 2 lb. tins of preserved fresh meat were received, to enable it to be issued to the troops on the march.

Bread was baked by contract at Suakin, and was, as a rule, of good quality. It was carried in crates to the various advanced posts, and issues of biscuit had seldom to be made. Had a further advance been made, field bakeries were ready to be at once put in operation, with a view to supplying the troops with fresh bread all along the line.

The troops were generally supplied with fresh vegetables but an occasional issue of compressed vegetables was made.

The forage for horses was chiefly obtained from England, in the shape of compressed hay, compressed forage, hay cake, and grain cake. Forage for horses and camels.

Camel forage was obtained from Egypt and India.

Wood was obtained from Egypt, Cyprus, India, and locally. At the advanced posts the troops cut wood. Fuel and water.

The packing, transport, and distribution of water, imposed an unusual duty on the Commissariat and Transport Department, in this campaign, the mere extra weight to be carried adding immensely to its work. While the gross weight of the ordinary food ration is a fraction under 4 lbs., the water ration weighed 12 lbs. The work of cleaning and filling the water tins was also very trying to both officers and men, having mostly to be done at night.

The tins had to be packed on camels (each camel carrying two tins of 12½ gallons each), carried to their destination, unloaded, either emptied into storage tanks or piled, guarded, and the water afterwards issued to the troops. The work was all done by the Commissariat and Transport Department, with the one exception of supplying the storage tanks.

Transport sent from England. Animals, whence supplied. The transport sent from England, consisted at first of four companies, and afterwards five, of the Commissariat and Transport Corps. Camels were sent from India, Egypt, Berbera, and Aden, and mules from Gibraltar, Malta, and Cyprus.

The strength of the transport towards the close of the operations, was :—

Europeans, 573; Indians, Aden men, &c., 6,500; horses, 250; mules, 1,050; camels, 6,800.

Organization into seven sections. It was divided into seven sections, which were told off respectively as follows :—

1. General convoys, expeditions, water transport, 2,500 Indian transport camels.
2. Base and local transport, Suakin, 7th Company, 900 camels, 32 mules.
3. Line of communications and railway transport, 3rd Company, 1,100 camels, 90 horses, 30 mules.
4. Brigade of Guards, 5th Company, 600 camels.
5. Infantry Brigade, 12th Company, 600 camels.
6. Hospital work, 2 bearer companies, 4 field hospitals, 330 camels, 230 mules.
7. Transport depôt for replacing casualties, 17th Company, 544 camels, 235 mules, 248 horses.

The whole of this transport, when not employed in the service for which it was detailed, became available for general transport service.

The transport for the brigades was so arranged that each brigade could move as a whole if so ordered.

34 mules per battalion were also detailed as regimental transport. This, when on the march, carried the regimental reserve of ammunition (30 rounds per man), intrenching tools, signalling apparatus, and water for the day. 205 camels and 175 mules were given to the Artillery and Ammunition Columns.

The labour required by the Commissariat Department was exceptionally heavy. The wharves had to be cleared of repeated accumulations of stores, which could be discharged from the ships with much greater rapidity than they could be removed afterwards. These stores had then to be piled on Quarantine Island, and afterwards loaded up on camels, to be unloaded again at H Redoubt, and the stores then rearranged. For every convoy going out, another laying out of loads and loading up of camels was involved. As the convoys started at daybreak, the loading had to be done at night.

With the Indian Camel Transport came 300 bhistis and 260 kahars. The former were at once told off to the filling of water tins and such like duties, and such of the latter as were not required as dhooly bearers were used as labourers.

Working parties were also obtained from the Indian contingent.

A contract for labourers was made in Cairo, and about 250 arrived.

The transport of the Indian contingent was almost entirely in regimental charge. It consisted of 1,973 mules, 150 bullock carts, and a corps of over 500 dhooly bearers. These latter were chiefly employed as labourers.

Labour required by the Commissariat Department.

Ordnance Store Department.

The Ordnance Store Department, which was in charge of Major E. G. Skinner, Assistant Commissary-General, was severely tried during the operations. It had not only to deal with a great amount of stores and munitions of war, but also with a large number of special articles of equipment. Like the other departments, the time available for its organisation was very short.

By working night and day, the department was able to land the stores as fast as the lighters were brought alongside, and no serious block ever occurred.

Arms, ammunition, and clothing, requiring cover, were stored in a building in Suakin under charge of a conductor, who was in sub-charge to the Ordnance Store Officer, but a direct accountant for clothing.

Ordnance Store Department.

Medical Department.

The Medical Department was in charge of Deputy Surgeon-General O. Barnett, Principal Medical Officer. The establishment consisted of one Principal Medical Officer, one Principal

Medical Department. British troops. Personnel.

Medical Officer, for the Base and Line of Communications, two Brigade-Surgeons (one a Sanitary Officer), 19 Surgeon-Majors, and 30 Surgeons.

Bearer Companies. Two Bearer Companies were employed, each under command of a Surgeon-Major, assisted by two Surgeons. No. 1 Company, which was attached to the Guards' Brigade, was equipped with ambulance wagons and dandies. No. 2 was attached to the Cavalry Brigade.

Hospitals. Four Field Hospitals were formed. Of these, No. 1 was in charge of a Surgeon-Major, assisted by a Surgeon-Major and two Surgeons. It was detailed for duty with the Cavalry Brigade. It was equipped with transport, and was ready for service in the field a few days after its arrival. No. 2 was in charge of a Surgeon-Major, assisted by three Surgeons. It was detailed for duty with the 2nd Brigade. No. 3 was in charge of a Surgeon-Major, assisted by two Surgeons. It was the last to arrive, and was permanently stationed in the camp, when, towards the end of the operations, it received sick from the Cavalry, Mounted Infantry, and other details. No. 4 was entirely used by the Brigade of Guards, and was at all times under the care of the Medical Officers of the Brigade.

A fifty-bed Stationary Field Hospital was established at Handub, under a Surgeon-Major, on the 14th April, and was used as a rest house for sick between the front and the base.

An Auxiliary Hospital was established on Quarantine Island, and was used to receive sick before the base hospital was established, and afterwards as a supplementary hospital.

Hospital ships. Two hospital ships were employed; the "Bulimba" and the "Ganges." The former was used for all cases, until the arrival of the "Ganges," and afterwards for the reception of slight cases. The latter was sent out fully equipped as a hospital ship, and was used for the treatment of the wounded, and all severe cases of sickness.

One hundred Lushai dandies, with 500 bearers, were sent from India for the use of the British force, to carry sick and wounded from the field.

Medical Department Indian Contingent.

Medical Department. Indian Contingent. Personnel. The *personnel* of the Department consisted of 1 Principal Medical Officer (Brigade-Surgeon J. H. Thornton) 1 Brigade-Surgeon, 2 Surgeons-Major, and 9 Surgeons.

Hospitals. Hospital provision was made on an estimate of 12 per cent. sick for the troops, and 3 per cent. for the followers; this estimate being given on the understanding that all sick who were not likely to be fit for duty in the field, should be sent back to India every fortnight.

Two field hospitals, of 100 beds each, were formed, each under charge of a Surgeon-Major, assisted by a Surgeon. Of these, No. 1 was opened on the 9th March, and the sick of regiments taken over together with their hospital establishments. After the arrival of the other field hospital, it was arranged that it should receive the sick and wounded of the 28th Bombay Native Infantry, and of the 9th Bengal Cavalry and Sappers.

No. 2 field hospital was opened on the 16th March, and received the sick of the 15th Sikhs and 17th Native Infantry. It was afterwards moved to a building in Fort Euryalus, and became the stationary field hospital.

A base hospital of 288 beds, under charge of a Brigade-Surgeon was also provided.

The transport "Czarewitch,' which arrived on the 13th March, was selected as a hospital ship for the Indian Contingent; but much work had to be done to her, and she was not ready for the reception of patients till the 23rd March. She contained 125 beds. *Hospital ship.*

The amount of ambulance transport provided was at the rate of 5 per cent. for troops, and 1 per cent. for followers. It was originally intended that the whole should consist of Lushai dandies with covers. 12 dhoolies were, however, sent in addition to the 189 dandies, which accompanied the contingent. *Ambulance transport.*

Veterinary Department.

The Veterinary Department of the expedition was in charge of Inspecting Veterinary Surgeon, W. B. Walters. *Veterinary Department.*

The *personnel* consisted of one administrative officer, and nine executive officers. *Personnel.*

In order to facilitate the treatment of the more serious cases of sickness and lameness amongst the horses, a sick horse depôt, with shelter sheds for 80 horses, was established at the base. *Sick horse depôts.*

An advanced sick horse depôt was also established at Handub on the 18th April, for the reception of all sick and lame horses at that station, and, as far as practicable from the next advanced post. An ample supply of medicines and veterinary stores was kept at this depôt.

194   HISTORY OF THE SUDAN CAMPAIGN.—PART II.

Camel lazaretto.

On account of the presence of contagious skin diseases amongst the camels landed for the expedition, and the necessity of isolating these diseased animals, a camel lazaretto zeriba was formed, which was so successful, that by the 14th April, parasitic mange was practically stamped out. The establishment was then turned into a general infirmary for sick camels, and worked well.

On the arrival of the reserve medicines and surgical appliances from England, a veterinary store was established on Quarantine Island, whence supplies were sent to the various officers as required.

Shoes and shoeing.

The new pattern machine-made shoes and nails were used in this campaign with great success. The iron is so malleable that the shoes can generally be fitted cold, thus doing away with the necessity for a heavy field forge, and its accompanying plant and fuel.

All animals landed, and all ships bringing them, were carefully inspected by a Veterinary Officer.

Balloon detachment.

Balloon Detachment.

A new departure in this expedition was the employment of a balloon detachment, which was under command of Major J. L. B. Templer, 7th Battalion King's Royal Rifles, and was attached to the Royal Engineers. Unfortunately the prevalent high winds generally made it impossible to employ the balloon.

Changes in the ordre de bataille of the Expeditionary Force.

Some changes in the *ordre de bataille* of the Expeditionary Force were made previous to the commencement of active operations. It was arranged that the 9th Bengal Cavalry, while remaining with the Indian Contingent, should, as a rule, form part of the Cavalry Brigade. G/B., R.H.A., was told off as Corps Artillery, but was available for duty with the Cavalry Brigade. A Gardner Battery (4 guns) was formed of men from the Royal Artillery and from the Royal Marine Artillery. This battery was formed on the lines of a Field Battery, with mules, led by men on foot. A detachment with two 7-prs. of 200 lbs., and two rocket troughs, and also an Ammunition Column were formed by 6/1 S.D., R.A., and Artillery drafts. A Naval Brigade with Gardner guns was also landed.

Night alarms.

The constant small night attacks on the part of the enemy

THE THEATRE OF OPERATIONS. 195

which the extended character of the camp facilitated, were very harassing to the troops, depriving them as they did of sleep, often for many nights in succession. Sir G. Greaves, therefore, on his arrival did all he could to mitigate this evil by drawing the camp in closer; but he considered that the advantages of a complete change of site would be more than counter-balanced by the great amount of labour which such a change would entail on the troops. As a consequence of the altered dispositions, the night alarms, which had caused such annoyance, almost ceased.

Shortly after his arrival at Suakin, Sir G. Graham received a letter from Osman Digna. This was of a defiant character, and a reply was sent warning Osman Digna of the results that would follow an attitude of hostility on his part. Osman Digna was at this time stated by spies to be at Tamai with about 7,000 men; a force of from 1,000 to 1,200 of the enemy were in occupation of Hashin, and Tokar was said to be held by a small force. *Letter from Osman Digna.*

As will have been seen by the instructions from the Secretary of State for War, given on page 180, two distinct phases of the campaign were contemplated. *Two phases of contemplated campaign.*

1st. The destruction of the power of Osman Digna, and the clearance of the country for the construction of the railway.

2nd. The construction of the railway, and the location of the troops for its protection, at points where the summer heats could be best endured.

Having arranged for the organisation of the force and its transport, Sir G. Graham turned his attention to the first of these points.

Before describing the operations which ensued, it may be well to glance briefly at the general features of the country in which they were conducted.

From the sea coast of Suakin a sandy plain rises gently, in a westerly direction, for a distance of 10 or 12 miles, to where, at an elevation of from 200 feet to 300 feet above the sea level, it meets the foot of the volcanic range of mountains which bounds it on the west. The country in the immediate vicinity of Suakin, for a mile or two to the north and west, is fairly open. But beyond this radius, and to the south-west, towards Tamai, it is for the most part covered with a thick scrub composed of prickly mimosa bushes, varying in height from six feet to eight feet, and intersected by belts of lower bushes, lining the numerous khors or water-courses, which, *Features of the country.*

(S.C.2)   O

running generally in a north-easterly direction carry off the summer and autumnal rains from the mountains.

Tactics of the enemy. The tactics of the enemy were admirably adapted to the country in which they fought. They consisted in long range firing from cover followed by desperate hand-to-hand assaults from the bush, through and under which the Arabs could steal unobserved. Their movements were stealthy and sudden, and their onslaught was carried out with extraordinary rapidity by small groups of spearmen.

Direction of the railway. The line to be taken by the railway followed the caravan route to Berber, and lay in a north-westerly direction from Suakin. A part of this country was inhabited by friendly or neutral tribes.

Position of enemy round Suakin. At the time when the force was ready for an advance, the enemy occupied the line Tamai, Hashin, Handub, south to north, but his main position was at Tamai, where about 7,000 men were reported to be concentrated.

As Osman Digna's power had to be crushed before the construction of the railway could be proceeded with, it was necessary to make two distinct advances, one to Tamai, and after returning thence to Suakin, another along the line of the railway.

Reason for advance on Hashin. As, however, the occupation of Hashin by a smaller force of the enemy threatened the right of any advance on Tamai, and as it was also a convenient position from which to organise the night raids that were so harassing to our troops, Sir G. Graham determined that, before engaging in any other operation, he would break up the concentration of the enemy at Hashin. Accordingly, at 7.45 a.m., on the 19th March, the Cavalry Brigade, supported by the Infantry of the Indian Contingent, advanced from the West Redoubt towards Hashin. They were accompanied by Sir G. Graham and the Headquarter Staff; their orders were to reconnoitre as far as the village of Hashin, examine the wells there, and avoid an engagement if possible.

Hashin lies almost due west of the town of Suakin. For the first seven miles the march led across a level sandy district, studded with scattered mimosa trees and patches of low scrub.

Seven miles from Suakin, there rises abruptly from the surrounding plain, a group of black rocky hills (A, B, C, D, F, in the sketch, facing page 200). The highest of these, an oblong ridge (B, C, D), was afterwards called Zeriba Hill. This group of hills marks the commencement of a zone of thicker under-

ADVANCE TO HASHIN.

growth, that extends westwards, almost without interruption, to the base of the Waratab Range. About a mile and a half further on, a conspicuous isolated hill or rather ridge, about a mile in length, and running from east to west, with the culminating point almost in the centre, forms a remarkable feature. Its slopes are exceedingly steep and rugged, destitute of vegetation, and at certain points almost precipitous. The bush about its base, is from 6 to 8 feet in height, and forms in places dense thorny thickets. This hill is known as Dihilbat, or Hashin Hill.

To the north of Dihilbat Hill, and separated from it by a ravine some two or three hundred yards wide, is a lower eminence with gentler slopes, which was christened Beehive Hill. Immediately in rear of this lies the village of Hashin, a cluster of squalid huts and shanties encircled by a jungle of mimosa. Beyond Hashin, and running between Dihilbat Hill and the volcanic chain of mountains known as the Waratab Range, is a wide khor almost choked up with scrub. This may be said to mark the limits of the Suakin plain on the Hashin side.

Little opposition was encountered till the troops approached Hashin.

At about 9.30 a.m. the enemy, in small force, was seen occupying the eastern group of hills, A, B, C, D, but retreated, apparently falling back on the main body at Hashin. Later on the whole force retreated westwards, a small portion of it, however, remaining in occupation of the Dihilbat Hill, whence it fired occasionally upon the cavalry which advanced into Hashin village. One private of the 20th Hussars was killed and Lieutenant J. R. K. Birch (East Surrey Regiment), of the Mounted Infantry, and a sergeant of the 20th Hussars were wounded. *[March 19th. Reconnaissance to Hashin.]*

At 10.15 a.m. a retirement was ordered, and the force returned to camp at 12.30 a.m.

The country near Hashin was found to be very difficult, being rough and covered with a dense scrub, in which the enemy could conceal himself perfectly within a short distance of our vedettes.

On the following morning, the following force, under the command of Sir G. Graham, advanced towards Hashin at 6.20 a.m. *[March 20th. The action at Hashin.]*

(S.C.2)

	Officers.	N.-C.O.'s and Men.	Horses.	Mules.	Camels.	Followers.	Guns.
Guards Brigade Second Brigade (except Shropshire Light Infantry) Indian Contingent Cavalry Brigade G Battery B Brigade R.H.A. R.M.A. (Gardner Battery) Ammunition Column Royal Engineers	306	7886	1192	210	735	317	10

The infantry advanced in the following order:—

The 2nd Brigade in line of company columns in fours, with the Guard's Brigade and Indian Contingent in columns of companies, on the right and left. The infantry thus formed three sides of a square, the rear being open. Inside the square were the rockets and Gardner guns, the Engineers and the Transport. The cavalry covered the front and flanks.

The infantry reached the foot of the detached group of hills to the east of Hashin (B, C, D, in sketch) at 8.35 a.m., and General Graham, with his staff, posted himself on the small detached hill (A), about $1\frac{1}{2}$ miles to the east of Dihilbat Hill, and remained on it during the action.

On arrival on the ground, the Royal Engineers and Madras Sappers and Miners, supported by the East Surrey Regiment, proceeded at once to form redoubts on the hills marked B, C, D, and F, on the sketch, and a zeriba at E.

In the meanwhile the enemy had, on the arrival of the advanced guard, fallen back on Dihilbat and Beehive Hills, and Sir G. Graham determined to dislodge them from their position. He accordingly gave orders for the infantry to advance. The 2nd Brigade (Berkshire Regiment and Royal Marines) under Sir J. McNeill, supported by the Indian Contingent, and followed by G Battery, B Brigade, Royal Horse Artillery, were ordered to occupy Dihilbat Hill. The Guards' Brigade moved in support of the whole, and the cavalry protected the flanks.

The Berkshire Regiment advanced up the steep slopes of the hill in attack formation, with 4 companies of the Royal Marines in support. The other half battalion of the Royal Marines advanced on the right rear of the Berkshire Regiment. On reaching the crest of the first spur a heavy fire was opened by the enemy, which was answered by volleys, with such good effect that the enemy were gradually forced from the summit.

This with a spur on the left, was taken possession of by the Berkshire Regiment and they were able to pour an effective fire on the enemy as he retired across the plain.

The Indian and Guards' Brigades with the Horse Artillery and Gardner Battery, had, in the meanwhile advanced and occupied the gorge between Dihilbat and Beehive Hills.

Considerable difficulty was experienced in moving through the bush in compact formation, and the advance was slow. The enemy showed in some force but every attempted attack was checked before the spearmen could come to close quarters.

Two squadrons of the 9th Bengal Cavalry while in pursuit of the Arabs, who, driven from the Dihilbat Hill, were retiring towards Tamai, were charged from the bush by a considerable force. One of the squadrons was dismounted for the purpose of firing volleys, but being taken at a disadvantage, was driven back, with a loss of nine men, towards the Guards' square.

On the right, the 5th Lancers and two squadrons of the 9th Bengal Cavalry charged with great effect, and completely checked a body of the enemy, who were endeavouring to advance down the Hashin valley, to turn the British right flank.

At 12.45 a.m. Sir G. Graham recalled the Indian Brigade, which, formed in three sides of a square, had advanced to the far side of the gorge between Dihilbat and Beehive Hills. The Horse Artillery had come into action on the western spur of Beehive Hill. The retirement was covered by the 2nd Brigade. The two brigades then retired in square to the south of the hill marked A. Dihilbat Hill was reoccupied by the enemy. The Guards' Brigade and the Horse Artillery, which had retired on to it from the Beehive Hill, remained at the foot of Dihilbat Hill till 1 p.m., when they also retired (the Guards in square) to the south foot of the hill A. During their retirement they were subjected to a hot fire from parties of the enemy concealed among the bushes, and suffered some loss, one officer, Captain M. D. Dalison, Scots Guards, being killed. This fire was, however, eventually silenced by the steady volleys of the Guards.

At 2.30 p.m. the whole force assembled at the hill, and retired under cover of fire from the Horse Artillery guns, posted on that hill. The force reached Suakin at 6 p.m., with the exception of the East Surrey Regiment, which was left to hold the zeriba and redoubt constructed by it, the

Return of force to Suakin.

200   HISTORY OF THE SUDAN CAMPAIGN.—PART II.

Royal Engineers, and Madras Sappers and Miners during the action. The losses sustained by the force in this engagement amounted to 1 officer and 8 non-commissioned officers and men, killed, and 3 officers (Major A. B. Harvey, 5th Lancers, Major D. H. Robertson, 9th B.C., and Surgeon-Major Lane, M.S.), and 36 non-commissioned officers and men, wounded. The strength of the enemy was estimated at 3,000. The success of this action was shown by the fact that from the time that the post at Hashin was held, the trying night attacks on our troops were discontinued.

March 22nd. Force sent out to establish post on road to Tamai under Sir J. McNeill. Composition of force.

Having broken up the enemy's concentration at Hashin and established a post there, the next step was to crush Osman Digna at Tamai. Before doing so, however, it was necessary for reasons of supply, to establish an intermediate post in the desert, and for this purpose Sir G. Graham despatched on the 22nd March the following force under command of Sir J. McNeill:—

British.

1 Squadron 5th Lancers.
Berkshire Regiment.
Battalion Royal Marines.
1 Field Company Royal Engineers, with section of Telegraph Battalion.
Detachment Naval Brigade, with 4 Gardner guns.
Ammunition Column.

Indian Contingent.

15th Sikhs.
17th Bengal Native Infantry.
28th Bombay Native Infantry.
1 Company Madras Sappers and Miners.

Formation and advance of force.

The force was formed up in two squares, at 7 a.m. and moved off in a south-westerly direction; the British square in advance under the command of Sir J. McNeill, and taking a line leading directly to Tamai. Sir G. Graham proceeded with the force about two miles and a half, and then returned to camp.

Sir J. McNeill's orders.

The orders given to Sir J. McNeill, with a view to the formation of an intermediate depôt for the supplies and water required for an advance in force on Tamai, or on Tamanib,

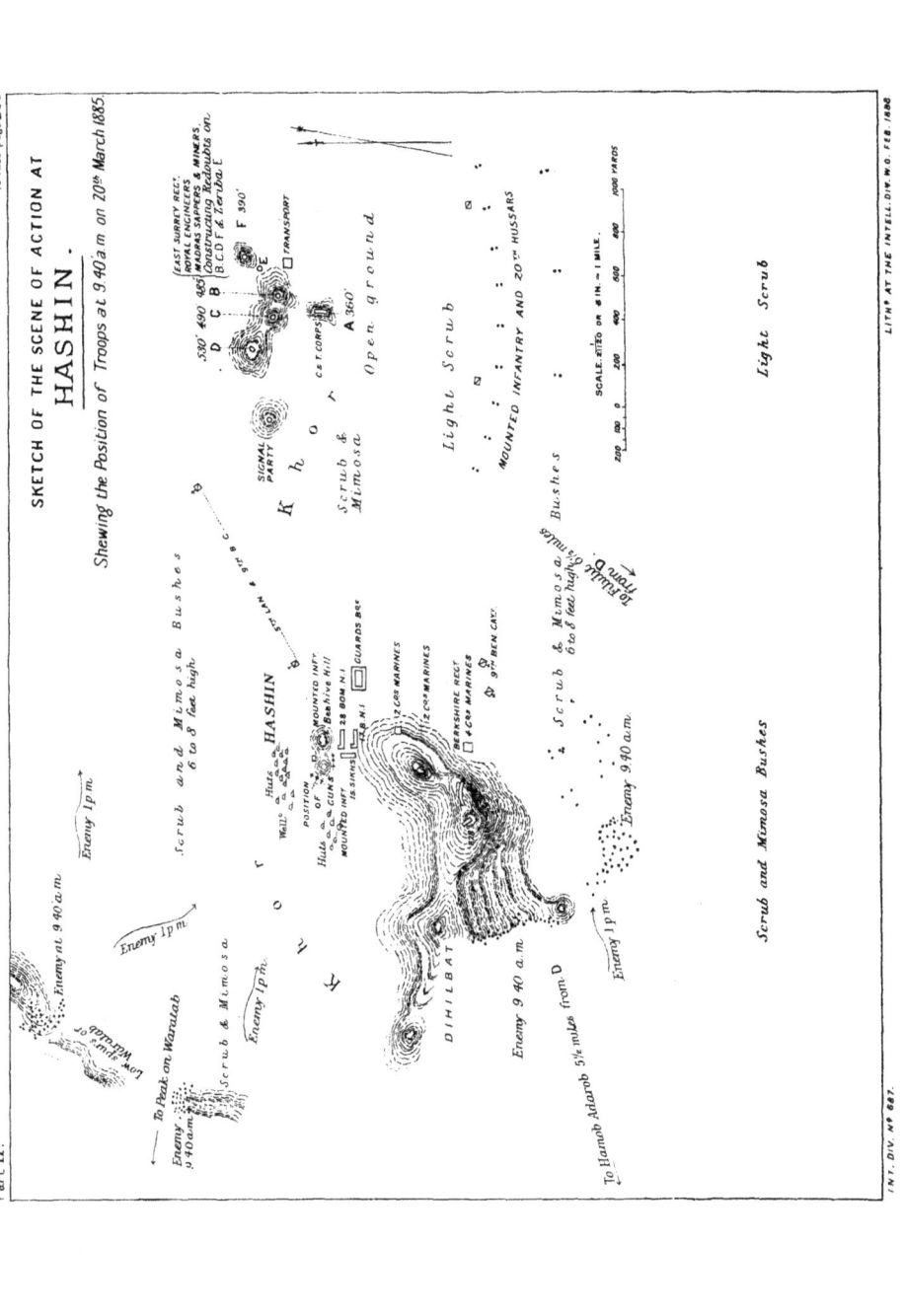

should operations in that direction be subsequently required, were as follow:—He was to march eight miles out from Suakin, there to make three zeribas; one capable of holding 2,000 camels, with flanking zeribas to hold one battalion each.—The Berkshire Regiment, Marine Battalion, 4 Gardner guns with the Naval Detachment, and the Company of the Royal Engineers were to remain in these zeribas. The Indian Brigade was to march back with the empty transport. When about half-way to Suakin it was to make an intermediate zeriba, in which one battalion was to be left, the remainder then continuing the march to Suakin.

The Indian Brigade, under the command of General Hudson, followed the British square, in echelon on the right rear. Within this square were placed some 1,400 or 1,500 transport animals—consisting of camels, mules, &c., laden with food, water, and ammunition; there were also a number of water carts.

The squadron of cavalry preceded the first square, acting as scouts. In the British square were the guns, telegraph cart (by which communication was kept up with Suakin), water carts, and spare ammunition.

Marching in this formation the force soon experienced much difficulty from the dense scrub in the watercourses that run between Suakin and the hills. The baggage animals had been in many cases overladen through carelessness. The thick and prickly bush impeded the movements of the animals, and loosened their loads, many of which were constantly falling off. All this necessitated frequent halts, and the average rate of progress was little more than a mile and a half an hour.

Almost immediately after the advance began, the Cavalry reported the enemy to be in front in small parties, retiring towards Tamai.

On arriving at a point about five miles from Suakin, Sir J. McNeill found that the great convoy of camels was rapidly falling into confusion, and, on consulting with General Hudson, concluded that it would be impossible, with any regard to military precaution, to proceed to the eight-mile point, form the zeribas, and then to send back the Indian Brigade to form an intermediate zeriba. This would have caused the Indian Contingent to be out until a late hour in the night.

A modification of the plan was agreed to, and Colonel E. Wood, R.E., who acted as guide, was ordered to form the zeriba about six miles from Suakin. This alteration was reported to Sir G. Graham by telegraph, and approved.

202 HISTORY OF THE SUDAN CAMPAIGN.—PART II.

Force halted at Tofrik.

About 10.30 a.m. the force reached the halting ground, known as Tofrik, a horse-shoe shaped clearing, of which the part corresponding to the toe pointed to Tamai. On halting the troops were disposed as follows (see the plan, facing page 208):—

Disposition and construction of zeribas.

The British Brigade, in square, was marched to the east, clear of the ground intended as site for the zeribas; and the Indian Brigade having left their camels to unload, water, &c., at the place indicated, formed (in three sides of a square) a large covering party, protecting the north, west, and south faces. The Sikhs were to the west, and the 17th Bengal Native Infantry and the 28th Bombay Native Infantry respectively on the south and north faces. The east, or rear face, was assumed to be protected by the British square. Subsequently it was found that the bush in front of the 28th Bombay Native Infantry was very dense, whereas in front of the 17th Bengal Native Infantry it was comparatively open, therefore two companies of the 17th were marched across and placed on the right of the 28th, in order to strengthen and prolong the right face, and more effectually to cover the working parties employed in constructing the small zeriba at the north-east corner.

Inside the British square were placed the spare ammunition, telegraph cart, guns, &c. It also formed a rallying point in case of attack before the zeribas were finished.

An orderly was sent to halt the cavalry, who were at work as a line of vedettes; and small piquets were thrown out, about 150 yards, in front of the Indian Brigade. These piquets were taken from the flanks of companies of various regiments. The Cavalry remained as vedettes and Cossack Posts about half a mile in advance; the bush being so thick that they could neither see, nor be seen from, the main body.

The zeribas were traced out as shown in the sketch. The south zeriba (A, B, C, D), was told off to the Berkshire Regiment with two Gardner guns and detachment of Naval Brigade. The north zeriba (E, F, G, H), was given to the Royal Marines, with two Gardner guns and detachment of Naval Brigade. The central zeriba (P, C, O, F), was to contain the stores.

The animals were directed through the large zeriba (where their loads were removed) to a "park" in rear of the 17th Bengal Native Infantry. Building, cutting, unloading and covering parties were detailed, and work went on rapidly. The working parties furnished by the Indian Brigade were

FORMATION OF ZERIBAS. 203

taken from the alternate ranks of alternate sections, thus preserving the front rank always intact.

Men were out on all sides cutting and dragging in the materials for the zeribas, but more than two-thirds of the force remained by their arms. The Indians were standing easy, in line, with their arms in their hands, and bayonets fixed. Ammunition was loose in the ball bags.

At 1 p.m. Major F. J. Graves, 20th Hussars, who had received orders at Suakin, at 10 a.m., to take his squadron and proceed along the line of telegraph wire, in order to keep up communication with the advance force, reported his arrival at the zeriba. He reported having seen on his way stray parties of the enemy, who retired before him. *Arrival of a second Squadron from Suakin. Its return.*

At 1.30 p.m., having received a despatch from Sir J. McNeill, he started with his squadron on the return march to Suakin.

The northern zeriba now approached completion, and was garrisoned by the Royal Marines, and supplied with two Gardner guns from the British square. The guns were mounted; and Sir J. McNeill now turned his attention to the Berkshire zeriba, which it was desirable to complete as soon as possible, in order to release the Indian Brigade.

Shortly before 2 p.m., the officer commanding the Berkshire represented that his men had had no food since 4 a.m., and had been marching and working in the heat since sunrise. They were ordered to receive dinner by half battalions. The first half battalion having received its rations, was marched immediately, with the two Gardner guns, into its zeriba. The other half-battalion received its rations on the original ground about 250 yards east of the zeriba, where it was held in reserve, and with a view also to preventing camels and followers from straying back towards Suakin.

After this, Sir J. McNeill met General Hudson in conference at the north-eastern angle of the Berkshire zeriba, and informed him that he hoped to be able to release the Indian Brigade and transport at 3 o'clock; the second defensive work being nearly complete.

At this hour, the disposition of the force appears to have been as follows:—

One half-battalion of the Berkshire Regiment was outside of their zeriba, cutting brushwood, close to the 15th Sikhs, who were in line facing the west, with parties 150 yards in their front. The 28th Bombay Native Infantry, and two companies of the 17th Bengal Native Infantry, were in line facing the north. The Marines were inside their own zeriba. The remaining six companies of the 17th Bengal Native Infantry were in line facing the south; their left flank being somewhat "*en l'air.*" The men of the other half-battalion of the Berkshire were having their dinners at the spot where they had been left in reserve, to protect the left flank of the 17th Bengal Native Infantry, which could not be doubled back as that would have too much reduced the space for unloaded camels. The disposition of the force is shown in the sketch.

The camels that had been unloaded in the central zeriba had begun to file out, in order to be formed up outside for the return march. They were chiefly to the east of the zeribas, and near to the half-battalion of the Berkshire, which was outside.

The attack on the Tofrik zeriba. The Generals had scarcely finished their conference, when, shortly after 2.30 p.m., an orderly arrived to report "the enemy collecting in front," followed immediately by another with the news that they were "advancing rapidly."

Sir J. McNeill gave notice to General Hudson, and gave orders to call in the working parties. He had scarcely given the orders when he saw the cavalry galloping in, close behind them being the enemy, in the usual small groups.

The working party of the Berkshire Regiment rushed back into their zeriba, and stood to their arms. The native infantry piquets ran in on the flanks of their companies, and the lines at once opened fire.

The right flank of the 17th Bengal Native Infantry was somewhat disordered by the 5th Lancers riding through it, and Sir J. McNeill observing that the regiment was unsteady, although the officers were doing their best, ordered some of the Berkshire, from the other face of their zeriba, to move over. But it was too late. The six companies of the 17th Bengal Native Infantry broke after firing one volley; the two companies on the right, whose ranks had been broken by the cavalry, retired in confusion into the Berkshire zeriba, and were rallied on the south front after some of the Berkshire had been moved over by Sir J. McNeill to their support. Others retired towards Suakin. The left of the line fell back in a more regular formation to the zeriba manned by the Marines.

On the retreat of the 17th Bengal Native Infantry, the Arabs instantly stampeded the animals collected to the left rear of that regiment, driving them hither and thither, but especially on to the half-battalion square of the Berkshire, east of the zeribas.

The enemy swarmed over the low bush fence, and over the unfinished sand-bag parapet at the south-west salient, into the Berkshire zeriba, stabbing and cutting everywhere. It was here that Lieutenant Seymour and men of the Navy, in charge of the Gardner guns, were killed; and here that the Berkshire had their greatest loss. The Gardner guns were being placed in position at the time, and could not be got into action, so that their detachments, who stood their ground gallantly, suffered severely.

Large bodies of the enemy rushed round in every direction, charging on the fence with the utmost courage. They came in masses between the zeribas and the transport animals, hence the enormous destruction of the latter. The native bearers and servants fared badly, for it was impossible to distinguish them from the enemy, and it is feared that many of them were killed and wounded by the fire of the troops.

The right half-battalion of the Berkshire Regiment, which was at work outside with some Royal Engineers and Madras Sappers, made a most gallant resistance, after getting to its arms, which were piled inside. One hundred and twelve of the Arabs who had entered the zeriba at the first rush were killed. The Berkshire also captured a flag, which the enemy had planted on the sand-bag parapet at the south-west salient. Two soldiers of the Berkshire were saved from certain death by the magnificent daring of Subadar Goordit Singh, commanding the left flank company of the 15th Sikhs, who, placing himself between the pursuers and their prey, killed three Arabs in succession by three rapid sword-cuts. This was one only among many feats of personal courage which this day produced.

The 15th Sikhs, and 28th Bombay Native Infantry stood firm, maintaining an intact line; receiving and repulsing successive attacks with a heavy fire, as also did the two companies of the 17th Bengal Native Infantry, which were in a line with the 28th Bombay Native Infantry. There never was a doubt as to the result of the attack on these regiments. The Sikhs were most severely attacked, and hundreds of dead Arabs were afterwards counted in front of their position. The Bombay regiment was less directly attacked, but fought steadily, and added its quota to the slain.

To turn to the other half-battalion of the Berkshire, which was outside the zeriba, having dinner about 250 yards to the east of it, when the alarm was given. The men formed rallying square, and succeeded in repelling two successive attacks without loss; they held their ground until the firing ceased, when they marched back to the zeriba. They killed over 200 of the enemy.

Small bodies of men, who were outside the zeribas at the moment of attack, were similarly collected by the exertion of the officers, and many others succeeded in making their way back to the zeribas.

The Marines held the northern zeriba, and with the Berkshire cleared the central one also.

The first shot was fired at 10 minutes to 3 o'clock, and at 10 minutes past 3 Sir J. McNeill sounded the "cease-fire"; yet in that short space no fewer than 1,500 Arabs were killed, and probably a large number were wounded, out of the force of about 5,000 which attacked. Over 1,100 were buried during the three following days, many more being left in the bush.

Major Graves' two squadrons.

As previously noticed, Major Graves, of the 20th Hussars, left the zeriba at 1.30 p.m., with his squadron, for Suakin. He had proceeded about two miles, and had met a squadron of the 9th Bengal Cavalry advancing to relieve him, when he heard heavy firing at the zeriba.

He took command of the two squadrons, and hastened back. About one mile from the zeriba they came upon a number of camel drivers, some native infantry, a few British soldiers, and a number of camels, mules, &c., all in full retreat on Suakin, closely pursued by the enemy, who were in much greater force, and who were cutting them down and killing them in large numbers.

The two squadrons were at once formed into line, and changing front to the right, cut into the line of pursuit. On the enemy being checked, every available man was dismounted, and several volleys were fired, which stopped the pursuit. The cavalry, having remounted, pressed on to within 300 yards of the enemy and delivered several more volleys. These had such good effect, that the Arabs turned and retreated towards the zeriba, leaving a number of dead and wounded on the ground. Some feigned death, and jumping up close to the troops were killed in hand to hand combat.

It was now observed that the enemy were trying to turn the left flank of the cavalry, with a view, no doubt, to again falling on the retreating transport. One troop was sent to intercept them.

The cavalry force being joined by one troop 5th Lancers, pressed on and drove the enemy, by dismounted fire, past the eastern side of the zeribas; here they were so effectually enfiladed, that they dispersed towards the sea, and did not again assemble in any numbers.

A strong cavalry cordon was formed round the transport and baggage, patrols were sent out, and Major Graves being entrusted with a second despatch, announcing the attack and repulse of the enemy, returned to Suakin.

After the engagement was over, desultory firing at Arabs, who attempted to rise and rush on, continued for some twenty minutes. Parties of Marines and Sikhs then moved out to examine the field; they found that the enemy had disappeared, and by 4 p.m. all was quiet.

During the action, and for nearly four hours later, the zeriba was in telegraphic communication with headquarters, as the wire laid by the Royal Engineers was not cut until 6.40 p.m.

On first hearing firing, Sir G. Graham ordered out two battalions of the Guards, with the battery of Royal Horse Artillery, and advanced two and a half miles towards the zeriba. He retired to Suakin on receipt of a telegram from Sir J. McNeill that no more troops were wanted.

As soon as possible the zeriba was completed, and by 7 p.m. was very fairly strong.

A sharp look-out was kept all night, parties of the enemy being heard prowling about, but with the exception of a false alarm at 8.30 p.m., the night passed quietly.

The casualties in the action of the 22nd March were—

	Killed or died of wounds.	Missing.	Wounded.
BRITISH.			
Officers	6	..	3
Serjeants	3	..	3
Rank and file	55	14	57
INDIAN BRIGADE.			
European officers	2	..	2
Native officers	2	...	..
Non-commissioned officers and men	49	10	90
FOLLOWERS.			
Followers	33	124	19
Total	150	148	174
CAMELS.			
Camels	501 killed and missing.		

The 5th Lancers, who were out as scouts, lost one officer (Lieutenant Richardson) and five men.

The Royal Artillery lost four men; and one officer, Lieutenant G. E. Benson, wounded.

The Royal Engineers suffered heavily, being out working when attacked, and lost two officers (Captain F. J. Romilly, and Lieutenant E. M. B. Newman), one sergeant, 12 rank and file killed and missing; one officer, Captain C. B. Wilkieson, and three men wounded.

The Berkshire Regiment, one officer (Lieutenant G. S. Swinton), one sergeant, and 21 rank and file killed; two sergeants and 28 rank and file wounded.

The Commissariat and Transport had 12 men killed and missing.

Quartermaster C. Eastmead of the Ordnance Store Department was killed.

The Naval Brigade lost Lieutenant M. H. Seymour and six men; one officer (Surgeon M. Digan) and five men wounded.

The Royal Marines had one sergeant and six men killed, one missing, 16 wounded.

Major J. M. Von Beverhoudt, of the 17th Bengal Native Infantry, was killed; Lieutenant F. G. M. Edwards, 28th Bombay Native Infantry, died of wounds; the Indian Brigade had 59 men killed and missing, two European and two Native officers, Lieutenant F. M. Drury, Lieutenant W. A. Thompson, Jemadar Venaigmoorthy, Jemadar Lachman Pandy, and 90 men wounded.

The Medical Staff Corps had two men killed, four men wounded.

The 20th Hussars, one sergeant wounded (with Major Graves' squadron).

Royal Sussex Regiment, one man wounded.

Staff, one officer (Lieutenant Hon. Alan Charteris, Coldstream Guards, Aide-de-Camp to Sir J. McNeill) wounded.

Subsequent movements. Convoys sent out. 23rd to 30th March.

The following day, 23rd March, Sir G. Graham arrived at the zeriba with three battalions of the Guards and a convoy of 1,200 camels. The wounded and baggage animals, with the Indian Brigade and Grenadier Guards, returned to Suakin, leaving the Coldstream and Scots Guards at the zeriba. The zeriba at Tofrik was generally known as McNeill's zeriba.

On the 24th March another convoy of 425 camels, 818 carts, with 8,000 gallons of water proceeded to McNeill's zeriba, escorted by the following force:—

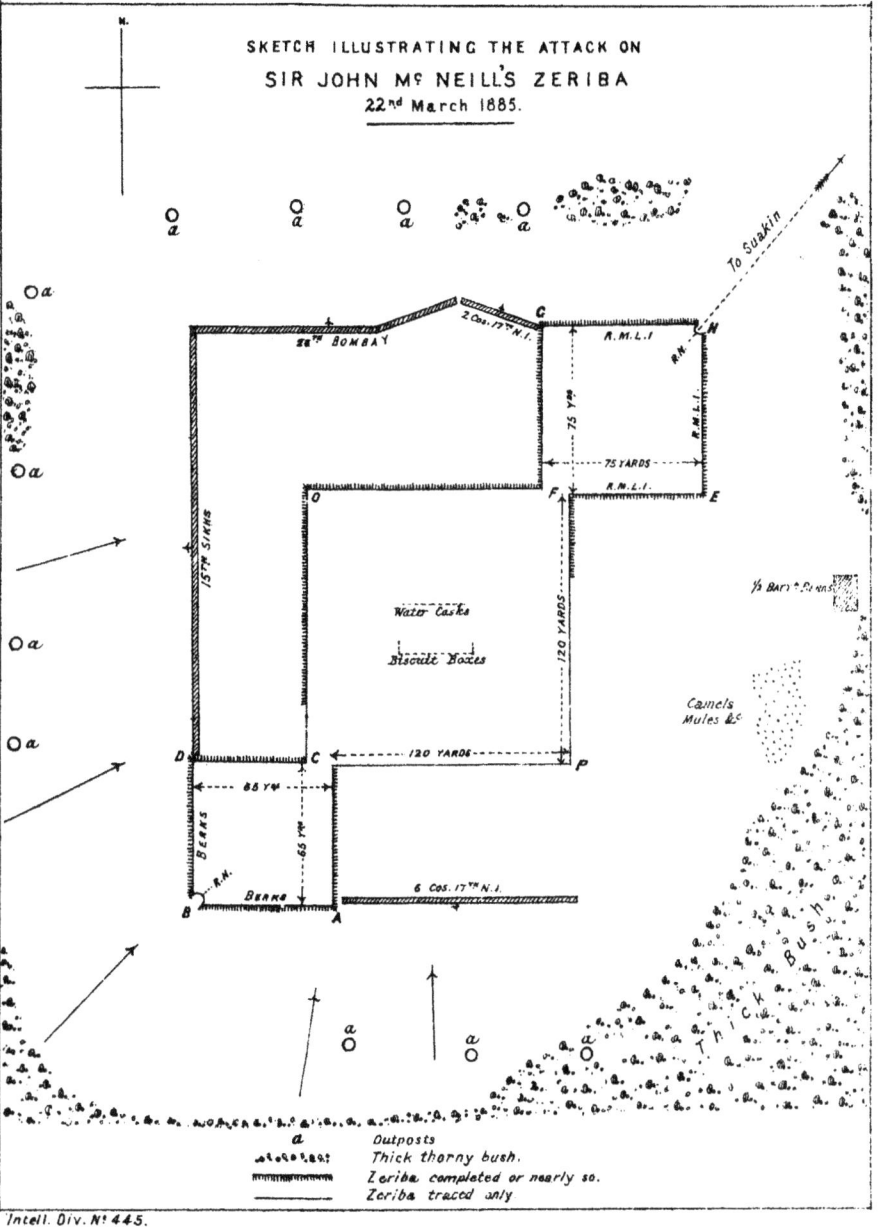

ADVANCE ON TAMAI.

15th Sikhs.
28th Bombay Native Infantry.
9th Bengal Cavalry.

At a distance of about three miles from the zeriba the force was met by an escort composed of the Coldstream Guards and Royal Marines, who had come out to take over the convoy. On its way back to the zeriba the escort was attacked by the enemy in considerable force, and in closing up the square, 117 camels were left outside and either killed or lost. During the skirmish one man was killed and three officers (Captain Hon. North Dalrymple, Scots Guards; Lieutenant J. L. R. Maclurcan, R.M.L.I., Lieutenant A. E. Marchant, R.M.L.I.), one non-commissioned officer, 19 men, and five followers, were wounded.

On the 25th March another convoy of 500 camels with 3,480 gallons of water, escorted by a force of about 2,100 men, was sent to McNeill's zeriba, and returned without having seen any traces of the enemy. On this occasion the captive balloon, under Major Templer, was for the first time used with success.

On this day the East Surrey Regiment and the details that had been holding the zeribas near Hashin since the 20th, were withdrawn, and the zeribas were dismantled.

On the following day (26th March) a larger convoy, of 600 camels and 300 mules, carrying 9,000 gallons of water, and escorted by the following force :—

2 guns G/B R.H.A.
1 squadron each from the 5th Lancers and 20th Hussars.
Grenadier Guards.
East Surrey Regiment.
Shropshire Light Infantry.
9th Bengal Cavalry.
15th Sikhs.
28th Bombay Native Infantry.

under command of Sir G. Graham, proceeded to McNeill's zeriba at 6 a.m. The infantry advanced in square. The Grenadier Guards and Shropshire Light Infantry formed respectively the front and rear faces, each with a front of two companies.

After two hours' march the enemy were seen in small

groups, and a few shots were exchanged between them and the cavalry, and by 9.15 they were seen swarming in the bush which had by this time got very thick. At the end of half-an-hour of desultory firing, a rush was made at the right front corner of the square, but was immediately repelled. After the bush had been cleared in front, the force was able to continue its advance to the zeriba, the only casualty being one slight spear wound. The force was joined by the Coldstream Guards, and, having handed over its load, returned to Suakin without further engagement.

On the 28th and 30th March convoys were sent to McNeill's zeriba and returned without opposition. The Marines were brought back to Suakin on the 28th, and the Scots Guards were relieved by the Grenadier Guards on the 30th; the Berkshire Regiment declined to be relieved. The zeriba had been strengthened, and had been altered so as to require only one regiment as a garrison. It was intended to hold 1,500 camels.

On the 31st March, it was reported that Osman Digna's force had been withdrawn from Tamai. The Mounted Infantry and a troop of the 9th Bengal Cavalry were sent to that place, and on their return reported that the village was still held. In consequence of this report (McNeill's zeriba being by this time complete with water) Sir G. Graham issued orders for an advance on Tamai on the morrow.

April 2nd. Force marched for Tamai.

At 3 a.m. on the 2nd April the following force paraded at Suakin and marched off at 4.30 a.m.

Corps.	Officers.	N.-C.O.'s and Men.	Horses.	Mules.	Camels.	Guns.
Headquarter Staff	40	50	52	...		...
Guards Brigade	79	1945	26	...		...
2nd Brigade	66	1715	23	...		...
Royal Engineers	5	143	11	...		...
R.A. and R.M.A. (4 Mountain and 4 Gardner Guns), rockets and Ammunition Column G/B, R.H.A. (6 guns)	24	324	154	171		14
Cavalry Brigade	31	743	773	...		...
Indian Contingent	25	1585	24	...		...
Medical Staff Corps	16	164	22	...		...
Balloon Detachment	2	15	10	...		...
Commissariat and Transport	16	200	16	...		...
Total	304	6884	1111	171	1639	14

The force was formed in one large oblong square with a

OCCUPATION OF TAMAI.

front face of three companies, about 70 yards long and 750 yards deep, the convoy being placed inside.

McNeill's zeriba was reached at 8.30 a.m., and a halt was made for breakfast. The 28th Bombay Native Infantry, and 2 Gardner guns manned by the Royal Marine Artillery, were left as garrison. The force was joined by the Grenadier Guards, Berkshire Regiment, 24th Company R.E., and also by the Mounted Infantry and troop of the 9th Bengal Cavalry which had been sent out the previous day. At 10.15 a.m. the march was resumed, the force having a total strength of 8,175 of all ranks. At 4.30 p.m. the force reached Tesela Hill, behind which a zeriba about 300 yards square was formed and the troops bivouacked for the night, being only disturbed at midnight by a short period of long range firing from the enemy, which was speedily silenced by the guns. The cavalry was sent back to McNeill's zeriba to water. *[margin: Halt at Tesela. Map 9.]*

At 8 A.M. on the following morning the troops, with a strength of about 6,300 officers, non-commissioned officers, and men, under Sir G. Graham, marched off in the following formation:— *[margin: April 3rd Advance on Tamai.]*

The 2nd Brigade (Berkshire Regiment, Royal Marines, and 15th Sikhs) under General Hudson in front; the Berkshire Regiment in line in the centre, with the Royal Marines and the 15th Sikhs in column of companies on the flanks.

The Guards' Brigade, including the battalion of the New South Wales Contingent, in line of columns in rear. The mountain guns, rocket battery, ammunition column, &c., were placed in rear of the Berkshire Regiment. The Horse Artillery was placed on the right flank.

Sir J. McNeill, with the East Surrey Regiment, Shropshire Light Infantry and the Gardner guns, remained in the Tesela zeriba to protect the transport.

The cavalry and mounted infantry reconnoitered to the front and covered the advance. The right flank was covered by the 5th Lancers, the right front by a squadron of the 9th Bengal Cavalry supported by the mounted infantry, and the left and left rear by the 20th Hussars, and remainder of the 9th Bengal Cavalry.

Sir G. Graham's object was the occupation of Osman Digna's headquarters at New Tamai, a village lying between Tesela Hill and the Khor Ghoub, and the occupation of the wells in the khor. The ground between Tesela and the khor was broken by three low ridges, between which lay the village; this was occupied without serious opposition by *[margin: Occupation of Tamai.]*

(s.c.2)   P

9 a.m., and by 9.20 the square had reached the edge of the khor, firing being kept up all the time between the mounted infantry and the enemy's scouts. The 2nd Brigade, under General Hudson, was then crossed to the far side of the khor, supported by artillery fire, a high point in the centre being occupied by the Berkshire Regiment, while the 15th Sikhs crossed the heights or detached hills to the left and front. G/B, battery R.H.A., and the mountain guns then came into action on the far side of the khor. The Guards' Brigade and New South Wales contingent were in support of the 2nd Brigade, crowning the ridges on the north side of the khor. The Arabs gradually withdrew into the mountains to the south-west.

On descending the khor to a point where, during the operations of the previous year, a running stream had been found, it was discovered that there were no signs of water beyond a little brackish moisture.

Return of force. Judging, therefore, that it was useless to attempt to follow the enemy to the hills into which he had fled, and considering the enormous difficulty of supplying the force with water, Sir G. Graham ordered a retirement. After burning Osman Digna's village and destroying large quantities of ammunition, the force marched off at about 10.30 a.m., and reached the Tesela zeriba at noon. Part of the artillery and cavalry were sent back to Suakin, the remainder of the force moved to the Tofrik zeriba in the afternoon, and returned to Suakin on the following day. The 28th Bombay Native Infantry and a detachment of the Naval Brigade, with two Gardner guns, were left at Tofrik as a guard.

It is noteworthy, that, of the 1885 transport animals that went out with this expedition, all but three returned, and one of these was killed in action—affording striking evidence of the efficiency of the transport.

Second phase of operations. The enemy having now been driven from the positions he had taken up at Hashin and Tamai and his force destroyed or dispersed, Sir G. Graham commenced the fulfilment of the second part of his instructions, and proceeded to open up the route for the railway. McNeill's zeriba being of no further use was closed on the 6th April, all stores being withdrawn in one convoy of 1,269 mules and 2,165 camels under escort of 4 battalions.

Attempted alliance with neutral tribes. The first step taken towards opening the country for the railway was an attempt to form an alliance with the neutral tribes dwelling on or near the Berber road; but it was soon discovered that any such alliance must be dependent on a fixed policy on the part of Her Majesty's Government. The tribes appeared to be anxious to come in and thoroughly tired of the terrorism established by Osman Digna, but they one and all said that they could not join us, unless they were assured of our future protection against Osman Digna, and unless we undertook that we should not go away as we had done in the previous year. In a telegram to the Secretary of State for War, dated 12th April, 1885, Sir G. Graham asked whether he might give this assurance. In reply, the following telegram was sent to Lord Wolseley on the 15th April, by the Secretary of State for War: "Construction of railway for any considerable distance to be suspended pending further consideration. Suakin to be held for the present, and any position in neighbourhood necessary for protection from constant attack, as last year. You should report on point to which railway should now proceed, and instruct Graham, with reference to his message of 12th, not to enter into engagements with tribes inconsistent with this policy."

On receipt of the instructions conveyed in the above telegram, Sir G. Graham requested General Fremantle, who was acting as political officer, to explain to the Amarars that we wished them to be independent of, but friendly to, Suakin, and that we would help them at any rate at first; that if they were prepared to strike for their own supremacy and independence of Osman Digna and his Hadendowas, they would not only have assistance but cooperation; and that if they made the best of their opportunity then, it would, even if the English went away later, be out of Osman's power to retaliate.

On the 6th April (the day on which McNeill's zeriba was evacuated) a force composed of:— *Formation of No. 1 station.*

> The Coldstream Guards,
> New South Wales Infantry,
> 17th Company Royal Engineers,
> 2 Guns 5/1 S.D., R.A. (7-prs.),
> Mounted Infantry,

under command of General Fremantle, proceeded to a point about half-way between Suakin and Handub (afterwards known as No. 1 Blockhouse), constructed a zeriba and occupied it, and on the following day this post was reinforced by the Scots Guards and 2 more guns of 5/1 S.D., R.A.

214 HISTORY OF THE SUDAN CAMPAIGN.—PART II.

April 8th. Occupation of Handub.

On the 8th April, the force sent to No. 1 Station on the 6th inst., augmented by one company Mounted Infantry and one squadron Bengal Cavalry, proceeded to Handub, and during the following week, convoys were daily despatched to Handub to place supplies there.

April 16th and 19th. Occupation of Otao and Tambuk.

On the 16th April Otao ($4\frac{1}{2}$ miles beyond Handub) was occupied without opposition, and on the 19th Tambuk (5 miles beyond Otao) was occupied by

The Scots Guards.
Half 17th Company Royal Engineers.
2 Guns 5/1 S.D., R.A. (7 prs.).
Detachment Madras Sappers and Miners.

Progress of the railway.

In the meanwhile the railway was steadily advancing, and on the date of the occupation of Otao had reached within a mile of Handub.

Camel Corps formed.

The arrival of camels from India, made it possible, at this date, to organize a camel corps, which did good service during the short period of its existence, and would have proved invaluable as supplying moving troops, had the campaign been prolonged.

Sir G. Graham had asked for 500 camels from India for this purpose before he left England, but they did not arrive at Suakin until the beginning of April, 195 being landed on the 6th April and 290 on the 17th. Owing to the impossibility of sparing enough men from the Infantry, however, to utilize this number, only 300 men were at first employed for service with the Camel Corps, the remainder of the camels being used to carry infantry on the "ride and tie" system, to which the New South Wales Contingent and the Grenadier Guards were specially trained.

On the 16th April, orders were issued for the immediate formation of a camel corps, to consist of 400 British and 100 native soldiers, with about 200 native drivers, divided into five companies, as follows:

1st Company, Brigade of Guards.
2nd Company, Royal Engineers, East Surrey Regiment, Royal Marine Light Infantry.
3rd Company, Berkshire Regiment, New South Wales Contingent.
4th Company, Shropshire Light Infantry.

5th Company, 15th Sikhs, 17th Bengal Native Infantry, 28th Bombay Native Infantry. The whole to be under the command of Major W. C. James, Scots Greys.

The camels carried two men each, three camels carrying between them five fighting men and one native driver.

Since the break up of Osman Digna's Headquarters at Tamai, the enemy, beyond some desultory firing at night, and occasional attempts to injure the telegraph and railway lines, did not cause any annoyance. But although the Arabs appeared to be cowed, every precaution was taken to meet any attempt to interrupt the progress of the railway, and several successful reconnaissances were made in advance, and also into the neighbouring valleys, to clear them of Arabs, who according to information received were collecting for the purpose of harassing our line of communications. Of these the reconnaissance to Khor Abent, on the 18th April; towards Es Sibil on the 24th April; and to Khor Adit on the 29th April, were the most important. *Reconnaissances westwards.*

On the 30th April, that is to say, in a little over three weeks after the final dispersion of the enemy's forces, the railway was completed as far as Otao.

On the 2nd May Lord Wolseley arrived in the s.s. "Queen," at Suakin, to inspect that station with a view to determining what permanent garrison would be required there. *May 2nd. Arrival of Lord Wolseley.*

It having been reported by the Intelligence Department that a certain Mohammed Adam Sardun, a Sheikh of the Amarar tribe, had collected a force at T'Hakul in the Abent Valley for the purpose of harassing our line of communications, Sir G. Graham determined to attack him. This was the more necessary from the fact that not only was Mohammed Sardun one of Osman Digna's most trusted lieutenants, but also that he was in command of the only organized body of the enemy then remaining in that part of the country. This body was also one that had not been seriously engaged at the action of Hashin, and had not been present at all at the attack on McNeill's zeriba; consequently having suffered little loss, it was less disheartened than the majority of the tribes. *Hostile gathering at T'Hakul.*

Sir G. Graham, having settled to break up this force, made arrangements for a combined attack from Suakin and Otao on the chieftain's stronghold, which was about 18 miles in a direct line west of the former and 10 miles south of the latter place.

216   HISTORY OF THE SUDAN CAMPAIGN.—PART II.

*May 6th.
Advance on
T'Hakul.
Suakin
column.*

At midnight on the 6th May a column composed as follows—

> 9th Bengal Cavalry,
> 2 Companies Mounted Infantry,
> Camel Corps,

paraded at Suakin, and marched off at 12.50 a.m. under the personal command of Sir G. Graham.

At 2.40 a.m. Hashin was reached, and the force then entered the valley of the Abent, a broad shallow khor, flanked by thick bush. At daylight the force reached the head of the T'Hakul Valley, which runs at right angles to that which had been followed. At this point a party of the 9th Bengal Cavalry were detached to the south-west, to cut off any possible retreat of the enemy in that direction, while the main body advanced and closed the south entrance to the valley.

Otao column.

In the meanwhile the Otao column, composed of—

> 1 Company Mounted Infantry,
> 15th Sikhs, and
> 200 Friendly Natives,

under command of Major D. W. Inglis, 15th Sikhs, had arrived at the north end of the valley at 5.40 a.m., drawing the enemy, who was unaware of the approach of the Suakin column, out to attack them. The Arabs were driven back in confusion by the fire of the Mounted Infantry, who, with the Friendlies, pursued them with great effect to the south-west, capturing over 1,100 sheep, goats, and some camels. At the same time, two companies of the Mounted Infantry of the Suakin Force were pushed to the front and crowning successively the lower heights on the west, quickly gained the higher ridges and drove the enemy from spur to spur.

The 9th Bengal Cavalry and the Sikh Company of the the Camel Corps were at this time actively pursuing the enemy along a lateral valley; they also swept the main valley, capturing the flocks of sheep and goats which the Arabs were endeavouring to drive off.

The enemy did not make any determined resistance, but kept firing from the hill tops, from which they were gradually driven until the whole district was clear. By 7 a.m. all firing had ceased. The enemy's encampment, which was found to be about one mile from the mouth of the valley, was then occupied, and how complete had been the surprise was proved by the confusion in which his property was left. Camel saddles, grain, food, clothing, household implements, skins of water, were littered about, showing beyond doubt that Sardun's men had barely had time to seize their arms and rush to the hills, before troops swooped down upon them.

At 9 a.m. the column from Otao returned to that place, accompanied by Sir G. Graham, and at 10 a.m. the Suakin column returned to camp, under command of Colonel A. P. Palmer, 9th Bengal Cavalry. On the march back it met some parties of the enemy coming from the direction of Tamai, which were afterwards ascertained to have been reinforcements, on their way from Osman Digna to Mohammed Sardun. These opened fire on the column from the bush, but this was soon silenced by the steady volleys of the Mounted Infantry and Camel Corps. Return to Suakin.

That this action bore good results is shown by the fact that within a few days a body of the tribes made an offer to submit to the British flag. Offers of submission.

The enemy lost 100 men killed, 10 prisoners, and 3 standards. The casualties in the two columns were 1 officer (Lieutenant A. Austen, Shropshire Light Infantry) and 2 non-commissioned officers wounded.

With the break-up of the force under Mohammed Sardun the political question of the eastern Soudan may be said to have been solved for the time being; large numbers of the Amarars placed themselves unconditionally at the disposal of Sir G. Graham; and a decided movement, which embraced even some of the Hadendowa clans, was on foot against the Mahdieh. At this date, however, Her Majesty's Government gave orders for the withdrawal of troops from the Sudan, and the evacuation of the advanced posts was at once commenced. On the 17th May the withdrawal of the Expeditionary Force from Suakin began with the departure of the Guards' Brigade and the New South Wales contingent, General Lyon Fremantle accompanied his brigade. Sir G. Graham left the same day; his final despatch is given in Appendix 65. Orders for withdrawal.

On the 19th, Lord Wolseley left for Cairo. The cavalry

and the Berkshire and East Surrey Regiments sailed on the 20th and 21st, Sir J. McNeill leaving on the latter date. Sir G. Greaves remained temporarily in command to superintend the withdrawal of the troops and to carry out the defensive arrangements that Lord Wolseley had decided upon.

CHAPTER XIV.

CONCLUSION.

ON the 27th June Lord Wolseley handed over the command of the troops in Egypt to Sir F. Stephenson, and with his personal and headquarter staff left for Alexandria *en route* for England.

As already stated, on receipt of Lord Wolseley's orders to continue the evacuation of the Sudan, General Brackenbury had on the 5th July, 1885, evacuated Dongola.

On the 6th July, leaving the headquarters and four companies of the Royal West Kent Regiment at Hafir, whither they had rowed from Dongola in whalers, General Brackenbury proceeded with all other troops in boats to Fatmeh. Here he relieved Colonel Maurice and Staff, and the garrisons of Fatmeh and Kubudeh, who then left for the north. The rear squadron of the 19th Hussars and two guns crossed the river from Hafir, and marched to Fatmeh.

On the 7th July one troop of the 19th Hussars and two guns marched from Fatmeh by the east bank for Halfa; the rear guard remaining being then:—

Hafir: headquarters and 4 companies Royal West Kent Regiment.

Fatmeh: 1 troop 19th Hussars, 3 companies Royal West Kent Regiment.

Kubudeh: 1 company Royal West Kent Regiment.

On the 10th July, it having been reported that Kajbar was clear of stores, Captain Boardman, R.N., the Senior Naval Officer, was informed that nothing now detained the rear guard above Kajbar except the steamers, and that, as soon as he could pass these down, the rear guard could proceed to Abri. To this the Senior Naval Officer replied that he did not yet consider the river sufficiently high for the steamers to descend the 3rd Cataract; he, however, succeeded in passing down four pinnaces.

On the same day Abdullah Hamza, a merchant of Khandak, came into Fatmeh from the south and reported the death of Mohammed Ahmed, the Mahdi, at Khartum.

(S.C.2) Q

Marginal notes: June 27th. Departure of Lord Wolseley for England. Evacuation of the province of Dongola. July 10th. Reported death of Mahdi.

On the 14th July the Senior Naval Officer reported that he would be prepared to send the steamers down the cataract on the 16th and 17th. The Headquarters and four companies of the Royal West Kent Regiment were therefore moved from Hafir to Fatmeh on the 15th, and one company with the three companies at Fatmeh, proceeded over the cataract to Kubudeh, relieving the company there, which with the three companies from Fatmeh, passed below Shaban.

On the 16th July, four companies of the Royal West Kent Regiment reached Kajbar and relieved the Egyptian garrison, which proceeded northwards.

On the same day, the Mudir's steamer, towing the hospital and other nuggars, passed over the cataract. Two steam pinnaces also passed down, one of them, with the four pinnaces already at Kajbar, passing over the rapid at that place.

On the 17th, the "Lotus" passed over the 3rd Cataract to Abri, followed by the last steam pinnace. It arrived at Kajbar and passed that cataract at 1 p.m.

July 17th, Evacuation of Fatmeh.

Orders were then telegraphed to the Officer commanding the Royal West Kent Regiment at Fatmeh to disestablish the telegraph and come down. This was done at once, the last boat leaving Fatmeh at 3.20 p.m., and reaching Shaban the same evening.

The troop 19th Hussars left Fatmeh at 3 p.m., reaching Kajbar at 2 p.m.

On the 18th July, the Headquarters and four companies of the Royal West Kent Regiment reached Kajbar at 3 p.m. and passed the rapid. The troop of 19th Hussars left Kajbar at 3 p.m. and proceeded to Absarat, the Egyptian garrison of which had been relieved on the previous day by two companies of the Royal West Kent Regiment.

On the 19th July, the two steam pinnaces, with nuggers in tow, and the Headquarters and six companies of the Royal West Kent Regiment, reached Absarat from Kajbar; and on the same day the troop of 19th Hussars marched from Absarat to Koyehmatto.

On the 20th July, the Royal West Kent Regiment complete, with the two pinnaces and nuggers, descended the river to Koyehmatto, and, having sent on the Egyptian garrison, went on to Dorkehmatto. The troop of 19th Hussars marched from Koyehmatto to Koyekeh and relieved the Egyptian garrison there.

On the 21st July, the entire rear guard arrived at Abri, and General Brackenbury handed over the command of the troops composing it, to General Grenfell, who had been appointed to the command of the Frontier Field Force, with the local rank of Major-General, on Lord Wolseley's departure for England.

July 21st. Command of frontier handed to General Grenfell.

By this date the Guards' Camel Regiment, Heavy Camel Regiment, Light Camel Regiment, and Mounted Infantry Camel Regiment, had left Egypt, and were followed on the 26th August by the Royal Sussex Regiment and the Royal Irish Regiment. On the 9th September, 1885, the Gordon Highlanders, the last of the regiments of the Nile Expedition to leave, embarked at Alexandria.

As already stated, the command of the Frontier Force was given to General Grenfell. The following despatch from Lord Wolseley, the suggestions in which were acted on, will show the extent of his command and that of General Hudson, who, on the departure of Sir G. Greaves, took over the command of the troops at Suakin. Both of these officers were under the command of Sir F. Stephenson, who after Lord Wolseley's departure again became Commander-in-Chief in Egypt.

"*Cairo, 27th May,* 1885.

"My Lord,

"1. In confirmation of telegrams sent on various occasions, I have the honour to report that the following are the arrangements which I recommend for the protection of the Egyptian frontier, and for the garrisons of Egypt proper, and of Suakin.

Lord Wolseley's recommendations for protection of Egypt.

"In the recommendations which concern the frontier and Egypt proper, Sir Evelyn Baring and General Sir F. Stephenson concur; and in those concerning Suakin, General Graham, General Greaves, and Brigadier-General Hudson concur.

"2. The frontier force, that is to say, the troops at and south of Assuan, should consist of—

1 Regiment of Cavalry.
1 Battery of Royal Artillery.
1 Company of Royal Engineers.
4 Battalions of Infantry.
Proportion of departmental corps.

"In addition to the above British troops, there will be an almost precisely similar force of the Egyptian Army.

"3. The garrison at Cairo should consist of—

> 1 Regiment of Cavalry.
> 1 Battery Royal Horse Artillery.
> 1 Mountain Battery, Royal Artillery.
> 1 Garrison Battery, Royal Artillery.
> 2 Companies Royal Engineers (of which one field)
> 7 Battalions of Infantry.
> Proportion of departmental corps.

"4. The garrison of Alexandria should consist of—

> 1 Garrison Battery Royal Artillery.
> 1½ Battalions of Infantry.
> Proportion of departmental corps.

"5. The Suakin garrison should consist of—

> 1 Squadron Indian Cavalry.
> 1 Garrison Battery, Royal Artillery.
> 1 Company Madras Sappers and Miners.
> 1 British Battalion.
> 3 Indian Battalions.

150 Men, Mounted Infantry (to be taken from British Battalion, which should be correspondingly increased).
100 Men, Camel Corps (taken from the Indian Battalions).
> Proportion of departmental corps.

"6. At Suakin only the ground up to the West Redoubt will be held. To hold more, say, for instance, to Otao, or even only to Handub, would require the retention at, and in the neighbourhood of, Suakin, of a British force very considerably larger than I have just named. This force would certainly suffer severely from the climate, and to a certain extent from the enemy's attacks. The garrisons of isolated spots, such as Otao and Handub, might at any moment be surrounded by Osman Digna's forces, and the investment thus formed, would have to be broken by a flying column from Suakin itself. Operations of this kind in a climate such as that of Suakin, during the summer months, mean the greatest fatigue and exhaustion to the troops, much sickness and loss of life from the sun, and in addition, the casualties of action. No compensating military advantage is gained, for, should the advance on Berber be resumed, Otao could be re-occupied with far less loss than would result from holding it through the summer; while as regards the protection of the railway, the existing line is so badly constructed, that if it were ever required for permanent traffic the whole would have to be relaid. As at present made, a large portion must be washed away during the autumn rains, as no culverts have been made in any parts of it. It is not, therefore, worth the loss of British soldiers' lives, to protect it from now till the floods break it up in September or October.

"7. For these reasons the concentration of the Suakin garrison within the immediate neighbourhood of the town is, in a military sense, most advisable. Waterpipes will be laid to all the forts round Suakin, and these posts will be connected by an 18-inch gauge light railroad, which will be of use, not only for the transport of stores, but also for the rapid movement of troops to any threatened point.

"8. The retreat from the positions at present occupied by our troops on the Upper Nile commenced yesterday, Merowi having then been evacuated. Their movement into their new positions will take between two and three months. It is difficult to estimate the time at all exactly, as much depends upon a very uncertain element, namely, the manner in which the Nile rises; but, by the middle of August, I anticipate that the greater part of the troops will, should nothing unforeseen occur, be echeloned along the river in the manner indicated at the commencement of this despatch.

"I have, &c.,
(Signed) "WOLSELEY, General.
"The Right Hon.
"Marquis of Hartington."

During the evacuation of Dongola by the British troops the Mahdieh had not been idle; before, however, following the steps of their pursuit, it may be well to glance at their position when the retreat was ordered.

On the retreat of the Desert Column from Gubat on the 14th February, the Mahdi, feeling that he was safe from further attack for the present, at once turned his attention to the subjugation of the tribes in Kordofan, among whom considerable disturbances had broken out. He accordingly withdrew from Metemmeh the reinforcements of 6,000 men which had been sent down to that place under Wad en-Nejumi and Abu Anga, and despatched them under the latter

Movements of the Mahdieh.

Chief to restore order in the Takalla mountains, leaving Wad en-Nejumi, with 8,000 men, in command of Metemmeh.

Mohammed-el-Kheir was sent to Berber to make preparations to resist the expected British advance from Suakin, and small posts of observation were established at the Gabra wells (on the Debbeh-Khartum road) under Wad Garaish, and at Sarni (near Merowi), under Ez Zein.

Fall of Sennar and Kassala. On hearing, about the middle of May, that the British Government had determined to retire from the Sudan, the Mahdi must have realised that the retention at Metemmeh of Wad en-Nejumi and his force was no longer necessary, and that if he wished to carry out his programme of conquest, it was necessary that every available man should be forthcoming. In order to arrive at this it was necessary to relieve the large force which was at that time locked up, besieging Sennar. An army was accordingly despatched in May, under Wad Jubara, to reinforce the besiegers there, and another of 10,000 men in July, under Wad en-Nejumi. Before the arrival, however, of the latter force, the town capitulated to Wad Jubara on the 18th August. Almost at the same date Kassala capitulated to troops that had been sent against it by Osman Digna, on the retirement of the English from Suakin.

Advance on Dongola. On the 26th May, Berber being no longer threatened from Suakin, Mohammed-el-Kheir received orders to follow the English into Dongola. On the 15th June, Merowi was occupied by Ez Zein from Sarni, and by Abd-el-Majid el-Kalik, who had followed the River Column as far as Berti and had there remained during the spring.

20th June, 1885. Death of Mahdi. Advance delayed. While the advanced guard of the Mahdieh was still at Merowi, and before the British rear guard had evacuated Dongola, the Mahdi was taken suddenly ill, and died on the 20th June.

This event, for the time being, delayed the hostile advance. In spite of the energetic measures taken by the Khalifa, Abdullah et-Taaishi, who at once assumed command, and issued proclamations stating that the Mahdi had prophesied his own death and had appointed him his successor, it took the spirit out of all, and many of the leaders, anxious to gain greater power under the altered condition of affairs, hurried to Khartum to do homage to Abdullah et-Taaishi. As, however, the last thoughts of the Mahdi had been directed towards the conquest of Egypt, his followers agreed that the orders of the "great master of all" must be carried out, and the concentration in Dongola was continued. It was not, however, till the 17th August that Abd-el-Majid el-Kalik reached Dongola with his advanced guard of 3,000 men. {August 17th. Dongola occupied by Dervishes.}

From this date the concentration steadily progressed till it culminated in the advance on, and investment of, Kosheh in November, and in the defeat of the Mahdieh by Sir F. Stephenson at Ginnis on the 30th December, 1885. {December 30th. Battle of Ginnis.}

Before leaving Cairo Lord Wolseley wrote the following final despatch to the Secretary of State for War:— {Lord Wolseley's final despatch.}

"*Cairo, 15th June*, 1885.

"Sir,

"1. All the troops on the Upper Nile have now quitted Dongola. Some have already embarked for England and the others are on their way to their allotted destinations. The withdrawal of our forces to a defensive position on the Wady Halfa railway in accordance with the orders I have received is now nearly completed. I therefore think it desirable that, before leaving Egypt for England, I should place on record my opinion as to the manner in which all ranks under my command have carried out their respective duties. I wish also to bring to your notice the names of some officers who have specially distinguished themselves, almost all of whom I think it would be in the interests of the service to promote whilst they are still young and efficient.

"2. It is a source of great pride to me as a soldier, and of satisfaction as a British subject, that upon each fresh occasion when I am brought in contact with Her Majesty's troops in the field, I find the army more efficient as a military machine than it was the last time I was associated with it on active service. This improvement is evident in all grades, and in all arms and departments, but it is, I think, most marked in the rank and file. Military spirit—the essence of military efficiency—is now established in our army in a higher form, and on a sounder basis than formerly. I attribute the improvement in moral tone that undoubtedly exists, in no small degree to the abolition of flogging, and I believe that amongst the officers who have lately had practical experience in the field, even those previously in favour of retaining the lash as a punishment on active service, now fully recognise that many advantages have resulted from its total abolition. The soldier is prouder of himself and of his calling than he used to be, and his self-esteem has also been raised by the healthy feeling of liberty arising from the knowledge that if the army does not suit his tastes, he can easily quit it, instead of being bound to it for ten or twelve years. Our rank and file are morally better, and militarily more efficient than formerly. The general conduct and bearing of our men in the Sudan left nothing to be desired, and was not only creditable to the British army, but should be also a just source of pride to the British nation.

"3. The physical appearance of the soldiers who assembled at Korti in last December and January, spoke well for the efficiency of our present recruiting service. I have never seen a finer body of troops in the field, and both their appearance and the noble spirit which animated them, made me feel that I was safe in relying on them to accomplish any enterprise where success was possible. The great bulk of these men had reached Korti in the whalers expressly built in England for the navigation of the Nile, and the bodily training obtained by rowing, tracking, and portaging, gave to these young soldiers the toughness, as well as the outward look, of veterans. No men have ever done harder work than they did, and to their lasting credit be it said, they did it cheerfully and without a murmur.

"4. It would be impossible for any commander to have been more ably seconded by his Chief of the Staff than I was by Major-General Sir Redvers Buller, V.C., K.C.M.G., C.B. To his already well-established reputation as a daring and skilful leader in action, he has now added that for great administrative capacity. When the late Major-General Sir Herbert Stewart was wounded, and Colonel Burnaby, whom I had appointed to command at Metemmeh, had been killed, I ordered General Sir Redvers Buller to take command of the desert column, and he carried out to my entire satisfaction the difficult operation of withdrawing it from Gubat to Jakdul in the face of an active enemy—an operation requiring great nicety of execution, and a thorough knowledge of the military art. When I received orders that the army was to fall back from its summer quarters on the Nile, to the Wady Halfa railway, I entrusted him with the details of this movement, which was also most ably effected. I beg to recommend this officer to your favourable consideration.

"5. Major-General Sir Evelyn Wood, V.C., G.C.M.G., K.C.B., was the General of Communications, and brought the utmost zeal to bear upon the arduous and difficult duties of that position. Our line of communications by rail, river, and desert, from Alexandria to Gubat, was about 1,500 miles in length. The responsibility of supervising it was great, but, thanks to Sir E. Wood's ability and energy, and to the efficient support he received from the large staff of officers under his command, the army operating in the front was well fed and provided with all it required. The officers and men of the Egyptian army, under General Wood's immediate orders, worked along this line with indefatigable earnestness, and with the best possible results to the welfare of the expedition.

"6. It is very desirable to utilise to the full the opportunity which active service affords of gauging the military ability of our officers. Every campaign enables a selection to be made among those officers, whose proved skill in the field, and thorough knowledge of their profession, mark them out as fitted for higher rank. Brigadier-General Brackenbury, R.A., comes, I consider, prominently under this category, and, in the interests of the army and the State, I would strongly recommend him to your favourable consideration. When Major-General Earle was killed at Kirbekan, Brigadier-General Brackenbury assumed command of the Nile column, and led it in its advance towards Abu Hamed. In this, and throughout the operations in the Sudan, he proved himself to be one of the ablest officers in Her Majesty's army, and he would be a most valuable addition to our present list of general officers.

"7. The column intended to operate from Suakin in the direction of Berber, and to construct a railway to that place, was despatched last February, partly from England and partly from India, with a rapidity that was highly creditable to our military and naval organisation. Great numbers of camels and other transport animals were safely and quickly disembarked at Suakin during the month of March, and three brigades of infantry and one of cavalry took the field there before the end of that month, destroying Osman Digna's power in the hard fought action of the 22nd March, under Major-General Sir J. McNeill. The quickness with which this column was organised for active service is most creditable to Sir Gerald Graham, and to the zeal and ability of the officers under his command. He speaks in high terms of the manner in which Major-General Sir George Greaves, K.C.M.G., C.B., performed the duties of Chief of the Staff to his force. I do not believe there is any officer who has a more extensive knowledge of the working of our army than Sir George Greaves, nor one who can use his great staff and admistrative experience to better purpose.

"8. I attach to this despatch a list of those officers, non-commissioned officers and men whose services are, I consider, specially deserving of mention, and in it I have included those of the Suakin Force who, I think, have done the best work.

"9. The various Departments were administered to my entire satisfaction by the following Officers:—In the Intelligence Department, Colonel Sir C. Wilson, K.C.M.G., C.B., R.E., kept me fully supplied with information as to the enemy's doings and intentions, and showed himself eminently qualified to conduct the duties of that Department. At Suakin similar information was furnished by the exertions of Major Grover and Major Chermside, both of the Royal Engineers. The last-named was Governor-General of the Red Sea Littoral, and has rendered valuable service to the State for a lengthened period.

"The Medical Department was administered with ability by Deputy Surgeon-General O'Nial. I have never seen the sick and wounded better cared for. The arrangements were good, and the Medical Officers worked with untiring zeal, and great devotion to their duties. At Suakin Deputy Surgeons-Generals Barnett and Hinde directed all medical matters with great credit to themselves and to their Department. Both there and on the Nile, the work done by the nursing sisters was highly appreciated by doctors and patients. The Commissariat duties were well performed throughout, the Department being excellently directed by Assistant Commissary-General Hughes. At Suakin Assistant Commissary-General Robertson did good work; all his arrangements were satisfactory.

"Lieutenant-Colonel Furse, the Director of Transport, carried on his duties in a most creditable manner, and produced good results under considerable difficulties. The system of separating these duties from those of the Commissariat, answered admirably, and I hope it may be established as the rule in future. Lieutenant-General Graham speaks in high terms of Lieutenant-Colonel Walton, who was the Director of Transport to the Suakin Force, and of Lieutenant-Colonel Beckett, who was in charge of the Indian Transport.

"Assistant Commissary-General of Ordnance Pease, on the Nile, and Assistant Commissary-General Skinner, at Suakin, evinced a thorough knowledge of the detail and working of the Ordnance Store Department. All the officers under them worked zealously and well.

"Owing to the great length of the line of communications up the Nile Valley, and to the number of stations upon it, the work of the Pay Department was difficult and very heavy. Great credit is due to Colonel Olivey for the efficient manner in which it was performed. The pay duties at Suakin were satisfactorily carried out by Lieutenant-Colonel Craig.

"The Rev. J. Brindle, the Senior Chaplain with the Army up the Nile, won the esteem of all by his untiring devotion to his sacred duties, and by his unfailing and cheerful kindness.

"Veterinary-Surgeons Burt and Walters well performed the work that fell to them.

"The Volunteers were represented by men of the Volunteer Engineers and of the Post Office corps, who, both by their zeal and their soldierlike bearing, sustained the reputation of the service to which they belong.

"10. The Indian Contingent, under Brigadier-General Hudson, C.B., showed high soldier-like qualities, and was of the utmost value in the operations round Suakin.

"11. The assistance rendered by the Royal Navy was willingly given, and of the greatest importance. I cannot praise too much the manner in which officers and men under the command of Captain Boardman, R.N., helped us in fitting out our boats, in working them over the worst cataracts of the Nile, and in keeping open our line of communications along that river. In previous despatches I have dwelt upon the excellent services rendered by the Naval Brigade, under Captain Lord C. Beresford, R.N., an officer, whose readiness of resource and whose ability as a leader, are only equalled by his daring. At Suakin, Commodore More-Molyneux was untiring in his exertions to help the troops; and the naval transport duties were most successfully carried on, under the direction of Captain Fellowes, R.N.

"12. Great credit is due to Colonel Butler, C.B., and to Lieutenant-Colonel Alleyne, R.A., for the care and thought with which the whalers for Nile service were designed and fitted out, under their immediate superintendence. The experience they had gained in boat work during the Red River expedition of 1870 enabled them to bring to this matter, and later on to their work on the Nile, an amount of special knowledge possessed by few men. Without these whalers, or had they been less efficiently equipped, the assembling of the troops at Korti, at the date it took place, and the subsequent advance of the two columns, one across the desert and the other up the Nile, would have been impossible. The great bulk of the provisions taken with the first column, and the whole of those taken with the second, were conveyed to Korti in our English whale boats. In a similar manner the retirement just effected from our positions on the Upper Nile, extending from Merowi to Abu Fatmeh, would have been extremely difficult save for these boats, as the river at this season is unnavigable by nuggers or other native craft.

"13. This is the first time that colonial troops have been employed outside the colonies in any of our wars. The result has been so satisfactory that I earnestly trust the noble and patriotic example set by New South Wales may, should occasion arise, be followed by other colonies. The Officers and men of the New South Wales contingent, under Colonel Richardson, were a credit to their colony, and to the parent race from which it sprang.

"The Dominion of Canada supplied us with a most useful body of boatmen under the command of Colonel Denison of the Ontario Militia. Their skill in the management of boats in difficult and dangerous waters, was of the utmost use to us in our long ascent of the Nile. Men and Officers showed a high military and patriotic spirit, making light of difficulties, and working with that energy and determination which have always characterised Her Majesty's Canadian forces.

"15. The Officers of my personal staff are named in the margin,* and I beg to recommend them to your favourable consideration. I cannot lay too much stress on the valuable services rendered by General Zohrab Pasha, of the Egyptian Army. His knowledge of Eastern languages, his intimate acquaintance with the manners and customs of the Sudanese people, and his tact in dealing with the native authorities, enabled him to assist me in a way that no British Officer could have done. Lieutenant-Colonel Swaine, C.B., Rifle

---

* Lieut.-Colonel Swaine, C.B. ... } Military Secretaries.
Lieut.-Colonel Grove .. ..

General Zohrab Pasha .. ..
Captain Lord C. Beresford, R.N.
Major Creagh, R.A. .. .. } Aides-de-Camp.
Major Childers, R.E. .. ..
Major Adye, R.A. .. ..
Dr. Simson Pratt .. ..

Brigade, was my Military Secretary until unfortunately his health broke down, and to my great regret he had to leave for home. The duties of Military Secretary have since then been carried out by Lieutenant-Colonel Grove, East Yorkshire Regiment, with the greatest ability. He is highly educated as a Staff Officer, and, previous to taking up this work, had done excellent service in superintending the fitting out of the English whale boats at Gemai. To all my Aides-de-Camp also my thanks are specially due.

"16. In conclusion I would only add, that, though the expedition was not crowned with success, the spirit and behaviour of the troops which took part in the operations, whether on the Nile or at Suakin, may be viewed with satisfaction by every Englishman. The army under my command was unable to accomplish the object set before it, and to save the lives of the gallant General Gordon and of the garrison of Khartum. But this was from no fault of its own, from no lack of courage, of discipline, of dash, or of endurance. It overcame physical difficulties of the greatest magnitude; it swept from its path, in every encounter, an enemy almost its equal in bravery, and greatly its superior in numbers, and its advanced guard reached the outskirts of Khartum only two days too late. No one can regret more than I do the fall of that place, but in common with all my countrymen, I look back with pride to the gallant struggle made by our troops to save Khartum and its heroic defender.

"I have, &c.,
(Signed)   "WOLSELEY, General.
"The Right Hon. the Secretary of State for War."

Inclosure.

LIST OF OFFICERS, NON-COMMISSIONED OFFICERS AND MEN WHOSE SERVICES ARE DESERVING OF SPECIAL MENTION.

ROYAL NAVY.

Captain F. R. Boardman
Captain Lord C. Beresford.
Commander T. F. Hammill.
Commander Julian A. Baker.
Lieutenant R. A. J. Montgomerie.
Lieutenant W. T. Bourke.
Lieutenant C. Reeve.
Chief Engineer H. Benbow.

CAVALRY.

1st Life Guards.

Lieutenant-Colonel Hon. R. A. J. Talbot.
Major the Hon. C. C. G. Byng.
Lieutenant D. V. Pirie.

2nd Life Guards.

Major the Earl of Dundonald.
Lieutenant W. F. Peel.

Royal Horse Guards.

Captain J. F. Brocklehurst.
Lieutenant Sir J. C. Willoughby, Bart

3rd Dragoon Guards.

Major F. M. Wardrop.

1st Dragoons.

Captain F. W. Rhodes.

4th Hussars.

Brevet Lieutenant-Colonel H. F. Grant.
Captain C. W. Peters.

5th Lancers.

Captain E. C. W. Gilborne.
Captain A. C. Little.

7th Hussars.

Brevet Lieutenant-Colonel H. McCalmont.
Captain C. F. Thomson.
Captain T. H. Phipps (since dead).
Captain H. Paget.

10th Hussars.

Major R. C. D'E. Spottiswoode.
Captain the Earl of Airlie.
Regimental Sergeant-Major B. Turner.

14th Hussars.

Brevet Major the Hon. G. H. Gough.

16th Lancers.

Major T. Davison.
Private W. Ilsley.
Private H. Newton.

19th Hussars.

Lieutenant-Colonel P. H. S. Barrow, C.B., C.M.G.
Major J. C. Hanford Flood.
Captain J. C. K. Fox.
Troop Sergeant-Major W. Beale.
Sergeant Chislett.

20th Hussars.

Lieutenant-Colonel C. Mangles.
Major F. J. Graves.

21st Hussars.

Captain C. B. Pigott.

ROYAL ARTILLERY.

Colonel F. Duncan.
Colonel H. Brackenbury, C.B.
Brevet Lieutenant-Colonel J. F. Maurice.
Brevet Lieutenant-Colonel J. Alleyne.
Major R. MacGregor Stewart.
Major A. E. Turner.
Major W. Hunter.
Brevet Major F. G. Slade.
Brevet Major A. G. Creagh.
Brevet Major J. Adye.
Captain A. N. Rochfort.
Captain H. C. Sclater.
Captain R. A. Bannatine.
Captain G. F. A. Norton.
Captain H. M. L. Rundle.
Lieutenant J. M. Grierson.
Lieutenant F. R. Wingate.
Sergeant T. Lee.

ROYAL ENGINEERS.

Colonel J. B. Edwards, C.B.
Colonel Sir C. W. Wilson, K.C.M.G., C.B.
Colonel E. P. Leach, V.C.
Brevet Lieutenant-Colonel J. C. Ardagh, C.B
Brevet Lieutenant-Colonel T. Fraser, C.M.G.
Brevet Lieutenant-Colonel E. Wood.
Major G. E. Grover.
Major W. FitzH. Spaight.
Major J. F. Dorward.
Brevet Major D. A. Scott.
Brevet Major H. C. Chermside, C.M.G.
Brevet Major H. H. Kitchener.
Brevet Major E. S. E. Childers.
Captain D. C. Courtney.
Captain H. H. Settle.
Captain H. A. Yorke.
Captain C. B. Wilkieson.
Captain F. W. Bennet.
Captain G. F. Wilson.
Captain A. H. Bagnold.
Lieutenant F. C. Heath.
Lieutenant A. G. Thomson.
Lieutenant H. M. Lawson.
Sergeant-Major Dalton.
Lance-Corporal J. Dale.
Sapper W. Leitch.
Sapper T. Bennet.

INFANTRY.

Grenadier Guards.

Colonel R. T. Thynne.
Lieutenant-Colonel H. E. Colvile.
Captain E. M. S. Crabbe.
Captain the Hon. F. W. Stopford
Captain H. P. St. J. Mildmay
Lieutenant J. T. St. Aubyn.
Sergeant-Major Hall.
Colour-Sergeant G. Ditchfield.
Private R. Cragg.

Coldstream Guards.

Colonel A. Lambton.
Lieutenant-Colonel the Hon. E. E. T. Boscawen.
Captain the Hon. H. C. Legge.
Sergeant-Major Dikenson.
Sergeant-Major Birch.

Scots Guards.

Colonel the Hon. W. R. Trefusis.
Lieutenant-Colonel Mildmay W. Willson.
Lieutenant J. W. A. Drummond.
Colour-Sergeant Livesay.

East Kent Regiment.

Captain R. G. Kekewich.

Royal Fusiliers.

Lieutenant E. M. Barttelot.

Somersetshire Light Infantry.

Captain H. A. Walsh.

East Yorkshire Regiment.

Brevet Lieutenant-Colonel C. Grove.
Lieutenant H. St. L. Wood.

Royal Irish Regiment.

Lieutenant-Colonel H. Shaw, V.C.
Captain H. W. N. Guinness.
Lieutenant B. J. C. Doran.

Yorkshire Regiment.

Captain F. B. Briggs.
Captain H. Bowles.

Lancashire Fusiliers.

Lieutenant F. Hammersley.

Royal Scots Fusiliers.

Serjeant Duggan.

Scottish Rifles.
Major C. T. Barrow.

East Lancashire Regiment.
Captain A. G. Leonard.

East Surrey Regiment.
Colonel W. H. Ralston.
Major F. H. Maturin.
Lieutenant J. R. K. Birch.
Quarter-Master Serjeant H. Curson.

Duke of Cornwall's Light Infantry.
Captain H. P. Carden.
Lieutenant G. A. Ashby.
Lieutenant H. G. Morris.
Serjeant R. B. Briscoe.

Royal Sussex Regiment.
Colonel J. O. Vandeleur.
Major M. S. J. Sunderland.
Captain L. J. Trafford.

South Staffordshire Regiment.
Lieutenant-Colonel H. Beal.
Major J. Emeris.
Lieutenant H. N. C. Heath.

South Lancashire Regiment.
Captain D. P. Chapman.

Welsh Regiment.
Major C. C. Smyth.

Royal Highlanders.
Colonel W. Green, C.B.
Lieutenant-Colonel R. K. Bayly.
Captain A. Scott Stevenson.
Captain Lord A. Kennedy.
Lieutenant J. G. Maxwell.
Colour-Serjeant F. Tweedie.
Colour-Serjeant T. Connan.

Essex Regiment.
Major F. Ventris.
Captain W. G. Carter.
Captain H. S. Fleming.
Lieutenant R. J. Tudway.

Derbyshire Regiment.
Lieutenant F. R. Gregson (3rd Battalion).

Berkshire Regiment.
Lieutenant-Colonel A. G. Huyshe.
Captain F. W. N. MacCracken.
Quarter-Master T. Ford.
Serjeant-Major Mathieson.
Colour-Serjeant Cloke.

Royal West Kent Regiment.
Colonel E. Leach.
Captain H. D. Armstrong.
Lieutenant F. Wintour.

South Yorkshire Regiment.
Major A. S. Wynne.
Captain G. E. Lloyd.

Shropshire Regiment.
Lieutenant-Colonel R. H. Truell.
Captain J. H. W. Eyton.

King's Royal Rifle Corps.
Colonel (local Major-General) F. W. Grenfell.
Major C. Holled Smith.
Major R. S. R. Featherstonhaugh.
Captain Lord F. Fitzgerald.
Lieutenant E. J. Montagu-Stuart-Wortley.
Lieutenant R. L. Bower.
Private B. Fagan.

Gordon Highlanders.
Lieutenant C. H. Payne.
Serjeant Pitman.

Cameron Highlanders.
Major E. Everett.

Royal Irish Rifles.
Captain the Hon. F. L. L. Colborne.

Rifle Brigade.
Brevet Lieutenant-Colonel L. V. Swaine, C.B.
Captain C. R. Orde.
Private G. Wood.

2nd West India Regiment.
Major C. H. W. Tyndale.

ROYAL MARINES.
Brevet Major J. H. Sandwith.
Brevet Major W. H. Poë.
Captain A. C. Pearson.
Lieutenant D. J. Kysh.
Serjeant-Major Scudamore.

GENERAL OFFICERS AND OFFICERS ON HALF-PAY.

Lieutenant-General Sir G. Graham, V.C., K.C.B.
Major-General Sir E. Wood, V.C.
Major-General Sir J. C. McNeill, V.C., K.C.B., K.C.M.G.
Major-General Sir G. R. Greaves, K.C.M.G., C.B.
Major-General Sir R. H. Buller, V.C., K.C.M.G., C.B.
Major-General A. J. Lyon-Fremantle.
Colonel H. P. Ewart, C.B.
Colonel H. B. H. Blundell.
Colonel W. Arbuthnot.
Colonel R. Grant, half-pay, R.E.
Colonel G. B. Wolseley.
Colonel W. F. Butler, C.B.
Colonel K G. Henderson.
Lieutenant-Colonel G. A. Furse.
Lieutenant-Colonel F. T. Lloyd, half-pay, R.A.

INDIAN ARMY.

Brigadier-General J. Hudson, C.B., Bengal Staff Corps.

9th Bengal Cavalry.

Colonel A. P. Palmer, Bengal Staff Corps.
Major D. H. Robertson, Indian Army.
Ressaldar Hakm Singh.

15th Sikhs.

Colonel G. R. Hennessy, Bengal Staff Corps.
Major D. W. Inglis, Indian Army.
Captain H. A. Abbott, Bengal Staff Corps.
Subadar Goordit Singh.

17th Bengal Native Infantry.

Captain T. E. Spencer, Bengal Staff Corps.

28th Bengal Native Infantry.

Lieutenant-Colonel F. C. Singleton, Bombay Staff Corps.
Captain R. E. D. Reilly, Bombay Staff Corps.
Subadar Rama Kurrikur.

Bengal Staff Corps.

Brevet Major Norman Stewart.
Brevet Lieutenant-Colonel E. S. Walcott, Bombay Infantry, Principal Commissariat Officer.
Brigade-Surgeon J. H. Thornton, M.B., Indian Medical Staff, Principal Medical Officer.
Lieutenant-Colonel S. Beckett, Bengal Staff Corps, Director of Transport.
Major E. H. H. Collen, Bengal Staff Corps, Assistant Military Secretary.
Major G. R. J. Shakespear, Bengal Staff Corps, Director of Transport.

AUSTRALIAN CONTINGENT.

Colonel J. S. Richardson.
Lieutenant-Colonel W. W. Spalding.
Major Mackenzie.
Major Morris.

CANADIAN MILITIA.

Lieutenant-Colonel F. Denison.
Dr. Neilson.

DEPARTMENTS.

Chaplains' Department.

The Rev. W. H. Bullock.
The Rev. R. Brindle.
The Rev. R. F. Collins.
The Rev. J. Mactaggart.

Commissariat and Transport Staff.

Lieutenant-Colonel E. Hughes, C.M.G., Assistant Commissary-General.
Lieutenant-Colonel C. E. Walton, Assistant Commissary-General.
Lieutenant-Colonel J. T. Skinner, Assistant Commissary-General.
Major W. Robertson, Assistant Commissary-General.
Major R. A. Nugent, C.B., Assistant Commissary-General.
Major A. A. Baker, Assistant Commissary-General.
Major M. E. Rainsford, Assistant Commissary-General.
Captain M. Graham, Deputy-Assistant Commissary-General.
Captain J. Whitley, Deputy-Assistant Commissary-General.
Captain J. A. Boyd, Deputy-Assistant Commissary-General.
Quartermaster M. P. Wasp.
Quartermaster J. M'Loughlin.
Quartermaster W. J. Barrell (hon. Captain).
Quartermaster H. Joyce.
Conductor Haycock.
Staff-Sergeant P. O'Malley.

Medical Staff.

Deputy Surgeon-General J. O'Nial, C.B.
Deputy Surgeon-General S. A. Lithgow, M.D.
Deputy Surgeon-General O. Barnett (since dead).
Deputy Surgeon-General G. L. Hinde.
Surgeon-Major E. C. Markey.

Surgeon-Major G. C. Gribbon.
Surgeon-Major R. Waters, M.D.
Surgeon-Major G. E. Will.
Surgeon-Major C. H. Harvey, M.D.
Surgeon-Major T. F. O'Dwyer, M.D.
Surgeon-Major F. Ferguson, M.D.
Surgeon-Major B. B. Connolly.
Surgeon T. J. Gallwey, M.D.
Surgeon W. H. Briggs.
Surgeon J. Magill.
Surgeon W. B. Allin.
Surgeon H. L. Donovan, M.D.
Staff-Sergeant Arbeiter.

Ordnance Store Department.

Lieutenant-Colonel T. Pease, Assistant Commissary-General of Ordnance.
Major E. G. Skinner, Assistant Commissary-General of Ordnance.
Captain F. G. Wintle, Deputy-Assistant Commissary-General of Ordnance.
Captain F. E. Mulcahy, Deputy-Assistant Commissary-General of Ordnance.
Quartermaster C. L. Sheppard.
Conductor P. Mullen.

Pay Department.

Colonel W. R. Olivey, C.B.
Major R. G. Craig.
Major T. W. Drage.
Major F. N. Woodall.
Major G. T. C. St. J. Kneller.
Major A. P G. Dowdall.

Veterinary Department.

Inspecting Veterinary Surgeon W. B. Walters.
Veterinary Surgeon, 1st Class, W. Burt.
Veterinary Surgeon, 1st Class, C. Phillips.
Veterinary Surgeon, 1st Class, A. E. Queripel.

APPENDICES.—PART II.

APPENDIX 39.
(See page 1.)

DISTRIBUTION OF THE NILE EXPEDITIONARY FORCE AND STATE OF TROOPS AT KORTI PREVIOUS TO THE DEPARTURE OF THE DESERT COLUMN.

I.—*Distribution of Troops, 25th December, 1884.*

Corps.	At Korti.	Debbeh to Korti.	Dongola to Debbeh.	Abu Fatmeh to Dongola.	Dal to Abu Fatmeh.	Sarras to Dal.
Mounted Corps.			Sections.			
Heavy Camel	4	2	4	...	...	...
Light Camel	3	3	3	...	...	...
Guards' Camel	3 Cos.	1 Co.	...	...	...	...
Mounted Infantry Camel	Regt.	...	...	...	...	...
Royal Artillery Battery	...	6 Guns	...	...	...	...
Egyptian Battery	...	...	...	...	...	...
Egyptian Camel Corps	...	...	...	...	...	...
Bearer Companies	About ¼	R	R	...	...	...
Commissariat and Transport Corps	About ¼ 9th and 10th Companies	...	...	...	R No. 10 Co.	R No.
Field Hospital	1¾	...	¼	...	...	...
			Boats.			
South Staffordshire	Regt.	...	...	...	...	...
Royal Sussex*	Head-Qrs.	...	...	...	...	...
Essex	...	...	11	23	R	...
Duke of Cornwall's Light Infantry	...	...	8	30	R	...
Black Watch	...	...	...	19	R	...
Gordon Highlanders	...	...	...	...	Regt.	...
Royal West Kent	...	...	...	...	...	Regt.
Royal Irish	...	...	...	...	...	Regt.
Naval Brigade	...	...	...	...	½	½
Cameron Highlanders†	...	...	...	...	...	...

* Detachments at Debbeh and Dongola.   † At Korosko.

Troops having arrived at a station, but not yet left, are shown as being in the succeeding stages.
Regt. signifies a complete Regiment.
R. signifies remainder of a Regiment.

II. State of Troops, &c.,

Corps.	Officers and Men.						Horses.							
	Fit for duty.		Sick.		Total.		Fit for duty.				Sick.			
							Officers.		Troop.		Officers.		Troop.	
	Officers.	N.-C.O.'s and Men.	Officers.	N.-C.O.'s and Men.	Officers.	N.-C.O.'s and Men.	English.	Native.	English.	Native.	English.	Native.	English.	Native.
Headquarter Staff	14	34	1		14	35	5		24					
Brigade Staff	5	1			5	1	13							
Heavy Camel Regiment	10	153	3		10	156								
Light Camel Regiment	6	113			6	113								
Guards' Camel Regiment	15	278		8	15	286								
Mounted Infantry Camel Regt.	22	389		3	22	392								
19th Hussars	15	275		8	15	283			336					17
Royal Engineers	5	52			5	52								
1st Battalion Royal Sussex Regiment	3	163			3	163								
1st Battalion South Staffordshire Regiment	18	528		7	18	535	5							
1st Battalion Berkshire Regiment		1				1								
Commissariat and Transport Corps	2	27			2	27								
Ordnance Store Department	1	4			1	4								
Medical Staff	14				14									
Medical Staff Corps		37		1		38								
Army Chaplain	1				1									
Army Pay Department	2				2									
Veterinary Department	1				1									
Total	134	2055		31	134	2086	23		360					17

APPENDIX 39.

Korti, December 25th, 1884.

Total				Camels						Mules	Interpreters	Natives	Remarks
Officers		Troop		Fit for duty		Sick		Total					
English	Native	English	Native	Riding	Baggage	Riding	Baggage	Riding	Baggage				
	5		24	10				10			4	13	One officer, 16 non-commissioned officers and men, Egyptian Army, attached to Headquarters Staff.
	13			5	7			5	7		1	7	
				177		9		136				5	
				128		19		147					
				303		18		321			1		
				441	4			441	4		1	4	Private camels are not included.
			343							7	1		
				32	7	2	6	34	13		1		
	5										1		
				9	199		108	9	307		1	90	
				4				4				25	
	23		367	1109	217	48	114	1157	331	7	11	144	

APPENDIX 40.

(See page 5.)

SIR H. STEWART'S DESPATCH, REPORTING THE OCCUPATION OF JAKDUL.

HAMBOK,
January 4th, 1885, 10 *a.m.*

Sir,
I have the honour to inform you that in accordance with the orders I received, I left Korti on the 30th ultimo at 3 p.m. with the troops as per margin,* and proceeded to Jakdul where the forced arrived at 6.45 a.m., on the 2nd ultimo.

There were traces of Arabs on the road, but not in any numbers, and the march was manifestly a complete surprise to the inhabitants. As a rule, they retired before the advancing force, but several were interrogated and sent away with directions to bring in cattle and supplies to the troops.

Nearing Jakdul a party of men wearing the uniform of the Mahdi, *en route* from Metemmeh, with 11 camels, were captured and will be brought into camp as prisoners. These men are supposed to be emissaries of the Mahdi *en route* for Sheikh Wad Kinkain.

At Jakdul, a strong post, securing the water supply and practically impregnable, was established under the command of Colonel the Hon. E. E. T. Boscawen, Guards' Camel Regiment, and a garrison of 21 officers and 401 non-commissioned officers and men left for its defence, together with 9 horses and 10 camels. The remainder of the force left the same night on its return march, arriving here at 9 a.m. this morning. A post will be established for the improvement of the water supply here and the troops will arrive at Korti to-morrow about noon.

In conclusion, I have to report that the officers and men I have had the honour to command upon this convoy, have been called upon to carry out very unusual and very arduous work. It would be impossible for me to exaggerate the admirable spirit which has animated the force throughout. Every difficulty has been overcome by the exertion of the officers and men, and the wearisome plod of the baggage camel, and the still more wearisome labour of loading him, has been borne with a cheerfulness which must have been seen to have been thoroughly appreciated.

* Page 2.

I am glad to be able to state that there are no sick amongst the troops.

The casualties amongst the camels are as follows:—

Destroyed, 14. Turned loose, 17, but of the latter a few have been recovered whilst returning. . . . . .

I have, &c.,
(Signed) HERBERT STEWART, Brigadier-General.

APPENDIX 41.

(See page 10.)

SIR H. STEWART'S REPORT ON HIS SECOND MARCH TO JAKDUL.   Maps 1 and 3

JAKDUL,
January 14th, 1885.

Sir,

I have the honour to inform you that in accordance with your orders dated 6th instant, I proceeded with the force therein laid down to Jakdul, leaving Korti at 3 p.m. on the 8th January.

Owing to the small quantity of dhura taken with the force it was necessary to march comparatively slowly in order to enable the camels to graze or the men to cut grass with which to feed them.

On arrival at El Howeiya on the 10th instant, the detachment of the Mounted Infantry there, was relieved by a detachment of the Essex Regiment, and full instructions were left with Captain Carter, commanding the latter detachment, as to the defence of his post and the improvement of the water supply.

At El Howeiya a company of the Heavy Camel Regiment was also left temporarily. This company having had a considerable amount of work as rear guard on the morning of the 10th instant, would not without halting have had time to feed its camels. This company rejoined at Jakdul on the afternoon of the 12th instant. Some variations in the route of the entire force was also made in the case of the 19th Hussars in order to relieve the horses and facilitate their watering.

In order to show more clearly the march of the force, I beg to attach an itinerary of the main force, and also of each portion that marched at any time independently before arrival at

Jakdul. I found that Colonel Clarke's convoy had arrived on the preceding afternoon at 3 p.m., and that officer has been desired to forward to you direct a report of his movements.

The post at Jakdul has been vastly improved by Lieutenant-Colonel Hon. E. Boscawen and the Guards' Camel Regiment during the 8 days they have been quartered there. Two strong forts built of stone have been constructed completely commanding the water supply. Roads and footpaths have been made over the stony ground in all directions. A water supply for camels has been arranged by which 50 camels at the least can be watered in 10 minutes, and equally good arrangements have been made for obtaining water for the men from the upper reservoir.

I think it right to state that nothing but extreme hard work on the part of officers and men could have effected so complete a metamorphosis in this post, and I venture to submit that it reflects the highest credit on the Guards' Camel Regiment.

Seeing the improvement alluded to above that has been made in the access to and egress from Jakdul, I have deemed it unnecessary to construct a post on the main camel track, so that the garrison, consisting of the headquarters and 150 men of the Sussex Regiment, will now occupy the forts to be vacated by the Guards Camel Regiment.

A further improvement in the roads will be carried out by Colonel Vandeleur, and by this means convoys passing Jakdul will be but little delayed by the detour to obtain water.

In order to give rest to the camels, it seemed desirable to halt here one clear day. During this halt the transport has been entirely rearranged, so that the movement on Metemmeh may be carried out in accordance with your orders.

The health of the troops has been excellent, and their cheerfulness under circumstances which have been rendered at times sufficiently trying by the scarcity of water and the toilsome march of the camel, has been admirable.

Colonel Stanley Clarke's convoy left this morning on its return journey to Korti.

A convoy under Colonel Burnaby arrived this afternoon.

I propose leaving Jakdul with the force detailed in your orders of the 6th instant, this afternoon, after watering all animals.

I anticipate arriving at Abu Klea on Friday, 16th instant, and occupying Metemmeh, Sunday, 18th instant.

I have, &c.,
(Signed) HERBERT STEWART, Brigadier-General.

APPENDIX 41.

Enclosure.

I.

Officers.	N.C.O.'s and men.	Natives, including interpreters.	Egyptians.	Camels, riding and baggage.	Horses.	Mules.
90	1,509	296	8	2,228	155	2

Left Korti ... ... 2.45 p.m. 8.1.85.
Halt ... ... 6.0 ,, ,,
Marched ... ... 3.30 a.m. 9.1.85.
Halt (Abu Gîr) ... ... 9.30 ,, ,,
Marched ... ... 2.0 p.m. ,,
Halt (Abu Neshki) ... ... 5.45 ,, ,,
Marched ... ... 3.30 a.m. 10.1.85.
Arrived Hambok ... ... 6.45 ,, ,,
Arrived El Howeiya (halt) ... 9.30 ,, ,,
Marched ... ... 2.15 p.m. ,,
Halt (Zobrik el Kelb) ... ... 7.15 ,, ,,
Marched ... ... 4.0 a.m. 11.1.85.
Halt (Abu Harote) ... ... 9.0 ,, ,,
Marched ... ... 11.0 ,, ,,
Halt (Abu Halfa) ... ... 1.30 p.m. ,,
Marched ... ... 6.0 a.m. 12.1.85.
Jakdul ... ... 10.0 ,, ,,

II. Rear guard of above force, consisting of:—

1 Company Heavy Camel Regiment.

Officers.	N.C.O.'s and men.	Camels.
4	80	88

Arrived El Howeiya ... ... 11.30 a.m. 10.1.85.
Marched ... ... 9.0 ,, 11.1.85.
Halt ... ... 1.0 p.m. ,,
Marched ... ... 2.0 ,, ,,
Halt ... ... 5.30 ,, ,,
Marched ... ... 6 a.m. 12.1.85.
Halt ... ... 8 ,, ,,
Marched ... ... 9.30 ,, ,,
Arrived Jakdul ... ... 2.30 p.m. ,,

III.—Cavalry of above force:

Corps.	Officers.	N.C.O.'s and men.	Horses.	Camels.	Mules.	Drivers.
19th Hussars ...	8	120	146	76	2	18

Marched (from Abu Neshki) ...	3.0 a.m.	10.1.85.
Halt (El Howeiya)	3.30 ,,	,,
Marched	12.15 p.m.	10.1.85.
Halt (Zobrik el Kelb)	4.0 ,,	,,
Marched	3.30 a.m.	11.1.85.
Halt (Abu Halfa)	12.5 p.m.	,,
Marched	12.45 a.m.	12.1.85.
Arrived Jakdul	4.15 p.m.	,,

Taken on with force from El Howeiya 11.1.85:

Corps.	Officers, including one Medical Officer.	N.C.O's and men.	Camels.
Mounted Infantry ..	5	58	22

Left of above force at El Howeiya, 11.1.85.:

Corps.	Officers, including one Medical Officer.	N.C.O.'s and men.	Camels.
Mounted Infantry ..	..	8	8
Essex Regiment ..	3	55	..

APPENDIX 42.   Map 3.
(See page 10).

WORK DONE AT THE JAKDUL WELLS.*

Report of Major Dorward, R.E.

"*Jakdul Wells.*—The trench made for conveying water from the lower pool for camels, was deepened and widened (partly by use of gun cotton); a well was formed at the end, out of which three pumps on a platform raised it about 9 feet into wooden V troughs (which had been improvised out of biscuit boxes), and thus conveyed it on trestles into a puddled drinking trough, raised about 18 inches from the surface of the ground and curling back into the gorge, where it was stopped by the necessity of leaving an entrance for the men's drinking place. This channel was 130 feet long, and could water 60 camels at a time, all from one side. A rough stone wall regulated the access of animals to the trough, and another divided it off from the men's drinking place. Their drinking water was drawn by a pump (placed in the gorge just above the lower pool) from the middle pool. From the pump it was led by a pipe, formed out of suction and canvas hose (about 120 feet long), along the bed of the lower pool, into a cistern made out of 15 100-lb. biscuit boxes connected together and containing about 600 gallons, This cistern was placed in an excavation which had supplied earth for the camel trough. . . . . The delivery into the reservoir was only 420 gallons per hour, owing to the length and varying materials of the conduit, and we had no material available to make a second one. The conduit was broken on the ground level, by passing through a large biscuit box; so there were 16 boxes from which men could fill their skins and tanks at once. A canvas trough was provided for water bottles.

"That these arrangements were fairly successful was shown by the following tests:—

"On the 11th inst. Colonel Stanley Clarke's convoy of 1,066 camels, about 50 horses and 450 men, commenced watering at about 4.30 p.m. They had suffered from thirst during their march, and the consumption was large, and difficulty is always experienced in watering convoys where several

* See Map 3.

camels are looked after by one native, (who invariably leaves his animals tied tail to head and goes to get water for himself). This watering was completed by about 9 p.m. On the following morning the convoy watered again, and at 11 a.m. Sir H. Stewart's column arrived, 2,500 camels and 1,600 men, and were well watered in seven hours.

"On the 13th the watering arrangements were in constant work, and on the 14th the whole force was carefully watered in preparation for the forward march between 6 a.m. and 12.30 p.m. At that hour the arrangements were dismantled, as all the pumps (except two left for watering camels) were going forward with the Royal Engineer detachment.

"*Little Jakdul.*—These pools, discovered by chance, consisted of an upper and lower reservoir, and bore a general resemblance to the main wells. I measured them on the 10th inst., and found the contents to be—

Upper pool.. ..	3,675 gallons.
Lower pool.. ..	1,757 gallons.

"Wooden shoots made out of biscuit boxes were put up, and all the water pumped into the lower pool for the use of animals, except about 900 gallons left in the upper one for native drivers.

"A rough pathway for camels, to and from the lower pool, was cleared, and six camels could water at a time. . . . . In addition to the above, several other pools were discovered in the torrent beds, the most important being two in the same ravine as the main wells, but three-quarters of a mile higher up. They were measured by Lieutenant Count Gleichen to contain 320,000 gallons, and the water was good for drinking. . . . .

"*Redoubts.*—The wells were defended by the construction of two redoubts, one (Fort Boscawen) on hill south-east of entrance to basin, the other (Fort Stewart) on the hill immediately over the east side of the wells. Both were strong works, the profile consisting of a rough stone wall about 2 feet 6 inches thick, with a thorn entanglement in places, and the trace was decided by the form of the hills and the garrison available. Both were defiladed by traverses. Fort Boscawen was a closed work which could be held by half a company.

"The gorge of Fort Stewart was formed by a rock scarp, and in it was a capital natural redoubt formed by rocks. It could well have been defended by half a company, but was intended to hold two. The gorge leading up to it was closed at the lower end by a work formed of Commissariat stores and at its upper end by a wall and abatis. It was a most interesting work, as from whichever side the attack came, there was covered access to the wells (or would have been had the works been continued).

"*Roads.*—The Royal Engineers afforded no assistance in making these beyond the issue of tools.

"*Survey.*—A tolerably accurate triangulation, made with a view to determine the ranges of various points from the two redoubts, was completed by Lieutenant D. Dawson.* A good military sketch, on a small scale, of the whole neighbourhood was made by Count Gleichen.

"*Equipment.*—The equipment with which the work was done was necessarily of the most limited description. There was a very large amount of quarrying for the forts, and it was all done with two crowbars and three sledge hammers"

* This sketch was at once sent to Korti for the information of Lord Wolseley.

APPENDIX 43.

(See page 14.)

APPROXIMATE STATE of Troops, &c., at Abu Klea on 17th January, 1885.

Corps	Name of Commanding Officer.	Officers.	N.C.O.'s and men.	Egyptian soldiers.	Natives and Interpreters.	Horses.	Camels.	Guns.	Remarks.
Staff	...	10	6	...	13	5	26	...	
Naval Brigade	Captain Lord Charles Beresford	5	53	...	11	...	91	...	1 Gardner gun.
1st Battery 1st Brigade Southern Division Royal Artillery	Captain G. F. A. Norton	4	39	8	12	...	90	3	
19th Hussars	Lieut.-Col. P. H. S. Barrow, C.B., C.M.G.	8	127	...	19	155	73	...	
Guards' Camel Regiment	Lieut.-Col. Hon. E. E. T. Boscawen	19	365	...	...	...	406	...	Royal Marines form part of Guards Camel Regiment.
Heavy Camel Regiment	Lieut.-Col. Hon. B. A. Talbot	24	376	...	5	...	420	...	
Mounted Infantry Camel Regiment	Major Hon. G. H. Gough	24	359	...	4	...	424	...	
1st Battalion Royal Sussex Regim't	Major M. S. J Sunderland	8	250	...	4	2	...	...	
Royal Engineers	Major J. F. Dorward	2	25	...	4	...	40	...	
Bearer Company	Surgeon A. Harding	2	40	...	57	...	146	...	Surgeon - Major Ferguson, Principal Medical Officer.
Movable Field Hospital	Surgeon W. H. Briggs	2	20	...	12	...	54	...	
Transport Detail	Assistant Commissary-General R. Nugent, C.B.	7	33	...	202	...	1,118*	...	*Including 258 conveying Detachment Royal Sussex Regiment.
Total	...	115	1,687	8	343	153	2,888	3	

APPENDIX 44.
(See page 21.)

DESPATCHES ON THE BATTLE OF ABU KLEA. *Map 4.*

CAMP, KORTI,
26th *January*, 1885.

My Lord,

I forward herewith the copy of a despatch from Brigadier-General Sir Herbert Stewart, K.C.B., in which he describes the action he fought on the 17th instant at Abu Klea.

I am now awaiting reports from him as to his further proceedings subsequent to that battle, and I reserve comments upon his operations until I am in receipt of them.

At present, I shall content myself with remarking that all he has done proves him to be a real leader of men and an able General. All ranks under his command have displayed that discipline, and those high fighting qualities for which Her Majesty's Army has always been renowned.

I deeply deplore our loss, which was considerable in proportion to the numbers engaged; but this must generally be the case where we have to contend with a brave and determined enemy, five or more times our strength, and who invariably comes to close quarters and hand-to-hand fighting.

I have, &c.,
(Signed)   WOLSELEY, General.

The Right Hon.
The Marquis of Hartington, M.P.

Enclosure.

From Brigadier-General Sir H. Stewart to the Chief of the Staff.

ABU KLEA WELLS,
18th *January*, 1885.

Sir,

In continuation of my report of the 14th instant, I have the honour to inform you that the force under my command has made the following movements in carrying out your orders.

On the 14th instant the force left Jakdul at 2 p.m., and marching until dark, bivouacked for the night some 10 miles on the road to Metemmeh.

On the 15th instant a distance of 24 miles was accomplished, and a bivouac formed among the hills marked Jebel Es Sergain on the map.

On the 16th instant, the force left camp at 5 a.m., and halted for breakfast at 11.30 a.m., at the spot marked in the map by the 840th kilometre.

Whilst halted a report was received from Lieutenant-Colonel Barrow, 19th Hussars, who had been sent forward with his squadron to reconnoitre the neighbourhood of the Abu Klea Wells, informing me that he had seen about 50 of the enemy standing in groups on the hills about four miles north-east of Abu Klea.

Shortly afterwards the whole force was advanced—the Guards' Camel Regiment, Heavy Camel Regiment, and Mounted Infantry Camel Regiment, moving on a broad front in line of columns at half distance, the ground being favourable.

It soon became manifest that the enemy was in force, and looking to the hour (2 p.m.), it did not seem desirable to attempt to attack until the following morning. Another bivouac was therefore selected, protected from the enemy's fire so far as the ground would permit, and various small works were constructed.

During the night a continuous light fire at long ranges was kept up by the enemy, doing little damage.

Upon the 17th instant it was plain that the enemy was in force. During the night they had constructed works on our right flank, from which a distant but well aimed fire was maintained. In our front the manœuvring of their troops in line and in column was apparent, and everything pointed to the probability of an attack upon our position being made. Under these circumstances no particular hurry to advance was made, in the hope that our apparent dilatoriness might induce the enemy to push home. The camp having been suitably strengthened to admit of its being held by a comparatively small garrison—viz., 40 Mounted Infantry, 125 Sussex and details—and the enemy still hesitating to attack, an advance was made to seize the Abu Klea Wells.

The force moved on foot in a square, which was formed as follows:—Left front face, two companies Mounted Infantry; right front face, two companies Guards, with the three guns Royal Artillery in the centre. Left face, two companies Mounted Infantry, one company Heavy Camel Regiment. Right face, two companies Guards, detachment Royal Sussex. Rear face, four companies Heavy Camel Regiment, with Naval Brigade and one Gardner gun in the centre.

The advance at once attracted a fairly aimed fire from the enemy in front and on both flanks, which, in order to enable the square to continue moving, it was absolutely necessary to hold in check by the fire of skirmishers.

The enemy's main position was soon apparent, and by passing that position well clear of its left flank, it was manifest that he must attack or be enfiladed. As the square was nearly abreast of the position the enemy delivered his attack in the shape of a singularly well organised charge, commencing with a wheel to the left.

A withering fire was at once brought to bear upon the enemy, especially from the more advanced portion of the left front face of the square. The rear portion of this face, taking a moment or two to close up, was not in such a favourable position to receive the enemy's attack, and I regret to say that the square was penetrated at this point by the sheer weight of the enemy's numbers.

The steadiness of the troops enabled the hand to hand conflict to be maintained, whilst severe punishment was still being meted out to those of the enemy continuing to advance, with the result that a general retreat of the enemy, under a heavy artillery and rifle fire, soon took place.

After reforming the square, the 19th Hussars, who had been acting in difficult ground supporting our left flank, were pushed on to seize the Abu Klea Wells, and at 5 p.m. those wells were completely in our possession.

Detachments of the corps then returned to the bivouac of the 16th instant to bring up the camels and impedimenta left there, thus completing the force here this morning at 8 a.m.

The strength of the enemy is variously estimated from 8,000 to 14,000 men. My opinion is that not less than 2,000 of the enemy operated on our right flank, 3,000 in the main attack, and 5,000 in various other positions; but it is difficult to estimate their numbers with any exactness.

Their losses have been very heavy; not less than 800 lay dead on the open ground flanking our square, and their wounded during the entire day's fighting are reported by themselves as quite exceptional. Many are submitting.

I deeply regret that the necessity of obtaining water, delays my immediate advance on Metemmeh, but I trust this may be overcome in a few hours.

I cannot too deeply lament the loss of the many gallant officers and men that the force has suffered; but looking to the numbers of the enemy, their bravery, their discipline, and accuracy of fire of those possessing rifles, I trust that this loss, sad as it is, may be considered as in some measure inevitable.

In conclusion, I would add that it has been my duty to command a force from which exceptional work, exceptional hardships, and, it may be added, exceptional fighting, has been asked. It would be impossible for me adequately to describe the admirable support that has been given to me by every officer and man of the force.]

A return of casualities is attached. Every possible care is being taken of the wounded. Tents have been pitched, and a strong post established over the wells, garrisoned by a detachment of the Sussex Regiment.

      I have, &c.,
    (Signed) HERBERT STEWART,
             Brigadier-General.

ENCLOSURE.

Intelligence Report.

WELLS OF ABU KLEA,
18*th January*, 1885.

The force opposed to Sir H. Stewart, on the 17th, consisted as far as can be ascertained, of 2,000 Ababdeh, Bisharin, and other Arabs from Berber, under Abd-el-Majid,* nephew of the Emir of Berber, who was wounded in the arm, and retired towards Berber.

60 soldiers of the old Egyptian Army from Berber, under Mohammed Effendi Wahabi and Beshir Agha.

The men from Berber arrived at the Wells on the 12th January.

2,000 men, Arabs, and others from Metemmeh, under Ali-wad-Saad, the Emir, who was killed; these men arrived on the 14th January.

1,000 men of the Mahdi's Army, 400 with rifles, and from 4,000 to 6,000 Arabs, of various tribes from Kordofan, arrived on the morning of the action. Sheikh Musa, the Emir of the Hamar Arabs, was killed.

Total from 9,000 to 11,000 men; the principal attack was delivered by the men from Omdurman.

Prisoners captured, report that the fort of Omdurman has been taken by the Mahdi's troops; and a portion of his army is thus set free for operations northwards.

The steamers under Khasm-el-Mûs are at Shabluka, and visit Metemmeh occasionally. There are at Metemmeh two, and at Shendi one, guns in position against the steamers on the river bank; they were brought up from Berber.

Prisoners differ as to probability of resistance at Metemmeh; they say that the force at the Wells was confident of victory, and that the defeat inflicted on the enemy was very severe; they do not think those who fought yesterday will again offer a serious resistance.

The Berber force, which had a contingent of about 250

---

* Abd-el-Majid Khojali.

APPENDIX 45. 259

horsemen, retreated towards Berber, but many of the Arabs are still assembled to the north of the roads, probably watching the force.

From numerous papers addressed to Ez Zein, which were found on the field, it would appear that he was present. The other letters found, including one from the Mahdi, and several from the Emir of Berber, relate chiefly to supplies, to an attempt to enlist Khasm-el-Mûs in the Mahdi's cause, and the best way of attacking him and his steamers.

The Omdurman force retired, partly with the men from Metemmeh, towards that place, and partly towards Omdurman.

As far as can be ascertained from the prisoners, the Mahdi intends to offer a stubborn resistance to the British advance on Khartum, but the effect of the defeat of his troops yesterday had not then been felt.

Intelligence of the advance from Jakdul was given to the enemy by scouts, whose tracks were seen to the side of the road on the 1st.

. . . .

(Signed) C. W. WILSON, Colonel,
D.A.G.

Brigadier-General Sir H. Stewart, K.C.B.,
Commanding the Column.

Forwarded,
HERBERT STEWART, B.G.
18. 1. 85.

APPENDIX 45.

(See page 27.)

DESPATCHES ON OPERATIONS NEAR METEMMEH. *Map* 1.

CAMP, KORTI,
29th *January*, 1885.

My Lord,
I have the honour to forward for your Lordship's information, the accompanying copy of a despatch from Colonel Sir Charles Wilson, K.C.M.G., dated 22nd instant. In it he describes the operations of the column lately under the command of Major-General Sir Herbert Stewart, K.C.B., subsequent to the 18th January, the date of that officer's despatch, which I sent to your Lordship on the 26th instant. When Sir H. Stewart was

most unfortunately wounded on the 19th instant, the command devolved upon Colonel Sir Charles Wilson, R.E., as next senior officer.

In common with every soldier in this army, I most deeply deplore the incalculable loss which we have suffered, in being deprived of the valuable services of Sir H. Stewart at this moment; and I am sure I express the feelings of all ranks, when I venture to hope that he may soon be restored to health, and again able to serve Her Majesty.

In the action of the 19th instant, it will be observed that no guns accompanied the square when it moved upon the enemy's position.

I hear from all sides that the enemy's loss was very heavy, both in killed and wounded, but that his final charge was not delivered with that firm determination which characterised his fighting in the action at Abu Klea.

The result of these successfully executed operations has been to place us in the possession of the desert route from this place to the Nile, in the vicinity of Metemmeh, near which place we are now firmly established, cutting off in great measure the enemy's forces north of Shendi from those besieging Khartum and thus rendering still more difficult than before, the feeding of the Mahdi's army, already very short of provisions.

I am in great hopes that the position thus gained on the Nile, will materially facilitate the capture of Berber by General Earle's column, as the steamers from Khartum now at my disposal, manned by the Naval Brigade and by detachments of infantry, will be able to assist in that operation.

I am now, also, enabled to communicate by steamer direct with General Gordon in Khartum, and thus raise the veil which has so long hung round that city, preventing one from ascertaining its real condition, or from communicating my plan to the heroic soldier, who has so long and so nobly defended it under most adverse and extremely trying conditions.

I forward herewith a list of the killed and wounded.

When the nature of the operation, the fine fighting qualities of the enemy, and the great results achieved are duly considered, I do not think that our losses since the 17th instant have been excessive.

Her Majesty has to deplore the death of many brave soldiers of all ranks; but the discipline, steady courage, and the noble spirit of her troops cannot fail to be a matter of congratulation and of pride to every British subject.

         I have, &c.,
      (Signed) WOLSELEY, General.

The Right Hon.
 The Marquis of Hartington, M.P.

APPENDIX 45.

ENCLOSURE.

From Colonel Sir C. W. Wilson, R.E., to General Lord Wolseley.

CAMP, NEAR METEMMEH,
22nd *January*, 1885.

My Lord,
I have the honour to inform you that the column under Brigadier-General Sir Herbert Stewart left the wells of Abu Klea at about 3.30 p.m on the 18th. After passing the wells of Shebakat the column moved to its right, as it was Sir H. Stewart's intention to turn Metemmeh and attack it from the south. The column which had been halted for a short time before daylight, marched, at dawn, for the Nile, which was at that time about six miles distant. At about 7 a.m. on 19th, when between three or four miles from the river, the enemy showed in considerable force on the left flank, and were noticed working round our front to intercept our march to the Nile.

Sir H. Stewart at once halted and formed square round the camels. At 8 a.m. the enemy's sharpshooters commenced a well-sustained fire on the square, and Sir H. Stewart directed the formation of a zeriba of camel saddles and boxes to protect the men.

At 10.15 a.m., Sir H. Stewart having been severely wounded, I assumed command of the force as senior officer.

After consultation with Sir H. Stewart and Lieutenant-Colonel the Hon. E. E. T. Boscawen, I determined to strengthen the position, and, after leaving a garrison there, to march to the Nile. A fort was constructed to protect the hospital, and a small work was erected on a knoll, which commanded the zeriba at a distance of 80 yards on the south-west. These works were thrown up under heavy fire, which I regret to say caused several casualties.

A company of the Guards' Camel Regiment, and one from the Mounted Infantry, were thrown out as skirmishers to protect the troops whilst forming up outside the zeriba. The troops marched in square formation towards a gravel ridge where a large force of the enemy was seen with banners, and left the ground at about 3 p.m.

The enemy's sharpshooters kept up a brisk fire on the square during its march, and on approaching the ridge the spearmen, led by several Emirs on horseback, charged the troops. About 250 of the enemy, including five Emirs, were killed, and many more were wounded. The others fled towards Metemmeh. The troops then marched to the Nile and bivouacked on its bank.

I entrusted the immediate command of the square to Lieutenant-Colonel Boscawen. . . . . .

Nothing could exceed the coolness of the troops, both whilst exposed to the fire of the sharp-shooters in the morning, and to the charge of the spearmen in the afternoon. None of the enemy arrived within 30 yards of the square.

On the 20th, a village, on a gravel terrace near the Nile, was occupied and placed in a state of defence. A small garrison was left in it, and the troops then marched back to the zeriba to commence removing the stores to the new position. Unfortunately, they could not all be moved at once, and the small work on the knoll was again left for the night. The wounded were, however, safely brought down to the village before sunset.

On the 21st, a reconnaissance in force was made of Metemmeh, when it was found to have been placed in a state of defence, with loop-holed walls, and three guns in position. During the reconnaissance, four Egyptian steamers, under Nusri Pasha, appeared, and landed men and guns to take part in the operation.

The remainder of the stores were brought down to the village, and a change was made in the disposition of the camp. The camp was moved down to the water's edge, and the village was held as a fortified outpost.

The important news received from Khartum, rendering it, in my opinion, imperative that I should carry out my original mission, and proceed at once to that place, I handed over the military command to Lieutenant-Colonel the Hon. E. E. T. Boscawen.

On the 22nd January, I went down the river with three steamers and two companies of Mounted Infantry, to make a reconnaissance in the direction of Shendi, and returned the same day.

. . . .

I have, &c.,
(Signed)   C. W. WILSON, Colonel.

Supplementary Despatch from Colonel Sir C. Wilson to Chief of Staff.

KORTI, 14*th March*, 1885.

Sir,

As a supplement to my report of the 22nd January last, I have the honour to furnish the following additional particulars, respecting the movements of the force which left Jakdul on the

14th January, from 10.15 a.m. on the 19th, when Brigadier-General Sir Herbert Stewart having been seriously wounded, I assumed command as senior officer.

After consultation with Sir Herbert Stewart and Lieutenant-Colonel the Honourable E. T. Boscawen, the next senior officer, I determined to strengthen the zeriba, and after leaving a garrison in it to march for the Nile. The hospital within the zeriba was protected by a strong wall of commissariat and ordnance stores, in which openings were left for the guns and Gardner. The zeriba round the camels was strengthened, and a small redoubt was built on a knoll occupied by our skirmishers, which commanded the zeriba at a distance of 80 yards. These works were thrown up under fire, and the boxes for the wall of the redoubt were carried across from the zeriba by the officers and men of the Heavy and Guards' Camel Regiments, assisted by a detachment of Royal Engineers.

Mr. Burleigh, correspondent of the *Daily Telegraph*, volunteered his services, and took an active part in this arduous duty.

Two companies, one from the Guards and one from the Mounted Infantry Camel Regiment, were thrown out as skirmishers to keep down the enemy's fire whilst the zeriba was being strengthened, and preparations were being made for the march to the Nile. The fighting force was formed up in square, on the least exposed side of the zeriba, and about 3 p.m. marched towards a gravel ridge on which a large force of the enemy, with several banners, was collected. As the square moved round the zeriba a warm fire was opened upon it, and several men fell and were carried back to the hospital. The enemy's riflemen, who were well concealed in the high grass, kept up a continuous fire upon the force until it arrived within 600 yards of the gravel ridge; at this moment the fire became much heavier, and there were several casualties, but it suddenly ceased as the spearmen, led by several men on horseback, came running down the hill; the appearance of the spearmen, which indicated an approaching crisis in the fight, was greeted by a loud cheer from the men, who were at once halted to receive the charge. The enemy left from 250 to 300 dead on the ground over which they charged, but it was ascertained afterwards that many more were killed in the long grass and in rear of the ridge, and that a number of wounded were carried off to Metemmeh : amongst the killed were five Sheikhs or Emirs of the Baggara Arabs. On the defeat of the spearmen, a strong force of the enemy, which had taken up a position to the left front of the square, and been kept in check by a well-directed artillery fire from the zeriba, dispersed in the direction of Metemmeh. The square then marched without further opposition to the Nile, and bivouacked on its bank shortly after dark.

The fighting force in the square was composed of half the Heavy Camel Regiment, Lieutenant-Colonel the Hon. R. A. Talbot, 1st Life Guards; the Guards' Camel Regiment, Lieutenant-Colonel Willson, Scots Guards; the Mounted Infantry Camel Regiment, Major Barrow; a detachment Royal Sussex Regiment, Major Sunderland; a detachment 19th Hussars, dismounted men, Lieutenant Craven, and a detachment Royal Engineers, Lieutenant Lawson, acted as a reserve within the square. I entrusted the executive command of the square to Lieutenant-Colonel the Hon. E. T. Boscawen, Coldstream Guards.

The garrison of the zeriba consisted of the 1st Division, Naval Brigade, Captain Lord Charles Beresford, R.N.; 19th Hussars, Lieutenant-Colonel Barrow; half the Heavy Camel Regiment, Major Davison, 16th Lancers; three guns, Royal Artillery, Captain Norton; and a detachment Royal Engineers, Major Dorward. Lieutenant-Colonel Barrow commanded the troops under Captain Lord Charles Beresford, who was in command as senior officer. The garrison of the zeriba covered the advance of the square by a well-directed fire, and the guns were served until the enemy charged down the hill.

I would beg to draw special attention to the exceptional hardships which the men of the force had undergone prior to the engagement. From the afternoon of the 16th, when they went into zeriba near Abu Klea, they had had little rest; during the night of the 16th–17th they were exposed to a long-range dropping fire; on the 17th they fought at Abu Klea; on the night of the 17th–18th they were engaged in breaking up the zeriba and removing the wounded to the wells; and from 3.30 p.m. on the 18th, to 7 a.m. on the 19th, they were engaged in making a night march over an unknown country, partly covered with a dense growth of high tufted grass and thickets of mimosa. The spirit of the men was, however, excellent, and nothing could exceed their coolness, both whilst exposed to the fire of the sharpshooters in the morning, and to the charge of the spearmen in the afternoon; so good was the fire discipline that none of the enemy arrived within 30 yards of the square.

On the 20th, leaving Lieutenant-Colonel the Hon. R. A. Talbot with an escort to protect the wounded, I proceeded to occupy a small village on a gravel terrace near the Nile. As soon as the occupation was assured, the wounded were brought up, and the village placed in a state of defence. A small garrison was detailed under Major Lord Arthur Somerset, who had been wounded on the previous day, and the force was then formed up to march back to the zeriba; as however, a large number of the enemy were seen collecting near Metemmeh, it was moved in that direction. A few volleys were fired, and the enemy having been dispersed, the force resumed its march to the zeriba, which it reached without opposition.

The zeriba was at once dismantled, and the wounded and a large portion of the stores were brought down to the new camp before sunset.

Owing to the heavy loss of camels from the fire of the enemy, and the weakness of those that remained from want of food and water, the stores could not all be removed at once, and a small garrison was left in the redoubt on the knoll, under Major Davison, 16th Lancers. During the day it was ascertained that the enemy who disputed the march of the force to the Nile on the 19th, consisted of a strong reinforcement from Omdurman under Nur Angar, and that another force under Feki Mustapha was marching northwards.

The expected arrival of Nur Angar's force at Metemmeh on the 18th or 19th was known in the afternoon of the 18th through prisoners, and it was partly I believe this information, which led Sir Herbert Stewart to march for the Nile some distance above Metemmeh, with the intention of securing himself there before fighting Nur Angar and attacking Metemmeh.

On the 21st, a garrison having been left in camp to protect the wounded, the force marched towards Metemmeh, which was found to be a long village of mud houses with loop-holed walls, and two or three mountain guns. Whilst the reconnaissance was in progress four Egyptian steamers, under Nusri Pasha, appeared and landed a contingent under Khasm-el-Mûs Bey which took part in the operations. Whilst the guns were attempting to form a breach in the wall, Khasm-el-Mûs informed me that he had seen the force under Feki Mustapha marching down the left bank, and that it would reach Metemmeh before sunset, or very early next morning. It was, therefore, probable that the force would have to fight an unbeaten portion of the enemy within the next 24 hours, and, as it had already lost one-tenth of its effective strength, and there were over 100 wounded in hospital, I hesitated to press an attack which could not have been carried to a successful issue without further heavy losses. I also considered that the town was too large for the force to hold, after the losses it had sustained and the return of the convoy and escort to Jakdul. Under these circumstances, I determined to withdraw without pressing the attack, and, at the same time, made arrangements for bringing in Major Davison and the stores which had been left at the zeriba.

In view of an expected attack from Feki Mustapha the camp was moved down to the bank of the Nile, and the village was held as an outpost. It was afterwards ascertained that Feki Mustapha halted his force about 12 miles from the camp, and that he remained halted until the steamers passed up the river towards Khartum, when he retired to the position of Wad Habeshi, where he fought the action with Lord Charles Beresford on the 3rd February.

On my return to camp, I received the letters which General Gordon had sent down by the "Bordein" on the 14th December, and the note dated 29th December stating that Khartum was all right and "could hold out for years." I then determined to carry out my original mission, as explained in my report of the 11th February last; but, before taking away two of the steamers from the small force, I considered it necessary to ascertain the truth of the report that a new force of the enemy was advancing from Berber. The 22nd was occupied in a reconnaissance to Shendi, the 23rd in changing crews, as mentioned in my report of the 11th February. On the evening of the 23rd the convoy left for Jakdul, Lieutenant-Colonel the Hon. R. A. Talbot commanding, and Captain Lord Cochrane acting as guide. Captain Pigott, Mounted Infantry (Camel Regiment), carrying despatches, accompanied the convoy.

On the morning of the 24th the steamers left for Khartum.

I regret that I was unable to send the convoy or despatches earlier, but the camels were absolutely in need of rest; they had had no water and hardly any food from the 13th to the 20th, and on the 17th and 19th they had been tightly tied down in the zeribas. The horses of the 19th Hussars were equally in need of rest.

. . . . . .

I have, &c.,
(Signed)   C. W. WILSON, Colonel,
Deputy Adjutant-General.

APPENDIX 46.
(See page 31.)

SIR C. WILSON'S EXPLANATION OF DELAY AT GUBAT.

CAIRO,
13th *April*, 1885.

My Lord,
I have the honour to forward a letter from Colonel Sir C. Wilson, R.E., giving the reasons for the delay in the departure of the steamers from Gubat.

I do not propose to add any remarks of my own to this letter. The reasons given by Sir Charles Wilson must speak for themselves.

I have, &c.,
(Signed) WOLSELEY,
General.

The Right Hon. the Marquis of Hartington, M.P.

Lord Wolseley,

The steamers from Khartum reached Gubat on the 21st January, whilst we were engaged with the enemy at Metemmeh, and I received the letters which General Gordon had sent down between 3 and 4 p.m. on that day. I at once determined to proceed to Khartum, but several considerations led me to delay my start. It may, however, be observed that if I had left on the morning of the 22nd, and travelled at the same rate as I did, I should only have reached Khartum at midday on the 26th, after it had fallen.

The considerations which guided me were:—

1st. The military position. The force had been much weakened by its heavy losses on the 17th and 19th; it was to be still further weakened by the return of the convoy and its escort to Jakdul, and it was hampered by the large number of wounded. Sir H. Stewart had been severely wounded and Colonel Burnaby, who was to have commanded at Metemmeh had been killed; the horses of the 19th Hussars were so "done up" they could not reconnoitre any distance from camp, and the camels also required rest and food. On the 18th, we heard

(S.C.2)   T

that reinforcements for the enemy were advancing from Omdurman and Berber; on the 19th we fought the reinforcement from Omdurman, and I had every reason to believe that the report of a force advancing from Berber, which came from the same source as the other, was correct. On the 20th I heard that another force under Feki Mustapha was advancing from Omdurman, and a repetition of the report about the Berber force. On the 21st, Khasm-el-Mûs Bey told me he had seen Feki Mustapha's force on the march, and that it would reach Gubat before sunset or early on the 22nd. My information thus led me to expect an advance of the enemy from the north and south, and I felt that I could not leave the small British force in its position on the Nile without first ascertaining whether it was liable to an immediate attack. I therefore went down the river on the 22nd, as far as Shendi, to see if any force of the enemy were advancing.

2nd. General Gordon, in a most characteristic letter, addressed to the Chief of the Staff or to the Officer Commanding the British advanced guard, insisted strongly on our taking actual command of the steamers, and removing from them all Pashas, Beys, and men of Turkish or Egyptian origin. He wrote in strong terms of the uselessness of these men in action, and begged that if the boats were not manned by British sailors, they should be sent back to him with none but Sudanese crews and soldiers. It was originally intended that the steamers should be manned by the Naval Brigade, but Lord Charles Beresford was in hospital, unable to walk, and all the other officers of the Brigade, and several of the best petty officers and men, had been killed or wounded. It was therefore impossible to carry out the original plan, and though Lord Charles Beresford, in the most gallant way, offered to accompany me, I felt that I could not deprive the force of the only naval officer with it, especially as the steamers left behind might be called upon at any time to take part in active operations against the enemy. It was therefore necessary to select Sudanese officers, crews, and soldiers from the four ships, and to transfer them to the two steamers going to Khartum. This was the chief reason for the delay on the 23rd.

3rd. I knew that Omdurman was in the hands of the Mahdi, and Khasm-el-Mûs told me that the enemy had several guns mounted on the river bank. I expected, therefore, to have to fight my way up the river, with Sudanese crews, in steamers like the penny boats on the Thames, which a single well-directed shell would disable, and to encounter a very heavy fire from Omdurman when running into Khartum. It was consequently necessary to have the engines overhauled, and, as far as time would allow, to prepare the steamers for the heavy fire they would have to encounter. In all these preparations I received much advice and assistance from Lord Charles Beresford and aid from his artificers.

N.B.—On ascending the river we found that the gun in the battery near Gandatu had been taken to Shendi the previous day, and that the guns at Wad Habeshi had been taken away by Feki Mustapha, whose force we saw on the left bank, about 12 miles above the camp.

4th. I was aware, from General Gordon's letter of the 11th November 1884, and from the letters sent down by the "Bordein" on the 14th December, that he expected Khartum to fall about Christmas Day. I was also aware, from information received before leaving Korti, that provisions were very scarce in the city. I knew that Khartum must be still holding out, and there was nothing to show that the expected crisis which had been delayed so long, would occur within the next few days. I rather hoped that the result of the battle of Abu Klea, which was known to Khasm-el-Mûs the same evening, and must have been known in the Mahdi's camp on the 19th and possibly in Khartum the same day, would have delayed the crisis. Unfortunately, it appears to have had the opposite effect.

The only day which might have been saved was the 22nd, as the reconnaissance showed that the force had nothing to fear from the Berber direction; but, I think, that if I were again placed in similar circumstances I should act in the same way. From the moment the steamers started on the morning of the 24th no time was lost.

No one can regret the untimely death of General Gordon more than I do, or could have been more anxious to relieve him, but I do not think that any action of mine could have saved his life, or averted the fall of Khartum.

(Signed)   C. W. WILSON,
Colonel, D.A.G.

Korti, 23rd March, 1885.

APPENDIX 47.

(See page 38.)

NOTES ON THE FALL OF KHARTUM BY MAJOR KITCHENER.

The last accurate information received about Khartum is contained in General Gordon's diary, and dated the 14th December, 1884.

The state of the town was then very critical, and General Gordon states "the town may fall in 10 days."

The fort of Omdurman had been cut off from communication with Khartum since the 3rd of November; it was at that date provisioned for $1\frac{1}{2}$ months, and the commandant, Farag Allah Bey, had requested further supplies of ammunition.

The garrison may therefore be considered to have been in great difficulties for food and necessaries, after the 20th December.

General Gordon had so weakened himself by sending away five steamers (four to meet the English Expedition and one with Colonel Stewart), that he found it impossible to check the Arabs on the White Nile, and therefore to keep open communication with the fort of Omdurman.

According to General Gordon's statement, there were in the stores at Khartum on the 14th December, 83,525 okes of biscuit, and 546 ardebs of dhura. From the almost weekly statement of the amounts in store, it is calculated that, although General Gordon was able to reduce considerably the issue of dhura, the biscuit ration to the troops had not been reduced up to the 14th December. The amount in store would represent approximately 18 days' rations for the garrison alone. Gordon had already, on the 22nd November, found it necessary to issue 9,600 lb. of biscuit to the poor, and he then says: "I am determined if the town does fall the Mahdi shall find precious little to eat in it."

There is little doubt that, as the siege progressed, it was found necessary to issue considerable amount of provisions to the poorer native inhabitants of Khartum. It may, therefore, be considered that even on reduced rations the supply in store must have been almost, if not quite, exhausted about the 1st January, 1885.

The town was then closely encircled by the rebels, who doubtless increased the intensity of their attack as they approached nearer and nearer to the works.

The Mahdi was fully aware from deserters, of the straits to which the garrison were reduced for want of food; and it was his intention that the town should fall into his hands without fighting, being obliged by famine to surrender.

About the 6th January, General Gordon, seeing that the garrison were reduced to great want for food, and that existence for many of the inhabitants was almost impossible, issued a proclamation, offering to any of the inhabitants who liked, free permission to leave the town and go to the Mahdi. Great numbers availed themselves of this permission, and General Gordon wrote letters to the Mahdi, requesting him to protect and feed these poor Moslem people, as he had done for the last nine months.

It has been estimated that only about 14,000 remained in the town out of the total of 34,000 inhabitants, the number obtained by a census of the town in September.

General Gordon kept heart in the garrison by proclamations announcing the near approach of the English relief expedition, and praising them for the resistance they had made, as well as by the example of his unshaken determination never to surrender the town to the rebels.

It appears probable, though the precise date cannot be exactly verified, that the fort of Omdurman fell into the hands of the rebels on or about the 13th January. The garrison were not injured, and Farag Allah Bey, the commander, was well treated in the rebel camp, as an inducement for any waverers in the Khartum garrison to join the Mahdi's cause.

The fall of Omdurman must have been a great blow to the garrison of Khartum, who thus lost their only position on the west bank of the White Nile. The Arabs were able then, by the construction of batteries along the river bank, to entirely close the White Nile to Gordon's steamers. Having accomplished this, they could establish ferries on the White Nile (south of Khartum), and have constant and rapid communication from Omdurman village and camp to their positions along the south front.

About the 18th January the rebel works having approached the south front, a sortie was made by the troops, which led to desperate fighting. About 200 of the garrison were killed, and although large numbers of the rebels were said to have been slain, it does not appear that any great or permanent advantage was obtained by the besieged garrison. On the return of the troops to Khartum, after this sortie, General Gordon personally addressed them, praising them for the splendid resistance they had made up to that time, and urging them still to do their utmost to hold out, as relief was near; indeed, that the English might arrive any day, and all would then be well.

The state of the garrison was then desperate from want of food, all the donkeys, dogs, cats, rats, &c., had been eaten; a small ration of gum was issued daily to the troops, and a sort of bread was made from pounded palm tree fibres. Gordon held several councils of the leading inhabitants, and on one occasion had the town most rigorously searched for provisions; the result, however, was very poor, only yielding four ardebs of grain through the whole town; this was issued to the troops. Gordon continually visited the posts, and personally encouraged the soldiers to stand firm; it was said during this period that he never slept.

On the 20th January the news of the defeat of the Mahdi's picked troops at Abu Klea created consternation in the Mahdi's camp. A council of the leaders was held, and it is said a considerable amount of resistance to the Mahdi's will, and want of discipline, were shown. On the 22nd the news of the arrival of the English on the Nile at Metemmeh, which was thought to have been taken, led the Mahdi to decide to make at once a desperate attack upon Khartum, before reinforcements could enter the town. It is probable that next day the Mahdi sent letters to Farag Pasha, commanding the black troops, who had been previously in communication with him, offering terms for the surrender of the town, and stating that the English had been defeated on the Nile. Rumours were also prevalent in Khartum of the fighting at Abu Klea, and the arrival of the English at Metemmeh.

It has been said that helmets were exposed by the Mahdi's troops in front of their works, to induce the garrison to believe that the English had been defeated; but this has been distinctly denied by some who could hardly have failed to observe anything of the sort.

On the 23rd General Gordon had a stormy interview with Farag Pasha. An eye-witness states that it was owing to Gordon having passed a fort on the White Nile, which was under Farag Pasha's charge, and found it to be inadequately protected. Gordon is said to have struck Farag Pasha on this occasion. It seems probable to me that at this interview Farag Pasha proposed to Gordon to surrender the town, and stated the terms the Mahdi had offered, declaring in his opinion that they should be accepted. Farag Pasha left the palace in a great rage, refusing the repeated attempts of other officers to effect a reconciliation between him and Gordon.

On the following day General Gordon held a council of the notables at the palace. The question of the surrender of the town was then discussed, and General Gordon declared, whatever the council decided, he would never surrender the town. I think it very probable that on this occasion General Gordon brought Farag Pasha's action and proposals before the council; and it appears that some in the council were of Farag Pasha's opinion, that the town could resist no longer, and should be surrendered on the terms offered by the Mahdi. General Gordon would not, however, listen to this proposal.

On the 25th Gordon was slightly ill, and as it was Sunday he did not appear in public. He had, however, several interviews with leading men of the town, and evidently knew that the end was near. It has been said that Gordon went out in the evening, and crossed the river to Tuti Island on board the "Ismailia" to settle some dispute amongst the garrison there. This statement has not been verified by other witnesses, but owing to it, the rumour subsequently arose amongst the black troops in Omdurman that Gordon had escaped that night on board the "Ismailia." The facts, however, that both steamers were captured by the rebels, that the "Ismailia" was afterwards used by Mohammed Ahmed when he visited Khartum, and the very full and complete evidence that General Gordon was killed at or near the palace, entirely dispels any doubt on the matter. If he crossed the river to Tuti, there is no doubt he returned later to his palace in Khartum.

On the night of the 25th, many of the famished troops left their posts on the fortifications in search of food in the town. Some of the troops were also too weak, from want of nourishment, to go to their posts. This state of things was known in the town, and caused some alarm; many of the principal inhabitants armed themselves and their slaves, and went to the fortifications in place of the soldiers. This was not an unusual occurrence, only on this night more of the inhabitants went as volunteers than had done so on previous occasions.

At about 3.30 a.m. on the morning of Monday, the 26th, a determined attack was made by the rebels on the south front. The principal points of attack were the Buri Gate, at the extreme east end of the line of defence on the Blue Nile; and the Mesalamia Gate, on the west side, near the White Nile. The defence of the former post held out against the attack, but at the Mesalamia Gate, the rebels having filled the ditch with bundles of straw, brushwood, beds, &c., brought up in their arms, penetrated the fortifications, led by their Emir, Wad en-Nejumi. The defenders of the Buri Gate, seeing the rebels inside the fortifications in their rear, retired, and the town was then at the mercy of the rebels.

General Gordon had a complete system of telegraphic communication with all the posts along the line of fortifications, and there must have been great irregularity in the telegraph stations to account for his being left entirely unwarned of the attack and entry of the rebels. Doubtless Farag Pasha was responsible, to some extent, for this.

Farag Pasha has been very generally accused of having either opened the gates of Khartum himself, or to have connived at the entrance of the rebels; but this has been distinctly denied by Abdullah Bey Ismail, who commanded a battalion of irregular troops at the fall of the town, as well as by about 30 refugee soldiers, who lately escaped, and came in during the last days of the English occupation of Dongola. The accusations of treachery have all been vague, and are, to my mind, the outcome of mere supposition.

Hassan Bey Balmasawi, who commanded at the Mesalamia Gate, certainly did not make a proper defence, and failed to warn General Gordon of the danger the town was in. He afterwards appears to have taken a commission under the Mahdi, and to have gone to Kordofan with the Emir Abu Anga.

In my opinion Khartum fell from sudden assault, when the garrison were too exhausted by privations to make proper resistance.

Having entered the town, the rebels rushed through the streets, shouting and murdering everyone they met, thus increasing the panic and destroying any opposition.

It is difficult, from the confused accounts, to make out exactly how General Gordon was killed. All the evidence tends to prove it happened at, or near, the palace, where his body was subsequently seen by several witnesses.

It appears that there was one company of black troops in the palace besides General Gordon's cavasses; some resistance was made when the rebels appeared, but I think this was after General Gordon had left the palace. The only account, by a a person claiming to be an eye-witness, of the scene of General Gordon's death relates: "On hearing the noise, I got my master's donkey and went with him to the palace; we met Gordon Pasha at the outer door of the palace. Mohammed Bey Mustafa, with my master, Ibrahim Bey Rushdi, and about 20 cavasses, then went with Gordon towards the house of the Austrian Consul Hansel, near the church, when we met some rebels in an open place near the outer gate of the palace. Gordon Pasha was walking in front, leading the party. The rebels fired a volley, and Gordon was killed at once; nine of the cavasses, Ibrahim Bey Rushdi, and Mohammed Bey Mustafa were killed, the rest ran away."

A large number of witnesses state Gordon was killed near the gate of the palace, and various accounts have been related from hearsay, of the exact manner in which he met his end. Several reliable witnesses saw and recognised Gordon's body at the gate of the palace; one describes it as being dressed in light clothes.*

* * * * *

The massacre in the town lasted some six hours, and about 4,000 persons at least, were killed. The black troops were

---

* On a subsequent occasion this witness (the messenger who carried Lord Wolseley's letter of November 17th, 1884, see Part I, page 124) stated that he had recognised General Gordon's body, by its being dressed in dark clothes.

spared, except those who resisted at the Buri Gate and elsewhere; large numbers of the townspeople and slaves were killed and wounded. The Bashi Bazouks and white regulars, numbering 3,327, and the Shaikiyeh irregulars, numbering 2,330, were mostly all killed in cold blood, after they had surrendered and had been disarmed.

Consul Hansel was killed in his own house. Consul Nicola, a doctor, and Ibraham Bey Fauzi, who was Gordon's secretary, were taken prisoners; the latter was wounded.

At about 10 a.m. the Mahdi sent over orders to stop the massacre, which then ceased. The rebels fell to looting the town, and ordered all the inhabitants out of it; they were searched at the gate as they passed, and were taken over to Omdurman, where the women were distributed as slaves amongst the rebel chiefs. The men, after being kept as prisoners under a guard for three days, were stripped and allowed to get their living as best they could.

It has been stated that the Mahdi was angry when he heard of General Gordon's death; but, though he may have simulated such a feeling on account of the black troops, there is very little doubt, in my opinion, that, had he expressed the wish, Gordon would not have been killed.

The presence of Gordon as a prisoner in his camp would have been a source of great danger to the Mahdi, for the black troops from Kordofan and Khartum all loved and venerated Gordon, and many other influential men knew him to be a wonderfully good man.

The want of discipline in the Mahdi's camp made it dangerous for him to keep as a prisoner a man whom all the black troops liked better than himself, and in favour of whom, on a revulsion of feeling, a successful revolt might take place in his own camp. Morever, if Gordon was dead, he calculated the English would retire and leave him in peace.

The Mahdi had promised his followers as much gold and silver as they could carry when Khartum fell, and immense disappointment was expressed at the failure to find the Government treasury.

Three days after the fall of the town, Farag Pasha was brought up to show where the Government money was hid; as he was naturally unable to do this, owing to there not being any, he was killed on the public market place at Omdurman.

Many others were put to torture to disclose where their wealth was hid, with varying results.

On the third day after the fall of Khartum, many of the prisoners saw Sir Charles Wilson's steamers off Tuti Island, with the English on board; some were present in the batteries at Omdurman when the rebels opened fire on the steamers.

The number of white prisoners in the Mahdi's camp has been

variously stated; a Greek, escaped from Khartum, reports when the place fell there were 42 Greeks, 5 Greek women, 1 Jewess, 6 European nuns, and 2 priests; of these 34 Greeks were murdered. The survivors are all at liberty, but in extreme poverty.

Abdullah Bey Ismail relates that, "all the European ladies are at Omdurman, living in a zeriba, where they form a little colony, guarded by the European men. They earn a meagre sustenance by sewing, washing, &c. Not a single one was taken by the dervishes; they all wear Moslem dress."

A letter from the Mahdi was received, relative to the white prisoners, who, he declared, preferred to remain with him. The document bears 96 signatures of Europeans; but some of them are undoubtedly spurious, as that of Father Luigi Bonomi, who has since escaped from El Obeid, never having been at Khartum.

A large number of the Baggara Arabs left the Mahdi shortly after the fall of Khartum, much disgusted at their failure to obtain a larger amount of loot. On the Mahdi attempting to bring them back by force, they joined the party in Kordofan, who are now fighting against the Mahdi's cause.

The memorable siege of Khartum lasted 317 days, and it is not too much to say, that such a noble resistance was due to the indomitable resolution and resource of one Englishman.

Never was a garrison so nearly rescued, never was a commander so sincerely lamented.

(Signed) H. H. KITCHENER,
Major.

In compiling this memorandum Major Kitchener has had at his disposal all the information in this department, and I believe it is as accurate a statement of what took place as can be made out.

(Signed) A. S. CAMERON,
Colonel.

Intelligence Branch,
    Quartermaster-General's Department,
        18th August, 1885.

APPENDIX 48.

(See pages 63 and 108.)

Maps 1 *and* 8.

GENERAL BRACKENBURY'S REPORT ON ACTION AT KIRBEKAN.

From Brigadier-General Brackenbury, C.B., to General Lord Wolseley, G.C.B.

CAMP, OPPOSITE DULKA ISLAND,
10*th February*, 1885.

My Lord,
In my telegram, No. 99, of this date, I have informed you in general terms of the result of to-day's action before Kirbekan. I have now the honour to report more fully on the same subject.

On the night of the 8th instant General Earle received a report from Colonel Butler, who was in command of the advanced camp, that in reconnoitring that day, he had found the enemy in a strong position occupying some rocky knolls (or koppies), and holding a high razor-backed ridge of hills behind. Major-General Earle then ordered the advance of the 1st Battalion South Staffordshire and 1st Battalion Royal Highlanders in boats to an open camping ground which Colonel Butler had selected, about a mile short of the enemy's position, and ordered the squadron 19th Hussars, half of the Egyptian Camel Corps, and two guns of the Egyptian Artillery to advance to the same place.

On the 9th instant, Major-General Earle himself arrived here, and having personally reconnoitred the enemy's position, and sent Colonel Butler to make a wide reconnaissance towards the enemy's rear, he decided, upon receipt of Colonel Butler's report to attack the enemy's position this morning, in the manner in which the advance was made to-day.

A company of the Royal Highlanders was left in a strong zeriba to guard the boats, baggage, baggage animals, and all unarmed men, under the command of the Lieutenant-Colonel Eden, 1st Battalion Royal Highlanders, with Major Sandwith, D.A.A.G., as his Staff Officer.

Two companies of the 1st Battalion South Staffordshire Regiment and two guns were placed under the command of Lieutenant-Colonel Alleyne, A.A.G., who was instructed to take up a position on a rocky knoll in front of the enemy's position, and occupy his attention in front, while with six companies of the 1st Battalion South Staffordshire Regiment, and six companies of the 1st Battalion Royal Highlanders, Major-General

Earle marched about a mile and a half to his right front, completely turning the high ridge, and the whole of the enemy's position.

From this point the column marched under fire from the high ridge, over broken and rocky ground, then pivoting on the left the right of the column was brought round till it faced the rear of the enemy's position. It was found that the column formation, ready to form square, was unsuited to the nature of the ground, and the advance was made by companies, but not in extended order; and points of vantage in the rocky ground were occupied in succession.

Sending two companies of the 1st Battalion South Staffordshire about 9 a.m. to take the high ridge by working up its shoulder, Major-General Earle directed the right of the Black Watch to advance under cover of the river-bank, and take the knoll (koppie) nearest the river. This was successfully done, and the main koppie was thus enfiladed.

The remainder of the Black Watch then advanced from one rocky knoll to another, towards the rear of the position. At this time a considerable body of the enemy rushed down from their position towards the Black Watch, who, without altering their formation, received then with admirable coolness, and, killing many, completely turned them. A few only reached the river and escaped.

The Black Watch, under Colonel Green, then advanced, with pipes playing, and stormed the main koppie from front and flank most gallantly, killing every one of the enemy, who were in great numbers among the rocks and boulders.

At this time Major-General Earle, who had accompanied the advance up the koppie, was killed by a bullet, fired from a stone hut in which several men had taken refuge.

Meanwhile the two companies of the South Staffordshire sent to take the high ridge had been received by a heavy fire, Lieutenant-Colonel Eyre had been killed, and their ammunition was exhausted. I, therefore, on assuming command, directed Lieutenant-Colonel Beal to reinforce the attack and take the ridge. The operation was performed with skill and courage, and the enemy were driven from their last position by 1.30 p.m.

I cannot speak too highly of the conduct of both officers and men. Numbers of the enemy were killed by the bayonet.

Most of the enemy were armed with Remington rifles, and their position, which was a formidable one, was defended with desperate courage.

After guiding the column to the rear of the enemy's position, Colonel Butler made a wide sweeping movement to the rear with the cavalry and captured the enemy's camp, taking eight standards. Two also fell into our hands on the main koppie.

In the pursuit by the cavalry some of the enemy were killed, and the survivors only escaped by swimming the river.

APPENDIX 48.

It is difficult to estimate the enemy's numbers in the field, or the number of his dead; but the lowest estimate I can make of his killed, is 200. They lay thick in every nook and crevice of the koppie, and on the open ground, where they tried to rush through our troops; and the Staffordshire killed many at the main ridge of hills.

Prisoners report that the three chiefs in command were killed, viz.:—Mussa Wad Abu Hejel, Ali Wad Hussein, cousin, and Hamed el-Kalik, brother of Abd-el-Majid el-Kalik.*

Our own loss was as follows:—

STAFF.

Killed.—Major-General Earle.

1ST BATTALION SOUTH STAFFORDSHIRE REGIMENT.

Killed.—Lieutenant-Colonel Eyre, and three privates.

Wounded.—Captain Horsbrugh (severely); Lieutenant the Hon. J. G. R. U. Colborne (severely); 20 non-commissioned officers and men.

1ST ROYAL HIGHLANDERS.

Killed.—Lieutenant-Colonel Coveny and four non-commissioned officers and men.

Wounded.—Lieutenant-Colonel Wauchope (very severely); Lieutenant D. Kennedy (severely); and 18 non-commissioned officers and men.

Missing.—One private.

EGYPTIAN CAMEL CORPS.

Killed.—Two privates.

Wounded.—One private.

Surgeon-Major Harvey, Medical Staff, accompanied the column throughout the day, and his dispositions for the care of the wounded were all that could be desired.

Having so recently assumed command I refrain from bringing any names to your particular notice. Indeed, when the conduct of all was so gallant, it would be difficult to select any names for special mention.

The column will continue its advance to-morrow, and I shall endeavour to carry out your orders, with which Major-General Earle had made me fully acquainted.

I have, &c.,
(Signed) HENRY BRACKENBURY,
Brigadier-General, Commanding Nile Column.

* Abd-el-Majid el-Kalik commanded the Dervishes opposed to the River Column and it was to him that the remarkable letter, describing the fall of Khartum, which was found the following day, was addressed. See page 111.

KIRBEKAN,
13*th February*, 1885.

My Lord,

In my report of the 10th instant, on the action of Kirbekan I inadvertently omitted to mention the part taken by the Egyptian Camel Corps, under Major Marriott, who, under fire from front and flank, lined the foot of the hill afterwards taken by the Staffordshire, and engaged the attention of the enemy in front. I the more regret this omission on my part as the plucky conduct of the Camel Corps, who had two killed and one wounded, and who killed several of the enemy, was the subject of universal comment after the action.

I have, &c.,
(Signed)   HENRY BRACKENBURY,
Brigadier-General, Commanding Nile Column.

APPENDIX 49. (See pages 63 and 115.)

ESTIMATED AMOUNT OF SUPPLIES TO BE WITH RIVER COLUMN ON REACHING BERBER.

	Preserved meat.	Bread stuffs.	Tea and coffee.	Sugar.	Salt.	Erbswurst and preserved vegetables.	Lime juice.	Tobacco.	Soap.
Now with River Column, 8th February, less 30 per cent. bread, sugar and salt (in thousand rations)	210	182	321	222	117	192	363	150	90
Convoy from Korosko (in thousands)	10	100	84	110	110	73	110	192	192
Total	220	282	405	332	227	265	473	342	282
Deduct for 3,000 men, 8th February to 19th March	177	117	117	117	117	117	117	117	117
Deduct for 2,000 men 30 days									
Remain in Berber 19th March (in thousand rations)	43	55	228	155	50	88	296	165	105
For 1,000 men up to	1 May	13 May	2 Nov.	21 Aug.	8 May	15 June	9 June	31 Aug.	2 July
Wanted to complete up to 19th July in thousands	79	67	..	..	72	84	..	..	17
Whence obtainable	Morowi, Korti or Assuan				Korosko.	Korosko or Korti.			Korosko.

(Signed) S. HUGHES, D.C.G.
S.C.O., N.E.F.

13 2. 5.

APPENDIX 50.

(See page 74.)

MARCHING OUT STATE FROM ABU KLEA, 23RD FEBRUARY, 1885.

Corps.	Officers.			N.C. Officers and Men.			Camels.	Horses.	Natives.
	Available.	Sick.	Total.	Available.	Sick.	Total.			
Naval Brigade	11	—	11	102	2	104		—	
19th Hussars	1	—	1	13	1	14		18	
Light Camel Regiment	13	1	14	196	6	202		—	
Mounted Infantry Camel Regiment	20	1	21	311	5	316		—	
Royal Artillery	6	—	6	75	2	77		—	
Royal Engineers	2	—	2	24	—	24		—	
Royal Irish Regiment	21	1	22	596	13	609		6	
Royal Sussex Regiment	7	—	7	217	7	224		—	
Royal West Kent Regiment	1	—	1	21	—	21		—	
Commissariat and Transport Corps	6	—	6	38	—	38		—	
Medical Staff Corps	5	1	6	43	—	43		—	
Head-Quarter Staff	6	—	6	4	—	4		6	
Army Chaplain	1	—	1	—	—	—		—	
Total	100	4	104	1640	36	1676	1180	30	386

APPENDIX 51.

(See page 87.)

MEDICAL ARRANGEMENTS OF THE RIVER COLUMN.

Report by Surgeon-Major Harvey.

1. On the 8th January, 1885, I arrived at Korti by boat from Gemai, from which place I had started on the 22nd November, 1884, in charge of three whalers, and was at once informed by Surgeon-General J. O'Nial, Principal Medical Officer of the Nile Expeditionary Force, that I was appointed Principal Medical Officer of the River Column, then forming at Hamdab, under the command of Major-General William Earle, C.B., C.S.I., and intended to operate by the river route, in the direction of the Abu Hamed, Berber, and Khartum.

2. On the 9th I was summoned to an interview at the Surgeon-General's office, at which Brigadier-General Brackenbury, C.B., the Chief Staff Officer of the River Column, was present, and at which were explained and discussed the objective and general scheme of the advance, and the special points to be borne in mind in making the necessary arrangements; chief amongst the latter was the reduction and re-arrangement of No. 2 Field Hospital into eight sections, to be stowed by sections in eight whaler boats, each section to be so far complete in itself, as that it might be detached if required, and contain all essentials for the supply of a small field hospital.

3. The method of working the hospital was not then entered into, but left for subsequent adjustment.

4. On the 10th January I left Korti with Brigadier-General Brackenbury, C.B., and proceeded by steam pinnace to Abu Dom, arriving there about 1 p.m.

5. Here were stationed Surgeons-Major S. Flood and R. W. O'Donnell, and Surgeon H. O. Stuart, Medical Staff, and here I found the material of No. 2 Field Hospital stowed, as it had been landed, in a marquee. It was decided that I should remain at Abu Dom and make all the necessary arrangements for the medical service of the River Column.

6. The first preliminary was to make a correct inventory of all equipment actually there; next to make a division of this equipment into eight portions, each forming a small hospital complete in itself; lastly the reduction to such proportion as might be conveniently stowed in a whaler boat.

7. To effect this reduction it was decided that marquees should not be taken, but that boat tents should be used in their stead. Those articles of equipment not portable or useful, or indeed absolutely essential, were discarded, and everything reduced to the lowest limit commensurate with efficiency.

8. A scale of a proposed one-eighth section, and of what was termed the Headquarter or A section, and which contained some articles, necessary but indivisible, or of which only one could be taken, was drawn up and submitted for the consideration and approval of the General Officer Commanding the River Column and the Principal Medical Officer of the Nile Expeditionary Force.

9. . . . . . .

10. In addition to the supply of medical comforts carried in the field hospital boats, each whaler of the force was provided with the box of medical comforts provided for Nile Boat Service. In these, at the suggestion of the Principal Medical Officer, Nile Expeditionary Force, brandy had been substituted, as far as possible, for port wine, as giving greater value for the space occupied.

11. On the 15th January, Brigadier-General Brackenbury, C.B., Chief Staff Officer, visited the hospital, and with him were arranged details of manning and provisioning boats.

12. A ninth boat, to be called the Principal Medical Officer's boat, was given, and in this were carried excess articles, some that might be considered luxuries rather than absolute necessaries, and some additional medical comforts.

13. The sections, having been finally arranged, were lettered from A (or, as it was called, the Headquarter section) to H, and every article in each section was marked with the letter of that section.

14. It had been settled that the Detachment Medical Staff Corps should number 42 non-commissioned officers and men, these were distributed through the boats, four or five in each boat.

15. To complete the crews, so that each boat should row eight oars and a coxswain and bowman, men were detailed from the 1st Gordon Highlanders, who, in addition to their duty in helping to navigate the boats were to act as a guard.

16. The names of the Medical Staff Officers attached for duty with the field hospital were :—

Surgeon-Major S. Flood (in charge) Medical Staff.

APPENDIX 51.

Surgeon-Major A. L. Brown, Medical Staff.
Surgeon-Major R. W. O'Donnell, Medical Staff.
Surgeon J. J. Greene, Medical Staff.
Surgeon H. O. Stuart, Medical Staff.

17. Each of these Medical Staff Officers had charge of a boat, and the other three sections and boats were placed in charge of the three senior non-commissioned officers, viz., 2nd Class Staff-Sergeant H. R. Hobson, 2nd Class Staff-Sergeant A. Lee, and 2nd Class Staff-Sergeant J. Morris, Medical Staff Corps.

18. In the first instance, the field hospital was divided into halves, Surgeon-Major S. Flood, with A, B, C, and D sections, and Surgeon-Major A. L. Brown with E, F, G, and H; with Surgeon-Major Flood, were Surgeon-Major O'Donnell, C section; Surgeon H. O. Stuart, B section, and Staff-Sergeant Lee.

19. With Surgeon-Major Brown's section were Surgeon Greene, F section; Staff-Sergeant Morris, G section; and Staff-Sergeant Hobson, H section. Practically, never less than two sections, one of them in charge of a Medical Staff Officer, were detached; but occasionally one, always with a Medical Staff Officer, would be alone, as more equipment might seem likely to be required in one direction than another. But the usual grouping was two by two.

20. In addition to the sectional hospital equipment, each Medical Staff Officer had a special equipment, comprising a pair of field panniers, surgical bag, field companion, haversack, antiseptic dressings, &c.

21. Medical officers attached to regiments carried in their boats the usual regimental medical equipment and, in addition, a pair of field panniers, medical comforts, &c.

22. Medical Staff Officers attached to corps were:—

Surgeon D. L. Irvine, 1st South Staffordshire Regiment.
Surgeon R. Haselden, 2nd Duke of Cornwall's Light Infantry.
Surgeon C. A. P. Mitchell, Squadron 19th Hussars.
Surgeon F. H. Treherne, 1st Royal Highlanders.
Surgeon H. A. de Lom, 1st Gordon Highlanders.

23. Civil Surgeon R. Keatinge subsequently joined the Egyptian contingent.

24. To meet the exigencies of a column always moving forward, but of which the component parts were constantly changing their respecting places, breaking up, and re-uniting at uncertain times and various periods, an exceedingly mobile organisation of hospital arrangements was necessary.

25. Medical officers attached to corps were therefore affiliated,

(S.C.2)

as it were, to the field hospital, and the power of admission and discharge given to all; a diet sheet accurately filled in was the only voucher required of them.

26. In order to keep the regimental medical equipment always complete, Medical Officers in charge were directed to apply to any Medical Officer in charge of a section of the field hospital, that they might be near; and the Medical Officers of the field hospital were instructed to reimburse the former any expenditure of medical comforts, &c., on the production only of a diet sheet as a voucher. The resources of the field hospital were thus made available to the utmost.

27. Each corps carried its own sick. Sick of mounted corps were carried in the boats of the corps to which they were attached for rations.

28. Sick and wounded requiring lying-down accommodation, were carried on stretchers arranged either along ship, or athwart ship, at the stern of the boat, and were protected from the sun by extemporised awnings.

29. All being in readiness, the field hospital received orders to leave Abu Dom on the 20th January, and proceeded to join Major-General Earle's column at Hamdab, at which place the nine (one, Principal Medical Officer's), boats arrived on the 21st, all well.

30. The composition of the River Column was as under:—

*   *   *   *   *

31. On 23rd January I inspected the regimental equipment of Medical Staff Officers attached to corps, and found all in satisfactory condition.

32. On the 24th the column marched from Hamdab. A, B, C, and D sections of the field hospital advanced, sections E, F, G, and H standing fast, but with orders to come on with the Duke of Cornwall's Light Infantry, and 1st Gordon Highlanders.

33. It would be too tedious to relate the day by day advance of the column, painfully tracking up cataracts and rapids by day, and sleeping in zeriba at night, officers and men sleeping always accoutred. Tents were never used, except for the sick, and then but seldom, as circumstances permitted.

34. The enemy fell back as the column advanced, now and then exchanging a few shots with our advanced parties. Berti was evacuated, and the people deserted their villages and fled. Not until the 10th February did the enemy make a stand, when was fought the brilliant action of Kirbekan, a separate detailed account of which as far as medical arrangements are concerned is attached.

35. The wounded at this action were carried on day by day

in boats, sometimes they were landed and placed in tents, more frequently they remained in the boats, even during halts.

36. The Medical Staff Officer attached to the 1st South Staffordshire Regiment and Royal Highlanders, aided by the Medical Officers of the field hospital, from this date were hardly worked, as the dressing of the wounded patients early in the morning and late at night was both tedious and laborious when carried out in boats, and the provision for their wants in food, &c., involved much forethought and arrangement.

37. Fresh meat rations were issued whenever obtainable, and the wants of the sick were satisfactorily met by such extras as preserved milk, Liebig's extract, oatmeal and rice, cabin biscuits, jam, tea, arrowroot, sugar, lime juice, &c.

38. On 24th February, the column had reached to within 22 miles of Abu Hamed on the right bank, having crossed the river at Hebbeh on the 21st. Here orders were received for the column to retire on Korti, and the descent of the river was begun. The river had now fallen some feet, and cataracts and rapids had become more difficult to descend; but day after day, with an energy beyond all praise, the dangerous journey was made. On but one or two occasions were the sick or wounded moved from the boats and portaged, where cataracts were too dangerous; but in all other cases they remained in the boats, and were brought down, without injury or casualty that could be attributed to the nature of their transit.

39. The stowage of the field hospital whalers was, after consideration, arranged in the manner to be described. The points to be considered were the trim of the boat, that she should be sufficiently down by the stern to steer readily in rapid water, and that the contents should be accessible as they were more or less frequently wanted by different persons. To ensure these objects the boats were divided in, as it were, (imaginary) sections. In the stern were stowed the heavy divisional boxes, medicines, field panniers (generally transverse, side by side on the top), field companion, haversacks, dressings, &c., in convenient places. These were always thus ready to the hand of the Medical Officer.

40. Forward of these and amidships, medical comforts, boxes of preserved milk, &c., were stowed, and perhaps some of the heavy boxes of the Nile boat stores, such as beef, lime juice, &c.

41. Forward again of these would be provisions, such as biscuits, &c., so that there was a general rough division from aft, forward, into medical stores and appliances, medical comforts, and provisions, modified so as to maintain the turn of the boat.

42. The supply of stores, medical comforts, &c., taken, proved more than ample for the period the column was in the field.

43. Arrangements had been made to obtain fresh supplies of medical comforts and dressings, *viâ* the Korosko–Abu Hamed route, if possible; of course, these were not in the event sent.

44. The supply of medicines was amply sufficient, not only for the field hospital requirements, but also for those of the regiments, so that the regimental equipment of medicines and medical comforts was constantly replenished and maintained, as referred to in a previous paragraph, No. 26.

45. As regards medical arrangements, the outline I have above given will, I think, sufficiently indicate the lines that should be followed in the detailed medical arrangements for any future intended advance up the Nile *viâ* Abu Hamed and Berber on Khartum.

46. The quantity of supplies taken, would of course have to be considered, not only with reference to the size of the force and the probable duration of the campaign, but also to the possibility of replenishing exhausted supplies by the Korosko–Abu Hamed or Suakin–Berber routes, the probabilities of actions being fought, and provision having to be made for the requirements of the wounded, and the supply of posts that might have to be established on the lines of communications, or even independently, to maintain themselves in temporary isolation.

47. Application to meet these contingencies would have to be estimated and made accordingly, but these matters could only be settled in consultation with the General Officer in command.

48. The above report bears strictly on medical transactions and arrangements.

49. . . . . . .

50. In separate reports I have made some remarks on the filters supplied with the Nile boat equipment, and I offer some suggestions on the Nile boat scale of rations.

51. The health of the troops forming the river column of the Nile Expedition Force was excellent . . . . . .

      (Signed)   C. H. HARVEY,
          Surgeon-Major, Medical Staff.
Kurot, 25th April, 1885.

Annexures.

(A.) Report on medical arrangements at the action at Kirbekan.

 *   *   *   *   *   *

     (Signed)   C. H. HARVEY,
         Surgeon-Major.

Kurot, 25th April, 1885.

Annexure A.

MEDICAL ARRANGEMENTS AT THE ACTION OF KIRBEKAN, 10TH FEBRUARY, 1885.

1. In compliance with the instructions conveyed in paragraph 2, Nile Column Orders of the 12th instant, I have the honour to submit the following report of the part taken by officers of Medical Staff and non-commissioned officers and men, Medical Staff Corps, under my command during the action of Kirbekan.

2. On receipt of orders to myself on the 9th instant, received immediately after my arrival at Castle Camp, I proceeded by riding camel to the bivouac opposite Dulka Island, accompanied by Surgeon-Major Flood, the Medical Staff Officer in charge of No. 2 Field Hospital, and 12 non-commissioned officers and men of the Medical Staff Corps, taking with me a portion of medical equipment, &c., in accordance with the scale, which I had previously submitted for the consideration of the General Officer commanding, and which had received his approval.

3. This equipment formed three camel loads.

4. On my arrival in camp and reporting myself, two additional camels to carry water were also placed by you at my disposal.

5. The Medical Staff Officers doing duty with regiments and corps at the bivouac opposite Dulka Island were, Surgeon D. L. Irvine, attached to the 1st South Staffordshire Regiment; Surgeon F. H. Treherne, attached to the 1st Royal Highlanders; Surgeon C. A. P. Mitchell doing duty with the squadron 19th Hussars; and Civil Surgeon Keatinge doing duty with the Egyptian Camel Corps and Battery.

6. At the disposal of these officers was the usual amount of regimental equipment as laid down by regulation.

7. On the morning of the 10th February the various regiments and corps moved out, accompanied by their respective Medical Staff Officers as above detailed.

8. I myself accompanied the Infantry Column.

9. The instructions given by me to the Medical Staff Officers were to the following effect, viz.:—

- (a.) The Medical Officers in charge of regiments and corps should march with their regiment and regimental stretcher bearers, carrying with them a field companion, water-bottle, field haversack, and a very small quantity of medical comforts; and should accompany their regiment into action.

(b.) Surgeon-Major Flood and Surgeon H. O. Stuart, with the equipment carried on the five camels as referred to above in paragraphs 2, 3, and 4, and the non-commissioned officers and men of the Medical Staff Corps, were to form a dressing station and act, as far as their limited number permitted, as a bearer party, moving in the rear, and conforming, as well as circumstances would allow, with the advance of the troops, and carrying with them any wounded collected at the station.

10. As, from the character of the enemy and the nature of the country, it was imperative that all wounded men should be brought on quickly in rear of the troops, and not allowed to fall behind even for a short distance, strict orders were given to the bearers to stand by the stretchers and be ready to move forward at a moment's notice, and the Medical Staff Officers of the dressing station, viz., Surgeon-Major Flood and Surgeon Stuart, had strict orders to remain by the wounded and see that their removal was rapidly effected.

11. . . . .

12. The Medical Officers attached to the dressing station did not, however, confine their duties to those of a dressing station, but visited various parts of the field of battle as calls for assistance from various quarters reached them.

13. . . . .

14. . . . .

15. . . . .

16. Restoratives such as beef tea, which was prepared on the field, champagne and brandy were administered to the wounded, both during the action and previous to their being removed to camp.

17. The wounded were, as rapidly as all circumstances permitted, collected in three groups, and were thence removed by regimental stretcher parties to the bivouac opposite Dulka Island.

18. On arrival in camp, food was provided, dressings were readjusted when required, and their wants generally attended to and they were accommodated for the night on stretchers in boat tents.

(Signed) C. H. HARVEY, M.D.,
Surgeon-Major, M.S.,
P.M.O., Nile Column.

14th February, 1885.

APPENDIX 52.
(See page 121.)

ORDERS FOR TROOPS IN BOATS ISSUED BY MAJOR-GENERAL EARLE AT HAMDAB.

I. The daily routine of the troops moving up the river in whalers has hitherto been regulated mainly by considerations of convenience and rapidity of movement. Upon leaving Hamdab, circumstances will be altogether altered, and the troops will move in regular order with all military precautions.

II. Generally, the banks will have been reconnoitred and occupied previous to the advance of the flotilla, but on some occasions it will be necessary that part of the column should leave the whalers and march to occupy the bank some distance in advance, returning when relieved to bring up their boats.

Thus, unless specially ordered, it will not be necessary that the men when tracking should be armed and accoutred.

III. But, whatever precautions may be adopted the troops must be trained to disembark at any moment, armed, fully accoutred, with biscuit in their haversacks, water in their bottles, and with a reserve of about 30 rounds of ammunition per man. This reserve will be taken from the Captain's boat in 3 boxes, and carried by hand with the company, or distributed as may be ordered.

In order to give commanding officers an opportunity of teaching the companies of their battalions to disembark very quickly, the proceedings upon arrival at, and departure from, the nightly bivouac, will be exactly similar to those required when the troops are called upon to disembark or embark unexpectedly.

IV. It is essential, with a view to the economy of time, that when a halt or a start takes place, the boats and all gear taken from them, should be handled in a smart and orderly way. There must be absolute silence.

V. When the troops disembark either unexpectedly or for bivouac, they will at once be marched to the place indicated, where they will remain under arms until further orders are received, or until guards and piquets have been posted.

The troops will remain accoutred throughout the night.

VI. If the disembarkation is unexpected, 1 man (fully accoutred) will be left in each boat, ready as may be ordered, to join his company or to form up to defend the boats.

VII. If the disembarkation is for bivouac 1 man (fully accoutred) will remain to take charge of the boat, and to disembark the articles allowed in bivouac.

VIII. These will be strictly limited as follows:—
1 camp kettle (filled with water).
Fuel, to be brought from the previous bivouac.
2 axes.
1 spade.
1 roll of bedding, with mess tin, per man.
Bedding, &c., for each officer.
Fires will at once be set going and kettles put to boil.

IX. When all military precautions have been taken, Captains will be ordered to march their men to the boats to fetch bedding.

X. In the morning, directly the breakfast has been served, the man in charge of the boat will replace the kettle, &c., in the boat, and the men and officers' servants will be sent down in regular order with the bedding, at such hour as may be ordered regimentally.

XI. Arms will be passed in to be stowed just before the men embark, but they will not take off their accoutrements till actually on board.

XII. The usual routine will be to breakfast before starting, to dine without halting, and to halt in good time in the afternoon.

XIII. A memo. respecting soldiers who may be wounded or who become sick will be circulated.

XIV. A memo. respecting the issue of supplies and provision of fuel will be circulated.

XV. The orders of the 29th October, 1884,* and of 27th December, 1884,† on the subject of boats are in full force.

XVI. Commanding officers (of both half battalions, if half battalions move independently) will keep a copy of their journal filled up from day to day, and take every opportunity of sending it to the Chief Staff Officer, thus avoiding the necessity of special reports.

* See Appendix 32, Part I.
† These Orders were as follows:—

"*Orders for Troops in Boats.*

"From the time of leaving Korti, the company will be the unit by which boats will work. The utmost efforts must be made to keep companies together. In every case an officer will be with the last boat of the company, and it will be his duty to urge on and assist where necessary any boats of his company which may be falling behind its leading boats.

"Where there are two officers to a company, they might take this duty in turn. Where there is only one officer to a company he should invariably bring up the rear of the company.

"By Order,
"(Signed)   H. BRACKENBURY, Col., D.A.G.

"*Korti, 27th December, 1884.*"

XVII. A party of skilled officers and voyageurs under Lieutenant-Colonel Alleyne, A.A.G., will assist the different flotillas at difficult points of the river.

XVIII. A boat-repairing party under Major Martin, R.A., will move after the flotilla.

XIX. When a camp is pitched, it is left to commanding officers to decide what articles may be taken from the whalers for the comfort and convenience of the officers and men. The system under which they will be drawn from and returned to the boats should be laid down regimentally, and the remaining boat gear should be arranged and inspected daily by company officers.

APPENDIX 53.

(See page 89.)

REPORT ON THE MUDIR'S TROOPS.

The Chief of the Intelligence Department,

On receipt of an order for the immediate mobilization of all available Mudir's troops, I at once began to collect animals and supplies and to make inquiries as to the effective strength of the troops then stationed at Abu Dom. I found that, out of the 463 men said to be stationed there, only 310 were available for service; 67 were untrained recruits, 36 were unfit for service owing to ill health, and 50 were scattered over the Mudirieh in various civil employments. The remaining 310 were men of good physique, fairly disciplined and proficient in drill, but badly clothed and shod, many not having great coats, none having proper boots, and many no boots at all. They had 120 rounds of ammunition per man, and were all armed with Remington rifles and sword bayonets.

It was the wish of the late Major-General Earle that a small portion of this force should be mounted on good riding camels for scouting purposes; but the great demands made on the district by the English, in this respect, and possibly the fear that the animals would not be paid for, made it impossible to collect even the limited number (twelve) which General Earle had fixed upon.

Baggage camels and donkeys were, however, collected without much difficulty, and the force left Merowi on the 23rd instant accompanied by 200 of the latter, and 30 of the former. The donkey transport answered its purpose of conveying the supplies of the troops to Berti, but owing to the slow pace of the animals and the number of men required to attend to them, would probably have proved very inconvenient had the enemy been more enterprising.

The scouting was done by the Vakil, who was mounted on a horse, and by such of the officers as had good riding camels. In this respect the want of good riding camels was greatly felt. Reconnaissances had to be conducted on baggage camels which had generally been engaged during the earlier part of the day in carrying burdens, and which under the most favourable circumstances, could hardly be edged into a slow trot.

The lack of proper boots also made itself felt after a few days marching, and by the time the force reached Berti many of the men had to walk barefooted.

The men throughout appeared to be cheerful and contented, and perfectly under the control of the higher officers, but the subordinate officers appeared to carry little weight and to enjoy but little respect from the men.

With regard to the manner in which the orders of the General Officer Commanding were carried out; I think, that taking into consideration the fact that they were not habituated to unquestioning obedience, there is nothing to complain of in this respect, as far as the higher officers were concerned; while as regards the subordinate officers and men, I invariably found that my orders and wishes were carried out with the greatest willingness and alacrity.

I had no opportunity of seeing these troops in action, but, judging by the confidence exhibited by all ranks, at a time when a considerable portion of the enemy's force had crossed over to the right bank, and the small body of the Mudir's troops had every prospect of becoming engaged with them, without any prospect of help or support for a considerable time, I believe that they would have stood their ground well in the event of an attack.

Whether the withdrawal of the enemy from the right bank was due to the presence of the Mudir's troops or not, I am unable to say, but from the presence of scances left by them on the right bank near the Edermi cataract, it is evident that at one time the enemy fully intended to hold a strong position commanding that portion of the river, and from the appearance of the remains of fires, near the scances, I am of opinion that their withdrawal must have been coincident with the advance of the Mudir's troops from Merowi. In my opinion, however, it is in the collection of supplies and information, that the Mudir's troops were able to render the most valuable services.

During the short time that the English troops remained at Berti, they supplied them with 150 sheep and over 60 head of cattle, and such information as I have been able to give as to the movements of the enemy was obtained exclusively through the influence of the Vakil. The presence of that powerful chief Wad et-Turki in this camp, is entirely due to the Vakil's exertions, and it is also through his influence that Abu Bekr Suliman, the uncle of Suliman Wad Gamr was induced to throw in his lot with the English. As one of the nearest relations of the late Sheikh Naman, this man's influence with his tribe must be considerable, while his personal enmity with Suliman Wad Gamr will probably render him more willing than the majority of his tribe to render us assistance in bringing that Sheikh to justice.

(Signed) H. E. COLVILE, Lieutenant-Colonel,
Grenadier Guards.

Hebbeh, 20th February, 1885.

APPENDIX 54.
(See page 132.) *Maps* 1 & 8.

DESPATCHES ON THE OPERATIONS OF THE RIVER COLUMN.

CAMP, KORTI,
8th March, 1885.

My Lord,
I have the honour to forward for your information the enclosed report from Brigadier-General Brackenbury, C.B., who returned here to-day in command of the column lately engaged in the operations in the Monasir country.

In this report, he describes the movements made by his troops from the 10th February, the date of the action at Kirbekan, to their arrival at Korti.

It would be difficult to exaggerate the hard work done by the men of this column, or to speak too highly of the soldierlike spirit that pervaded all ranks. Everyone who shared in the expedition up the Nile will long remember their gallant leader General Earle, and deplore his loss as an able commander, a brave and daring soldier, and a good comrade.

When General Earle fell in the action at Kirbekan on the 10th February, Brigadier-General Brackenbury assumed command of the subsequent operations, and conducted them with great ability and success, and to my entire satisfaction.

I have, &c.,
(Signed) WOLSELEY,
General.

The Right Hon. the Marquis of Hartington.

Enclosure.

*From Brigadier-General Brackenbury, C.B., Commanding the
River Column, to the Chief of the Staff, Nile Expeditionary
Force.*

KORTI,
8th *March*, 1885.

Sir,
 I have the honour to report, that on the 11th February, the day following the action of Kirbekan, the column under my command continued its advance, carrying in the boats its wounded officers and men.

We traversed the difficult Shukuk Pass without opposition, though it had been prepared for defence by the enemy throughout its entire length of six miles. On the 17th, we occupied Salamat and destroyed the houses, palm trees, and sakiehs of Suliman Wad Gamr, the chief author of the murder of Colonel Stewart and the British and French Consuls.

On the 20th, we reached Hebbeh, the scene of the murder, and on that and the following day we swam over to the opposite bank (300 yards distant) the 800 horses and camels of the force with a loss of only five camels, ferrying over their equipment and loads in the boats. While the crossing was proceeding, the troops, not engaged in ferrying or protecting the crossing, were employed in destroying the houses and property of Fakri Wad Otman, the man in whose guest-chamber the murder was committed.

We then advanced towards Abu Hamed on the right bank.

On the night of the 23rd, the whole column was concentrated (after an advance of 11 miles that day) at the last cluster of huts in the Monasir country, about 26 miles distant from Abu Hamed; and our cavalry, who had scouted six miles to the front, were still without touch of the enemy.

2. Early on the 24th, just as the further advance was commencing, I received your orders to discontinue the movement on Abu Hamed and return to Abu Dom, opposite Merowi. Sending forward a strong patrol, which pushed to within sight of Mograt Island, I reversed the column, and reached Hebbeh (16 miles) the same day. On the 25th we halted to recruit the horses and camels, which absolutely required rest, and occupied the day in completing the destruction of the houses and palm groves of the villagers who had taken part in the murder, and in whose houses articles from the wrecked steamer had been found. Continuing the movement on the following day we reached a village opposite Salamat.

3. Having decided that our return would be effected more rapidly, and on the whole with less risk, by moving the mounted

troops and convoy independently on the right bank, I here entrusted the command of them to Colonel Butler, with orders to march to a position opposite Berti, and descended the river myself with the boats.

4. Reaching Berti on the 1st March, I requested the Vakil of the Mudir of Dongola to march his troops down the left bank on the following day, and directed Colonel Butler to continue his march by the right bank to Merowi, keeping touch as far as possible of the boats.

5. On the 5th instant, the entire force arrived at Merowi and Abu Dom. The crossing of the horses and camels to the left bank commenced at 2 p.m., and was completed in a gale of wind at 11.30 a.m. on the 6th instant.

6. On the 7th instant, leaving Colonel Butler in command at Abu Dom with a troop 19th Hussars, the Egyptian Camel Corps, two guns Egyptian artillery, a detachment Royal Engineers, the 1st Battalion Royal Highlanders, and 100 camels of 11th Commissariat and Transport Company, I advanced with the remainder of the column to Korti, arriving here on the 8th instant.

7. The crushing effect of the action of 10th Februrary at Kirbekan is best shown by the fact, that after that fight the enemy allowed us to march unmolested to the furthest limits of the Monasir country, to take successively all the positions they had prepared for defence, and subsequently to retire through the same positions, without firing a shot or offering us any opposition.

8. The difficulties we had to contend against were caused by the nature of the river, which, from a few miles above Abu Dom, presented a succession of rapids as far as Salamat. That we ascended these rapids, well-known to be among the most formidable obstacles to navigation on the river, and descended them at this late season, during an exceptionally low Nile, with a total loss by drowning, in ascent and descent, of only five lives, proves conclusively that at an earlier season of the year, and under ordinary conditions of the river, a force, constituted as ours was, could, with comparative ease, advance by river to Berber and Khartum.

I have, &c.,

(Signed). HENRY BRACKENBURY, Brigadier-General,
Commanding River Column.

APPENDIX 55.

(See page 147.)

LORD WOLSELEY'S TELEGRAM OF THE 11TH FEBRUARY WITH REGARD TO STEAMERS REQUIRED.[*]

"I require four steel stern-wheel steamers, with compound engines for wood or coal, each to carry 50 tons cargo, and tow two barges with 25 tons each. Steamer's draught not to exceed 30 inches when fully loaded, and beam not over 23 feet. Horse power about 80. Three large rudders; the tops of the outside rudders to be 8 inches out of the water when ship is laden. Present Yarrows vibrate too much. Add a steam syphon to each compartment. Each steam capstan to be for 6 tons. Provision for water ballast when empty. As steamers will probably be built south of Halfa, no piece should weigh above 5 cwt., except cylinders. Provide steel wire slings with proper fittings, countersunk in main deck for attaching foot of slings, which will carry military sick stretchers on Zavoavski's system. Brodmeir, of Yarrow, going home, will explain details. Require 10 steel open barges, each for 25 tons, to be towed in pairs by these steamers. Draught, loaded, not to exceed 2 feet. Freeboard, loaded, 2 feet. Beam, 10 feet. Four watertight compartments in the total length. Removeable deck planks. Great rudder power. Each boat to be in two lengths. Arrange to couple together when launched. Require also four barges, each in one length of 36 feet. Draught and freeboard as above. Beam, 10 feet. All the above to have square, overhanging bows, and long rudders; also lifting rings for untraining; also high trunk, with tumbler, for steel masts to raise and lower. Beam is limited by railway cuttings. Details as to rig by post. This is drafted after consultation with Brodmeir."

[*] Additional steamers and barges were ordered later. See page 159.

APPENDIX 56.
(See page 158.)

REPORT BY THE DIRECTOR OF TRANSPORT ON THE ORGANISATION OF CAMEL TRANSPORT FOR THE AUTUMN CAMPAIGN.

Chief òf the Staff,

The heavy losses which have been sustained by that part of the regular Transport Companies which has been employed across the Bayuda desert, between the 30th December, 1884, and the present day, make it evident that little of it in the way of camels will ever return to this station. Under these circumstances I may be pardoned for submitting some ideas as to the future arrangements I would propose for reforming our regular Transport, and for the future expansion of the same, when the time is approaching for renewed operations.

*   *   *   *   *   *

The experience of this campaign has gone far to prove that the European private is not a valuable addition to a Company of Transport composed of Europeans and natives. He neither understands the native nor the animal, and in place of supervising others, requires much looking after himself.

Most of the Transport officers of this force having recognised these facts, I would suggest that the privates of the two companies be either sent back to England, or transferred for work to the Supply Branch. What is required is a good working cadre of officers, conductors, non-commissioned officers, with their own establishment of artificers; these with good interpreters and headmen, and a fair body of Somali drivers, for whom an additional demand has been made, will be found to constitute as good a company for service as can be desired.

A painful occurrence which took place at the battle of Abu Klea, when several of our Aden drivers were killed, makes me suggest that a more distinctive dress be given to our Somali drivers in future. I propose for consideration the issue of a red jersey instead of the blue one, which would please the men, and would go far to make a repetition of the above-mentioned accident impossible.

For the summer months we would thus have two companies of regular transport at a reduced establishment of animals—say 400 camels each—and a transport train working on the line of communications between the railhead and Sarkamatto. This train is at the present moment being organised by Captain Allen and Lieutenant Wood, in conjunction with Colonel Clery and Colonel Henderson, the latter of whom is purchasing camels at Assuan, and forwarding them to Sarras.

The Bearer Company will also have to be reorganised. Suitable animals for the conveyance of litters and cacolets are not likely to be obtained from our present camels, and carefully selected ones will have to be purchased wherever they can be found. The Principal Medical Officer might be requested to consider what establishment of animals it is absolutely necessary to keep up during the summer months.

The Remount Depôt, as such, has ceased to exist, all the animals fit for work having, whenever a demand was made, been sent to the front, or issued to strengthen the Transport Companies, Bearer Company, mounting officers, guides, &c. Others have been formed into special convoys, and sent to Jakdul or further on. Keeping a depôt of this description here would be of no use, and it would seem preferable to move it somewhere north of this; it would then return to be a Remount Depôt later on when operations are about to be resumed. The workmen of the repairing establishment might move north with it, for keeping them here would add to the supply difficulties without any corresponding advantages. Both the Remount Depôt and repairing establishment might have at Korti a depôt of small dimensions if considered absolutely necessary.

Having reviewed the arrangements proposed to be made to meet the requirements of the troops retained in the neighbourhood of this place, I will now pass on to consider the best way for expanding the transport when the time for renewed operations approaches.

The experience of the past months has proved that the best camels for standing continuous work under unfavourable circumstances are those purchased at Assiut, Keneh, and Sohag, which are a cross of the delta and the desert camel, and from these places, for several important reasons, I would suggest recruiting our animals. We know now the resources of these localities, and the best men we can call upon to produce camels for purchase, whilst the owners are well acquainted with the stamp of animals we are likely to demand, the price they will get for them, and the certainty of ready payments. The most successful of our purchasing agents can be again employed in this work, and past experience will enable me to frame better nstructions for their guidance.

The chief paymaster has already prepared a code of instructions regarding all future purchases for Government, and how the accounts are to be rendered.

With regard to the objections likely to be raised against purchasing in districts too far north, I would make the following remarks. Experience has shown that the tribes about here do not wish to part with their best camels, and that we are not likely to secure a better animal for work, than the camels found north of Assuan. Our hiring operations of this year have shown that we can obtain here a large number of hired camels at any moment by the offer of a remunerative price, and that 600 or more camels will always be forthcoming to strengthen our transport and work on the line of communications. Further, it may be admitted that the employment of hired camels tends to keep the tribes in their own interest faithful to our cause. All these points being taken into account, I would propose not to encroach on this valuable reserve of transport, but to confine our purchases to districts further north, where there is a fair market for camels.

As to distance, if the purchases are commenced at an early period, and the convoys are moved slowly up, with sufficient periods of rest under careful officers, the animals would doubtless arrive here in good condition. We have plenty of time to mature our arrangements, have the experience of the past months, and a personal knowledge of the country passed through, which all put together, should render the operation easy and successful.

With regard to the extent of our purchases, it will be as well to leave out of consideration any camels retained in this neighbourhood during the summer, (which might, however, be looked upon in the light of a reserve), and to remount our regular transport entirely. For this purpose, 36 riding and 1,208 baggage camels will be required for two companies. Should three companies be required to meet the wants of the force on retaking the field, our purchases would have to be raised to 54 riding and 1,812 baggage camels. A total of 1,866 transport animals is none too many for the force which is now collected in this part of the Sudan, particularly if water has to be carried, and the camels have to be used for the temporary transport of troops. I would strongly urge obtaining the cadre for this third company from England, and completing it with headmen, interpreters, and Somali drivers, on its starting from Cairo.

The bearer company and battery of artillery require 195 and 131 camels respectively, a total of 326 to be added to the above. In all, the three transport companies, bearer company, and battery would require 2,192 camels, to which it might be thought desirable to add a 10 per cent. reserve to meet casualties, making a total of 2,400 animals in all. The 2,400 camels purchased by Brigadier-General Grenfell's agents, in the reach of the Nile from south of Assiut to Assuan, notwithstanding the difficulties experienced at first in obtaining money from the various Mudiriehs, and in spreading the news of our intention to purchase, were obtained in a period of nine weeks.

When shall we begin to buy? This must be determined according to the time the camels will be required up here. The furthermost market in our purchasing ground (Assiut), is 900 miles north of Korti, representing at the rate of 20 miles march a day, a 45 days' march; or at the rate of 15 miles a day, one of 60 days. Allowing an additional one-third for the first case, and one-fifth for the second, for necessary halts, the entire distance would be got over in 60 and 72 days respectively. On this calculation, all purchasing should be completed at Assiut by the 1st September, if the camels are required here by the beginning of November; and, allowing eight weeks for completing the purchases, the purchasing operations themselves should commence not later than the 1st July.

Depôts of forage (beans and tibben) might be formed leisurely along the line of march from Assuan to Dongola. This last winter there were no means for forwarding tibben from Sarras to Dongola; and as dhura stalks were not easily procured, the big-framed transport camel did not get all the nourishment he required. The stages on the line of march are now well defined and known to us, therefore the best localities for the forage depôts are fixed. With the railhead pushed much closer to Dongola, the difficulties of filling these large forage depôts would be greatly diminished. At certain stations along the line a greater supply of forage would have to be stored to enable the animals to remain there for one or two days to rest, as continuous marching tends to destroy the condition of the camel more than that of any other animal.

It has already been noted that a demand for 600 additional Somali drivers has been made; the wording of the demand was that they were to be supplied after all such as were required for the Suakin force. It might be as well to face the possibility of any of the present drivers being anxious to quit our service to return to their homes, which would necessitate our making a larger demand than the above.

Our requirements in saddlery and equipment can only be ascertained, when the returns of articles in possession are received from the various companies.

A good number of packsaddles, however, have been destroyed or lost, and of the remaining ones many are worn out, and barely worth the while repairing. The recommendations of some of our transport officers with regard to the necessary alterations in the present packsaddles, with drawings, have been sent to the senior ordnance store officer at Cairo, for guidance in the construction of the packsaddles required for the Suakin force. The result of these recommendations, if carried out, would give us a serviceable packsaddle free from all chance of injuring the bones of the loins and back, where a large number of our animals have been wounded on falling out of condition.

To keep the saddlery in a good state of repair by executing promptly petty repairs, as also to thoroughly fit the saddles, it would appear highly desirable to give to each transport company a small body of native artificers, with tools and supply of necessary materials. The companies should be independent of the large repairing establishment now attached to the remount depôt, as the necessities of active service often localise the latter in such a way as to preclude its affording any assistance to the transport companies. Both of the companies lately employed in advance of Korti could receive very little assistance from the repairing establishment, and it was considered inopportune to send part of this establishment forward to Jakdul when demanded.

As attaching the repairing establishment and sick lines to the moveable remount depôt tends to hamper its movements, it would appear a preferable arrangement to separate them entirely from it. The moveable remount depôt in that case would only contain animals thoroughly fit for work, and should accompany any column as a reserve, or follow it at a short interval.

Lists of equipment, repairing material, tools, &c., necessary for a given force can soon be prepared. All can be obtained from Cairo, being forwarded early to the front so as to thoroughly complete every part of the transport before the troops again take the field. Some of the native articles—for example, leather— have proved so very inferior that it would be preferable to demand a supply of it from home.

(Signed)   G. A. FURSE, Lieutenant-Colonel,
Assistant Adjutant-General,
Director of Transport.

Korti, 3rd March, 1885.

APPENDIX 57.

(See page 165.)

THE HUTTING OF TROOPS.

By line of communications order, dated 25th February, Commandants of stations were instructed to provide hut accommodation for the troops serving under their command. Where Royal Engineer officers were available, the hutting was carried out under their direction, but at many stations the work was ordered to be done regimentally, the type of hut and method of execution being left entirely to Commanding Officers. Thus, as regards dimensions and details of execution, the hutting at different stations on the Nile has varied somewhat. Commanding Officers in many instances were authorised to demand and draw from the Ordnance Store Department the materials required, or to procure these and native labour for themselves, sending in bills to Paymasters of station. The main difficulty to be contended with was the absence of timber suitable for roofing purposes, and the scarcity of straw for the manufacture of mats.

At Assuan, Korosko, and Wady Halfa, a certain amount of timber was obtained from Cairo; but at the latter place water transport ceased, and at stations to the south the resources of the country had to be depended on. The timber available consisted of the date palm, mimosa, and sunt wood. The palm trees were split and used as rafters for roofs : the mimosa and sunt trees are of stunted growth and very crooked ; the branches, rarely exceeding 10 feet in length, were largely used in the construction of huts. At some stations the walls of huts were built of sun-dried mud and bricks, or mud with a core of stones ; at other, the sides, ends, and roof, consisted of a framework of poles, such as could be obtained in the country, firmly braced and lashed with rope, and the whole covered in with straw matting. The roofs were generally made of a double layer of mats, and in some cases a layer of palm-leaves was inserted between the mats. Huts built in the open were laid out with their length running east and west, or as nearly as possible in the track of the sun, so that the ends of the huts only, and not the sides, were exposed to the early and late rays of the sun. The prevailing cool wind being from the north, doors and windows were given this aspect, ventilators only being made in the south walls of huts. The advantage of straw over mud huts is that they are less costly, require no skilled labour, and can be rapidly constructed. Thus, with all the materials on the spot, a party of 10 men can in 8 hours build a hut 40 feet long, 16 feet broad, and 8 feet high, capable of accommodating 20 men. A hut with mud-brick walls of same dimensions, would take 8 days to build. Mud huts are cooler than straw in the day-time, but warmer at night, the walls retaining the heat longer. The huts built at Wady Halfa of mud-brick walls 18 inches thick, and whitewashed, with a double-mat roof and layer of palm-leaves, have been very generally approved of. On a very hot day the temperature at noon in one of these huts was 92°, whereas on a diahbieh it was 108° and in a mess marquee 112°.

For temporary shelter, and when time presses, straw huts answer their purpose, but in consequence of the great danger arising from fire, this type of hut is not recommended for a standing camp. At Assuan, Korosko, and Wady Halfa, the three stations which are to be garrisoned by the army of occupation, the huts have all been constructed of sun-dried bricks.

At Korosko and other stations the roofs of huts were covered with a 2-inch layer of mud. This plan was, however, latterly abandoned. The layer of mud, though offering greater security against fire, increased the weight of roof, and consequently the strength and number of roof timbers, and the huts so covered were found much hotter than those constructed with a roofing of a double layer of mats.

* * * * * *

(Signed)   J. C. BARKER, Captain,
Brigade Major, R.E.

Wady Halfa, July 15th, 1885.

APPENDIX 58.

(See page 167.)

INSTRUCTIONS ISSUED TO THE PRINCIPAL MEDICAL OFFICER FOR THE WITHDRAWAL OF THE SICK DURING THE EVACUATION.

1. I have received orders for the evacuation of the Dongola district.
2. The withdrawal will commence in 15 days with the troop from Merowi, and will be continued as rapidly as possible, the troops being passed from left to right down the river.
3. On, or possibly before, the 15th day from commencement of move, the Royal Highlanders from Merowi will be beginning to leave Fatmeh.
4. Arrangements are being made on the Line of Communication for the establishment of rest camps with sun shelters, at intervals of about 10 to 12 miles, along the river from Fatmeh to Railend.
5. The troops will proceed from Fatmeh by march route in parties about 300 strong, and we hope they will be able to leave Fatmeh at the rate of about 1,500 men a week.
6. The Vakil has begged for 15 days' start, and that we will,

as far as possible, conceal our intentions during that time, in order to enable him to take what steps he can, to mitigate the murder and rapine for which our retirement may be the signal.

7. Please, therefore, while making such arrangements as are necessary, do so under cover of their being intended for the better evacuation of the sick.

8. Arrangements have been made by the General Officer Commanding Line of Communications for the immediate removal of 300 sick from Fatmeh, at the rate of about 30 a day, which is the largest number we can send across the desert from Akasheh to Railhead.

9. Provision for 200 sick has been made at Akasheh, and for 100 at Dal.

10. I will let you know the number of rest camps when Colonel Fraser, who is now locating them, reaches the telegraph. It is for your consideration whether medical officers should be attached to each camp, or to each marching unit; if possible, I should prefer the latter.

11. I telegraphed last night to General Officer Commanding Field Force, and desired he would send Surgeon-Major Price and the medical stores from Tani down in the "Lotus."

(Signed) REDVERS BULLER, Major-General,
Chief of Staff.

Dongola, 12th May, 1885.

APPENDIX 59.
(See page 170.)

MOVEMENT OF THE NILE FORCE FROM THE SUDAN IN JUNE AND JULY, 1885.

"*Memorandum by the General of Communications.*

"*Abri, July 4th,* 1885.

"*Troops south of Abri.*

"Previous to this movement there were echeloned from Merowi to Hafir the following troops, viz.:—

"British: Naval Brigade, 8 battalions of infantry, 1 battery,

3 squadrons 19th Hussars, 4 camel regiments, departmental troops.

"Egyptian : 1 battalion Egyptian Army (blacks), 1 company Egyptian Army (infantry), 1 camel company, 2 camel battalions.

"*Orders for movement.*

"The headquarters line of communication was warned on the 6th May that the movement might have to take place, and on the 14th May authority was given by the Chief of the Staff to make the necessary preparations; the probable commencement of the move from Fatmeh being fixed at the 5th or 6th June.

"It was ordered that the route should follow the river from Kajbar to Akasheh; marches to be about 10 to 12 miles

"*Shelter stations.*

"Arrangements were accordingly made to open new stations at Delko, Said Fanti, Koyeh Matto, Dorkeh Matto Koyekeh, and Mograka, and to provide at these, and at Kajbar, Absarat, Sarkamatto, Akasheh,· and Tanjur road, shelter for 300 men and their officers, with the necessary accessories, and for piers for landing when required.

"Not less than 5,000 rations and the necessary forage had to be put down at the new stations, while a larger quantity was reserved at the original stations.

"*Hospitals.*

"New hospitals for 25 beds were ordered at Koyeh Matto and Abri, and a commandant, a commissariat issuer, and a detachment of 1 officer and 25 Egyptian soldiers were placed at each new station.

"*March from Fatmeh to Kajbar.*

"Arrangements were made by Colonel Grant at Fatmeh for columns marching from Fatmeh to Kajbar, a distance of some 23 miles, the troops to march in the evening, accompanied by camels to carry water as far as the halting place, where the columns were to bivouac for some hours, and proceed to Kajbar.

"This march was severe.

"Shelter.

"At the rest station shelter sheds, about 12 feet wide, and of length sufficient to allow a yard per man were made of poles and straw mats. In nearly all cases the materials were hired, and the labour paid for at a total cost of about 22l. per station.

"Camels and Guides.

"Among other arrangements, seven or eight camels were put down at stations to accompany columns one station north, and guides and saddle donkeys were held in readiness.

"Departure of Guards.

"On the 24th of May, the General of Communications informed the Chief of Staff that the arrangements would be completed during the week. On the 2nd June, the first column (Guards' Camel Regiment) marched across the desert from Fatmeh to Kajbar, and reached Alexandria on the 3rd July.

"Whaler Transport.

"Previous to this, the Chief of the Staff had consented to the employment of whalers in large numbers for the movement of troops down the Nile, on the representation of the General of Communications that they could pass down without difficulty, and this means of transport was in consequence largely used, as many as 19 to 21 men per boat (including pilots), with their baggage and rations, were carried rapidly from Fatmeh to Sarkamatto, under arrangements made by Colonel Grant and Captain Settle, D.A.A G.

Marching Column.

"The marching column of half battalions and corps were accompanied by four or five whalers, which took down their baggage and preceded them to the next station, where their food was always prepared for them on their arrival.

"The troops appreciated being able to eat and lie down after their march; shade temperature in the day varying from 100 to 121 degrees Fahrenheit in the afternoon.

"Most of the columns preferred to make an evening march, after which the men had tea, and lay down for part of the night, marching early enough to reach their next station shortly after sunrise. Their whalers halted with them.

"*Sick.*"

" Up to the present, not a man had been left in hospital at the rest stations, and few fell out on the march.

"With one exception all the columns marched daily between Kajbar and Abri.

" Most of the marching columns were carried from Abri to Sarkamatto in whalers, and all were taken from Dal to Akasheh in the same way.

"*Akasheh.*"

" From Akasheh they marched to Tanjur road, and next day to Railhead, and thence to Halfa by train.

"*Halfa.*"

"From Halfa they were at once despatched to Assuan and Cairo in fitted barges, towed by steamers, as arranged by Commander Hammill, R.N., under the direction of Colonel Clery.

* * * * * * *

"The removal of some 600 to 700 tons of stores and supplies from Dongola and Fatmeh, is being effected by 14 vessels and 65 convoy whalers, in addition to 6 nuggers and 19 small vessels from Dongola on the Fatmeh-Kajbar reach, and by 27 vessels and 130 convoy whalers on the Kajbar-Dal reach.

  (Signed)   " F. GRENFELL, Brigadier-General,
         " General of Communications.

Transport of Troops by Water from Fatmeh to Akasheh, on evacuation of the Sudan.

Report by Captain Settle, R.E.

The following arrangements were made on the various reaches :—

Fatmeh-Kajbar Reach.

(a.) Troops proceeding by desert route (24 miles).

The whaler convoys on this reach were broken up into sections of 5 to 6 whalers, and to each half-battalion a whaler section was allotted to convoy the baggage. The whalers left Kubudeh (north end of Hannek Cataract) in the morning of the day of march and reached Kajbar in the evening. They unloaded and left the following morning for Kubudeh, reaching there in two or three days, depending on the wind; four days were allotted for the round trip.

(b.) Troops proceeding by water (30 miles).

The troop boats were passed down Hannek Cataract by Kroomen to Kubudeh, the baggage was then put on board and the troops embarked. A pioneer-boat was at first detailed for every four boats, but later one to two pilots were placed in each, to steer them through the bad water ending in the Shaban Rapid. The troops reached Kajbar the same day, disembarked and handed over their boats to Egyptian soldiers who passed them down the Kajbar Cataract.

Kajbar-Abri Reach.

(a.) Troops proceeding by road (75½ miles).

The whaler convoys were broken up as before into sections, each section accompanying its half-battalion, as far as Abri and halting for the night at each rest station along the route. The first section generally started one hour before the troops marched, to enable it to reach the next station in time to have the men's teas ready on their arrival.

Seven days were allotted for the passage down, and five days to return to Kajbar.

The return journey was, however, done in two or three days.

(b.) Troops proceeding by water.

Regiments were told off into company sections of four or five whalers, and to each section two Egyptian soldiers, taken from the whaler convoys, were posted as pilots. These men were placed in the whaler of the officer commanding the section. This whaler took the lead, and after passing through a rapid, halted till the remaining boats were safely through.

Each section was ordered to keep together and proceed north as fast as possible.

Abri-Sarkamatto Reach.

(a.) Troops proceeding by road (20 miles).

With the exception of the following detachments, viz.:—

Commissariat and Transport Corps, 3 officers, 55 men.

Royal Sussex, 8 officers, 299 men.

the whole of the troops up to date were taken down to Sarkamatto in whalers.

For those marching, five to six whalers were detailed from the convoys plying on this reach, as owing to the bad water (especially the rapids of Shaban, Mograka, and Ferkeh) it was not deemed advisable to let the baggage boats from Kajbar proceed beyond Abri. The baggage boats left Abri at 4 p.m., and reached Mograka rest station at 7 p.m. The troops started at 5 p.m., and arrived at 9 p.m.

(b.) Troops proceeding by water.

As this reach abounded in intricate and dangerous channels at low water, two pilots were detailed per boat, one to take the helm, the other to be in the bows. The pilots were drawn from the Kroomen and Dongolese convoys.

Troop-boats arriving at Abri up to 10 a.m. were at once furnished with pilots, who were always held in readiness, and proceeded after an hour's halt to Sarkamatto which they reached the same day.

The quickest passages on this reach were made by the left half-battalion, Black Watch. Leaving Abri at 6 a.m., the first boat touched Sarkamatto at 10.30 a.m., and the last at 12.15 p.m.

At Sarkamatto the boats were handed over to the Station Commandant.

The pilots on their return brought up spare boats to Abri, which were furnished with new crews, Egyptian and Dongolese, and employed to supplement the existing convoys on the Abri-Kajbar and Abri-Sarkamatto Reaches.

A boat was also sent to each of the rest stations along the line to be used for station purposes and eventually for the evacuation of its small garrison

Dal-Akasheh Reach (9 miles).

All troops after crossing the portage were taken to Akasheh in whalers, 28 being employed for the purpose. They were furnished with two pilots per boat from convoys, the remainder of the crews marching by road to Akasheh, where they took over their boats and returned to north end Dal to await the next embarkation.

In all the reaches troop-boats were ordered to keep an interval of at least 50 yards when passing down rapids.

Orders were also given that the last boat but one was never to part company with the last boat.

No hitches whatever occurred throughout the line.

Provision was also made for sick convoys which ran at times simultaneously with troop-boats, and for which selected crews had to be kept in reserve.

The pilots did their work well, more particularly the Kroomen and native reises on the Abri-Sarkamatto Reach.

* * * * * *

HENRY H. SETTLE, Captain,
D.A.A.G. of Boats.

Abri, July 2, 1885.

APPENDIX 60.
(See page 184.)

INDIAN TRANSPORT FOR THE BRITISH FORCE AT SUAKIN.

1.—*Camel Driver Corps, 2,000 strong, for Camels to be taken charge of at Suakin.*

This corps consisted of Major Sir B. P. Bromhead, Bart., B.S.C., and eight other officers, with 18 Warrant, or non-commissioned officers, 9 clerks, 90 jemadars, 180 duffadars, 1,656 camel drivers, 9 munshis, 9 cattle agents, 9 naib chowdries, 18 weighmen, 45 saddle carpenters. Total of all ranks, 2,035.

This corps was to take over 4,500 camels, or nine war divisions, each division consisting of 500 camels, 1 officer, 2 Warrant, or non-commissioned officers, 1 clerk, 10 jemadars, 20 duffadars, 185 camel drivers (*i.e.* 1 to 3 animals, and 10 per cent. spare), 1 munshi, 1 cattle agent, 1 naib chowdry, 2 weighmen, 5 saddle carpenters.

APPENDIX 60.

2.—*Two Corps, each of 3,000 camels, with drivers and equipment complete.*

First Camel Corps.—Senior Officer Major G. H. E. Elliott, Deputy-Assistant Commissary-General, Bengal, and 5 other officers, 12 Warrant, or non-commissioned officers, 6 clerks, 60 jemadars, 120 duffadars, 1,104 surwans, 6 munshis, 6 cattle agents, 6 naib chowdries, 12 weighmen, 30 carpenters. Total of all ranks, 1,356.

The corps was divided into six war divisions of 500 camels each, as follows:—500 camels, 1 Transport Officer, 2 Warrant, or non-commissioned officers, 1 clerk, 10 jemadars, 20 duffadars, 184 surwans (*i.e.* 1 to 3 animals, and 10 per cent. spare), 1 munshi, 1 cattle agent, 1 naib chowdry, 2 weighmen, 5 saddle carpenters.

Second Camel Corps (not completed).—Senior Officer, Major Cummins, Madras Staff Corps, and five other Officers, 12 Warrant, or non-commissioned officers, with complete establishments and attendants of 1,350, divided into war divisions, each division with its own Officers and establishments, as noted in the organization of the first corps.

3.—*500 Riding Camels.*

This corps was organized as a war division of camels with two officers, 2 non-commissioned officers, 2 clerks, 10 jemadars, 20 duffadars, 184 drivers (*i.e.* 1 to 3 camels, and 10 per cent. spare), 1 munshi, 1 cattle agent, 1 naib chowdry, 2 weighmen, 5 saddle carpenters.

4.—*150 Riding Ponies for Mounted Infantry.*

These were sent in charge of one non-commissioned officer, 3 jemadars, 6 duffadars, 55 drivers (*i.e.* 1 to 3 animals, and 10 per cent. spare), 1 salutri, 1 shoeing smith, 2 saddlers, 1 carpenter, 1 blacksmith, 1 hammer-man, 1 bellows-man, 1 cattle agent, 1 weighman, 1 peon.

5.—*A Corps of 300 Muleteers.*

2 Officers, 3 non-commissioned officers, 3 clerks, 15 jemadars, 30 duffadars, 300 muleteers, 3 weighmen, 3 peons, 3 salutries, 3 shoeing-smiths, 6 saddlers, 3 carpenters, 3 blacksmiths, 3 bellows-men, 3 hammer-men, 1 gomashta 1st class, 1 gomashta 2nd class.

This corps of muleteers was organized in three peace divisions of men, to take over each a peace division of 250 mules, with 24 animals over.

6.—*A Corps of* 300 *Bhisties.*

1 Officer, 1 non-commissioned officer, 1 clerk, 6 jemadars, 12 duffadars, 300 bhisties, 1 gomashta. Total, 320 natives.

7.—*A Corps of* 500 *dhooly-bearers with Lushai dandies.*

2 Officers, 2 non-commissioned officers, 2 clerks, 10 sirdas, 20 mate bearers, 500 bearers, 1 gomashta. Total, 533 natives.

APPENDIX 61.
(See page 184.)

STAFF OF THE SUAKIN FIELD FORCE.

Appointment.	Rank.	Name.	Corps.	Remarks.
Com. Suakin F.F.	Lt.-Gen.	Sir G. Graham, V.C., K.C.B.	R.E.	
Assist. Mil. Sec.	Major	E. H. H. Collen	Ben. S.C.	
A.D.C.	Lieutenant	Hon. J. M. Stopford	Gr. Guards.	
,,	,,	W. C. Anderson	R.A.	
,,	,,	C. G. Lindsay	R.N.	
Chief of Staff	Major-Gen.	Sir G. Greaves, K.C.M.G., C.B.		
A.D.C.	Captain	A. N. Rochfort	R.A.	
A.A. and Q M.G.	Colonel	D. S. Warren	Half-pay	Subsequently transferred to Base.
	,,	G. F. Gildea, A.D.C.	Half-pay.	
	,,	J. M. Leith, C.B.	Cam. Highlrs.	Succeeded Col. Gildea when the latter was invalided.
D.A.A. and Q.M.G.	Major	R. H. L. Anstruther	Half-pay.	
	,,	W. Cooke-Collis	R.I.R.	
	Major	G. E. Grover	R.E.	
D.A.A. and Q.M.G. (Intelligence Department).	Captain	W H. Sawyer	The King's Own Royal Lanc. Regt.	Subsequently employed in Q.M.G.'s Department.
	,,	P. H. N. Lake	E. Lanc. Regt.	
	,,	G. H. More-Molyneux	Ben. S.C.	
Provost Marshal (A.A. and Q.M.G.)	Bt.-Lt.-Col.	R. W. F. Gordon	Argyll and Sutherland Highlanders	
Assistant Provost Marshal (D.A.A. and Q.M.G.)	Major	J. Morris	R.M.L.I.	
C.R.A.	Lt.-Col.	S. J. Nicholson	R.A.	
Adjutant	Captain	R. A. Bannatine	R.A.	
C.R.E.	Colonel	J. B. Edwards, C.B.	R.E.	Half-pay.
In charge of signalling	Major	E. T. Browell	R.A.	
Brigade Major R.E.	Bt.-Major	H. W. Smith	R.E.	
S.C.O.	A.C. Gen.	J. L. Robertson	Com. and Trans. Corps	
S.O. S.O.	A.C. Gen. of Ord.	E. G. Skinner	Ord S. Corps	
District Paymaster	Staff-Paymr.	R. G. Craig	A.P. Dept.	
P.M.O.	Dep. S. Gen.	O. Barnett, C.I.E.	M.S. Corps.	
Principal Vet. Surg. in Egypt	Insp. Vety. Surgeon	W. B. Walters	Vety. Dept.	

Special Service Officers.

D.A.A. and Q.M.G.	Captain and Bt.-Col.	R. H. Murray	Seaforth Highlanders	Attached to Chief of Staff, subsequently to Adj.-General's Dept.
,,	Major	J. H. Barnard, C.M.G.	R.M.F.	Base.
,,	Captain and Bt.-Major	C. W. H. Douglas	Gordon Highlanders	Attached to A. G. Dept.
,,	Major	R. C. D'E Spottiswoode	10th Hussars	Base.
,,	,,	H. Hare	R.M.F.	Base.
,,	Captain	G. S. Clarke	R.E.	Acting Assistant Military Secretary, subsequently attached to Intelligence Branch.
,,	Lieutenant	J. M. Grierson	R.A.	Attached Q.M.G.'s Dpt.
,,	Captain and Bt.-Major	W. C. James	2nd Dragoons	Attached A.G. Dept., subsequently command of Camel Corps.

Appointment.	Rank.	Name.	Corps.	Remarks.
		Brigade of Guards.		
A.D.C.	Major-Gen. Captain	A. J. Lyon-Freemantle. Hon. F. W. Stopford	G. Guards	Subsequently Brigade-Major, Brigade of Guards.
Brigade-Major	,,	Hon. N. de C. Dalrymple	S. Guards	
		Infantry Brigade.		
Brigadier-General	Major-Gen.	Sir J. C. McNeill, V.C., K.C.B., K.C.M.G.		
A.D.C.	Lieutenant	Hon. A. D. Charteris	C. Guards.	
Brigade-Major	Bt.-Lt.-Col.	W. F. Kelly	Royal Sussex Regiment.	
		Cavalry Brigade.		
Colonel on the Staff	Colonel	H. P. Ewart, C.B.	Half-pay.	
Brigade-Major	Captain	C. F. Thomson	7th Hussars.	
		Indian Contingent.		
Brigadier-General	Bgdr.-Gen.	J. Hudson, C.B.	Ben S.C.	
A.A. and Q.M.G.	Major	R. McG. Stewart	R.A.	
D.A.A. and Q.M.G.	Bt.-Major	N. R. Stewart	Ben. S.C.	
,,	Major	A. J. Pearson	R.A.	
Brigade-Major	,,	J. Cook	Ben. S.C.	
Provost Marshall	Captain	H. R. L. Holmes	Ben. S.C.	
		Base and Line of Communication.		
Brigadier-General	Major-Gen.	C. B. Ewart, C.B.	R.E.	
A.D.C.	Lieutenant	C. R. McGrigor	K.R.R. Corps	
Commandant Base (D.A. and Q.M.G.)	Colonel	W. Arbuthnot	Half-pay	Subsequently in charge of Adj.-Gen.'s Dept.
A.A. and Q.M.G.	Bt.-Lt.-Col.	H. G. MacGregor	Half-pay.	
D.A.A. and Q.M.G.	Major	A. Garstin	Mid. Regt.	
		Naval Brigade.		
Commanding	Commander	Domville	R.N.	

APPENDIX 62. (See page 184.)

EMBARKATION TABLE OF TROOPS FOR SUAKIN EXPEDITION.

Corps.	Officers.	N.-C.O.'s and Men.	Horses.	Followers.	Mules and Ponies.	Camels.	Per Steamship.	Date of Arrival.
15th Sikhs	8	309	3	192	145	...	Sirdhana	3 3 85
,, ,,	4	201	4	62	...	...	Madura	4 3 85
,, ,,	5	299	3	215	140	...	Zambesi	5 3 85
17th Bengal Native Infantry	9	400	...	219	...	...	Clive	5 3 85
Staff of Officers Commdg. Indian Contingent	8	5	19	84	160	...	Nerbudda	6 3 85
9th Bengal Cavalry	10	94	91	131	93	2	,,	6 3 85
24th Company, R.E.	4	261	87	...	...	...		
Intelligence Department, Staff	12	288	78	...	...	...	Queen	7 3 85
Commissart. and Transport Corps and details	10	80	1	...	...	...		
Nos. 1 and 2 Field Hospitals	4	65	1	...	...	...		
No. 1 Bearer Company	11	251	...	...	...	...		
3rd, 5th, and 12th Company Commissariat and Transport Corps								
5th Batt. 1st Brigade Scottish Division, Royal Artillery	2	43	1	...	...	...	Arab ...	8 3 85
Commissariat and Transport Corps	1	82	29	...	299	...	Mareotis	8 3 85
1st Batt. Coldstream Guards	31	800	6	2	...	...	Mandra	8 3 85
17th Bengal Native Infantry	2	200	3	114	93	...	Goa ...	8 3 85
9th Bengal Cavalry	8	95	108	114	97	...	Bancorra	8 3 85
17th Bengal Native Infantry	8	233	2	122	138	...	Gulna	9 3 85
2nd Batt. Scots Guards	30	808	6	...	...	...		
Staff Clerks	...	4	...	...	...	...	Pembroke Castle	9 3 85
Medical Staff Corps	1	25	107	...	46	...		
9th Bengal Cavalry	2	106	3	3	...	...	Golpora	10 3 85
3rd Batt. Grenadier Guards	31	799	6	...	...	...	Australia	10 3 85
Shropshire Light Infantry	24	775	3	...	...	...	Deccan	11 3 85
Royal Marine Light Infantry	6	135	95	...	54	...		
9th Bengal Cavalry	2	185	...	68	68	...	Canning	11 3 85
Hospital	...	100	102	70	280	...	Hazara	11 3 85
9th Bengal Cavalry	1	1	...	113	147	...	Shubzada	11 3 85
Indian Contingent	1	249	3	169	...	...	Ellora	12 3 85
28th Bombay Native Infantry	2	238	211	169	...	...		
9th Lancers	10	2	43	...	...	...	Lydian Monarch	13 3 85
Staff	5	342	4	170	121	207	Bangalore	13 3 85
Head-quarters Bombay Native Infantry	1	...	...	68	...	...	Nyanza	13 3 85
20th Hussars	14	247	214	...	...	...	Italy ...	14 3 85

318 HISTORY OF THE SUDAN CAMPAIGN.—PART II.

EMBARKATION TABLE—*continued.*

Corps.	Officers.	N.-C.O.'s and Men.	Horses.	Followers.	Mules and Ponies.	Camels.	Per Steamship.	Date of Arrival.
Royal Artillery and Departments	4	4	...	4*	...	...	Ganges	15 3 85
Royal Engineer Hospital	1	150	...	570	...	...	Pelshawur	15 3 85
Madras Sappers and Dhooly bearers	1	10	...	55	158	...	Tenasserim	15 3 85
Ordnance Store Department	...	13	...	...	...	...		
Departments	4	124	137	...	...	...	Romeo	15 3 85
Mounted Infantry	8	50	82	1	...	...	Lochard	16 3 85
Royal Horse Artillery	1	13	13	...	...	...		
Mounted Infantry, Police	1	28	40	...	...	...	Persian Monarch	17 3 85
Commissariat and Transport Corps	...	17	...	89	...	248		
Native Indian Troops	15	275	3	...	...	...	Calabria	17 3 85
Medical Staff Corps	2	72	2	...	6	...		18 3 85
6th Batt. 1st Brig. Scots Division, Royal Artillery	3	61	117	...	1	...	Queen	18 3 85
Mounted Infantry	3	16	1	...	...	...		
Royal Marine Light Infantry	1	2	...	218	324	423	Sird Hind	19 3 85
Bombay Staff Corps	1	20	...	165	193	...	Nordshera	
5th Batt. 1st Brig. Scottish Division, Royal Artillery	3	114	12	2	...	...		
Commissariat and Transport Corps	1	1	...	522	100	211	Mareotis	20 3 85
Native Indian Contingent	1	1	...	100	...	99	Secundra	21 3 85
" "	3	...	5	186	...	252	Sceptre	22 3 85
" "	1	15	...	706	...	300	Baghdad	22 3 85
Indian Transport	1	...	...	98	...	...	Rosina	22 3 85
"	1	2	...	268	...	...	Roma	22 3 85
" Ambulance Corps	1	7	...	522	...	...	Chupra	22 3 85
" Labourers	2	5	...	423	...	...	Darien	23 3 85
Departmental	7	100	...	409	...	383	Argo	25 3 85
Indian Staff Corps	2	1	...	...	...	...	Nuddea	26 3 85
Royal Marine Light Infantry	1	...	...	...	83	...	Queen	27 3 85
Commissariat and Transport Corps	...	...	...	...	...	...		
Lady Nurses	1	...	...	10	...	244	Elliott	27 3 85
Transport animals	1	12	7	106	...	...	Kildare	27 3 85
Commissariat Department	1	2	3	520	...	370	Clan McKay	29 3 85
Bengal Staff Corps	1	4	5	175	...	238	Kangra	29 3 85
Hydrabad Contingent	4			411				

*Lady Nurses.

APPENDIX 62

Corps.	Officers.	N.-C.O.'s and Men.	Horses.	Followers.	Mules and Ponies.	Camels.	Per Steamship.	Date of Arrival.
New South Wales Contingent. { Staff	4	3	...	...	...	...	Iberia ...	29 3 85
Artillery ...	2	54	25	...	...	...		
Ambulance Corps	1	32	...	...	...	...		
Infantry ...	17	515	...	...	...	...		
Chaplains ...	2	...	...	...	...	...		
Bengal Staff Corps ...	3	5	...	553	...	...	Abergeldie ...	30 3 85
New South Wales Artillery	6	130	159	...	...	205	Australasian ...	31 3 85
Transport	3	18	197	...	...	300	Dilston Castle ...	31 3 85
Aden Transport ...	...	...	...	159	...	198	Sirdhana ...	1 4 85
Indian Transport ...	...	...	...	106	...	...	Bandora ...	5 4 85
Royal Engineers ...	5	143	9	228	...	...	Kinsembo ...	7 4 85
28th Bombay Native Infantry	5	...	...	16	...	...	Nazara ...	13 4 85
Royal Artillery	3	57	2	28	...	290	Deccan ...	13 4 85
Transport	...	...	...	530	187*	...	Nevada ...	16 4 85
Labourers for Suez ...	1	7	2	101	...	...	Mareotis ...	17 4 85
„ India ...	...	...	...	1,191	...	...	Geelong ...	20 4 85
							H.M.S. Jumna ...	6 5 85
Total ...	391	9,996	2,054	10,507	2,933	3,973		
Troops at Suakin before assembly of Field Force	109	2,526	187	63	28	339		
Grand Total ...	500	12,522	2,241	10,570	2,961	4,312		

* 155 donkeys.

APPENDIX 63.
(See page 217.)

Maps 9 and 10.

SIR G. GRAHAM'S FINAL DESPATCH.

Alexandria,
30th May, 1885.

MY LORD,

Her Majesty's Government having decided to withdraw the greater portion of the Suakin Field Force from the Eastern Sudan, I have the honour to submit my final report on the operations of the campaign which has now been brought to a close.

2. I was appointed on the 20th February to the command of the troops to be collected at Suakin, and my instructions of the same date, from the Secretary of State for War, directed me to organize a field force, and to make such transport arrangements as were possible, so as to secure the first and most pressing object of the campaign, viz., the destruction of the power of Osman Digna.

3. I was directed to arrange next for the military occupation of the Hadendowa territory lying near to the Suakin-Berber route, so as to enable the contractors to proceed with the railway which it was proposed to construct from Suakin to Berber. In the Secretary of State's letter, of the 27th February, 1885, my attention was again drawn to the necessity for rapidly constructing this railway. The direction of the works was to be entirely under my orders; their details and execution being in the hands of the contractors.

4. It will thus be seen that there were two distinct phases of the campaign contemplated, after organizing the force and its transport, viz.:—

> 1st. The destruction of the power of Osman Digna, and the clearance of the country for the construction of the railway.
>
> 2nd. The construction of the railway, and the location of the troops for its protection, at points where the summer heats could be best endured.

5. In the first days of March, the troops began to arrive in quick succession, and on the 12th of that month, when I landed at Suakin, a force of 10,482 Officers, non-commissioned officers, and men had been collected.

The work of disembarkation of men, animals, supplies and stores, the formation of camps, the completion of the defences,

APPENDIX 63.

the arrangements for the water supply, the general organization of the force in every branch and department was heavy and unceasing. A week before the above date there were only two or three Officers of the Commissariat and Transport Staff and very little transport, but an accumulation of supplies. Officers and men soon, however, began to arrive from home, also camels from Egypt, Berbera and Aden. The Government of India furnished large numbers of camels with drivers, organized in divisions, under Transport Officers, and thoroughly equipped. The organization and allotment of 10,000 animals and 7,000 transport men, collected from various sources, and of the supply establishments for a large force, was necessarily a work of magnitude, but, by the 18th March, both supply and transport arrangements were fairly efficient.

6. From the sea-coast at Suakin a sandy plain rises gently in a westerly direction to an elevation of a few hundred feet above the sea-level, in a distance of 10 to 12 miles, where it meets the foot of the mountains which bound it on the west. These mountains are of volcanic or metamorphic formation, and in many of the passes, there stand up huge water-worn boulders of granite. In the immediate vicinity of Suakin towards the north and west, the country is fairly open for a mile or two, but beyond this radius, and south-west towards Tamai, the bush is thick.

The scrub is chiefly composed of the prickly mimosa bush, growing sometimes to a height of 6 or 8 feet, and of a growth of small shrubs in belts, following the shallow beds of the numerous watercourses or "khors," which carry off (in a north-easterly direction) the water flowing to the sea from the mountains during the periodical summer and autumnal rains.

The slope of the plain being so very gradual, these watercourses or khors are rarely deep or abrupt, except at special points—as, for example, the "Khor Ghuob," near which Tamanib and Tamai are situated. This great khor is 50 yards to 200 yards wide at the bottom, and from 20 feet to 60 feet below the general surface of the ground.

7. To appreciate properly the operations and the work of the troops in this campaign, it is necessary to bear in mind not only the nature of the country, but also the style of warfare practised by the enemy, which consists in long-range firing from cover, combined with desperate hand-to-hand assaults from the bush, through, and under which, they can steal unobserved.

8. The main difficulty in this campaign has been want of water. Here and there a well of brackish water might be found, and with labour the supply could be developed. But such an operation requires time, and for a force moving quickly it would be impracticable. Thus it became a principle that water to drink must be carried for the men, and this entailed the employ-

ment of a large number of transport animals, which all require 1 water to drink, whether that water were carried for them or derived from the scanty local supply obtainable at the place of halt.

9. The line to be taken by the railway was in a north-westerly direction from Suakin. This, the caravan route, passes through a country, part of which is inhabited by friendly or neutral tribes, and is the easiest line for the railway. The military operations would have been simplified had Osman Digna's position and head-quarters lain on this line. As it was, it was necessary to advance on Tamai, which is in a south-westerly direction from Suakin, and having accomplished the task of overcoming him, and of clearing the country for the construction of the railway, to make a fresh advance in a north-westerly direction.

10. Early in March the enemy occupied the line Tamai, Hashin, Handub, south to north; but the main strength of their force was at Tamai, where about 7,000 men were reported to be concentrated. Handub was subsequently evacuated by the enemy, and Hashin became a position of some importance as it threatened the right flank of my advance on Tamai. Screened by the bush and mountains, the enemy were able to reinforce this point from Tamai, and it was from here that they sent parties to creep up through the bush and harass our camps. During the first period, up to the advance on Hashin on the 20th March, the troops were subjected to continual night alarms. The enemy showed great audacity at this period, creeping through the advanced posts unseen, in small parties, and attacking isolated sentries, stragglers, &c.

11. The first operation necessary, therefore, was to break up the concentration at Hashin. Having ascertained by a cavalry reconnaissance on the 19th March that the enemy were in force, I attacked them on the following day, the 20th, and established a post for a short time to discourage them from re-occupying the position. I have already reported in detail on this reconnaissance and action, in my despatch of the 21st March. Although the troops behaved admirably, the action at Hashin was not decisive, as the enemy would not charge our squares at close quarters as they did on the next occasion.

12. On the 22nd March the action under Sir John McNeill was fought at the zeriba, six miles on the road to Tamai. The position of this post was selected with a view to making it a depôt for operations against either Tamanib or Tamai, according to circumstances. The attack of the 22nd March was the only serious attempt of the enemy to stop our advance. They were driven back with great slaughter, though not without severe loss on our side.

13 The next week was occupied in storing the zeriba with

supplies and water, and in preparing for the advance on Tamai. On the 23rd, 24th, 25th, 26th, 28th, and 30th, strong convoys proceeded to the zeriba. Those of the 24th and 26th were attacked in the bush, the enemy being repulsed on each occasion with great loss.

As the enemy were reported to have withdrawn from Tamai, a reconnaissance was made on the 1st April which proved that they were still in some force, and I determined to advance and endeavour to compel them to fight.

14. And here I may be permitted to remove a somewhat confusing idea that Osman Digna is a great and warlike leader. The facts as ascertained are that he himself never appears on, or near, the scene of conflict, but is content to urge on his men from some safe position or inaccessible fastness.

15. On the 2nd April the force advanced to the zeriba, and thence to the Tesela Hills, near Tamai, and on the 3rd occupied and destroyed Tamai itself, the absence of any formidable opposition proving that Osman Digna, notwithstanding his boasted intention of driving the British forces into the sea, had not forgotten his defeat at the battle of Tamai last year, and that the actions at Hashin and the zeriba, and the repulse of the attacks on the convoys, had rendered him quite unable to collect any body of men to meet us in the field.

16. I did not advance to Tamanib, because there seemed little or no probability of the enemy making any stand, and much labour would have been required to make the water at Tamai sufficient for the horses and transport animals of the force, preparatory to a further move.

17. The enemy had now been driven from the line of positions they had taken up at Hashin and Tamai, and their forces were destroyed or dispersed. I, therefore, determined to endeavour to fulfil the second part of my instructions, and to proceed to open up the route for the railway. This work could not have been commenced earlier with advantage. Indeed, had time permitted, it would have been better to have delayed the commencement of the railway until more rolling stock and plant had been disembarked.

18. The troops returned on the 4th April, and as there was no reason to continue to occupy the zeriba, the garrison was withdrawn on the 6th April. On that date an advance was made towards Handub, which was occupied on the 8th, Otao on the 16th, and Tambuk on the 19th. The railway reached Otao on the 30th April, in a little over three weeks from the date on which the dispersion of the enemy's forces was completed.

19. Looking upon all these operations merely as trying the qualities of the troops, it cannot be denied that they were severe tests, and that no troops could have stood them better. The harassing night alarms with enemies having all the stealthy

cunning and ferocity of wild beasts, prowling about in their midst, only served to increase the vigilance of the men in outpost duties, and, while teaching caution, made them more eager to meet their enemy in fair fight. The long marches and toilsome convoy duties under a tropical sun; the repulse of the enemy's sudden charges in the bush; the toilsome ten nights' watch in the zeriba, amid the carnage of a battlefield, are achievements of which any troops may be proud. As an instance of the high spirit that animated the whole force, I may mention that the 1st Battalion Berkshire Regiment, who bore so glorious a share in defeating the enemy's sudden and desperate onslaught of the 22nd March, continued to form part of the garrison of the zeriba until the final advance, and, though suffering great hardship, declined to be relieved.

20. During the progress of the railway the troops were not annoyed by the enemy, beyond desultory firing at night, and some attempts to injure the telegraph and railway. They had, however, heavy duties to perform in clearing the bush, and the heat continued to increase. Although the enemy was now cowed, full preparation had to be made to meet any attempt to interrupt the progress of the railway, and successful reconnaissances were directed in advance, and also into the neighbouring valleys to clear them of Arabs who, according to the information received, were collecting for the purpose of harassing our line of communication. The troops who took part in the reconnaissance showed great spirit and powers of endurance. On one occasion the 2nd Battalion Scots Guard marched a distance of nearly 20 miles over rough mountain passes, without a man falling out. The 15th Sikhs, on several occasions, displayed their splendid marching powers, and, at the surprise of and attack on Mohammed Adam Sardun, in the T'Hakul Valley, the Camel Corps and Mounted Infantry marched all night, dismounted at daybreak, came fresh into action, and then, after climbing steep hills in pursuit of the enemy, they returned to camp, having made a march of over 40 miles, half of which had been under a hot sun. This was done without any loss from over fatigue.

21. Not only did the troops cheerfully undergo the strain put upon them by their heavy duties in such a climate, but they readily responded to any call on them for extra duty, especially for any service involving some chance of adventure. Volunteers were easily obtained for night ambuscades on the railway, or for service in the armoured train; and the Camel Corps was to a great extent manned by volunteers. Before the great heat came on, men also volunteered for work on the railway.

22. It was found here, as elsewhere, that a certain amount of work, even during the hot season, tended to keep the troops in condition, and enabled them better to resist the enervating

APPENDIX 63. 325

effects of the climate. The troops in the front, at Tambuk and Otao, suffered less than those nearer the base, and the medical statistics of the campaign tend to show that, had the operations been prolonged into the summer months, the best chance of keeping the troops in health would have been by moving into the hills, and by not keeping the men too long in the same spot.

23. It was unfortunate that the campaign should have been closed just when I had obtained the means of organizing flying columns so as to move across the country as I did on the 6th May. The Camel Corps was most successful, but, owing to the lateness of the arrival of the camels, its organization could not be commenced before the 18th April. 500 riding camels had been asked for by me before leaving England, and that number was ordered from India; out of these only about 300 were used for service with the Camel Corps, as no more men could be spared from the Infantry. These riding camels were very fine animals, and were equipped with saddles for two men each, so that 300 camels could carry about 500 fighting men, besides one native to every third camel. The remaining camels were employed to carry infantry on the "ride and tie" system. The New South Wales Battalion, and the 3rd Battalion Grenadier Guards, were specially trained in this mode of camel riding, and as the Camel Corps could also apply the "ride and tie" system to any untrained infantry, I had the means of moving for an emergency about 1,800 Infantry, one-half being always mounted. With the Camel Corps, Mounted Infantry, and Cavalry, I could form a formidable flying column, and was preparing to make a simultaneous advance on Sinkat and Tamanib, when the announcement of the intended recall of the troops rendered further movements on an extensive scale inadvisable.

24. At the same time that the Camel Corps furnished me with the means of rapid movement notwithstanding the great heat, the arrival of pipes and pumps under the contract of Messrs. Edwards & Tweddle promised to solve the greatest difficulty of the campaign, the want of water. The supply of water to troops in the front before the railway was made, and in advance of the line, was a most difficult service involving great labour and responsibility. The weight of water for each man's daily ration was at least 12lb., his ordinary rations weighing less than 4lb. The work of cleaning and filling the water tins preparatory to a march, had to be done at night. They had to be packed on camels, every camel carrying two tins of $12\frac{1}{2}$ gallons each, and were then started off before daybreak to join the convoy. On arrival at their destination the tins were either emptied into storage tanks, or piled and guarded preparatory to issue to the troops. Much water was, of course, lost in transit, from leakage and other causes. Incessant vigilance was required

to guard the water amongst soldiers and camp followers, many of whom suffered from intense thirst, and the fact that so little was stolen is another proof of the high sense of duty and discipline that pervaded the force.

25. From the date of my arrival at Suakin, I endeavoured to establish confidence on the part of the Amarar tribes, hoping to be able to induce them to form a league which would include all tribes hostile to Osman Digna, or wearied of his cruel despotism. Little progress in this direction could be made, however, until the preliminary operations were concluded, and the advance along the Berber road began. On the 20th April, I appointed Major-General Lyon Fremantle as political Officer at the front, furnishing him with detailed instructions for his guidance. The main difficulty with which it was necessary to contend, was the impossibility of giving any formal guarantee of protection to the tribes.

26. The capture on the 15th April, of a large number of cattle intended for Osman Digna, acted as a strong discouragement to those of the Amarar tribes who were still supplying him with provisions; while the break up of the force under Mohammed Adam Sardun, on the 6th May, produced a deep impression throughout the country. As a result, many chiefs at once opened direct communication, and large numbers of tribesmen gathered at and in the neighbourhood of Otao. Had the force remained in occupation of this advanced post, the whole of the Amarar tribes lying north of the Berber road would have been at our disposal, and I have no hesitation in saying that large numbers of the nominal adherents of Osman Digna would have followed suit.

27. At the period at which the evacuation of the advanced posts commenced, the political question was practically solved. A large number of the Amarars had placed themselves unconditionally at my disposal, and a movement in our favour, which even embraced some of the Hadendowa clans, was on foot. It will be a matter of regret, if the evacuation of the advanced posts prevents any advantage being derived from this movement, and the more so since the dissolution of the Amarar league in its infancy, may serve to restore Osman Digna's prestige, and to throw increased power into his hands.

28. This campaign will be at least memorable as the first in which Her Majesty's Colonial Forces have taken a part with British and Indian troops.

The New South Wales Contingent took its share in all hardships and dangers. The New South Wales Infantry had three men wounded at Tamai, and during subsequent operations they were always in the front. Had the contemplated advance on Sinkat and Tamanib taken place, they would have formed a portion of the troops engaged. The Officers and men were, as I have stated previously, trained to camel riding, in which they soon acquired sufficient proficiency. The New South Wales Battery moved to Handub, and by constant drilling became fairly efficient, considering the many difficulties it had to contend with. The spirit of good fellowship between the men of the Australian Contingent and the British troops was very noticeable. The highest credit is due to Colonel Richardson, and to the Officers under him, for the excellent discipline and cheery readiness shown on all occasions.

29. In bringing to special notice the admirable conduct of the troops I had the honour to command, I wish to record my sense of the loyalty and devotion shown by the Staff and regimental Officers, who never spared themselves, and set the troops a bright example of courage and endurance. The Departmental Officers also worked with the utmost zeal and intelligence.

* * * * *

50. My warmest thanks are due to all ranks of the Suakin Field Force for the loyal help they have given me. That force was composed of the British troops of Her Majesty, and of the native soldiers of Her Empire in India, and with them were united Her Majesty's Colonial Forces, and detachments of English Volunteers. But though the troops were drawn from so many different sources, all were animated and bound together by a firm determination to preserve untarnished the reputation of the British Army.

By their efforts the power of Osman Digna was so broken that for all practical purposes the country was completely cleared; the railway was being pushed on as fast as the plant could be landed; the tribes were rapidly submitting to us; so that, had circumstances permitted the continuance of the great enterprise on which the force was engaged, it would, I am convinced, have been successfully carried out.

I have, &c.,

GERALD GRAHAM, *Lieut.-General.*

The Right Hon.
The Marquis of Hartington.

SKETCH MAP TO ILLUSTRATE THE HISTORY
OF THE
SUDAN CAMPAIGN

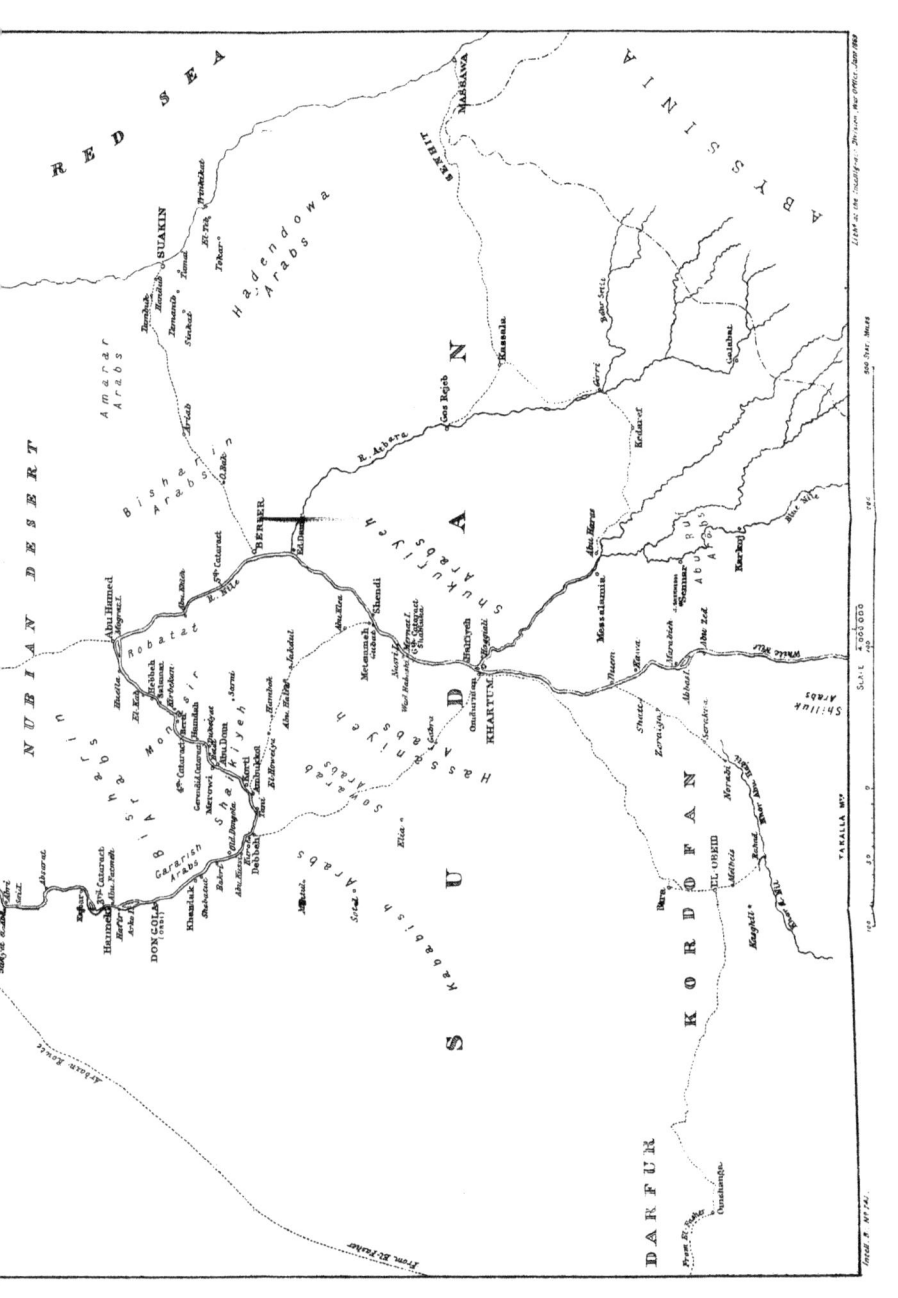

www.ingramcontent.com/pod-product-compliance
Lightning Source LLC
Chambersburg PA
CBHW070718160426
43192CB00009B/1232